ALSO BY GEORGE HOWE COLT

The Enigma of Suicide

THE
BIG HOUSE

A Century in the Life of an American Summer Home

GEORGE HOWE COLT

SCRIBNER

NEW YORK   LONDON   TORONTO   SYDNEY   SINGAPORE

SCRIBNER
1230 Avenue of the Americas
New York, NY 10020

For information regarding special discounts for bulk purchases,
please contact Simon & Schuster Special Sales at 1–800–456–6798
or business@simonandschuster.com

Designed by Kyoko Watanabe
Text set in Janson Text

Manufactured in the United States of America

7 9 10 8 6

Library of Congress Cataloging-in-Publication Data

Colt, George Howe.
The big house: a century in the life of an American summer home/
George Howe Colt.
p. cm.
1. Historic buildings—Massachusetts—Cape Cod. 2. Vacation homes—
Massachusetts—Cape Cod. 3. Cape Cod (Mass.)—Social life and customs.
4. Colt, George Howe. 5. Cape Cod (Mass.)—Biography. 6. Colt family.
I. Title.

F72.C3 C57 2003
974.4'92043'092—dc21
[B]
2002191138

ISBN 0-684-84517-2

For my father and mother

Contents

PART TWO

✳

✳

Prologue

T HE DOORS that are always open have been closed and locked. The windows are shut tight. The shades are drawn. No water runs from the faucets. The toaster—which in the best of times works only if its handle is pinned under the weight of a second, even less functional toaster—is unplugged. The kitchen cupboards are empty except for a stack of napkins, a box of sugar cubes, and eight cans of beer. The porch furniture—six white plastic chairs, two green wooden tables—has been stacked in the dining room. The croquet set, the badminton equipment, the tennis net, and the flag are behind closet doors. The dinghy is turtled on sawhorses in the barn, the oars angled against the wall. The roasted-salt scent of August has given way to the stale smell of mothballs, ashes, mildew.

Here and there are traces of last summer: a striped beach towel tossed on the washing machine, a half-empty shampoo bottle wedged in the wooden slats of the outdoor shower, a fishing lure on the living room mantel, a half-burned log in the fireplace, a sprinkling of sand behind the kitchen door. Dead hornets litter the windowsills. A drowned mouse floats in the lower-bedroom toilet. The most recent entry in the guest book was made five months ago. The top newspaper in the kindling pile is dated September 29. The ship's clock in the front hall has stopped at 2:45, but whether that was A.M. or P.M. no one can tell.

After gorging on summer for three months, the house has gone into hibernation. They call it the off-season, as if there were a switch in the cellar, next to the circuit breakers, that one flipped to plunge the house from brimming to empty, warm to cold, noisy to silent, light to dark. Outside, too, the world has changed color, from blues, yellows, and greens to grays and browns. The tangle of honeysuckle, *Rosa rugosa*, and poison ivy that lapped at the porch is a skein of bare branches and vines. The lawn is hard as tundra, brown as burlap. The Benedicts' house next door, hidden from view when I was last here, is visible through the leafless trees. The woods give up their secrets: old tennis balls, an errant Frisbee, a lost tube of sunblock, a badminton birdie. Out in the bay, the water is the color of steel and spattered with whitecaps; without the presence of boats to lend perspective, the waves look ominously large. On the stony beach, the boardwalk—a set of narrow planks we use to enter the water without spraining our ankles on the algae-slicked rocks—has been piled above the tide line, beyond the reach, we hope, of storms.

A summer house in winter is a forlorn thing. In its proper season, every door is unlocked, every window wide open. People, too, are more open in summer, moving through the house and each other's life as freely as the wind. Their schools and offices are distant, their guard is down, their feet are bare. Now as I walk from room to room, shivering in my parka, I have the feeling I'm trespassing, as if I've sneaked into a museum at night. Without people to fill it, the house takes on a life of its own. Family photographs seem to breathe, their subjects vivid and laughing and suspended at the most beautiful moments of their youths: my father in his army uniform, about to go off to World War II; my aunt in an evening gown, in a shot taken for a society benefit not long before her death at twenty-eight; my grandfather as a Harvard freshman, poised to win an ice hockey game; my cousins in the summer of 1963, gathered on the sunny lawn. I am older than all of them, even though many are now dead.

In this still house, where is the summer hiding? Perhaps in the mice whose droppings pepper the couch, the bats that brood in the attic eaves, the squirrels that nest in the stairwell walls. They are silent now, but we will hear and see them—and the offspring to which they will soon give birth—in a few months. For if the house is full of memory, it is equally full of anticipation. Dormant life lies everywhere, waiting to be picked up where it left off, like an old friendship after a long absence: that towel ready to be slung over a sweaty shoulder, that tennis ball to be thrown into the air, those chairs to be set out on the porch, that fishing lure to be cast into the bay, that guest book to be inscribed with a day in June. Even on the coldest winter morning, this house holds within it, like a voluptuous flower within a hard seed, the promise of summer.

PART ONE

I

Arriving

SOMEWHERE north of Wareham, the land began to flatten. Maple and birch gave way to scrub oak and pitch pine, and the air tickled with salt. In the backseat of our overstuffed and overheated Ford station wagon, my younger brother Ned and I stopped playing got-you-last and sat up, alert as bloodhounds. My older brother, Harry, looked up from his Hardy Boys book. We shouted as we spotted each familiar milestone: the first cranberry bog; the first seagull, floating incongruously over an inland ocean of green pine; the first glimpse of salt water, a brackish inlet rimmed with rickety-looking docks, which led, we knew, to a tidal creek, which flowed to the bay, which, at some distant point, emptied into the ocean.

Four decades later, the subtle change in landscape still effects a physical change in me as surely as if I had taken a drug. I breathe faster, my legs go weak, and excitement rises within me like a tide. It is a sweltering August day, but I turn off the air conditioner in our rented red Toyota and roll down the windows. My sweat feels good. In the backseat, six-year-old Susannah, who has been reading *Little House on the Prairie* and occasionally bursting into "Ninety-Nine Bottles of Beer on the Wall" (if Anne and I keep our objections to ourselves, she usually peters out at sixty or seventy), sits up and looks out the window.

"Are we in Cape Cod?"

"Almost," I say.

Even eighteen-month-old Henry senses something. When Anne points out a boat to him and he puts down his pacifier to repeat the word, he is too excited to ask for it back. After having exceeded the speed limit most of the way from New York City, I find myself, as always, instinctively slowing down here, not because I am more interested in what's outside my window—although I am—but from habit, as if I have entered my parents' old bailiwick and they might be watching.

I have been making this trip for forty-two years. My family has been making it for nearly a century, starting in 1903, when my great-grandfather brought his family down by horse and carriage along the dirt road that curled from town to town before this highway was built. In those days, the journey from Boston to Cape Cod took six hours. Today it takes us less than that to get from Manhattan to the Cape. Families came for the entire summer back then. We are staying for a month. But as always, the summer doesn't begin until we get to the Big House. And as we draw closer, I almost forget for a moment that this will likely be the last time we make this trip.

For many years, the highway ended seven miles from the Cape Cod Canal in a jumble of warning signs, flashing lights, and—lest anyone fail to heed these—a cement roadblock. Motorists were forced to detour onto Route 6, an old two-lane thoroughfare ambitiously known as the Cranberry Highway, which made its way to the Bourne Bridge through a gantlet of motels, clam shacks, dairy bars, antiques stores, trailer parks, and bait shops as garish and alluring as a carnival midway, offering a glimpse of what to my dazzled childhood eyes passed for sin: shopping, squalor, bad taste.

As a boy, I longed to browse the Sand 'n Surf Largest Basket and Gift Shop, whose front yard was festooned with lobster pots, fishermen's nets, duck decoys, cement angels, and every object that could conceivably be fashioned out of wicker, none of which I was tempted to buy, but which, in the aggregate, presented an irresistible vision of plenty. Though we had never been inside the Mezza Luna Restaurant-Lounge, on whose neon sign a silver-haired Italian grandmother was juxtaposed with a sug-gestively tilted martini glass (budget and tradition limited us to Howard Johnson), I felt as fond of it as if I had been one of its most loyal patrons. And though Katie seemed a rather tame name for a fortune-teller, I would have given anything to know what took place in the white one-room cabin adorned by a hand-painted sign: KATIE'S PALM READING (and whether the proprietor might, perhaps, with a slight spelling change, be moonlighting at Katy's Beauty Salon next door). I wished we could spend a night at the Starlight Motel—or the White Pines, the Rosewood, or any of a half dozen other motels with beguilingly sentimental names—with its tidy one-room cabins clustered like Monopoly houses around a small, pallid pool, and out front, a wooden VACANCY sign with a removable NO. In front of each cabin was parked a station wagon with a license plate from a distant state. Who were these families? Were their cars full of wicker baskets and cement angels? Were they going to a house like mine?

Although my grandfather dismissed such places as "tourist traps," they were beloved milestones on our annual pilgrimage, as essential to our vision of Cape Cod as any lighthouse or sand dune. Indeed, throughout my youth I assumed that the highway had been deliberately designed to end prematurely so that every motorist could experience Route 6 as a sort of ecological transition zone between mainland and Cape. The real reason, as I would learn many years later, was less practical: the state had planned to link the highway directly to the Bourne Bridge, but the elderly woman who owned the property through which the road would run had refused to sell, fearing that construction would damage local cranberry bogs. For years the issue was argued in the courts, and the road got no farther than that cement wall.

Although a compromise was finally reached ten years ago, and the highway was extended to the bridge, I continue to take the older, slower road. Over the years, most of the gift shops and clam shacks have been supplanted by gas stations, shopping plazas, and health clubs. Each summer we look to see what new stores have opened and which old favorites haven't survived the winter. Most of the motels have been razed—people prefer to stay in time-shares and condominiums now—but the Starlight still stands, though we never see more than three or four cars parked in front of its dilapidated cottages, and the VACANCY sign is always up. The few antiques stores that remain are antiques themselves. I'm comforted to see that Katie/Katy is still telling fortunes and styling hair, though her cabin now sits cheek by jowl with a Burger King. In downtown Buzzards Bay, the only business that seems to be thriving is the Port O' Call, a bar whose name frequently turns up in the local newspaper's police log, and whose always-wide-open door frames a gloomy, seductive darkness even on this bright August afternoon. Everywhere, there is change. Perhaps that's why I continue to drive this way: it reminds me, by contrast, how little the house we are going to has changed. Indeed, the Big House has always been a place whose very *goal* is never to change. Now it is on the verge of changing forever.

And then we are lifted into the air by the Bourne Bridge, the great gray rainbow-shaped steel arc that vaults over the western end of the Cape Cod Canal. The bridge has seemingly supernatural powers of levitation—when we cross it I feel that we might drive right off into the sky. When I was a child, my grandmother always told us that if you saw a boat in the canal as you drove over it, you'd have good luck for the entire summer. The bigger the boat, the better the luck. My brothers and I would scan the gray water, claiming each distant tug, sloop, scow, and cruiser. One summer, as we crested the bridge, we were dismayed to see not a single boat—not so much as a dinghy—in the entire canal. We were horrified: What kind of summer awaited us? Just then, Ned let out a cry, and we watched, incredulous, as a massive steel bow nosed out from under the bridge. It belonged to a tanker so large it seemed the sailors on deck could leap onto the bridge and shake our hands. That was the summer I caught my first fish.

This year, we see no such behemoths (the anti-suicide fencing installed several years ago doesn't make the viewing any easier), but Susannah counts two small sailboats and three sport-fishing boats. "There's a boat!" she announces, raising herself as high as her seat belt will allow. "And there's one! And there's one!"

I used to believe that the Bourne Bridge had been named for its powers of resurrection, its ability to make us feel, as we passed over it, reborn. (In fact, the bridge was named for Jonathan Bourne, a nineteenth-century whaling tycoon who was, by all accounts, a practical and decidedly earth-bound man.) For although the gentle, pine-covered hills into which the bridge releases us look little different from what we've left behind, we feel we have been delivered to an entirely different place. I still feel this, despite the fact that for nearly thirty years the first things I've seen on the far side of the bridge are the words CAPE COD—as if I needed to be told—spelled out in topiary two feet tall on an artificial hill in the Bourne Rotary. To me, this seems an apt synecdoche for what much of the Cape has become: a collection of tacky, self-promoting artifacts around which traffic gradually comes to a standstill. But different generations have different traditions. "'Cape Cod' spelled in grass!" says Susannah happily. "I *always* see that when we come here."

We follow a back road along the eastern shore of Buzzards Bay, through stretches of pine forest punctuated by clusters of summer cottages. Each turn we make sheds more people, more houses, more cars; adds more salt, more wind, more water. Each turn leads to ever more familiar territory. Susannah calls out landmarks as we pass: "There's the Singing Bridge!" "There's the Whack House!" "There's the Rainbow House!" The roads get increasingly narrow and rough—a soothing regression. And then we come to the edge of the marsh that marks the entrance to our own particular world. On the far side lies Wings Neck, a spit of land that reaches into Buzzards Bay like a gull wing into the sky. Although Wings Neck is technically a peninsula, the marsh makes it seem like an island, separating it from the rest of the world the way a moat defines a castle.

Beyond the marsh, the road disappears into the woods. It gently bends and undulates—up a hill, down a hill, up a hill—in a geological roller coaster exhilarating to a boy on a bicycle. The trees on either side nearly meet overhead. Although the road is never much more than a hundred yards from the water, one would never know it, the woods are so thick. Every so often, a path or a driveway burrows into the pines. Some of the driveways are marked with a family name daubed on a fragment of an oar or a piece of driftwood, but the houses themselves are rarely visible, aside from an occasional gable or chimney. As we pass each driveway, Susannah announces the familiar names. The road turns gradually to the left and heads downhill past a small beach. "There's the Big Cove!" she exclaims. Nailed high on the trunk of an oak tree at the entrance to a driveway not far beyond the Big Cove is a warped white board that says COLT—a sign so small and so hard to spot that guests often pass right by. We turn in, and, as I hear the crackle of gravel kicking up like popcorn beneath the car, I feel a simultaneous lifting and settling in my heart.

When I was small, our driveway was a source of great pride to me. It was the longest on Wings Neck, and to a child raised in the suburbs, it seemed endless. Like most driveways on the Neck, it was nothing more than a spine of weeds flanked by troughs of dirt and gravel, with occasional handfuls of crushed clamshells discarded after their innards had been slurped up at cocktail parties. I learned to drive on this driveway, sitting on my father's lap, steering while he worked the pedals, and I know it so well that I could drive it with my eyes closed (and did, many times, as a teenager coming home late from a party, filled with liquor and a youthful belief in my own immortality): the gradual uphill through the pine, oak, and sassafras; the gentle leftward curve past the tennis court; the sharper bend where the path to our neighbor's house cuts through the woods; and the final straightening as the driveway forks, the right branch leading to the main house, the left to the barn and cottage.

In the cleft of that fork, a decaying wooden sign with faded green letters announces LOOK OUT FOR CHILDREN. (As a child, I was never quite sure whether it was intended to keep visitors from running over us, or to warn them—in the manner of a BEWARE OF DOG sign—that difficult and possibly dangerous youngsters lay ahead.) "'Look out for children'!" reads Susannah. "But there's no children on the road now, there's only children in the car and that's us!" The sign was put up by my great-grandfather, and the children to whom it originally referred—my grandmother and her brothers—have been dead for many years. Susannah is one of the fourth generation for whom the sign has stood sentinel, although there have been summers when the house was nearly empty, and there were no children to look out for. But when I was a child there were a great many of us. And every time we heard a crackle on the driveway, we would hurry—from the tennis court, from the beach, from the croquet pitch, from the hammock, from the barn—and converge on the car to see who it was. As we turn the last corner now, I half expect to see cousins and aunts and uncles materialize; to see my grandparents emerge from the house, Grandma beaming and waving, and Grandpa, in his worn gray cotton suit and white sneakers, looking on with a quizzical smile. But when we pull up in front of the house, everything is quiet aside from the southwest wind that shakes the tops of the trees, the shush of the waves on the Bluff, and the sound of Susannah (who has, Houdini-like, managed to shed her seat belt, shoes, and socks in the time it has taken to drive up the driveway) crying out in excitement, as she opens the door and leaps from the car, "We're here!"

When I was a child, this was the moment we had been waiting for all winter. As the car slowed to a stop, my brothers and I would kick off our shoes. Then we'd spring from our seats to run barefoot from place to place, making sure the things we had dreamed of during the last nine months were still there. We'd run down to the beach to test the water with our toes, a foretaste of the hundred swims that lay before us. We'd patrol the rocky shore for sea glass, jingle shells, and the skates' egg cases that my grandmother called mermaids' purses (but that to me looked more like devils' pillows). We'd touch the dinghy from which we'd fish for scup. We'd race across the lawn to the barn, where we'd run our fingers across the winter's dust that furred the pool table's protective plastic cover. And then, like the child at supper who saves his favorite food for last, we'd turn to the house.

These days I make a slower, but no less passionate, circuit: I walk to the Bluff to see whether the tide is high or low; I walk the perimeter of the house, past the garden, past the catalpa tree my great-grandfather planted, past the clothesline; I walk out to the huge green barn. Susannah darts about in a delirium, racing through the garden, taking a test ride on the swing, inspecting a daddy longlegs, sniffing the honeysuckle that climbs the piazza. ("Piazza"—the word my grandparents used— always made the simple back porch on which they sipped martinis and watched sailboats go by sound like the balcony of a villa in Capri.) Henry, too, seems intoxicated. Last summer, when he was six months old, he visited Wings Neck for the first time and screamed most of the way there. But when we pulled into the driveway long after dark and lifted him from the car, he looked up, saw the stars, and was suddenly hushed. Over the last few weeks, as we talked to him about the upcoming trip, we wondered whether he would remember this place. Tugging on Anne's hand, he looks around him at the broad, scraggly lawn, the pine trees beyond. And then, almost as an afterthought, he notices the gigantic building towering above him. He toddles toward it, pointing. "House!" he cries, as if in disbelief. "House! House! House!"

It is an extraordinary structure, a massive, four-story, shingle-style house as contorted and fantastic as something a child might build with wooden blocks. My grandmother once wrote that while growing up she had been embarrassed by its whimsical appearance until, reading a book of fairy tales, she came across an illustration of a castle of similar design. The peaked roof, covered with bays, gables, and dormers, is pitched as sharply as a wedge of cheese stood on its rind. The walls are ringed with porches and breezeways. Two huge chimneys lie diagonally along the roof, as if they had toppled during a storm and miraculously come to rest with every brick in place. Children love to count the rooms, of which there are nineteen (or, if you count the bathrooms—as children usually do—twenty-six). There are eleven bedrooms, seven fireplaces, and a warren of closets, cupboards, and crannies that four generations of Wings Neck children have used for games of Sardines. From the water, the house appears to rise from the pines like a ship from an enormous green wave. The most prominent house on Wings Neck, it has been a familiar landmark to generations of sailors approaching the harbor. Several years ago, I was at a party in Boston, talking with someone about sailing in Buzzards Bay, and I mentioned that my grandparents had a summer house on Wings Neck. As I began to describe it, he interrupted me: "Oh, you live in the Ghost House!" Wings Neck children also know it as the Haunted House, the Wicked Witch of the West House, and the House of the Seven Gables. (Actually, it has eight.)

My family calls it, simply, the Big House. Each summer for forty-two years I have traveled here from winter homes across the United States. The Big House is where I learned how to swim, play tennis, sail. The Big House is where I first kissed a girl, first got drunk, first experimented with drugs. My most vivid dreams and nightmares are set here. It is where I read the books my father, grandfather, and great-grandfather read as children, and where I wrote my own first book. It is where I decided to get married. It is where my wife and I buried keepsakes to remind us of two miscarried babies, not far from where my grandfather's ashes are buried. I have come to recognize the peculiar rattle each window makes in its casement, the luffing of each window shade, the texture of each forest path under my bare feet, the sound of each screen door slamming, the nine-second pause between the beam from Cleveland Ledge Light that stripes my wall as I lie in bed at night. Although I have spent only a month or two here each year for four decades, I have always thought of it as home, if home is the one place that will be in your bones forever.

I am only one of many people who have thought of the Big House as home. It has been a gathering place for my family for five generations. The house has watched over five weddings, four divorces, three deaths, several nervous breakdowns, an untold number of conceptions, and countless birthday parties, anniversaries, and love affairs. My aunts, uncles, and cousins have crisscrossed the country, moving from job to job and from winter home to winter home, but they have always come back. For nearly a century, my family has thought of the Big House as an unchanging place in a changing world, a sanctuary we have assumed we would always be able to return to, as would our children and our children's children.

And yet—I can hardly believe it even as I write these words—we are selling the Big House. Like many extended families throughout the Northeast whose rambling summer houses were built in another, palmier era, we can no longer afford to keep up the place. The financial issues are entwined with emotional issues far more formidable. The house has come to mean something very different to each of the siblings in my father's generation who jointly inherited it after my grandmother's death in 1986. During two years of meetings whose veneer of civility could not wholly conceal the strong feelings that lay beneath, the family was unable to come to an agreement that would enable them to keep any part of the place. Four years ago, it was put up for sale.

For three years, as the real estate market staggered through the economic recession of the early nineties, we received not a single offer. Over the last twelve months, however, as the selling price was lowered and the economy revived, the family has received a flurry of bids, among which the principals are currently choosing. We have come here for what we know may be our last summer.

We lug our bags to the thick green oak door. Instinctively throwing my shoulder against the top while kicking the bottom where the door sticks, I open it wide. Inside, we are enveloped by an unmistakable smell, one that might be difficult for even the most expert chemist to break down, but that seems to be composed, in various measures, of salt, wind, dust, sunlight, moonlight, sand, pine, mildew, mothballs, leather, old books, disintegrating bricks, and dead bluebottle flies. It is a smell so evocative and precious, so irresistibly redolent of both life and decay, that I wonder why it has never been bottled and sold as a perfume.

"It smells like the Big House," I say.

Susannah laughs happily. "Daddy, it *is* the Big House."

For a building this large, the Big House has a surprisingly cramped front hall—no more than a stairwell, really—as if the architect had been impatient with social niceties and decided to devote space only to living itself. As we stand there, familiar objects take shape in the midafternoon shadows: the rack of my great-grandfather's canes; the blue denim mailbag with my grandmother's initials; the charcoal portraits of my father and his siblings; the carved wooden buck's head on the wall, its antlers festooned with baseball caps, battered old Panamas, and Grandma's broad-brimmed straw gardening bonnet. The hallway, which is several feet lower than the rest of the first floor, receives so little sunlight I feel as if I'm underwater, swimming up toward the mosaic of light that plays in the living room window. Walking up the four stairs that lead to the landing is like stepping up onto the deck of a boat.

This nautical feeling is reinforced by the Chelsea ship's clock that hangs on the wall directly ahead, next to a haphazardly thumbtacked tide chart. My great-grandfather bought it in 1903, the year he built this house. Round as a porthole, encased in what I used to think was solid gold but is only well-polished brass, it is, nevertheless, the only thing of real value in the house, according to my father. Although summer is the season in which we may be least beholden to time—in which, in fact, we try to ignore its existence—this clock has always been one of the house's most essential artifacts. As a child I consulted it only to learn how many minutes I had left to play until bedtime, yet I seemed always to be aware of its ticking, and at night I'd wake to hear it tolling downstairs, a surprisingly dainty sound, and try to decipher, in my sleepiness, the confusing mathematics of ship's bells, which chime every half hour, up to eight chimes. Did seven chimes mean that it was 11:30 P.M. or 3:30 A.M.? I felt as if I were a sailor and the house a boat, floating somewhere on the Atlantic. Although not much larger than a saucer, the clock was so solid and magisterial-looking that I half believed it kept time not just for this house but for the entire world, at least during the summer. Indeed, as the clock approached the end of its weeklong cycle and began to slow down, it almost seemed that *everything* was growing lethargic, and that time itself might soon grind to a halt.

My father says that when the Big House is sold, the clock is the only thing he wants from it, although when I ask him why, he can't explain, other than to say, "I've always wound that clock. And when I was a boy I watched my grandfather wind that clock." Like my father, I find the act deeply satisfying. Using two hands, as on a ship's wheel, I unscrew the brass-rimmed glass cover, its heaviness and finely beveled threads giving me the sensation of spinning the tumblers of an expensive safe. Rummaging among the golf tees, thumbtacks, rubber bands, and pennies in the wooden bowl on the shelf, I fish out the brass key. Fitting it into the square slot in the face of the clock—a strangely intrusive gesture—I turn it to gradually increasing resistance, and the ticking begins, metallic and light as the clicking of a barber's scissors. As I wind this clock, the traditional first ritual of opening the house, I feel, in a larger sense, that I am starting time again, starting the summer, setting the heart of this house, here in this narrow hallway, to beating once more.

While Anne takes Henry upstairs to unpack, I dump the contents of my pockets—wallet, change, keys—on the sideboard in the dining room, a symbolic stripping down. Then I walk from room to room, raising windows, noting another broken sash cord, checking on leaks, opening the two ancient refrigerators, turning on the hot water heater in the cellar. I'm not just taking inventory, I'm greeting the house. As I go, I find myself touching things to make sure they're still there, the way Henry, even though he no longer nurses, keeps a tiny, proprietary hand on Anne's breast when they snuggle. I trace the gold-leaf letters on my great-grandmother's set of Dickens in the living room bookcase; I run my finger over the bone-handled silverware; I notice to what letter my grandfather's dictionary is open on its stand; I slide the guest book from the desk in the corner of the living room and read the latest entry. As I see once again the worn spot on the pantry door where hundreds of hands have opened and closed it, the graffiti of white scratchings inscribed by thousands of matches on the ash-blackened fireplace, the pentimento of labels (DOUBLE FITTED, TWIN FLAT) on the linen closet shelves, I feel an interlayering of generations that is delicious but slightly disorienting. Each room holds so many memories that its contents are measurable not just in three dimensions but in a fourth—time. Here and there I intersect with Susannah, who is making a nostalgic tour of her own, revisiting her favorite things from summers past: the small wooden rocking horse in the living room, the blocks in the third-floor Playroom, the set of Beatrix Potter books in the Little Nursery. "I drank from that little blue glass last year; I'm going to drink from it again this year," she tells me, fondling my grandmother's miniature plastic water glasses in the pantry.

I have always done this fossicking, like a dog sniffing out its territory, although on recent visits I have had a more practical reason for doing so. For the last four years, we have been renting out the Big House for most of the summer to help cover the cost of taxes and maintenance. Each time I arrive after renters have been here, I cannot help feeling as if I'm entering the house after a burglary. Nothing is broken or missing today, but traces of occupation are everywhere: dishes misshelved in the pantry; twelve garbage bags of soda cans, wine bottles, and milk jugs in the back hall; a Tupperware container, housing a brownish lump I can't identify, in the freezer. The front hall is stippled with dust balls, the kitchen floor hasn't been swept, and the screens on the back porch doors are ripped. The badminton net has been set up on the side lawn, where croquet is usually laid out. The lawn itself is strewn with cigarette butts and stray tennis balls. The barbecue sits in the garden, far from its accustomed place on the kitchen porch. I know these small changes are no more than a foretaste of what will happen after the house is sold. But things have been the same here for so long that any deviation rankles. I return the dictionary stand from the dining room to the living room corner, the ladder-back chairs from the porch to the dining room. It's not that I want things pristine; in fact, I prefer a slight disorder, but I want it to be *our* disorder.

Then we settle in. When I was a child, I usually slept in one of the former maids' rooms in the kitchen wing, and I recall the excitement I felt on returning to it after nine months' absence. Anne and I have graduated to a large, sunny room overlooking the bay, the door of which has a sign that says GRANDMA'S BEDROOM. There are signs on most of the bedroom doors, painted in the early sixties by my mother and our baby-sitter, who came from a neighboring Wings Neck family. Each bears the room's name and a watercolor of a flower or a bird. The paint has faded, but we still call the rooms by these names: Grandma's Bedroom, Grandma's Dressing Room, Grandpa's Dressing Room, the Little Nursery, the Yellow Room, the Sunny Room, Oliver's Garden Bedroom, the Balcony Room. (The signs have the effect of freezing these rooms in time. Thus, the small bedroom under the eaves on the third floor is still known as Mariah's Room—after the nurse who cared for my father and his siblings in the twenties and thirties—although Mariah has been dead for decades.) I help Anne make the bed. I hide my papers, my office telephone list, and everything else that says New York in the back of a drawer. Meanwhile, Susannah arranges her things in Grandma's Dressing Room, a large, airy chamber with two single beds and a chaise longue. She thinks of it as *her* room, her favorite, she says, in all the world. As usual, she takes the bed by the west window, from which, at night, she can see the stars over the bay.

As soon as we are unpacked, we head down to the Bluff, the name we have always used for the rocky beach that rings the house on two sides. The house sits on a promontory. When you walk from the house toward the bay, you can't see the beach, so it looks as if you are walking straight off into deep water. "I'll race you," says Susannah, and we run across the back lawn, then make our way down the rickety wooden stairs to the beach. "Be careful, because it's very steep and there's poison ivy," she says, before I can say it. It's windy and the waves crash on the rocks. The end of the boardwalk has broken off and washed away. Susannah makes a bee-line for the driftwood clubhouse she made last year; she's excited to find many of the planks still there. We pick up sea glass, throwing back pieces that haven't been rubbed smooth and translucent so that—according to Susannah, who doesn't believe we're really selling the house—"we can find them again next year." Bare for the first time this summer, our tender feet cringe from the stones and boat shells. We seek the soft furl of seaweed at the tide line.

Henry, who graduated from crawling not so long ago, does not wish to be carried to the water. He insists on walking: a perilous journey over rocks that to him must seem the size of boulders. As he picks his way along, holding Anne's hand, I can see his feet already making instinctive choices: when he steps on a thin, sharper rock, before planting too much weight on it he steps off onto a lower, flatter one. It takes them five minutes to travel the ten yards to the water's edge. When they get there, he points at the waves as they approach his toes. "Ocean," says Anne. He repeats the word. Then he points at a sloop coming into the harbor. "Boat," he says. He points at a cormorant flying low over the water toward the setting sun. "Bird!" He points out the faint half-moon in the pale sky and says, "Me!" (That's his word for moon.) He is pointing out all the things I love about this place.

That night, after the children are asleep, Anne and I lie in bed listening to the wind. I love the sound of wind, whether it is soughing through the pines in the Sierras or whistling around the steel and stone corners of lower Manhattan. But there is something especially eloquent about the sound of wind coming off water. As a child, I liked the idea that the very wind that knocked against my bedroom window had originated far out to sea. The Big House looks directly down Buzzards Bay, and thus faces directly into what people around here call the "teeth" of the prevailing southwest wind. The Wampanoag Indians, who lived on Cape Cod before the arrival of the Pilgrims, called this wind Sowwanin, "the wind of good fortune," and believed it blew departed souls to the land of plenty. When the wind races up Buzzards Bay, as it does almost every afternoon, it plays the Big House like a flute. Each year, the wind and rain further erode the corners of the eaves and the window frames, creating an ever more pliant, ever-louder instrument. By now the house is so worn that even the gentlest breeze can produce a sigh.

In a heavy wind like tonight's, I can hear several different parts, each of which, as I lie in bed, I like to separate and identify. There is the low, querulous whistle of the wind in the eaves, its pitch fluctuating with the air's changing velocity—in big gusts it spikes a higher, flighty soprano that reminds me of my grandmother singing. This is surmounted by a sharper descant at the very peak of the attic, the way a perfect, resonant note sung in a cathedral may produce a hovering fifth. In the background, you can hear the general whoosh of the wind through the trees. The farther up you go in the Big House, the higher and louder the sound, so that as you walk upstairs, you hear a gradual crescendo, and by the time you reach the third floor, it's so loud that as a child I liked to believe that the Big House Playroom had been the setting for the George MacDonald tale *At the Back of the North Wind*.

Then there is the syncopated rattling of the windows in their casements, a sound that kept me awake as a child until I could account for every last shudder. Even now, I like to figure out where each individual rattle is coming from, whether it be the mutter of the leftmost window on the west wall of Grandma's Dressing Room; the sporadic banging of the windows in Oliver's Garden Bedroom, which sounds just like someone rapping at the door, pausing, then rapping again; or the insistent quiver of the Playroom windows, which sounds like someone pacing the third floor. The house has sixty-seven windows and, in a big wind like tonight's, almost every one of them joins the chorus. (I have often wondered whether it might be possible, if one hurried from room to room, from floor to floor, opening and closing windows to various heights, for the wind to produce some faintly recognizable melody, the way we used to fill soda bottles to different levels in order to puff out "Three Blind Mice.") And there is a percussion accompaniment: the smack of the green window shades as they are sucked against the frames and released, the occasional slam of a distant door. Underlying all of these is the steady *sssssh* of the waves on the Bluff.

The sound of the wind is one of the first things guests notice about the

Big House. Some find it exciting. Some write in the guest book about its soothing, soporific effect. Some are frightened by it and feel it's a sure sign that the house is haunted. To me, the sound of the wind is as much a part of the house as the ivy on the trellis or the chimneys on the roof. Indeed, when I read *The Merchant of Venice* in eighth grade, I imagined that the music of the spheres must sound like the wind through the Big House. And later, I chose to relocate a favorite T. S. Eliot poem, "Rhapsody on a Windy Night," from the back streets of London to Buzzards Bay.

"Oh, if only these walls could talk," guests in the Big House often say. I've always felt the walls *do* talk, and the sound they make is sometimes a wail, sometimes a sigh, and sometimes a joyous hullabaloo. The wind seems to come not from outside but from inside. To me it is the house's song, a blend of the voices of all the people who have lived here over the last hundred years. Now that we are selling the house, the voices sound more urgent than ever, trying to make themselves heard. And as I lie here, Anne sleeping beside me, Susannah in Grandma's Dressing Room, Henry in the Little Nursery, I wonder: When the house is sold, what will happen to the wind?

II

The Family Tree

S USANNAH has developed an interest in her ancestry. A few nights
ago, at the Big House dining table, we sketched out her family tree.
On my half of the page, we filled in the brackets back through the First
World War, past the turn of the century, past the Civil War: a dendri-
form thicket with so many limbs, boughs, and twigs that Susannah's
handwriting shrank to near-illegibility. We were still going strong when
it was time for bed. Anne's half, however, was mostly empty. Although
she can trace her roots on her mother's side back to Mormon pioneers
who traveled to Utah in covered wagons, the paternal line comes to a
halt at her grandparents, Russian Jews who fled the pogroms at the turn
of the century. She does not even know her great-grandparents' names.
The Fadimans had no old family portraits to hang on their walls, no
crumbling photograph albums, no boxes of disintegrating letters. Was
this sad? Was this enviable? Both, I felt. A few years ago, a cousin of
Anne's hired a genealogist to try to fill in some of the gaps in the Fadiman family tree. "Your family doesn't need to hire a genealogist," Anne
told me. "Everyone *in* it is a genealogist."

In the Big House, family seeped into us like the salt air or the
mildew—not only in the form of the cousins and aunts who kept its sixteen beds full throughout my youth, but in the ancestors who lurked in
every corner. In the attic there were trunkfuls of photos of unidentified
relatives: women in chin-to-toe dresses sitting on the porches of Victorian houses; Union officers posed like schoolboys in a studio before
going off to battle; debutantes in gauzily lit Bachrach portraits on thick,
creamy poster board. The desk drawers held unfinished family trees, old
leather-bound guest books, typed lists of birth and death dates, notes to

distant cousins tracking down information on still-more-distant cousins. Cloistered behind the latticed glass doors of the elaborately carved breakfront in the dining room, on each end of which a hooded monk prayed atop a scroll, were the family books: hymnals, prayer books, biographies, genealogies, bound collections of correspondence, privately printed memoirs dictated by elderly forebears "for the sake of my children and my children's children." When I was a boy, the bookcase would swell with humidity each summer until it seemed an impenetrable ancestral tomb. I'd finally pry open the doors with a butter knife, and a faint, damp warmth would creep out, like the sigh of a very small ghost.

I was the archaeologist; my ancestors were the bones. As I unearthed each one—the captain killed in King Philip's War; the seventeenth-century bride whose father gave her her weight in shillings as a wedding gift; the farmer who tethered his cow on Boston Common; the great-great-great-great-grandfather who fought the British at Lexington; the girl who was kissed on the hand by the Marquis de Lafayette; the great-great-great-uncle who married Ralph Waldo Emerson's daughter; the great-great-grandfather who was wounded at Gettysburg—I was surprised to learn that my family had been present at important events, that we had once been *players* in a way we no longer were. This made me feel larger (I was related to famous people!). But it also made me feel smaller, a speck in a long ancestral line, not entirely free to be me because it had been ordained, long before I was born, that I was one of them.

In the attic of the Big House, among the trunks and hatboxes, there stood a curious object made of wood, steel, and asbestos. My brothers and I thought it might be an animal trap, or perhaps a primitive portable toilet—a companion piece to the enameled chamber pots, also stored in the attic, that we giggled over as we imagined them in use by our distinguished ancestors. It was, in fact, an Aladdin Oven, a sort of primitive Crock-Pot invented by our great-great-grandfather, Edward Atkinson.

Born in 1827, Atkinson was a Brahmin of orthodox lineage (his antecedents had come to America around 1630) who had been headed for Harvard—a fact he found it necessary to mention frequently in his writings—when the family merchant business failed. At the age of fifteen, he went to work unpacking crates in a dry goods store for thirty dollars a year. I have always wondered to what extent his subsequent career represented an attempt to compensate for his lack of formal education. Judging from his papers at the Massachusetts Historical Society—82 letter books (at 1,000 pages per volume), 45 boxes of miscellaneous correspondence, and more than 250 polemical pamphlets—Atkinson never saw an editorial that didn't need amending, a cause that didn't need defending, a congressman who didn't need correcting, or a young man (including Henry Adams, who praised him in *The Education*) who didn't need career advice. He contributed regularly to the *The Atlantic Monthly, Harper's Weekly,* the *North American Review,* and *The Nation,* which he had helped found. A self-taught economist, he became the treasurer of several cotton mills, counseled Lincoln on the South's financial future, and served as a behind-the-scenes adviser to Grant, Garfield, and Cleveland. An abolitionist, he raised money to ship John Brown some of the rifles he would use in the uprising at Harpers Ferry. An integrationist, he helped establish schools for newly freed slaves. "One thing will be easily granted by the reader;" wrote Mark Twain in *Life on the Mississippi,* citing Atkinson's position on river management, "that an opinion from Mr. Edward Atkinson, upon any vast national commercial matter, comes as near ranking as authority, as can the opinion of any individual in the Union."

But the achievement my great-great-grandfather was proudest of, that he thought would be of most lasting value to his country, was the contraption we found in the attic. It was his quixotic hope that the Aladdin Oven would enable working-class families to prepare inexpensive, nutritious foods. For a time, Aladdins were used at the Tuskegee Institute, the Elmira State Reformatory, and Chicago's Hull House. In the 1890s, Atkinson helped set up the New England Kitchen, a take-out restaurant in a blue-collar Boston neighborhood that sold Aladdin-cooked renditions of all the spectacularly drab Yankee classics I hated as a child: clam chowder, succotash, creamed codfish, corn mush, boiled hominy, baked beans, brown bread, Indian pudding, apple pandowdy. The Kitchen was awarded a contract to provide lunches for all nine Boston high schools—the first school lunch program in the country.

Although the citizens of New York City, Philadelphia, Providence, and Chicago were subjected to my great-great-grandfather's recipes when his restaurant opened branches there, the Aladdin never achieved widespread acceptance. Boston's immigrants rejected the bland New England food cooked on the Aladdin in favor of the spicier cuisine of their homelands. "I don't want to eat what's good for me—I'd rather eat what I'd rather," commented one woman after swallowing a sample. Labor organizer Eugene Debs derided the oven's inventor as "Shinbone Atkinson" and claimed he was looking for an excuse to reduce workers' wages. There were technical kinks, too: the Aladdin, which was heated by a kerosene lamp, took five hours to reach the boiling point and had an alarming tendency, if left unattended, to burn through the table on which it stood. Nevertheless, Atkinson continued, with a touch of obstinate pride, to have all his own meals prepared on the Aladdin—as well as those of his guests (governors, college presidents, Ceylonese monks), whose patience was tried not only by the menu but by the lectures their portly, white-bearded host gave between courses on the merits of his invention. "I do not remember what we had," recalled a friend, "but it all took a very long time."

It is not surprising that such an unconventional father would have unconventional children. I grew up hearing stories about the "Ats," as the Atkinsons liked to call themselves, an eccentric crew of seven siblings raised in comfort (except for the bill of fare) on Heath Hill, a rambling estate in Brookline, overlooking Boston, built by the wealthy family into which Edward Atkinson had married. There was Charlie, who, after being deemed most likely to succeed in Harvard's Class of 1885—among other achievements, he held the intercollegiate high-jump record—had a nervous breakdown and lived out the rest of his life in the care of an attendant in rural Vermont. There was Carla, a painter and political activist who chained herself to the railing of the Boston State House in order to protest the execution of Sacco and Vanzetti. There was Robert, who made pocket money at Harvard by performing as a one-man band, simultaneously playing piano, harmonica, kettledrum, Turkish cymbals, castanets, bells, and "humanotone," an instrument that, worn on the nose, produced a sound midway between that of a flute and a clarinet. (Alas, Robert married what family members sniffily referred to as a "Page from Philadelphia," who, not understanding that euphonious nose blowing and the culture of the Boston Brahmin were an excellent fit, vetoed his musical career and provided an object lesson for the rest of the family: Marry Bostonians.) There was Mary, a fine pianist. There was Anna, a mainstay of the Atkinson family chorus, which serenaded her father's guests while they awaited their Aladdin-cooked dinners. And there were the two brothers whose talent (on the one hand) and money (on the other) combined to build the Big House: William, its brilliant and eccentric architect, and Edward W., universally known as Ned, its owner, the eldest At son.

Every Brahmin family needs a member like Ned Atkinson, the prosperous striver who plays straight man to his insolvent, idealistic, humanotone-playing siblings. After graduating from Harvard, where he rowed crew, he worked for a company that imported machinery and raw materials for textile mills; by twenty-seven, when he became a full partner, its name was changed to Atkinson, Haserick & Company. After the deaths of his parents, he moved into the family home on Heath Hill, began to support his siblings financially, and became the stable emotional center around which the Ats revolved.

I grew up staring at a gold-framed portrait of Ned Atkinson: an extraordinarily handsome, fit-looking man with turquoise eyes, a thick, brown, upturned mustache, and the Atkinson nose (prominent and pointed). He wears a three-piece suit, a red tie, a gold stickpin, a gold fob. The impression is one of bankerly solidity: he looks important, but he doesn't look fun. By all reports, however, he was both—what in his day was known as a "hail-fellow-well-met." Atkinson belonged to fifteen clubs. He smoked oversized cigars and ate oversized meals. He was an avid sailor and a natural athlete who took up ice-skating in his fifties. (A rusty trophy in Mariah's Room attests that in 1919, at the age of sixty, he won the pairs championship at the Boston Skating Club, which he had founded, with a Mrs. Channing Frothingham.) He was something of a philanthropist, who, in addition to supporting his siblings, his church, and the usual Brahmin cultural institutions, helped sponsor the great African-American tenor Roland Hayes in the early years of his career, when Boston impresarios were unwilling to offer their stages to black performers. Atkinson himself had a powerful baritone that he rarely hesitated to use. My aunt Ellen remembers being woken each morning in the Big House by the sound of scales; my father still occasionally bursts into one of the Irish ditties his grandfather used to sing as they rode in the backseat of the family's chauffeured car. His voice was known far beyond Boston and Wings Neck. In the thirties, when my greatuncle Chis, then a Washington correspondent for the *Wall Street Journal*, was at a White House dinner, he found himself standing next to President Franklin Roosevelt when the band struck up "The Yellow Rose of Texas."

"Mr. President, have you ever heard Ned Atkinson sing that song?" my uncle asked.

"I certainly have," the president answered.

Ned Atkinson did not make the same mistake as his exogamous brother Robert: he married a Boston Brahmin—and not just any Brahmin, but a granddaughter of John Murray Forbes, a legendary Bostonian "merchant-prince," who by the age of twenty-four had amassed one of the country's largest fortunes by sailing tea and silk out of China and sailing cotton, tobacco, and opium in. (The moral ramifications of the opium trade were only partly appreciated, and completely ignored, at the time. "It was commonly asserted," wrote historian Samuel Eliot Morison, "that opium had no more effect on the Chinese than rum on Yankees.")

In 1857, Forbes had used the profits to purchase Naushon, a seven-mile-long island southwest of Cape Cod (and eleven miles south of Wings Neck), and due in large part to the money he left behind, his lineal descendants have been able to enjoy it as a communal summer retreat ever since. There is little doubt about who qualifies for this privilege, as the Forbes family tree, painstakingly maintained and updated by a cadre of aunts, is currently laid out on all four walls of a Naushon barn. In a kind of genealogical spiderweb that struck Anne speechless the first time she saw it, each of the six branches of the family is represented by a different color of yarn (more than two hundred yards in all), tracing its way through the burgeoning generations from John Murray Forbes to his 106 great-great-great-great-grandchildren. Whenever I look at the small piece of green cardboard in the northwest corner that says "George Howe Colt—m. Anne Fadiman, children Susannah Fadiman Colt and Henry Clifton Fadiman Colt," which is connected by five lengths of yarn to the blue piece of cardboard that contains the names of my great-great-great-grandparents, I feel literally tied to the past. Tied, and also tied *down*, like Gulliver trussed up in Lilliput. But I'm clearly not the only family member who has felt the need to break, or at least stretch, the ancestral yarn. The names on the walls are accompanied by photographs. In the first few generations, everyone looks alike, but beginning in the 1960s, the tree becomes a veritable Rainbow Coalition of African husbands, Japanese wives, and adopted Guatemalan babies.

In the nineteenth century, as now, Naushon had no written rules, but it did have a set of mores and traditions no less hallowed for their informality. Among these was that the small ferry to the mainland always left on time. One Monday morning, I'm told, my great-grandfather Ned Atkinson, who had an important meeting that day, was late for the early boat that allowed businessmen to catch a train to Boston for the beginning of the workweek. He arrived at the wharf just as the boat cast off. Although he called out to the captain, his entreaties were ignored, and the ferry steamed out of the harbor, leaving him harrumphing on the dock.

One morning not long afterward, Ned Atkinson again took the early boat—this time taking care to be on board well before its scheduled departure. But when the hour arrived, the ferry did not budge. A few minutes later, he saw why: the great John Murray Forbes himself, his gnomelike face topped, no doubt, by his favorite lumpish hat, was strolling in a leisurely fashion down to the dock. As soon as Forbes stepped on board, the ferry left. I can imagine that my famously scrupulous great-grandfather was apoplectic (inwardly, of course). He vowed never again to set foot on Naushon. He also decided to establish a summer retreat of his own, where, if rules were to be made, he would be the one to make them.

He was true to his word. Ned Atkinson never returned to Naushon, and several years later, at Wings Neck, he broke ground for the Big House.

There is hardly anyone on the walls or in the albums of the Big House who was not born in or near Boston. In 1859, the year of Ned Atkinson's birth, Boston was the centerpiece of what Van Wyck Brooks called "the flowering of New England": the nation's literary and artistic headquarters, the city where future presidents were educated, the fertile breeding ground for all the new isms—Unitarianism, Transcendentalism, abolitionism, feminism. "Boston commands special attention as the town which was appointed by the destiny of nations to lead the Civilization of North America," proclaimed Emerson. North America? Too small! To Oliver Wendell Holmes, it was nothing less than "the hub of the solar system."

Until my own generation, everyone in the Hub, it was said, knew everyone—although "everyone," of course, meant only the small sliver of Boston that constituted the Brahmin upper crust. My grandfather told his children that, by the end of his freshman year at Harvard, he could walk down Commonwealth Avenue as far as Hereford Street and know the name of the family behind each door. (On the other hand, if he'd turned left and walked ten blocks to the South End, he wouldn't have known a soul.) Marriages between second cousins were common; marriages between firsts were not unheard of. It was a society no less inbred than backwoods Appalachia—and, given its incidence of mental illness and alcoholism, may have similarly suffered from a lack of hybrid vigor. When I was a child, it seemed that every adult I met on Wings Neck was known not as Mr. or Mrs. but as Cousin or Aunt or Sister—some of them indeed relatives by blood, but most of them relatives by social class. The incestuousness of Brahmin nomenclature reached its semantic apogee in a neighbor who was introduced to me as "Cousin Sister." Marry outside Boston—even a Page from Philadelphia—and tongues would cluck. Marry a Nobody from Michigan (as a friend's grandmother did), and your name was likely to be dropped from "the lists"—the tally sheets of those deemed worthy of invitation to the waltzes, balls, and "evenings" that constituted Boston's social season.

The same families that had campaigned for progressive causes through much of the nineteenth century had become timorous xenophobes by the dawn of the twentieth, when "newcomers" outnumbered descendants of colonial stock by nearly three to one. In "Boston: Notes on a Barbarian Invasion," an article published in *Harper's* in 1928, Elmer Davis compared the arrival of the Irish in Boston to the Ostrogoth takeover of ancient Rome: "The old Bostonians, like the old Romans, keep out of their way, hiding in the crumbling palaces, each race despising and envying the other." The painter Thomas Gold Appleton coined the phrase "Cold Roast Boston" (referring to the Brahmin habit of serving roast beef every Sunday and cold roast beef the next day) to describe the stuffy parsimony of Brahmin society. "The best thing about Boston is the Merchant's Limited train going home," became the stock line of visiting Manhattan debutantes. Uncomfortable with the present, upper-class Boston turned for comfort to the past, first living off family money, and then, when that dwindled, trying to bask in the increasingly dim glow cast by once-powerful family names. "Boston—wrinkled, spindly-legged, depleted of nearly all her spiritual and cutaneous oils, provincial, self-esteeming—has gone on spending and spending her inflated bills of pure reputation, decade after decade," wrote Elizabeth Hardwick in an infamous 1959 essay. "Now, one supposes it is all over at last."

Indeed, by the time I was growing up in the sixties, it was hard to think of Boston as the hub of anything, let alone the universe. Much of Brahmin Boston had fled to the suburbs, and the empty downtown was a pale echo of its former self, like the ghostly horseshoe crab moltings we found on the Big House Bluff. There were a few pockets of resistance left, to which my grandmother escorted us from our suburban home: the hushed parlors of the Chilton Club; the acoustically perfect crucible of Symphony Hall; the gilt splendor of the Copley Plaza. The seven-story Romanesque headquarters of the S. S. Pierce Company, which had been serving Brahmin epicures (an oxymoron?) since 1831, had recently been replaced by a Back Bay parking lot, though my grandparents could still get their claret sauce delivered by telephone order. People still called the Brookline Country Club "The Country Club" and the Harvard-Yale football game "The Game," but ironic quotation marks were likely to be vocally implied. At family gatherings we still encountered people who were defined by their having quarterbacked the Harvard football team or stroked the St. Something's crew—people of whom it was said, as it would later be said of my own grandparents, "Well, you should have known them when they were young"—but of course they were all silver-haired. An increasing number of Boston WASPs were rebelling: marrying Catholics or people from Michigan, moving to New York, or becoming carpenters. ("From shirtsleeves to shirtsleeves in three generations," a family friend dryly observed.)

The Brahmin influence was vastly diluted in the suburban Boston home in which I grew up. Although my father took us to Harvard football games and my mother occasionally performed in Nucleus Club shows with my grandmother, my parents both worked full-time and were too busy making ends meet—albeit in order to put us through private schools—to reflect much on ancestral glories. I remember finding a copy of the *Social Register* on a family bookshelf when I was a teenager and being baffled not only by its obscure code (*P* meant Princeton, *M* meant the Myopia Hunt Club) and its bizarre vocabulary (I was a "Junior Mister," vacation homes were "dilatory domiciles"), but by its purpose. I certainly never saw my parents use the thing. Around the same time, they dutifully scraped together the money to enroll me in Miss Souther's, the venerable dancing school, lodged in a decrepit old auditorium in Jamaica Plain, where my father and grandmother had learned to waltz. Stuffed into a hand-me-down blue blazer, my sweaty palm resting on the exposed back of a girl officially certified as a Brahmin by what remained of "the lists," I struggled to master the box step, my feet stumbling as the ancient Miss Souther herself barked "right and left and left and right and left and right and right and left." My parents, bless them, didn't make me return.

Proper Boston may have been fading, but proper Bostonians still had their summer places, where nothing changed, where nothing *had* to change, where the best part of old Boston, it seemed, lived on. Here, on their tennis courts, in their leaky wooden boats, and on their rocky beaches, they did the same things they had always done, and were thereby allowed, in a certain sense, to stay forever young. I have often heard people call Wings Neck—and other summer communities like it—a retreat. And it was, it seems to me now, not only a retreat from the city, but a retreat from the ever-changing present into a safer, more orderly past, a past in which Boston—and our family—was still in its full flower. I cannot deny that as a child, I felt a thrill when my grandmother began a story with the words "Your great-great-grandfather, who fought Stonewall Jackson at the Battle of Cedar Mountain . . ." Or that part of me envied the casual sureness with which my grandmother spoke of "Alice Howland, née Forbes," or when my great-uncle Chis described someone by saying "He didn't make the A.D.," and the grown-ups nodded as if nothing more need be said. Or that, leafing through the gilt-edged pages of the Big House guest books, I felt a sense of wonder at seeing all those names lead from my great-grandfather's elegantly inked signature to my own felt-tipped scrawl. Or that, on a summer evening, looking from the ancestral portraits on the walls to the three generations of faces around the Big House dining table, I felt swollen with pride at being part of this family.

III

1963

WHEN I THINK of the Big House—and my family—at its greatest glory, I recall hot August weekends circa 1963, when I was
eight or nine. The house was filled with cousins; the dining table swelled
with extra leaves; the second refrigerator was pressed into service; and
every morning the frying pan turned out enough bacon to feed, as my
grandfather put it, "a small army."

I slept in the kitchen wing with my brothers and cousins. Its steep
stairs, low-ceilinged hallway, and small, sparsely furnished rooms led us
to believe that this part of the house had been made expressly for children, but it had, of course, been designed for servants, back in the days
when there were servants. The room I shared with my cousin Oliver
overlooked the bay. Each morning the smell of bacon lured us downstairs to the kitchen, where my grandfather was hunched over the stove,
an apron over his worn gray suit, straightening the slices that lay cooling
on a paper towel. We sat down at the vast, square kitchen table, reaching
for condiments we didn't really want so we'd have an excuse to spin the
lazy Susan (and wonder about the slothful girl for whom this marvelous
apparatus had been named) while Grandpa padded back and forth in his
sneakers, ferrying poached eggs, sausage patties, apricot nectar, and
steaming bowls of Cream of Wheat topped with butter and brown sugar.

Grandpa was particular about food. Once a week, a delivery truck
from S. S. Pierce would pull up at the kitchen door. Only Jones sausages,
Hellmann's mayonnaise, and Keiller's Dundee marmalade—spooned
from a cream-colored ceramic jar that, emptied and cleaned, would be
used to hold pencils—would do. Our eggs, purchased from a small farm
in Sandwich, were topped with Roman Spice, an herb blend Grandpa

told us had been used by emperors in 100 B.C. If a grandchild reached for a slice of bacon tinged with what he deemed excessive fat, he'd say, "You don't want that, old boy. That's not fit for human consumption." Into the garbage it would go (the only instance I can remember in which anything of possible utility was ever thrown out in the Big House). At the time, this fastidiousness seemed generous: nothing, it seemed to say, was too good for us. Later, I would see that my grandfather applied similarly uncompromising standards to people, and I worried that if he found even an ounce of fat on my character, I might be similarly rejected.

In his early sixties, Grandpa bore little resemblance to the curly-haired Harvard hockey player in the photograph on my grandmother's dresser. His lanky frame was stooped with age and sciatica, his handsome face was wrinkled and jowly, and his head was as smooth as a billiard ball. By then his chief sport was *The New York Times* Sunday crossword puzzle, and his most fearsome opponent was the catbrier he battled in the woods each afternoon. Once a summer, however, he'd appear at the top of the steps that led to the Bluff for his annual "swim," towel draped over one shoulder, baggy madras bathing suit drawn up over his pale belly. After contemplating the scene for a moment, he'd turn around and head back to the house. He was opposed to the beach on general principle, and if you were rash enough to tender a picnic invitation, he'd snort, "If I must have sand in my food, I prefer to have it brought to the table." The air of gentle, weary bemusement with which he regarded the world gave Grandpa an impression of premature age, an impression reinforced by the antiquated vocabulary with which, to our delight, he larded his conversation. A grandchild who brought his dirty dish to the sink had done "yeoman work"; a restive grandchild might provoke a stern "*douce-ment*"; a grandchild sitting out a tennis match was "*hors de combat.*" Letters from Grandpa invariably began with the salutation "My dear and gallant sir."

Grandpa was at his most delightful in the morning, before the appearance of Grandma, to whom—we could sense it, though we didn't understand it—he seemed something of a disappointment. To us, he was a kind of hero. None of us would think of missing the morning drive to the general store, a two-mile journey that took us off the Neck into what he called "civilization." Wearing the kind of Panama hat sported by his favorite golfer, Sam Snead, Grandpa hunched so low over the wheel of his ten-year-old Peugeot station wagon that he appeared to be monitoring the road through its spokes. In those pre–seat belt days, the children tumbled about in the metal-ribbed cargo area we called "the way back," waiting expectantly for each familiar landmark. When we approached the bump in the road near Johnny Hallowell's house, Grandpa would cry, as if we were climbing Pikes Peak, "HOLD ON TO YOUR HATS!" As we passed the pen where the heir to the Victor coffee fortune kept peacocks, he'd crow, "Whoop! Whoop! Whoop!" an exclamation we believed might induce the birds to display their plumage. The highlight of the journey was the "Whack House," a ramshackle home from which we'd once seen a child hauled forth and spanked by his mother. As we searched its dark windows for a glimpse of whatever terrors lay within, Grandpa would re-create that fateful day by imitating the sound of a smack—*Whack!*—followed by a child's falsetto howl, which sent us into uncontrollable laughter.

We bounced across the railroad tracks and arrived at the church, Laundromat, fire station, and general store that constituted the town of Pocasset, or, as Grandpa deliciously pronounced it, "Pokey-asset." Inside the one-room store, while he headed across the sawdust-covered floor to buy two pounds of bacon (barely enough for tomorrow's breakfast), a carton of Camels, and a *Boston Globe*, we converged on a glass case near the soda fountain, within which lay a sumptuous array of penny candy: orange slices, spearmint leaves, root beer barrels, malted milk balls, fruit slices, licorice sticks, sour apple gum, Pixy Stix, Mexican hats, sour balls, Smarties, red jelly coins, candy necklaces, fireballs, Bit-O-Honeys, Mary Janes, Tootsie Rolls, circus peanuts, watermelon slices, jawbreakers, and candy buttons. Best of all, there were bull's-eyes, whose cool peppermint centers were encased in chewy caramel skins, making it seem as if we were getting two candies for the price of one. As we fingered the dimes in our pockets, the elderly man behind the counter awaited our decisions with a patience I now realize was nearly superhuman, then dropped our purchases into a small brown paper bag that, by the time we reached home, would be empty except for a light dusting of fallen sugar.

Clutching our loot, we followed my grandfather next door to the post office, a small room enclosed on three sides by rows of gold mailboxes emblazoned with fierce-looking eagles. While Grandpa chatted with the postmistress, a kindly woman with tortoiseshell glasses who alerted my stamp-collecting brother Harry whenever a new commemorative came in, we'd rush to Box 338, through whose small glass window we could see a stack of letters. One of us, as tenderly as a safecracker, manipulated the twin gold wheels that, set to the proper combination, allowed the door to swing open. Emptied, the box was a portal to the secret commerce on the other side: towers of packages and baskets of unsorted mail coming from and going to the world beyond Wings Neck. Before we left, I'd drift over to the counter and flip through the sheaf of white pages that hung on the wall, each with a grainy black-and-white photograph of a desperate-looking man—or, occasionally, shockingly, a woman—glowering above a curriculum vitae brimming with foul deeds. I was exhilarated and terrified by the "Wanted" posters, which seemed a confirmation of both the safety of the Big House and the peril that lay in wait in "civilization."

By the time we returned to the Big House, the rest of the family was beginning to rise. On weekdays, the house was a matriarchy. Weekends, the house filled with fathers, uncles, guests. We'd rush to hug my father, a businessman who always arrived from Boston—or wherever his job had taken him—late Friday night, long after we were asleep. No matter how tired he was the next morning, Dad was always ready to join us for Wiffle ball or Ghost (a game of catch played with a tennis ball tossed atop the barn roof). I worshiped my father, who could throw a pop fly so high it seemed it would never come down, could make even the corniest knock-knock joke ("Ella who? Ella Vator!") seem hilarious, and was so tender that when one of his children felt sick or scared in the middle of the night, it was his name we called out.

My father, the eldest of five siblings, would be teasing someone—most likely my mother, who, while tidying the kitchen, would be trying to keep the children's noise "down to a dull roar" so we wouldn't wake Grandma. Uncle Jimmy, a young lawyer who came down most weekends from Boston, would be reading yesterday's *Globe*, looking up from the sports section to ask us about our trip. A tanned, athletic bear of a man, who, like his father, had played hockey at Harvard, he spoke in a deep, rich voice, leaning into you with an intensity that made you feel important. Aunt Mary, a husky woman with a forthright manner, would be bustling about the pantry, tending to a fallen child ("Just pick yourself up and dust yourself off") while making sandwiches for a picnic lunch ("We've got to get *organized* here"). Aunt Sandy, a long-legged beauty who worked for the Peace Corps in faraway Washington—she was the youngest of the siblings by six years, as close to my age as to my father's—would be leaning easily against the counter, watching everything with an amused smile. The only missing Colt sibling was Ellen, the eldest daughter, who was living in Argentina at the time with her businessman husband and five children.

The highest compliment in the WASP lexicon was to be called "attractive" (or, as the men put it, *damned* attractive), which seemed to mean not only physically appealing—that went without saying—but socially graceful: unself-conscious, athletic, able to put people at their ease. My father and his siblings were damned attractive. All of them (at least it looked that way to me) moved through life as if they had never encountered an obstacle and never would. All of them knew how to make the guests who flocked to the Big House feel perfectly at home: pretty blonde girlfriends of Uncle Jimmy's; prep school headmasters who had roomed with Grandpa at Harvard; cousins once and twice removed whose branches of the family I could never keep straight; pert elderly women who painted watercolors or could distinguish seven species of identical-looking warblers. As I sat in the kitchen, licking up the last specks of sugar in my bag, I wondered whether I would ever be half so attractive as my father and his siblings.

Around ten o'clock, the tinkling of a bell would be heard, and Grandpa would dispatch one of the grandchildren upstairs—we vied for the honor—with a breakfast tray, garnished with a bouquet of pansies and a copy of the *Christian Science Monitor.* Knocking on the door, we'd hear Grandma trill, "Come in, my darling!"

My grandmother was a hothouse flower, next to whom everyone and everything else in the Big House seemed a little rough and clumsy. She was, as my grandfather put it, "above the fray." She exuded a certain humid fragrance, produced, no doubt, by the 4711 Original eau de cologne she dabbed on her wrists and temples, as well as by the hot baths she took twice a day to ease her arthritis. Her room, with its row upon row of perfume bottles, its gauzy white curtains, its hot water bottle nestled under a pink satin quilt, and its view of the bay, seemed as precious as a Fabergé egg. At tea, while we shoveled sugar cubes from a bowl, Grandma plucked tiny circlets of saccharin from a cloisonné pillbox. While the interior of my mother's huge imitation-leather pocketbook was a jumble of nickels and pennies, Grandma's dainty red purse contained mostly quarters and dimes. While we devoured "Hoodsies"—paper cups of vanilla and chocolate ice cream—my grandmother nibbled spoonfuls of raspberry sherbet. The small, candy-covered nuts the rest of the house knew as Jordan almonds, she, with a perfect French accent, called "dragées." But since Grandma was a Bostonian, her elegance was always understated: sneakers under a floor-length gown; unadorned goldenrod as a dining-table centerpiece; a battered plastic bucket in which to dip our feet before entering the house after a swim. And like many Bostonians, she would struggle all her life between the temptation to laze in her good fortune and the energetic demands of noblesse oblige.

To us Grandma seemed a small but dazzling star around which drama and gaiety constellated. She pulled us into songs, charades, and musicales—descendants of the Naushon pageants she'd shone in as a girl. The apotheosis of our theatrical collaborations was a Fourth of July extravaganza, written and directed by my brother Ned, that intended to portray, among other historical vignettes, George Washington crossing the Delaware. Grandma was a one-woman production crew. She sewed the living room curtains into soldiers' costumes; rummaged through her closets and jewelry boxes to outfit Colonial maidens; lent a favorite shawl to a disappointed cousin when Ned awarded the part of Betsy Ross to a lissome blonde girl from Bassetts Island; sent out invitations on her rich, creamy stationery; and, on the day of the performance, distributed hand-lettered programs to an audience of several dozen Wings Neckers. The pageant began at the far end of the Bluff, where Ned, dressed as the Father of Our Country in his great-grandfather Colt's riding jacket and boots, stood in the bow of our fiberglass dinghy as his friends, a Continental Army outfitted with driftwood muskets and an assortment of Uncle Jimmy's old tennis hats, rowed him furiously into a stiff southwest breeze. Disembarking at the boardwalk, they marched solemnly behind an American flag up the steps to the back lawn, where my grandmother beamed with pride, led the audience in tumultuous applause, and informed the cook that it was time to bring out the cookies.

Except for our early-morning odyssey with Grandpa, we rarely left the Big House grounds. There was no need. The house itself, reverberating with the sound of screen doors closing (with a gentle click if Grandma was holding the knob, with a slam if we were), was a home base from which we ventured out into the familiar, thirteen-acre wilderness. There were the paths that veined the woods and took us behind the barn, or to the pump house, or to the Little Cove, the strip of shoreline Ned Atkinson had apportioned for the servants' use. There was the makeshift baseball diamond (more of a trapezoid, really) on the patchy grass between the house and the barn, with a Virginia-shaped slab of milky quartz as first base. The hammock, strung between pines, where we'd play desert island. The painted white rectangle on the side of the barn where budding Bill Monbouquettes would learn to throw strikes. The garden on whose wall we'd pretend to be tightrope walkers. The side lawn where we'd play croquet on a surface so irregular that balls often hit a tussock and hopped over the intended wicket. For hours we saw the grown-ups only in passing: my parents and aunts en route to a tennis match; Grandma tending her foxgloves; Grandpa trudging from the woods to the lower hall closet for a set of loppers, a Rorschach blot of sweat expanding from the collar of his khaki work shirt.

We spent much of the day at the Bluff, a messy-looking strand of glacial boulders broken by patches of dusty miller, goldenrod, Queen Anne's lace, broom, and *Rosa rugosa*. Houseguests invited for a swim were sometimes taken aback when we led them to this rocky strip, but I grew up under the impression that the Bluff was the very definition of a beach, so that years later, confronting the sandy expanse of the Jersey Shore, I found it disappointingly bland. To us the Bluff was a veritable amusement park of natural attractions. At high tide, we sat in the Bathtub, a trio of rocks that formed a natural Jacuzzi, and let the waves rush over us. We practiced our swashbuckling on the Pirate Ship, a fragment of a barge that had washed up years earlier. The Whale Rock, a pinkish boulder so named because its shape reminded us of a sperm whale, was our lookout tower. The Black Diamond Rock, a masssive cube, made an ideal wall for forts. And there was the Big Rock, the size and shape of a small elephant, which rose from the water just beyond the peeling green boardwalk and dominated the Bluff the way the Big House dominated the Wings Neck skyline. We learned to swim to the Big Rock, to dive from it at high tide, to roost like cormorants on its back and talk beyond earshot of the grown-ups, who lounged on the small wooden platform at the head of the boardwalk, chatting, smoking cigarettes, sipping Carling Black Label (*Best reason in the world to drink beer*, went the radio jingle), and watching tugs prod tankers toward the canal. The purr of their conversation was punctuated by the squawks of herring gulls, the rustle of sails as boats came about, and occasionally, the thunder of jets from nearby Otis Air Force Base breaking the sound barrier—a boom so loud that no one could speak for several seconds, although, looking up, I might see a pair of sleek silver jets emerge from a fat cumulus cloud moments before burrowing into another. (Coming as it did at the height of the Cold War, this earsplitting sound only added to my sense of well-being.)

Every day the incoming tide brought us new treasures. Over the summer, our windowsills became small museums of prized specimens: striped lucky stones (a *double*-striped lucky stone was the seaside equivalent of a four-leaf clover); whelk egg cases, whose brittle pods, resembling the rattles of a snake, we'd crack open to find dozens of miniature whelks within; stones glittering with fool's gold. We built grocery stores of driftwood and stocked them with milk cartons, wooden fishing lures, boiled lobster shells, beer cans, lightbulbs, suntan lotion bottles, and whatever else the waves delivered. Our currency was sea glass. Blue was most valuable, not just because it was the rarest, but because it was the most beautiful—a piece of the sea made solid. Red was next best, then turquoise. White, green, and brown were the equivalent of dimes, nickels, and pennies. We believed that anything—*anything*—might wash up. We dreamed of finding ambergris, the waxy gray substance found in a sperm whale's intestinal tract that, used to make perfume, was said to be worth more than its weight in gold. Once a friend and I thought we'd found some and raced back to the house, only to learn we'd discovered a worthless chunk of marl. On another memorable morning, I spied a dark shape bobbing on the waves out past Scraggy Neck, the next peninsula south. I couldn't tell what it was, but it was *big*. I scrambled down the beach, trying to calculate the point at which it might reach our shore. As it got nearer and larger, I saw it was a dinghy. Even as I crowed over my luck—a boat of my own!—I knew my parents would make me track down its owner. But for several hours it was mine, evidence of the sea's limitless bounty.

As a child, I sympathized with those fourteenth-century cartographers who believed the world was flat, for the bay looked so vast that if you sailed to the horizon—where, on clear, calm days Naushon Island appeared to be suspended in the air—you might fall off the edge of the earth. I believed Buzzards Bay was the ocean. When I imagined the "sailors tossing on the deep blue sea," according to the words of a hymn my grandmother sang to us before bed, I placed them somewhere out past Scraggy. It has been suggested by a few local historians that Vikings, exploring the Atlantic coast, may have sailed into the bay around 1007 and named it Straumfiord, or "Bay of Currents." It is more generally accepted that six centuries later, searching for a Westward Passage, Bartholomew Gosnold named the bay Gosnold's Hope, perhaps agreeing with the ship's officer who called it "one of the stateliest Sounds that ever I was in." (It was given its current name a few generations later, to commemorate the great number of ospreys—known as buzzards by the less ornithologically inclined—in the area.) During the War of 1812, British warships nosed up as far as Wings Neck. Tiger sharks and pilot whales have taken wrong turns and ended up in the bay; once I saw a small hammerhead shark at the Big Cove. The bay is even capacious enough to support its own sea serpent, according to the fisherman who in 1881 claimed to have spotted a twenty-foot-long, spotted, horned creature surfacing near Wings Neck Light.

High tide, when the boardwalk that led across the rocks left us in shoulder-deep water, was best for swimming. The children would dog-paddle out to the Big Rock, whose hump protruded a foot above the surface, making a small offshore island. My father and Uncle Jimmy floated on their backs, chatting, only their heads and feet visible, like the victims of a magician's trick. Grandma, in her white bathing cap, sidestroked far from shore with her eyes closed, as if she were pulling herself farther into a dream. Legend had it that she used to swim every day to Scraggy Neck and back, a distance of several miles.

Over the course of the morning, as the tide withdrew and the beach expanded, our favorite rocks climbed slowly out of the sea. Above the tide line, the rocks were blanched and pinkish under the sun; below, they were green and brown with algae. At low tide, the Big Rock stood completely out of the water, exposed, vulnerable, lopsided as a popover, a thick, white girdle of barnacles encircling its middle and a horde of periwinkles browsing its base. Swimming at low tide was only for the hearty. The boardwalk left one stranded at the water's edge; to proceed any farther over the slippery, barnacle-covered rocks required leathery feet and pinpoint balance. But low tide allowed us to walk on tiptoes along an underwater sandbar, and explore the tide pools, miniature maritime Brigadoons in which we'd find crabs, snails, and stranded, desperate minnows.

One day, at dead low, Uncle Jimmy led us offshore into water that seemed impossibly deep. He swam back and forth for a few minutes, gazing up frequently at the Big House. Suddenly, he pulled us up onto a huge, seaweed-covered rock whose top lay just below the surface. (He had found this landmark before and relocated it by lining it up with the chimneys.) To my younger cousins on the beach, it appeared that we were walking on water.

At five o'clock, we were summoned inside by the clanging of a bell rung by my grandfather. After being bathed two by two in the claw-footed bathtub and fed in the kitchen by our mothers, we spent the early evening swarming over the nubbly lawn in pajamas, chasing one another in endless games of freeze tag, pausing occasionally to suck nectar from a blossom of the yellow honeysuckle that climbed the trellis. Above us, the grown-ups sipped cocktails on the piazza, murmuring about how hot it must have been "up in town" today and who would be playing whom in what crucial tennis match tomorrow. That tableau seems to me now a sort of distillation of summer, its scent made all the more delicious by the knowledge that it would soon be coming to an end. Already, in mid-August, a coolness was insinuating itself into the salt air. In a few days we'd be lighting a fire in the living room hearth and getting the extra blankets out of mothballs. The water would become too cold for more than a quick dip, and the wind would turn and come from the northeast.

Though my grandmother always asked Martha Keady, the tender-hearted Irishwoman who had cooked for Ned Atkinson and still occasionally cooked for us, to serve dinner at seven, the cocktail hour often lengthened like the shadows on the lawn until the sun had dropped behind the woods to the west. Finally, the grown-ups would rise. Grandpa and Grandma repaired to their rooms to dress for dinner: he in a red velvet smoking jacket, tuxedo pants, bow tie, pumps, and a fresh application of bay rum; she in a thirty-year-old evening gown with a string of pearls. They'd sweep into the dining room and seat themselves at either end of the twelve-foot-long oak table, which had darkened to the color of black tea. Then everyone else took his or her appointed place, the men pulling out chairs for the women. After muttering the grace he'd learned half a century ago at St. Paul's School—"Bless this food to our use and us to thy service"—my grandfather bent over the table and began to carve a turkey with an ancient set of antler-handled knives or to mete out fillets of striped bass in cream sauce. To the children, who sneaked peeks from the living room, the scene seemed breathtakingly elegant: the bamboo place mats; the candles in their silver holders; the salt and pepper in their cut-glass dishes with tiny ivory spoons; the finger bowls; and, when lobster was served, the silver nutcrackers, miniature forks, and ramekins of drawn butter. We were usually invited in for dessert: a slice of peach pie, perhaps, or vanilla ice cream with a choice of S. S. Pierce claret or melba sauce. Careful to keep our elbows off the table, to chew with our mouths closed, and to rise whenever a woman entered or exited the room, we tried to follow the conversation, which flitted from subject to subject "like a fly on the open pages of the encyclopedia," as my grandfather was fond of saying. Even then, I was aware that the two ends of the table constituted different, often competing worlds. At one end, Grandma held forth, light, merry, seductive, slipping a favorite grandchild a treat from her plate and fomenting envy in the rest of us. At the other end, Grandpa told long, witty stories about General Patton's North Africa campaign, about Churchill's boyhood escapades, about the biblical character Potiphar and his licentious wife. But he was a good listener, too, and always took special notice of whichever grandchild seemed lost in the conversational swirl. And whenever a bat flapped into the dining room, he'd delight us with his mock-heroic response: leaping to his feet, fetching a broom from the kitchen, and shooing it out the door, crying, "Out, damned spot! Out, I say!"

After dinner, we squeezed next to Grandpa on the living room couch as he read to us in a gentle growl so embedded in my memory that I cannot read these books to my own children without hearing it. Hard as I try, I cannot match his falsetto rendition of Jeremy Fisher's "A minnow! A minnow! I have him by the nose!" or the crocodile tears he shed in imitation of Peter Rabbit caught in Mr. McGregor's garden. The Beatrix Potter oeuvre made such an impression that my youthful mind often confused my grandfather with some of its more sophisticated characters: dapper Johnny Town-mouse; plump, menacing Samuel Whiskers. Our other favorite was *Goops and How to Be Them*, a deadpan brief for Victorian manners, written by Gelett Burgess at the turn of the century, whose title characters, a horde of hairless, moon-faced children, ran amok to the consternation of their prune-faced elders: *The Goops they lick their fingers, / And the Goops they lick their knives; / They spill their broth on the tablecloth— / Oh, they lead disgusting lives!* Although my grandfather—who, with his large, bald head resembled a Goop at least as much as he resembled the grown-ups who tried to discipline them—made us laugh uproariously at his histrionic reading, I found the book unnerving. I was an obsessively "good" boy, and I wonder now how much of my eager-to-please behavior can be traced back to my horror of (and fascination with) the Goops.

Not long after the ship's clock chimed eight times, my grandfather would say, "I believe it's time for the arms of Morpheus." I pictured Morpheus as a benevolent god who waited on the second floor to fold me in his embrace, someone forbidding but tender, someone more than a little like Grandpa. After processing around the room to kiss the grown-ups good night, we trooped upstairs to bed. Grandma would come up to sing "Now the Day Is Over" to us, and I'd think about the sailors tossing on the deep blue sea. And then, watching the beam from Cleveland Ledge Light stripe the wall every nine seconds, I'd fall asleep.

IV

The Discovery of Cape Cod

THEY LOOK lost, these well-dressed Victorians in the photograph, as if they had been heading to a dinner party and had ended up instead on this desolate, boulder-strewn shore. The day is chilly and overcast. The sturdy old man with the bushy white beard, a cane in one hand and a cigar in the other, stands on a rock, looking off into the distance. The thin, elderly woman, black cape and shawl pulled so tightly around her that she has the sheathed appearance of a sleeping bat, sits on a washed-up piece of timber, clutching a fan. The young woman, her back to the others, stares at the water with a disoriented and anxious expression: *Why am I here?* A hand, presumably that of the person holding the camera, reaches out from the lower right corner of the picture, as if to warn them away from this place.

When I came across this photograph in the Big House—it was pasted in an emerald green album I found in the living room highboy—I, too, felt disoriented, as if I were looking at a photograph of something I had once dreamed. Who were these people? Where had they come from? Then, just beyond the old man, I recognized the Whale Rock. And in the distance I saw the Bathtub. The photograph had been taken at the Bluff. The portly man, I realized, was my great-great-grandfather. The severe-looking old woman was his wife, the young woman his daughter-in-law. The hand, I felt sure, belonged to his son, my great-grandfather Ned Atkinson, the man who built the Big House.

When I was a small boy, I believed that my great-grandfather had discovered Cape Cod. I had been told that he was among the first to settle

Wings Neck, and the Big House seemed so ancient that I assumed, with a child's self-centered grasp of history, that it was not only the oldest house on Wings Neck, but one of the oldest houses—if not *the* oldest— on Cape Cod, and perhaps in the entire United States. In my experience, the Big House had always been there; therefore, I believed it had been there forever. It was part of what I knew as "the olden days," an amorphous time frame that encompassed—in no particular order— everything from the appearance of the dinosaurs to the moment of my birth. In this skewed chronology, I imagined that my great-grandfather, like some turn-of-the-century Columbus, had discovered Wings Neck and, by extension, Cape Cod. I had an image of a pin-striped, watch-fobbed gentleman stepping ashore on the Bluff to a welcoming delegation of Indians from whom, after sharing a peace pipe and feasting on corn, quahogs, and lobster, he purchased Wings Neck for a handful of wampum.

In fact, by the time Ned Atkinson set foot on Wings Neck in September 1902, it was the last undeveloped peninsula on Buzzards Bay. Cape Cod was in the midst of a sweeping transformation whose roots could be traced back to October 1849, when Henry David Thoreau made the first of four visits. Two years removed from his sojourn at Walden Pond, Thoreau—carrying an umbrella, a guidebook, and an 1802 volume of the *Collections of the Massachusetts Historical Society* containing brief histories of Cape Cod towns—came to the Cape intending to write a magazine article. Traveling by stagecoach from Sandwich to Orleans, then on foot to Provincetown, he found a spartan landscape little changed since 1614, when John Smith described the Cape as "onely a headland of high hils, over-growne with shrubby Pines, hurts and such trash." (For the next two hundred years, most descriptions of Cape Cod were similarly dismissive. One nineteenth-century visitor considered it "about as poor a piece of real estate as ever a man took title to"; another called it "the earth's most unattractive region.")

Its inhabitants, too, seemed to belong as much to the seventeenth century as to the nineteenth: a gritty, provincial bunch (it was often observed that many Cape Codders had sailed to the Far East yet had never been to Boston) struggling to wrest a living from a barren land and a mercurial sea. By the time Thoreau arrived, the economy had begun to stagnate. With the spread of railroads to transport goods and people, shipbuilding was dying out, and the discovery of "earth oil" in Pennsylvania in 1859 was to sound the death knell for the whaling trade. The coast was dotted with abandoned windmills used in the once-thriving salt-making industry, which was now unable to compete with imports. (The salt was used by fishermen to preserve their catch.) Farming the sandy soil had never been profitable, and the "great store of cod-fish" that had astonished Bartholomew Gosnold in 1602 was thinning fast. Young people were leaving Cape Cod, lured by factory jobs in Boston, Lowell, Fall River, and New Bedford, or by the free land offered to homesteaders out West. By 1840, the population of Cape Cod had stopped growing; by 1860, it had begun to decline.

"Every landscape which is dreary enough has a certain beauty to my eyes," wrote Thoreau, who saw in the Cape's austere terrain an echo of what his country might have been like in its original state. He was equally impressed with its inhabitants, calling Cape Codders "some of the salt of the earth, who had formerly been the salt of the sea." Wearing a hat equipped with an interior shelf on which he stored interesting botanical specimens, Thoreau explored dunes, visited lighthouses, and even had the quintessential Cape Cod experience of eating a bad clam. But his real quarry was the sea, and when he saw it he was as giddy as any child on his first visit to the beach, collecting shells, handling jellyfish, identifying seaweeds, and poring over the fragments of old shipwrecks and the carcasses of whales. "It is a wild, rank place, and there is no flattery in it," wrote Thoreau. From the hermit of Concord, there could be no greater compliment.

In 1849, the notion of voluntarily traveling to Cape Cod to see the ocean—without planning to fish, build a ship, go whaling, or scavenge a wreck—would not have occurred to anyone except, perhaps, a man who had spent two years gazing into a small, dark pond. Cape Codders considered shorefront land nearly worthless. They built their houses inland, within a short ride of their ships but beyond easy reach of the tidal waves and "great storms" (the word "hurricane" had not yet come into use) that scrubbed the coast. Asked why he had built his house in the woods a half mile from the harbor, the sea captain who sold his Mattapoisett home to my great-great-grandfather Edward Atkinson, whose family began to summer there in 1872, replied that, having spent his days on the water, he wished to get away from it when he came home. Shorefront land was used for summer pasture; although the soil was salty, sandy, and over-grazed, the islands and peninsulas offered some protection from the wolves that tormented Cape Codders and their livestock until the early nineteenth century.

I have a map of Cape Cod drawn in 1858. Aside from an isolated lighthouse here and there, the land along the shore is unblemished. Houses are clustered in small settlements in the interior—and are sparse enough that the map has room to denote each dwelling place with a small square and spell out the name of almost every owner alongside. Cape Codders would have snorted if someone had told them their most valuable resource lay in those sere bluffs and forbidding shores. But Thoreau knew better: "The time must come when this coast will be a place of resort for those New-Englanders who really wish to visit the sea-side."

No historian has ever pinpointed when the first summer house was built—likely none has ever tried—but it's certain that as early as A.D. 100 the Italian coast near Rome was dotted with summer villas and palazzi. The ancient Romans found the sea physically and spiritually enchanting. They even developed a philosophical concept, called *otium*, to justify what we'd now call a little R and R: a few days of swimming, reading, and meditative strolls on the beach between periods of work in town. Well-to-do Romans considered a water view essential, and often cleared the land between their vacation houses and the coast to improve the vista. Pliny the Younger, the first-century Roman author and statesman, designed Laurentum, his famous thirty-four-room villa at Latium, west of Rome, to permit sea views from as many rooms as possible; his dining room was cantilevered over the water so that guests could enjoy the sight of salt spray splashing against the floor-to-ceiling folding glass doors. Competition for shorefront property along the coast from Rome to Naples became so fierce that in the sixth century, in order to protect sea views, Emperor Justinian found it necessary to pass an ordinance barring construction within one hundred feet of the water. (Fourteen centuries later, in order to protect the local environment, Cape Cod building authorities passed an identical ordinance.)

With the arrival of the anhedonic Dark Ages, the passion for the sea also faded. For the next ten centuries, the sea was regarded as the "great abyss" described in Genesis, a vast, mysterious expanse inhabited by monsters: the Orc, the Grampus, the Wasserman, the Kraken. Indeed, in *The Sacred Theory of the Earth*, seventeenth-century divine Thomas Burnet maintained that before the biblical deluge, the face of the earth had been "smooth, regular and uniform; without Mountains and without a Sea." The flood of divine retribution, in Burnet's view, rent the earth's surface and left a chaotic mess of cliffs, boulders, and chasms (the shore as we know it today). The thought of living by the ocean was anathema. The only people who swam were those attempting to survive shipwrecks.

In the eighteenth century, people timidly began returning to the sea. The impetus was medicinal. Wealthy Europeans had long been relieving their ailments by immersing themselves in mineral springs at inland resorts known as "watering places." Gradually the saltwater equivalent came to be considered equally therapeutic. Medical authorities asserted that breathing pure, oxygen-saturated sea air and bathing in salt water could cure ailments as various as Saint Vitus' dance, hysteria, gastritis, and asthma. Benjamin Franklin promoted swimming as a cure for diarrhea and insomnia. Sudden immersion in cold seawater was considered a kind of natural shock treatment for melancholy. Some further held that *drinking* seawater was an effective elixir for gout, worms, scurvy, jaundice, and leprosy. In *A Dissertation on the Use of Seawater in the Diseases of the Glands*, a physician named Richard Russell prescribed a daily regimen of ocean bathing, the consumption of a pint of seawater, and, in certain cases, a vigorous seaweed massage. (None of this would surprise the current Wings Necker who for three decades has washed his hair not with shampoo but with salt water from Buzzards Bay in the belief that it will forestall baldness. To see him safely through the off-season, he fills empty Perrier bottles with seawater and lugs several cases to his winter home.)

Invalids, hypochondriacs, and faddists flocked to the seaside. "No person could be really well, no person . . . could be really in a state of secure and permanent health without spending at least six weeks by the sea every year," wrote Jane Austen in *Sanditon*, an unfinished novel satirizing the resorts that proliferated along the English coast. (Austen was herself fond of sea bathing, although she never learned to swim.) Certain scholars furthermore proclaimed that ocean dips (the chillier the better) had beneficial effects on the character. Noting that the size and quantity of marine life increased as one moved from warmer to colder latitudes, the French naturalist Georges-Louis Leclerc de Buffon—who, apparently, had never seen a coral reef—concluded that Homo sapiens, too, grew sturdier and more morally fit as the temperature of his bathing environment decreased. At the same time, painters and poets of the

Romantic movement touted another attribute of the seashore: its beauty. The coast was no longer a visual abomination but a sublime setting for aesthetic contemplation. Gradually, it was discovered that one didn't have to be an invalid, or even a hypochondriac, to benefit from a summer by the sea. For the first time since antiquity, Europeans began buying land along the coast and crowning it with spas, hotels, and cottages.

Americans soon followed suit. In 1817, the year Austen died, Colonel Thomas Handasyd Perkins, a Boston merchant who had made a fortune in the China trade, decided to see whether a steady dose of ocean breeze might revitalize a sickly grandchild. He accordingly bought a swatch of desolate, treeless pastureland northeast of Boston on the peninsula of Nahant, and built what may well have been America's first summer home by the sea, a stone cottage from whose porch he could watch the family clipper ships heading off from Boston Harbor to the Far East (including, thirteen years later, the ship bearing his nephew and protégé, my great-great-great-grandfather John Murray Forbes, on his maiden voyage to Canton). History does not record whether the soft sea air cured the Perkins grandson, but it did have a salutary effect on the grandfather. In 1823, he opened a seventy-room hotel, complete with billiard room, bowling alleys, fresh- and saltwater pools, and a European bathing machine (a private bathhouse on wheels that could be rolled into the ocean). Overnight, Nahant became *the* place to go for proper Bostonians, many of whom bought up pastureland and erected houses of their own, to which they returned each summer to pursue a peculiarly Bostonian brand of *otium*: fishing, swimming, sailing, consuming chowder, playing croquet, beach-combing, sketching, sitting on the porch and watching the play of light on water. Nahant became the first enduring seaside resort in America.

Over the next half century, summer resorts boomed, spurred primarily by three factors. Increasing urbanization left many wealthy city-dwellers longing to escape the oppressive heat, fetid air, and cholera- and yellow-fever–ridden congestion of the metropolis in summer. In the breezy ambi-ence of the shore, they could "recuperate from the deleterious effects of the confinement of city life," as one of them put it. The seashore was con-sidered a refuge not just from physical pollution but from moral pollution as well: its simpler, slower pace and natural setting were said to provide an ethical and spiritual antidote to the city's corruption (the very corruption that provided many of the vacationers with the wherewithal to enjoy the shore's virtuous atmosphere). The rapid expansion of the railway system (track mileage more than quadrupled in the twenty-five years after the Civil War) made getting away from it all more feasible. Wherever the tracks went, vacationers—and land speculators—were sure to follow. Post–Civil War prosperity provided the necessary funds. After four years of war, the nation was in the mood for play, and whether it be a week in a two-room cabin in Cape May, New Jersey, or the entire "season" in a forty-room gilded palace in Newport, the notion of the summer vacation took hold. By 1886, the once-deserted New England coast would be lined, according to an article in *Harper's*, with "an almost continual chain of hotels and summer cottages." The phrase "watering place" referred no longer to a rural retreat where gouty elders immersed themselves in mineral springs, but to a fashionable summer settlement in which wealthy city folk immersed themselves in the social whirl.

The shorefront of Cape Cod remained a wild, rank place. Travel by stagecoach was difficult and uncomfortable, even though "Cape Cod buggies," as they were known, were equipped with extra-wide axles to negotiate the sand roads. It was not until the year before Thoreau's arrival that train tracks had even reached the Cape, and then only as far as Sandwich, to carry sand, coke, and coal to its glass factory. And there were few accommodations. By 1856, when the town of Cape May had twenty-four hotels, all of Cape Cod was served by a handful of rudimentary inns along the stagecoach line. The Cape's few visitors included well-to-do Boston sportsmen, who found its lakes and forests a rich source of trout, turkey, plover, and deer; Christian revivalists, for whom its severe beauty provided an ideal setting for spiritual reflection in camp meetings; and patronizing journalists, who wrote of Cape Cod and its inhabitants as if, like anthropologists, they had discovered a quaint, slightly dangerous country peopled by a primitive but endearing tribe. Indeed, at the time of Thoreau's first visit, visitors to the Cape were so rare that Provincetown locals assumed he and his traveling companion, the poet William Ellery Channing, were bank robbers. And though Thoreau's speeches and articles on Cape Cod were well received (of his first lecture, Emerson wrote that people "laughed till they cried"), his descriptions of the uninviting landscape and its flinty inhabitants were hardly likely to inspire a deluge of tourists. (As for following in Thoreau's footsteps, "I would as lief have marched with Napoleon from Acre, by Mt. Carmel, through the moving sands of Tentoura," observed a travel writer.) *The Book of Summer Resorts,* a popular travel guide published in 1868, described more than seven hundred worthy destinations. Unlike Albany, Yonkers, Schenectady, Swampscott, and Chicopee, Cape Cod was not even mentioned.

Then, in July of 1872, the Old Colony Railroad completed an extension down the east shoreline of Buzzards Bay to Woods Hole. The spur was built primarily to service the Pacific Guano Company on Long Neck, where bird droppings from island roosts in the Pacific were blended with oil pressed from locally caught menhaden to make fertilizer for farms out West—and, in the prevailing southwest wind, perfumed the streets of Woods Hole. But the railroad's lasting contribution was to enable summer visitors to get to the shores of Cape Cod more quickly. Farmers and sea captains were delighted to sell to these Bostonians and New Yorkers, whom they deemed crazy for paying $30 an acre for worthless coastland. "Negotiations for the sale of real estate near the shore are going rapidly and parties are realizing good prices," observed a Falmouth newspaper in 1873. "Several gentlemen are having tracts of land surveyed and laid out into cottage lots for the purpose of putting them into the market. We would advise those wishing to purchase eligible sites near the sea to procure them at once." The Barnstable County Atlas of 1880 contains page after page of developments laid out with extensive grids of newly named streets—on which few, if any, houses had yet been built. Interested parties scrambled to throw a better light on rugged Cape Cod. "It's dotted with fine old towns which haven't yet been spoiled by too many fashionable notions," trilled a promotional pamphlet published in 1884 by the Old Colony Railroad. "Why! there's a perfect harvest for an artist. It has plenty of forests and lakes, and even a simon-pure tribe of Indians."

Over the next twenty years, the old Cape Cod was overlaid with the new. Entrepreneurs bought up pastureland, divided it into lots, and built developments named for Indian tribes that had mostly disappeared. They catered clambakes for Bostonians who came down on specially chartered trains to view available parcels. Along the eastern shore of Buzzards Bay, considered the most desirable Cape Cod real estate because of its proximity to Boston, summer "colonies" took root in every fold of the coastline. A Boston family put up seven large summer homes on an old cabbage patch and called it Wild Harbor. A group of Brockton speculators carved a nameless ox pasture into five hundred small lots and called it New Silver Beach. The Wellesley owner of a shoe factory transformed Hog Island, where local farmers had once fattened their swine among the ship's litter left from the island's whaling and shipbuilding days, into a collection of summer estates named Chapoquoit. And in a twist that Thoreau might have found delicious, a wealthy businessman from Newton bought Long Neck, and over the razed remains of the Pacific Guano Company laid down Cape Cod's most opulent summer colony. Rechristened Penzance (the scythe-shaped neck reminded him of the English peninsula by that name), the land was divided into twenty-four lots of up to ten acres in size, on which the buyers erected vast stone-and-shingle mansions with names invoking the great manor houses of Britain: Izanough, Driftwood, Weatherside, Stone Groton.

All along Buzzards Bay, wealthy gentlemen built estates. The actor Joseph Jefferson, renowned for his portrayal of Rip Van Winkle, built a stone castle known as Crow's Nest on Buttermilk Bay. *Boston Globe* publisher Charles H. Taylor built three mansions in Bourne, one for himself and one for each of his sons. Future Secretary of State Richard Olney built a place in Falmouth. And in 1890, ex-president Grover Cleveland, after vacillating between spending his summers in the mountains or by the sea, bought a large, rambling house on a forty-acre fist of land two miles north of Wings Neck and named it Gray Gables. Cleveland became an active figure in the community, attending church, joining the Old Colony Club (where he became friends with Edward Atkinson), and spending "long weeks of perfect content in fishing," according to his biographer, Alan Nevins. His substantial silhouette, surmounted by an Abercrombie & Fitch–style hat, was instantly recognizable as he and his fishing partner sat in their dinghy casting for pickerel on one of several ponds (their stern, where Cleveland sat, riding perilously low in the water), or headed out past Wings Neck in his catboat *Ruth* in search of bluefish, sea bass, tautog, and squeteague. (Cleveland Ledge, the lighthouse in the middle of Buzzards Bay whose glance illuminated my bedroom wall, was built on the site of one of his favorite fishing spots.) When Cleveland was elected to a second term in 1893, Gray Gables became the first summer White House, and a small railroad depot was built for him nearby. He became something of a proselytizer for the area, writing in the local newspaper, "Those who enjoy the cool breezes of Buzzards Bay are favored above all others by a kind of Providence."

Some of the summer colonies were founded by entrepreneurs whose only goal was profit, others by wealthy people who sold to family and friends in order to create a community of like-minded people of their own social class. Each colony was self-contained and insular, and over the years developed its own ethos, its own history, its own traditions. Falmouth Heights, a warren of cheek-by-jowl cottages inhabited primarily by businessmen from Worcester, could hardly be confused with neighboring Penzance, whose homeowners, mostly New York and Boston financiers (the private road that wound past their estates became known as Bankers Row), were required to put up homes costing at least $5,000. Yet even the most ostentatious estate on Penzance would have been considered shabby on Ocean Drive in Newport. Cape Cod summer colonies were not watering places, where young women hoping to keep their names in the society columns might arrive with twenty-five trunks full of dresses for the season. The Cape concept of *otium* had a Bostonian restraint. "There is no costume *de rigueur*; there are no conventional hours; no bands, no hops, no receptions, but a general atmosphere of picnic and do-as-you-please," observed a visiting New Yorker in 1875. Of his summer home in Mattapoisett, Edward Atkinson observed, "It is the dullest, flattest, stupidest, pleasantest, most restful place on the whole coast. Nothing to do and we do it all the time." The boats were single-sailed catboats, not steam yachts. In one home, guests were required to wear shoes to Sunday dinner—but it didn't matter whose: the hostess kept dozens of pairs just outside the dining room. The author of an 1892 article extolling the joys of sailing, fishing, and bathing in Buzzards Bay wrote, "The aboriginal life here, on the sparkling water, in the bright sunshine, with sweet air to breathe, reminding one of the life of the old Wampanoags, is the kind of life to restore the nerves exhausted in the crowded city ways." (One doubts whether the old Wampanoags found time, while fighting off the Puritans, to lounge on the piazza or perfect their backstrokes.) Even the hotels had an unassuming feel. The Sippowissett House proudly advertised horsehair mattresses and a bathroom on every floor. In Henry James's *The Bostonians*, published in 1886, a wealthy Southerner arrives in Marmion (a fictional name for Marion, an old Buzzards Bay whaling-port-turned-summer-colony, where James had spent an August weekend):

> Ransom had heard that the Cape was the Italy, so to speak, of Massachusetts; it had been described to him as the drowsy Cape, the languid Cape, the Cape not of storms, but of eternal peace. He knew that the Bostonians had been drawn thither, for the hot weeks, by its sedative

influence, by the conviction that its toneless air would minister to perfect rest. . . . They wanted to live idly, to unbend and lie in hammocks,
and also to keep out of the crowd, the rush of the watering-place.

In 1904, when James returned to the United States after twenty-one
years abroad, he was disquieted by the commercialized landscape and
accelerated pace he found in the country of his birth. But on a three-day
side trip to Cotuit, he found that these changes had bypassed Cape Cod.
Each small seaside town, he wrote in *The American Scene*, "was practically
locked up as tight as if it had *all* been a question of painted Japanese silk."

The "salt of the earth who had formerly been the salt of the sea" grum-
bled and adapted. Shipbuilders became surveyors and carpenters; farmers became land speculators; sailors became charter boat captains, taking
summer visitors out for day sails or casting for bluefish in catboats, fifty
cents a head. (After chasing sperm whales across the Pacific, some old
salts found baiting tourists' hooks in Buzzards Bay maddeningly dull; for
diversion, retired whaling captains staged impromptu horse races down
the main streets of Falmouth.) More than a few Cape Codders seem to
have gone into public relations. Just as pioneers were said to be "taming
the wilderness" by pushing into the American West, there was a sense
that civilization—in the form of summer estates and graceful wooden
yachts—was pushing south from Boston. Some of the early tourist
brochures and town publications would have us believe that it was only
the introduction of wealthy, cultivated Bostonians that put Cape Cod on
the map, and the building of eight-thousand-square-foot mansions that
made the land beautiful. "To the inhabitants of Falmouth, twenty-five
years ago, it was a wild and rocky waste, suitable only for fishing and
gunning," wrote the authors of *Residential Falmouth*, in a description of
Sippewissett. "To-day, under the magic wand of John C. Haynes, of
Boston, the whole land has blossomed like the rose. Avenues of generous
width, parks of unlimited proportions, residences of pleasing architecture, invite those persons who seek a location for summer homes."

    For sheer chutzpah, few local boosters could rival Ezra G. Perry, a
Bourne candy maker turned real estate entrepreneur, who wrote and
published *A Trip Around Cape Cod: Our Summer Land and Memories of My
Childhood*, a collection of photographs of recently built summer estates,

many of which happened to be for sale by Perry himself. Essentially a lavish real estate brochure, the book concludes with a full-page advertisement for the author's business: I HAVE SOME EXTRA FINE TRACTS OF LAND FOR SALE WHERE IN A FEW YEARS MONEY INVESTED CAN BE MORE THAN DOUBLED. Although unabashedly self-serving, the book constitutes an invaluable portrait of a Cape Cod in transition, showing page after page of huge new summer homes rising from the freshly deforested hills around Buzzards Bay, as shockingly raw as the subdivisions being hewn from many of those very estates today. Perry saw this transformation as a moral achievement: "We find ourselves surrounded by scores of stately villas, with men and women more stately, owners of them—houses which are prophets, every one, of what is coming to the whole Cape; for the most hopeful sign in our summer visitors is not the number but the quality of them," he wrote. "Somehow the Cape appeals to the highest in man or woman, and so brings us that class as fellow citizens." One can almost hear the strains of "America the Beautiful"—whose lyrics were written by Katharine Lee Bates, a Falmouth schoolteacher—in the background.

By the time my great-grandfather, still smarting from his snub on the Naushon ferry, began looking for a place to build a summer home, the only substantial "unimproved" hunk of shorefront on Buzzards Bay was Wings Neck. That is not to say that it had never been inhabited. The first summer visitors to the area were the Manomet Indians, a sub-tribe of the Wampanoags of southeastern Massachusetts and Rhode Island, whose great sachem was Massasoit. They traveled from their winter homes in Manomet (present-day Bourne) to make their summer camps in the place they called Pokesit (Pocasset), meaning "where the waters widen." My grandmother once found an arrowhead on the Bluff, and I like to imagine that on the rocks where we now gather sea glass, Manomet men once gathered mussels; that in the firebreak where we pick blueberries, Manomet women planted and tended corn, beans, squash, pumpkins, and Jerusalem artichokes; or that in the cove on the north side, where we now catch minnows and jellyfish, the children skipped stones while their mothers collected bulrushes to splice among the saplings of their wigwams and their fathers caught eel and tautog in grass nets. A local legend—oft-repeated by my great-grandfather—has it that during King

Philip's War, Captain Church drove the proud king and his warriors out to the end of Wings Neck, from which they made a narrow escape by canoe.

What muskets couldn't accomplish, money could, and the Pilgrims and their descendants gradually bought up land from the Indians, paying for it with hoes, kettles, knives, beads, hats, shoes, cloth, and wampum, the sky blue interior of the quahog shell, which, as my aunt Mary frequently reminded us, the Wampanoags used for currency. By 1769, according to Sandwich town records, there were twenty-three houses and 169 "white people" in Pocasset, as well as "a few Indians without any land . . . living as servants, chiefly in English families." In 1722, a Wampanoag named William Numuck, Sr., who owned a great deal of the Upper Cape—and who sold it off over the years to farmers and shipbuilders—sold Wings Neck (or Wenaumet Neck, as it was known then) to John Handy, Ebenezer Wing, and Samuel Swift, descendants of Pocasset's founding families. They used it for sheep and cattle pasture, and harvested the marsh grass as hay. Early in the nineteenth century, Ebenezer's grandson, Judah, built a house on the south side of the Neck, cleared land for a sheep farm, and erected a gristmill powered by tidewater on the edge of the millpond where we now catch fiddler crabs. By 1840, Judah Wing owned the entire peninsula (which is presumably why its name was changed from Wenaumet Neck to Wings Neck). Wing had twelve sons, who jointly inherited his peninsula. None of them, apparently, thought of it as highly as their father had, for by the time my great-grandfather first saw it, there was no trace of the Wings or their farmhouse, and the Neck was wooded over again.

From Wings Neck's deserted shores, however, no matter what direction one looked, one could see change coming. In 1849, the government built a lighthouse on the tip of the peninsula to guide ships toward Monument Harbor, a few miles north. On the other side, packet schooners— some as large as four hundred tons—sailed past the Neck's southern shore to unload wheat, coal, apples, and cider at the Barlowtown wharf before departing with cordwood cut in Pocasset to sell in Newport and New York. Fishing boats from New Bedford crossed the bay to handline for tautog and bluefish in the nooks of Bassetts, a cleat-shaped island a stone's throw from Wings Neck.

In the second half of the century, the working boats were joined and, eventually, outnumbered by pleasure craft belonging to summer visitors.

An 1857 editorial in the *Register*, a local paper, touted Pocasset's virtues: "This is a beautiful little village, particularly in the summer, possessing fine natural scenery, in which are the blended attractions of hill, dale, woodland grove, pond and seashore, together with rare fishing and gunning for those possessing a taste for field sports. We can hardly think of a more favorable spot for summer residences, combining as it does the advantages of a moral neighborhood, delightful location, and eligibility to the city."

From Wings Neck, one could see woods cleared, farms broken up, and summer houses rising on the shores all around. Across the channel, a few modest cottages were visible in Cataumet, where in 1873 the Pocasset Grove and Shore Company had subdivided a chunk of farmland into eighty-five lots. Above the trees, one could see the roof of the Jachin Hotel, a no-frills hostelry with room for seventy-five guests, built in 1875 by Alden Davis, the Cataumet postmaster, station agent, and marble engraver who cut many of the stones in the Cataumet Cemetery. (The hotel and its owner came to a sad end in 1901, when a deranged guest poisoned all four members of the Davis family.) East of Bassetts Island, two men from Taunton bought an old summer pasture in the early 1880s and laid out the developments of Patuisett and Pocasset Heights, building six cottages on speculation. Looking northeast from the Bluff, one might have seen the mansard roof of the Pocasset House, a three-story, twenty-room hotel built around 1870, which catered to hunters, fishermen, salesmen, and an increasing number of summer tourists. On the near side of the sand road that led to Wings Neck, former ship's captain Jesse Barlow and his son, Captain J. Fred Barlow, carved up a portion of their ancestral lands into a development they called Wenaumet Bluffs, using their navigational skills to pace off lots to whatever size and shape the buyer desired. And directly across from Wings Neck, W. E. C. Eustis of Milton, a wealthy mining engineer and ardent yachtsman known as "The Copper King," bought the entire three-hundred-acre, flounder-shaped peninsula known as Scraggy Neck. The stone mansion he built there in the 1880s was said to have cost $100,000—small potatoes compared with the $2 million it cost Cornelius Vanderbilt II to build The Breakers in Newport, but a fortune considering that anyone who bought a lot in nearby Cataumet and put up a house for at least $600 was given a free second lot. To protect his investment, Eustis built a stone wall and iron gate at the entrance to

Scraggy Neck. He grazed sheep, not for their wool or meat but to keep his lawn clipped. His house was one of the first in the area to have electricity, down to the lamp hanging on its dock.

Yet except by locals who walked the cart path out to the lighthouse to picnic on the rocks, or who sailed over to pick the grapes that grew so abundantly along the north shore, Wings Neck itself was still untouched. It wasn't for lack of trying.

In *The New England Magazine* of September 1892, an article titled "On the Shores of Buzzards Bay" described the area's burgeoning fascination for summer visitors. It opened with a pen-and-ink sketch of Wings Neck in which a gaff-rigged catboat heads over calm waters toward a familiar-looking peninsula, appearing as untouched as it was in Wampanoag days except for a lighthouse on one end and, a little to the right, one lone, abandoned house. That house had belonged to Cyrus Augustus Bartol, the Unitarian pastor of the old West Church in Boston and a well-known author and Emersonian whose Beacon Hill home hosted many meetings of the Transcendental Club.

A small man whose elfin features were framed by his flowing snow-white hair and beard, Bartol possessed what his biographer called a "childlike simplicity." ("What a dear old man he is!" the author Bret Harte said of Bartol after their first meeting. "A venerable baby, nothing more!") In a photo taken in middle age, Bartol wears a distracted, ethereal look. He may have been preoccupied with spiritual matters. Or perhaps he was mulling over the killing he was making in real estate on Boston's North Shore. Bartol, who often preached on how we can find God in nature, particularly in the rugged grandeur of the seaside, had for many years summered on Cape Ann. In 1870, at the age of fifty-seven, no doubt hoping to help others find God, Bartol began buying up shorefront land in Manchester at $600 an acre, laying out roads and selling lots for as much as $12,000 apiece, becoming largely responsible for the development of one of the most exclusive resorts on the North Shore. Bartol built himself a mansion overlooking the rocky coast, as well as a four-story observatory, where, ascending a spiral staircase, he liked to sit in an easy chair and contemplate his expanding real estate empire. Asked by a parishioner why he was putting his money into shorefront property instead of a proper Boston bank, Bartol is said to have replied, "Ah, my friend, you and a lot of other folks seem to forget that the Lord Almighty has stopped making seacoast."

When Bartol ran out of seacoast on the North Shore, he turned to Cape Cod. One can't be sure how he set his sights on Wings Neck, but in 1879, Pocasset came to national attention when a local farmer, a devout Adventist who believed the Lord had demanded an extreme sacrifice of him, stabbed to death his three-year-old daughter in her sleep. Bartol was one of many clergymen across the country to preach about what newspapers called "the Pocasset Tragedy." (Several noted the contrast between the heinousness of the crime and the beauty of the setting. "Pocasset itself is a most charming place," observed a New Bedford minister. "There are few sheets of water in America more lovely than Buzzards Bay; and of the numerous summering places that dot its coast and overlook its placid waters, few are more favorably situated than Pocasset.") In 1888, although warned by the Pocasset locals that "it wa'n't worth nothin'," the seventy-five-year-old Bartol bought several large chunks of Wings Neck, where he built a three-story stone-and-shingle mansion on the southern shore, near the lighthouse.

But Bartol's dreams of another real estate bonanza went up in a cloud of *Aedes sollicitans*. "The last of the Transcendentalists," as he was known by then, was unable to transcend the mosquitoes, and lasted only one summer on Wings Neck before abandoning his mansion and retreating to Manchester. Seventy-five years later, whenever we passed the Bartol House—as it was still known, although several other families had owned it by then—I regarded the dark brown hulk with the same apprehension and fascination with which most children regarded the Big House. It was the only house on the Neck that was older than ours. It was said to belong to a man who was very rich; we never saw him. Neither did we ever see anyone on the beach in front of the house. Its aura of mystery was augmented by the fact that its owner was one of the few people on my paper route to take the Sunday *New York Times*. A huge dog began to bark as soon as it heard the sound of my bike in the driveway.

Cyrus Bartol's house was still empty in 1902, when my great-grandfather first set foot on Wings Neck. Ned Atkinson had seen the Neck before. In 1874, when he was fifteen, his father had presented him and his brothers with their first sailboat, a sixteen-foot Rapid Streak. That summer, he and a brother and a friend started across Buzzards Bay from Mattapoisett, the former whaling town on the bay's western shore,

where his father had been one of the first summer settlers. Passing
Wings Neck, my great-grandfather was intrigued. "The wind was southwest, rather strong, and the shore of Wings Neck looked wild and rocky
as we entered the harbor," he wrote many years later. They put in at Barlowtown landing, and spent the night at the Pocasset House before sailing home the next day.

Twenty-eight years later, Ned Atkinson joined a group of friends and
associates (they called themselves "the syndicate," a name that enthralled
me, making them sound more like a bunch of mobsters than a group of
proper Boston businessmen), and bought Wings Neck from Bartol's
widow and seven other landowners. They paid $84,350, about $214 an
acre. Many of the men in the syndicate had been at Harvard together.
Others were winter neighbors in Brookline, business associates, or
members of the same men's clubs. They wanted to buy the entire peninsula so they could make the place their own.

One day the twelve members of the syndicate met in an office in
Boston to determine which lot each member should have. Most wanted
lots inland, or on the more sheltered northern side. Ned Atkinson's
first choice was a seventeen-acre corner parcel on a bluff midway along
the south side of Wings Neck, from which—had he not been such a
gentleman—he could on a clear day have thumbed his nose at Naushon,
the island to which he had vowed he would never return. "It was a most
remarkable meeting because each member of the syndicate got the particular lot or lots that he wanted," he wrote. They divided the rest of
the land into five- to-twenty-acre parcels and proceeded to sell them to
their friends and associates. "In view of the developments of the shores
of Buzzards Bay in recent years, it is surprising that one of the most
attractive areas of land should have remained untouched," began the
"Prospectus" they published.

> Wings Neck has always been one of the most familiar landmarks to
> yachtsmen who have sought refuge in the harbors made by it, or taken
> their bearings from its lighthouse.
>
> While its aspect from the sea has been familiar to many, very few
> have had the opportunity to appreciate its land attractions. It is a high
> promontory two miles long, running into the bay in a southwesterly
> direction, and embraces about five hundred acres of land, varying in
> height from ten to fifty-six feet above mean low water mark . . .

All the land is high except the narrow neck joining the promontory to the main land. It is also dry and free from dampness. Pure water is abundant.

Almost all the land is available for attractive estates.

There are excellent harbors both on the north and south sides, affording unusually large areas of inland water.

The Neck has all the advantages in coolness of an island, the breezes coming off the water from whichever direction they blow. The deep water surrounding it renders the bathing deliciously fresh.

In order to guard against undesirable elements, the property is restricted within proper limits.

When I first read those words I believed that the "proper limits"—a matter of minimum acreage—were designed to keep thieves and con artists at bay. Proper Bostonians of that casually xenophobic era, however, surely knew that the "undesirable elements" discouraged by the high prices would include Irishmen and Italians—the same Irish who raised their children and cleaned their houses, the same Italians who dug their wells. In short, anyone not like themselves.

Although he had sailed by it many times, my great-grandfather had never set foot on Wings Neck before he bought it. When he did, he must have wondered whether he had made an expensive mistake. The following summer, in 1902, he came over from Mattapoisett with his father, his mother, and his wife to see the new land, taking the train to Pocasset, where they hired a horse and "sort of a beach wagon" and headed out the long sandy road toward Wings Neck. The entire peninsula was swampy and buried in catbrier. "The moment we crossed the causeway, the horse turned gray," recalled Ned Atkinson in a memoir of Wings Neck he wrote in 1939, a year before his death. "He was covered with mosquitoes." They drove down to the lighthouse, and on the way back they walked out to look at the lot he had chosen and picnicked on the rocky shore. "The mosquitoes were nearly as thick there," he wrote. "I now have a photograph of the lunch-party—my father vigorously smoking and the rest of the family with fans and twigs trying to keep away the mosquitoes during the lunch but with poor success."

And that was the photograph I found, ninety-four years later, in the emerald green album in the living room highboy.

V

Rooftree

ON RAINY days we used to play Sardines, that form of hide-and-seek in which one person hides and each of the other players tries to find him—without letting anyone else know—and hide with him. The hiding place gradually fills, becoming as crowded as a tin of sardines, until only one person is left searching.

I was thrilled and terrified by the game, which made literal one of childhood's archetypal fears: that there really *were* creatures under the bed. I could never decide which was the more frightening role, hunter or hunted: to be folded up in a dark closet below a rack of foul-weather gear, listening to the footsteps of a dozen boys and girls who were trying to track me down, or to walk through the house knowing that behind this cupboard or that door, a living, breathing someone might be watching. Actually *finding* that someone—to glimpse a hand beneath a pile of blankets, a face in the depths of a closet—was almost as bad. In Sardines, unlike hide-and-seek, the person hiding didn't jump out at you when you found him; he stayed silent and still as a statue, except for a barely perceptible nod or a grimace of acknowledgment as you crawled in beside him. Worst of all, if you were still hunting, was to realize that the number of your fellow seekers had dwindled, Agatha Christie–style, until the only footsteps you heard were your own. Several years ago I read a short story by Graham Greene in which a timid child, playing a form of Sardines at a birthday party, is literally frightened to death. Recalling our games in the Big House, I believed it possible.

Sardines requires a large house, the larger—and more rambling and convoluted—the better. With its eaves, alcoves, crawl spaces, and passageways, the Big House was an ideal site, and games of Sardines at the Colts' were legendary among Wings Neck children, often attracting such a crowd that it took the organizational steam of Aunt Mary to get us started. We each had our favorite hiding places. The space in the dormer above the closet in the Yellow Room. The passageway behind my grandmother's room on the second floor that was longer than a closet but narrower than a bedroom. The storage spaces off the front stairwell that lay behind small, oblong doors, the kind one might see on an elf's cottage, where one hid among a jumble of old boxes Grandma had saved for packaging Christmas and birthday presents—stiff blue-and-gold shirt boxes from Brooks Brothers; large, flimsy boxes from Jordan Marsh; small, elegant, cream-colored boxes that had held Crane's stationery. (These closets were obvious hiding places, but were so dark, so musty, and so often frequented by mice or squirrels—and who knew what else—that few seekers dared more than stick a head in for a cursory look.) There were rooms with four doors, each leading to a different room. There were doors one opened only to find *other* doors behind them. There were closets deep as mine shafts, and strange, wasted spaces that served no apparent purpose. And as well as I knew the house, there always seemed to be new hiding places I'd never thought of before.

During one game I found a small door in an alcove of the Playroom and climbed in. I crawled in pitch darkness over loose boards and old nails, feeling for a wall ahead of me, finding nothing, worrying all the while that, like Tom Kitten, I would suddenly tumble through a hole and into Samuel Whiskers's lair. Indeed, at one point I put down a knee and, touching nothing but air, nearly fell into what I later deduced would have been the Little Nursery. I finally saw a splinter of light. Inching toward it, I eventually pushed through a curtain and found myself looking out at the third-floor stairwell. The crawl space had run the length of the Playroom—only twenty feet, but in the dark it was as endless as Tom Sawyer's cave. Although I felt sure no one would have found me there—ever—I crawled out and chose another hiding place.

The Big House was so well suited to the game that I liked to believe the man who had designed it had Sardines in mind. On the theory that houses look something like their architects, I pictured a tall, eccentric, elderly gentleman with a large, declivitous brow, a steeply pitched nose, and a brooding, melancholy air.

Whether my great-great-uncle William Atkinson, the architect of the Big House, had Sardines in mind is something we cannot know, but that he was eccentric seems to be a fact universally acknowledged in our family, although its effect has been subject to interpretation. My grandmother called him "rather a genius," while my great-uncle Chis insisted that he was "a little off." There is evidence to support both views.

The fourth of the seven Ats, born one year after the end of the Civil War, William followed his older brothers to Harvard, where he sang in the Glee Club, helped edit the *Lampoon*, and joined the right gentlemen's clubs. But he left in the middle of his senior year and never graduated. Like his brother Ned, William was a tall, slim man with bushy eyebrows and a thick mustache, but he lacked Ned's dashing good looks and brio. He parted his hair in the middle, a style that gave him a sober, somewhat reserved appearance. My aunt Ellen tells me that, while perfectly friendly, he was, compared with his ebullient brothers, serious and somewhat shy. From a series of family silhouettes that Ned made, using a lantern slide, it is evident that William also inherited what is known in the family as the Atkinson nose, that genetic gift of which I was so embarrassed as an adolescent, despite my mother's assurance that it was not a *big* nose per se, but Roman and distinguished.

It was said of William Atkinson—as it has been said of more than a few members of our family—that he was a man of great talents who never quite found his niche. This was our way of saying that, after a certain point, he never seemed to feel the need or inclination to hold down a full-time job. William had inherited the curiosity of his father, the creator of the Aladdin Oven, but lacked his ambition and drive. He was a facile draftsman who enjoyed sketching. I recently came across a map in the Big House that he'd made for his father's houseguests, showing them how to get by trolley from Boston to the Atkinson place in Brookline; it was illustrated with charming, perfectly rendered drawings of Trinity Church, the Longwood Tennis Club, and other landmarks en route. William was an accomplished amateur musician who sang, played the piano, and composed and recorded several sonatas, copies of which remain in the Big House. He was a proficient engineer whom some credit with the creation of that peculiar source of modern frustration known as the traffic rotary. He was a fine mathematician, an amateur economist, an ardent genealogist (given his family, he had plenty to work on), and something of an inventor. At one point, he designed a one-story, solar-heated kindergarten for the town of Brookline and was, according to family legend, laughed out of a town meeting. Although the story smacks of the apocryphal, when Aunt Ellen moved into one of the old family homes on Heath Hill several years ago, she came across a set of blueprints, signed by William Atkinson, showing the front elevation of a futuristic-looking, one-story schoolhouse that seemed to be made almost entirely of glass.

In vision, William Atkinson may have been a twentieth-century man, but in personality he belonged to the nineteenth. He combined the meticulous perfectionism of an engineer with the woolgathering ideal-ism of a reformer. He read widely and kept abreast of current events— "public affairs," as they were then known—in the Boston *Evening Transcript* and the leading liberal journals of the day. Whenever he felt passionate about an issue, he would thoroughly research it, and, like his father, write and publish a pamphlet outlining his views. Few guests left his house without a copy of his latest work, be it "The Mystery of Loga-rithms" or "And Now, Bimetallism." Although he was married for thirty-five years, no one in the family remembers anything about his wife other than her name, and Uncle Bill and Aunt Mittie had no children. But he was devoted to the Ats, and he brought pencil and paper to every Thanksgiving and Christmas family dinner so he could make a seating chart, which he later copied into his journal "for reference." Like many of the Ats, he remained true to his conscience to a degree that seems both thoroughly admirable and slightly ridiculous. When World War II broke out, he was so angry that he destroyed all his German music. Aunt Ellen, who told me the story, doesn't know how he did it—whether he threw out the scores or merely lugged them up to the attic and aban-doned them—and though it is tempting to imagine William dancing a jig around a massive bonfire, I think it more likely that he gently laid his Bach, Beethoven, and Brahms in the fireplace, then sat back in an easy chair, smoked his pipe, and wondered what the world was coming to.

William Atkinson was thirty-six when his elder brother Ned asked him to design his summer house. From a personal standpoint, the choice was characteristic—part of Ned Atkinson's lifelong sense of financial responsibility toward his impractical and impecunious siblings. From a professional standpoint, however, it made less sense. Certainly, William Atkinson had had architectural training. After leaving Harvard, he had studied at MIT, where the first American architectural school had been established in 1865, and at the atelier of Henri Duray in Paris. Like most aspiring architects of the time, he had taken the obligatory tour of Europe, filling sketchbooks with drawings of arches, cornices, and pediments. Returning to the United States, he had set up his own practice in downtown Boston, and published sketches in architectural journals. But when his brother hired him, his practical experience—the actual translation of his designs from paper to wood and brick—consisted of one building: a seventy-two-bed hospital in Newport. The Big House would be his second commission.

In the fall of 1902, when William Atkinson sat down at his drafting table to design a summer house at Wings Neck, the architecture of American country houses was in its infancy. The summer houses of the mid-nineteenth century had been plain, undistinguished cottages, little different from winter houses of that era aside from the occasional Gothic arch or gingerbread trim. That changed in the decades following the Civil War, when wealthy city-dwellers began to escape to the salubrious seaside. In the decaying towns to which they flocked, architecture had changed little in the past hundred years. Houses were simple, squat, shingle-clad structures built with rough, native materials and central chimney columns. Interest in this colonial architecture was reinforced by the nation's centennial celebration. Future partners Charles Follen McKim, William Mead, and Stanford White took a celebrated walking tour of Boston's North Shore in 1877, measuring and sketching the sturdy colonial houses. Wealthy vacationers didn't want to be quite *that* simple, of course. Theirs would be a *symbolic* simplicity. They wanted to live the rustic summer life without giving up their full complement of live-in winter servants.

Led by Bostonian H. H. Richardson, young architects gradually devised a style that expressed this natural simplicity without sacrificing comfort. All along the northeast coast, they built large, rambling houses with gables, dormers, and towers. "Beside the sea, where the level line of the horizon is the characteristic feature, a stretch of sand or a line of bluffs and green fields making up the scenery, a long low structure, sloping roofs and broad verandas, and, above all, plenty of space, seem much more compatible with the surroundings," observed the author of an 1895 article called "Architecture at the Seaside." These houses were admirably adapted to coastal weather, built low to the ground to avoid storms, with steep roofs to deflect heavy winds and covered porches for protection from sun and rain. They were made of natural materials, often from local sources: roughly laid stone instead of marble or brick. (In 1887, when William Ralph Emerson, one of the most prominent of the new architects—and a distant cousin of Ralph Waldo—designed Stone House, a fifty-three-room structure on Naushon in which I've always wanted to play Sardines, he used boulders from the island's pastures and eighteenth-century stone walls, preferring those with "good weather-stained and lichen-covered surfaces.") Instead of clapboards, the architects used shingles, whose unpainted, rust-brown surface weathered silver-gray, making them shimmer, in some lights, like the scales of a breaching fish. Well suited to damp conditions, shingles had long been used to protect seaside houses, but late-nineteenth-century architects prized them for their flexibility. Unlike clapboards, whose length and thickness made them relatively rigid, shingles, being small and easily cut, allowed architects to work in curves so fluid that the roofs and walls seemed dynamic, a sinuous skin that wrapped around the contours of the interior space and rendered the framing of the house all but invisible. After nearly a century of turning to Europe for inspiration in a series of revivals—Georgian, Gothic, Queen Anne—our nation's architects had created the first distinctively American style, one that Witold Rybczynski recently described as "one of the highest accomplishments of American architecture." It was, however, a style that would go nameless for nearly a century until Yale professor Vincent Scully dubbed it "the shingle style" in a book of that title published in 1955, long after the style itself had fallen from favor.

Both in its design and in its materials, a shingle-style house was intended to relate to its environment, to seem an organic part of its site, to look, as Thoreau said of the colonial houses he passed on his Cape Cod rambles, "firmly planted." Of an Emerson house in Manchester, the influential art critic Mariana Van Rensselaer wrote in *Century Magazine*, in 1886, that the house "seems almost as much a part of nature's first intentions as do the rocks and trees themselves." Even the trim was painted to look natural—dark green was a common choice—so that, as Lewis Mumford wrote nostalgically of these houses in his 1926 essay "Architecture," "they mellowed into the landscape year by year, and their greens, yellows, crimsons, blues, and russet browns became as native to the land as the goldenrod, asters, and sumach."

For all the talk of integrating structure and landscape, the motivation was solely aesthetic. The shingle style was born in a time of prosperity, in which American land and money seemed limitless—to the wealthy, at least. No one found it ironic that these "simple," "natural" houses devoured the land at a terrific rate. In George William Sheldon's *Artistic Country-Seats: Types of Recent American Villa and Cottage Architecture with Instances of Country Club-Houses*—a two-volume compendium as lavish as its title, published in 1886–87, with photographs and floor plans of ninety-three estates—several of the houses are the size of small ocean liners, their properties the size of minor seas. Like most people at the time, Sheldon, an art critic, considered the transformation of rugged seacoast into manicured, mansion-crowned estates an unqualified improvement. "To him, the family that purchased 50 acres of land to protect its summer cottage was not greedily appropriating land that others might share, but artistically developing the American landscape," wrote historian Arnold Lewis in his introduction to a recent edition of *Country-Seats*. "Furthermore, he did not object if the owners erected a cottage large enough for ten families to live in simultaneously, and he did not raise questions if a family used its miniature hotel for only a fraction of the year."

And yet for their size, these homes were comparatively modest. Theirs was an informal style for an informal season. Inside, the emphasis was on ease: wide halls, gradual staircases, and large, open spaces in which one room flowed into the next. Previously, a house's exterior and interior had often seemed to have little to do with each other. In shingle-style houses, designed to accommodate lives lived largely outdoors, interior and exterior were interwoven by bay windows and wraparound piazzas, the latter, according to Herman Melville, who had one added to his farmhouse in the Berkshires, "somehow combining the coziness of in-doors with the freedom of out-doors." The piazza—essentially a porch vastly expanded and given a fancy foreign name—became such a staple of summer life that in 1903, Mariana Van Rensselaer decreed, "It is hardly needful to-day to affirm that an American country house without a piazza is in every sense a mistake and a failure."

It can be no accident that the shingle style reached its fullest expression on the New England coast, where old money Yankees found it an architectural manifestation of their idealized selves. Indeed, the adjectives used by architectural critics to describe these homes could describe many of the people who lived in them—or at least the way they liked to think of themselves: Relaxed. Calm. Reassuring. Generous. Gentle. Humane. Unpretentious. Unobtrusive. Orderly. Comfortable. Earnest. Secure. Simple. Confident of their social status, they didn't require their houses to be made of more formal materials. (The fact that shingled houses were half as expensive as those made of brick or stone surely didn't dismay Bostonians, whose financial circumspection was well known.) Even the names were unshowy and utilitarian. Naushon's shingle-style homes include Stone House, Shore House, Ridge House, Field House, Pony Pasture, Calf Pasture, and North Pasture, while three shingle-style houses erected on speculation in Manchester by Cyrus Bartol, and designed by the well-known architect Arthur Little, were given names of almost biblical austerity: Barn, River, Fort. A few intrepid homeowners felt secure enough to bestow no name at all.

Although these houses looked, in the words of one critic, as if they were "meant to endure," the shingle style itself was short-lived. Shingles and boulders were hardly grand enough for Gilded Age tycoons, a new breed of fabulously wealthy people who saw their country homes as extensions of their bank accounts. The last thing they wanted for their houses—or for themselves—was to blend in. By the turn of the twentieth century, architects were preoccupied with monumentality, volume, formality. The Northeast coast blossomed with French Renaissance châteaus, Italian villas, Genoese palaces, and twelfth-century Norman castles—limestone and marble manifestations of what, in 1899, Thorstein Veblen would call "conspicuous consumption." Here, like Marie Antoinette at Hameau, the lords of the manor could play at country life. (These anachronistic confections were equipped, of course, with electricity and central heating.) Arnold Lewis called them "pretentious and heavy academic machines that announced so clearly the frantic search of new wealth for historical and cultural trappings." The boathouses were the size of houses, the houses the size of hotels. They were given names like Bagatelle, Dosoris, Kykuit, Château-sur-Mer. The distance traveled from the shingle style could be seen most compellingly in the spring of 1902 in Newport, where, one mile and nineteen years removed from the modest, fluid, shingled masterpiece they had built for cotton trader Isaac Bell in 1883, McKim, Mead and White completed Rosecliff, a twenty-two-bedroom, twenty-two-bath, $2.5-million marble replica of the Grand Trianon at Versailles, for socialite Tessie Oelrichs. People were still talking about its forty-by-eighty-foot ballroom when William Atkinson began to design the Big House that fall.

The grand style never took hold on Cape Cod, where architectural statements had traditionally been muted. Touring the Cape in 1800, Timothy Dwight, the president of Yale, observed that nearly all the homes were snug, shipshape, shingled, one-and-a-half-story structures with central chimneys, small windows, and gabled roofs. He called them "Cape Cod houses," a name that stuck, and a style, synonymous with compact simplicity, that can today be found across the country. "In Cape communities, where pretension was abhorred, and where the homes of captain and crewman were undifferentiated, even painted clapboards were considered 'showy,'" according to *The American Heritage History of Notable American Houses*. When wealthy Bostonians began building shingled summer homes on Cape Cod, these were far less grand than their counterparts in Newport and Manchester. (Of the ninety-three houses photographed for Sheldon's *Artistic Country-Seats*, none was from Cape Cod.) And as the Gilded Age barons were erecting their palaces, the wealthy summer residents of Bourne, Sandwich, and Falmouth continued to build unpretentious houses in the shingle style. Even the Eustis mansion on Scraggy Neck was touchingly guileless in shape: a $100,000 shoebox.

Although it had a few unusual elements—indeed, it was sheathed in clapboard for several years before being shingled—the house William Atkinson designed for his brother was clearly rooted in the shingle style. Like river plantations in the South, where visitors were likely to arrive by boat, shingle-style houses along the coast often put their best face backward, with the seaward side designed to be the "front": more grand, more formal, more symmetrical, with a "front lawn" stretching from the house to the water. Although it could be seen by nearly everyone who sailed in Buzzards Bay, the Big House was invisible from the road, and because the driveway approached it from the side, visitors arriving by car saw the house only in profile. By the time they pulled up at the front door, they saw a more complicated arrangement of shapes: mismatched gables, a kitchen ell angling inward, a stairwell revealed by a series of windows climbing diagonally across the front of the house over the entrance porch. The house presented its full self to the bay. From a boat, one saw a neat slope of roof punctuated by four symmetrical dormers, overhanging the piazza that ringed the house on three sides and, in turn, overlooked the lawn where we played croquet, and the water beyond. From the land, the house seemed turned in on itself, brooding, introspective, shy. From the water, it was large, proud, expansive; it turned out as if flexing its muscles and basked in the sun. These contrasting sides reminded me of a Hollywood flat, with its painted magnificence on one side and, on the other, an unseen clutter of struts and buttresses.

In 1887, a visitor to a Berkshires resort wrote, "the comparison of views is the chief occupation of the resident summer population." At the seashore, water views assumed a status they hadn't enjoyed since Pliny built Laurentum. Houses that only a few years earlier would have been built two miles inland were now built close to the shore, often on spectacular natural sites, with windows and porches that enabled their inhabitants to admire the vista and inhale the sea breeze. William Atkinson perched his brother's house on a knob where the channel to Pocasset Harbor meets Buzzards Bay. Like sailboats, which can't head directly into the wind, seaside houses are often angled to avoid the prevailing breeze. The Big House, however, faces straight down the bay, heading directly, impertinently, into the teeth of the southwest wind. This orientation provided not only a sweeping view but ensured that if there was so much as the slightest zephyr, the house would feel it—and if there was a hurricane, it would bear its full force. While the main part of the house faced the bay, the ell was angled along the narrow channel between Wings Neck and Bassetts Island we know as "the Gut," mirroring the turn of the land into the harbor. In those pre-environmentalist days, William Atkinson could have built the house on the edge of the Bluff so that, like Pliny's, its rooms would be bathed in sea spray. But concerned about storms, wanting to give the house a sense of perspective, and prodded, perhaps, by a sense of Brahmin modesty, he set the house back seventy yards. (Today, if it weren't for the legal restrictions, seaside houses would probably be placed so close to the water you could dive out the back door.)

Most shingle-style homes were long and sprawling, built low to the wind, adapted to the elements like boats with their sails reefed. The Big House was under full sail. With three floors and an attic below it, the roofline rode forty feet above the ground, making the house the tallest structure in the area. (It is likely to remain so; the Bourne Planning Board has long since made it illegal to build any new residence taller than thirty-five feet.) Its silhouette has become a landmark for mariners—it is mentioned in *A Cruising Guide to the New England Coast*—almost as familiar as the lighthouse at the far end of the Neck. During World War II, its height made it a tempting objective for fledgling fighter pilots from nearby Camp Edwards; they'd swoop down as close as possible to the massive roof then veer away, a practice my grandfather put an end to with a few calls to his friends in the military. Its height also makes the house a target for lightning. The chimneys are struck every five or six years, leaving fragments of brick and shingles scattered across the lawn.

The Big House seems even taller because its roof, on the water side, sweeps down from the attic to the first floor in an audaciously steep, three-story expanse of shingles. The pitch of a roof is measured by comparing the horizontal run with the vertical. If the roof rises six inches in each horizontal foot, it is called a six-pitch roof. (Ranch-style houses are usually six pitch.) If it rises a foot in each horizontal foot, it is twelve pitch: a 45-degree angle. (Cape Cod houses have traditionally been twelve pitch, an aerodynamic shape intended to persuade stiff winds to sheer up and off.) The roof on the Big House is seventeen pitch, a 64-degree angle, far steeper than an Olympic ski slope—as steep, to be frank, as the Atkinson nose. Indeed, the roof is so "brutal," as an architect friend calls it, that it is difficult to find contractors willing to work on it. The last person to reshingle it found the experience so unnerving that he went home to his wife after the job was finished and vowed he'd never do it again. Called in recently to make an estimate on some chimney repairs, a mason took one look and said, "I'm not going out there." The only people I know to have ventured onto the roof without benefit of ropes or scaffolding are my father and his siblings, who used to climb out a third-floor window and clamber around the dormers. But they were children then, and possessed a child's sense of immortality.

Why did William Atkinson make the roof so steep? As much as I'd like to think he was working in metaphor—at various times, looking at the house from the water, I have been reminded of a wave about to break, the sail of a boat heeling in a stiff wind, or the Bluff itself—his most likely inspiration was not aesthetic but economic. "My father, at that time, had financial difficulties," my grandmother wrote in a brief reminiscence of Wings Neck, "and wished to build as inexpensively as possible—hence the height." (She was referring to a slump in Ned Atkinson's business that strained his ability to support three small children along with his six siblings.) The smaller—and simpler—the footprint, the cheaper the house, since the cost of foundations and roofs, which are more expensive than framing, is kept to a minimum. Building up, not out, is a way to get maximum volume at minimum cost. (Indeed, the entire first floor of the Big House could have easily fit inside Rosecliff's ballroom.) The sharp pitch of the roof ensured that the angle of the eaves was so close to vertical that the house could have a usable third floor *and* an attic.

For most of the previous two centuries, windows had been seen more as a potential source of heat loss than as a frame through which to admire the view or catch a breeze. Most houses didn't have large expanses of glass, which was expensive, and only corner rooms had more than one exposure. Cross ventilation was a heat-squandering disadvantage. With the advent of summer houses, used for only a few warm months each year, windows—including dormers and bow windows—became increasingly important, not only for views but for light and air. Cross ventilation was a necessity, since it coaxed breezes inside even on sweltering days. (It took the later invention of air-conditioning and plate glass to enable modern seaside homes to be more window than wall.)

Windows were an area of special interest for William Atkinson, whose obituary would describe him as "a pioneer in the field of orienting buildings for sunlight." Before siting and building a house, he suggested that a "sun plan" of the building and its neighbors be drawn, "and their positions considered with respect to the shadows they cast upon each other and upon the ground." He used geometry to calculate exactly where the shadows of a building would be cast throughout the day—and throughout the year, according to the earth's changing position. In 1904, a year after the Big House was built, he would appear before a committee considering legislation to regulate the height of buildings in Boston; at the time, the city was contemplating the example of New York, which was experiencing its first wave of skyscraper construction. Showing a sheaf of sun plans he had prepared, my great-great-uncle demonstrated exactly how much natural light buildings of various heights and angles would shut out from the city streets below. Whether due to his powers of persuasion or to innate Bostonian restraint, it would be decades before the city would permit its skyline to venture above 125 feet.

William Atkinson also invented something he called the "sun box," a glass, wood, and felt contraption equipped with a thermometer, which looked something like a sauna for dogs. He used this to measure the sunlight admitted by any particular window. He compiled extensive tables showing the amount of sunlight received by rooms of certain shapes with windows at certain angles at certain times of the day. He summarized his findings in *The Orientation of Buildings or Planning for Sunlight*, a graph-and-diagram-filled book published in 1912.

I have never come across a sun plan for the Big House, nor do I know whether he lugged a sun box down to Wings Neck, but, judging from the profusion of dormers, gables, and bow windows, William Atkinson clearly had sunlight and ventilation in mind. Anne once made an informal study of windows in the Big House. By her count, seventeen of the house's nineteen rooms have windows on at least two sides. Eleven rooms have windows on three sides. Three rooms have bow windows. One *closet* has three windows. For its time, the Big House was the ultimate air-cooled building. By the time the house's additions were completed, there were sixty-seven double-hung windows of different sizes, oriented at so many different angles that, walking through the house even now, I am occasionally surprised by an unexpected slice of sea and sky.

William Atkinson designed a simple interior built, in the colonial tradition, around a central chimney stack. Not only did central chimneys stabilize a house, being the fulcrum against which the framing took place, but they offered an early version of central heating. Like most shingle-style architects, he placed the living rooms on the "back" side of the house, facing the water and opening onto the piazza. The living room flowed into the dining room through double doors that were rarely closed. A corridor led from the dining room to a one-story kitchen ell, placed on the east side of the house so the servants would have the benefit of morning light as they prepared breakfast and heated water for the day's laundry on the huge cast-iron range. As in most large Victorian houses, the kitchen was separated from the dining room by a pantry, so the family wouldn't have to hear the hubbub of the servants and, one assumed, so the servants couldn't hear the family. The second floor was similarly simple: a congeries of bedrooms and nurseries off a short central hallway. On the third floor, there were two bedrooms for servants. (One reason houses of that era were bigger, of course, is that they had to have room for the staff.)

The dimensions of the interior details were, as in many nineteenth-century houses, generous by modern standards. The doors were wide, five-paneled, and made of fir. The stairs had a six-inch riser, as opposed to the seven that is now standard. One walked up the broad, shallow steps in a gentle shuffle; running, we could take them three at a time. Yet the rooms themselves were far from grand. The living room was only sixteen by twenty-eight feet, and when three generations of Atkinsons crowded in after dinner, half of them had to stand. There was no parlor, no drawing room, no library. The few frills in which William Atkinson indulged were on the exterior. On the back side, the dormers were bordered by delicately pinked shingles, and above the windows in each of the two larger dormers, in the triangle of the gable, he placed a shingled half circle, like a setting sun, an allusion to the Palladian windows he had, no doubt, seen and admired on his European tour. The piazza was edged by latticework fencing that canted inward, like ship's rails, mimicking the pitch of the roof and adding a nautical touch typical of Cape Cod homes, many of whose owners and builders were old mariners who craved a reminder of their days at sea.

People chuckle now to recall the false modesty with which rich home-owners referred to their massive turn-of-the century summer houses as "cottages." For a house its size, however, the Big House had some truly rustic touches. As in many summer homes, the interior finishes and detailing were crude. "There was no plaster used in the entire house," Ned Atkinson proudly observed, writing about the construction of the house many years later. Instead, the stairwell, hallways, and many of the rooms they led to had open-stud construction, with walls composed of a mysterious, rough, gun gray substance too thick to be cardboard, too thin to be wood. When you lean against it, you can feel its humidity-softened surface give a bit; thumped, it yields a disconcertingly hollow sound. You can't swing your elbows too aggressively in the hallway, or be careless when carrying a sharp-cornered piece of furniture up the stairs—one false move and a table leg could punch clean through the stuff. The stair-well still has three or four ragged-looking holes that make it look like the scene of an old family brawl. We've hung paintings or thumbtacked posters over them, like Band-Aids over cuts. Take away "The Dales of Derbyshire" and there is a lightning-shaped gash; remove the postcard of the Austrian Alps, written to my grandfather by an old friend in the fifties, and a fist-sized cavity is revealed.

Carpenters working at the house over the years have been baffled by the gray wallboard. Known as Sackett Plaster Board, after its inventor, a New Jersey manufacturer named Augustine Sackett, it consisted of two layers of plaster of Paris interleaved with three layers of gray paper, combining to make a board about the thickness, firmness, and durability of a slim volume of poetry. Sackett Board was much weaker and less attractive than the customary three coats of plaster on wood lath. But it was quicker and cheaper, and was therefore immensely popular at the turn of the century. (It became obsolete when its thicker, stronger descendant, Sheetrock, was invented in 1917.) The rough paper resisted the direct application of paint or wallpaper, so to spruce up the living room, dining room, and most of the bedrooms, William Atkinson settled on another economical practice common in summer homes of the time: he glued jute fabric over the Sackett Board and painted it white. In the stairwell, the hallway, the bathrooms, and a few of the bedrooms, however, the Sackett Board was left exposed, its leaden hue lending a certain gloom to the house, as if fog had drifted in.

We'd always been told that Ned Atkinson had run out of money and couldn't finish the walls—hence the Sackett Board. That, we assumed, was also the reason for what lay *behind* the Sackett Board. The house was insulated with eelgrass, tufts of which emerged, like stuffing from a couch, whenever a hole appeared in the wall. The eelgrass was dry and crinkly, the texture of the artificial grass that lines children's Easter baskets. I pictured Ned Atkinson carting it up from the Bluff and jamming handfuls in the walls. He wouldn't have been the first. Cape Codders had long used *Zostera marina* to bank their houses and barns for the winter. By the time the Big House was built, however, a Boston chemist named Samuel Cabot—one of the Cabots who, as the poem goes, "talk only to God"—had come up with a slightly more sophisticated technique. After washing and drying eelgrass raked from the shore in front of his summer home in Chatham, he sewed it between thin sheets of black paper into squares, resembling small pillows, four inches across and about an inch thick. Manufactured and sold in three-foot rolls, Cabot's Single-Ply Sheathing was sound from both an insulation and—long before the word "recycling" had been coined—an environmental point of view. But dried eelgrass is highly flammable, and contributed to the speed with which many shingle-style homes burned down. After the invention of fiberglass insulation, which can melt but not burn, eelgrass (much of which was killed off by blight in the 1930s) was no longer used. And no one seems to remember that it ever had been—until another old summer house is torn down and its interior secrets are revealed. Meanwhile, the Big House's insulation is further recycled by the generations of mice and squirrels who have gnawed into the walls and purloined the innards for their nests.

Ned and William Atkinson also saved money on wood. I had been impressed when I had read, in the specs, such spare-no-expense-sounding instructions as "Hard pine where called for to be best quality Georgia pine," but at the time, longleaf yellow pine was about the cheapest floor-ing available. As one carpenter told me, "In those big old nineteenth-century homes, you could tell just by looking at the floors which were the family's rooms and which were the maids'." The family rooms—living room, dining room, bedrooms—would have hardwood: oak, hickory, wal-nut, butternut, mahogany. The maids' quarters would have yellow pine. The Big House floors are almost all yellow pine. Later, when his business prospered and he made numerous additions to the Big House, Ned Atkinson had his wife's bedroom refloored with fir.

In the last few years, yellow pine has become a high-end wood. Agents list it as a selling point in real estate ads, and contractors reno-vating old shingle-style homes have gone to great lengths to track down vintage longleaf yellow pine lumber. Several years ago, the Cataumet sawmill bought the huge pine timbers that once supported the floors of a number of old factories in Quincy. Resawn and recycled, they are sold at a premium to make expensive new houses look old.

In March 1903, work on the Big House began. The contractor was G. W. Eldredge, who had built the Douglas shoe factories in Brockton. First, a local mason built the living room fireplace. Then the carpenters framed the house against the central chimney. Like many summer homes near the water, the Big House was built without foundations, on cedar and chestnut posts, so air could circulate underneath and prevent dampness. (In the thirties, brick piers and a concrete foundation were installed, just in time to save the house from sure destruction in the 1938 hurricane.)

By the turn of the twentieth century, Cape Cod had long since used up its own forests for timber to build ships; building lumber was hauled from Maine to Boston by boat, and then inland by wagon. The Big House was framed with pine and spruce. In those days the sawmills sold rough-cut lumber to the contractor, and the contractor planed it smooth as needed. When a contractor ordered a two-by-four, he got board lumber whose cross section measured two by four inches. These days, milling equipment is sophisticated enough to plane the lumber itself, and the boards end up slightly smaller than the rough size, a half inch or so off each side. In a lin-guistic shuffle, this is called "finished lumber." These days a two-by-four is really a three-and-a-half-by-one-and-a-half (a diminution not unlike that suffered by the therapeutic "hour," which has dwindled to fifty minutes). Although houses built with finished lumber still possess what contractors call "structural integrity"—meaning they won't fall down without provo-cation—houses built with true two-by-fours are, according to an architect friend, "built like a brick shithouse." Indeed, the Big House has survived three Category 4 hurricanes, numerous lightning strikes, and nearly a cen-tury of fierce familial affection.

The contractor used balloon framing, a technique said to have origi-nated in Chicago in 1832, in which the huge timbers of post-and-beam construction were replaced by many small boards. (This development was necessitated by the scarcity of large trees and made possible by the recent mass production of nails.) In post-and-beam, the tenon of one structural element fits into the mortise of the other. This creates a sturdy, somewhat rigid frame. Balloon framing, whose name comes from the empty sleeve of air between the exterior and interior walls, uses many smaller pieces of lumber nailed together. The vertical studs rise up the façade from the cellar to the attic without any horizontal break. Balloon-framed houses are faster to build, more flexible, and structurally sound, but the continuous air flow between the cellar and the attic creates mini-chimneys: once a fire starts, it can race up through the cavity and quickly engulf the building. Balloon framing is another reason why so many of these old summer houses have burned to the ground. In platform fram-ing, which replaced it, each new story is framed separately on the "plat-form" created by the story below; the vertical stud stops at the floor joists, and there is fire blocking at each level.

I sometimes try to imagine the Big House construction site. Every-thing was hand cut, using saws, adzes, and broadaxes—it would be sev-eral decades before the invention of the skill saw, the nail gun, and the other power tools carpenters use to build houses today. Everything was carted in by wagon over dirt roads: lumber from the mill in Brockton; bricks from the West Barnstable brickyard; square-headed nails from the Tremont Nail Factory in Wareham. The commute from Brockton—where the contractor and, in all likelihood, most of his employees lived—would have taken most of the day, so the crew probably put up rough shacks and camped at the site. A cook was hired to prepare meals. Did the workers think it was a waste of money to build such a large house in the middle of what must have seemed a wilderness? Did they stop and admire the view? As spring turned to summer, did they wash off their sweat at the Bluff? I imagine them cursing as they clung to the roof in a stiff southwest wind, nailing the shingles, made of cypress from the swamps of Louisiana, to the spruce sheathing, two nails to each shingle, carefully overlapping them like fish scales so water couldn't seep in. I wonder what the fishermen from Barlow's Landing must have thought as they saw the house rise above the trees.

It went up fast. Just as the London postal system was able to deliver the mail ten times a day in 1680, premechanized housing construction was often far more efficient than its high-tech counterpart. Despite a fortnight's strike, the Big House was finished in three and a half months. Today, if the owners were lucky, a house its size would take three times that long. And it was built well. Whenever a carpenter comes to make some minor repair, before he gets to work he invariably taps a beam or gazes admiringly at a gable and comments on the quality of the construction. "These days most summer houses aren't well thought out and they go up slam bang," says a local contractor. "But this house was built to last." No one knows how much the house cost, but judging by the prices paid for other houses of its size in the area, it was likely less than $10,000—not a small sum at a time when the skilled carpenters who worked on the place were paid fifty cents an hour, but a tenth the cost of the Eustis house across the bay.

When I look at a photograph taken shortly after the house was finished, and published in *A Trip Around Buzzards Bay Shores* (another compendium of summer estates compiled by Ezra Perry in 1903), I hardly recognize the place. To me, the Big House was as much a part of the landscape as the oak tree that shaded the kitchen wing or the ivy that worked its way between the shingles. It didn't occur to me that it had once been new—the lumber recently milled, the nails newly hammered, the paint wet, the shingles raw and orange-gold, the ground bare and brown. In the photo, the house looks as plunked down as Dorothy's farmhouse in Oz. It is a house without memories, a house without ghosts, a house waiting to become a home.

On July 3, 1903, Ned Atkinson and his wife, Ellen, traveled by train from Boston to Monument Beach. From there, they were driven by horse and carriage along the sandy roads to Wings Neck, and up the long driveway—a dirt swath recently hacked through the pines—to their new house. Following in their wake were several wagons filled with packing cases of blankets, linens, and towels; trunkfuls of clothes; enough barrels of flour, sugar, coffee, and tea to last the summer; and a complete set of Dickens that my great-grandmother had recently bought and inscribed with the words "Wings Neck." A few days later, the cook, the parlor maid, and the governess would bring down the children: five-year-old Edward, three-year-old Hal, two-year-old Mary. John, their "man," brought down the two family dogs and the cow, Bismarck—so they would be assured of milk from a reliable source—in a covered wagon. (Turn-of-the-century Brahmin families decamping to their summer houses sixty miles away managed to make the journey seem as daunting as if, like Anne's great-great-grandparents, they were heading two thousand miles west by prairie schooner.)

They opened the door and stepped inside. The house smelled of freshly cut spruce and pine. Everything was immaculate. They had decided to call their new house "Rooftree," a term for the main beam or ridgepole of a roof that also refers to the ritual, begun by medieval builders but occasionally still practiced today, of fastening a small tree to the ridge of a newly framed roof for good luck. Over time the word also came to signify the family beneath that roof, and the toast "To your rooftree" used to be offered in the same spirit as one might say "To hearth and home." Although the name wouldn't last—my father had never heard of it and, in my memory, no one has used any name other than the Big House—I find it moving. It seems to speak to Ned Atkinson's hope that this new house would provide a safe, loving refuge for his young family.

That evening, my great-grandfather opened a new leather-bound volume with the words WINGS NECK NO. I inscribed in gold lettering on the cover (that "No. 1" confidently implying that many volumes were to follow). He turned to the first blank, white, gilt-edged page and wrote:

Edward W. and Ellen F. Atkinson and Family
"The Rooftree"
Wings Neck
July 1903

VI

Renovations

T HEIR FIRST summer, the Atkinsons were alone on Wings Neck, aside from the lighthouse keeper on the point. The Bartol house, the Neck's only other dwelling, stood empty down the dirt road. It was, perhaps, an even simpler life than my great-grandparents had bargained for. Water was pumped from an outside storage tank to a cistern above the Little Nursery bathroom, from which it was gravity-fed to spigots throughout the house. At night, although a few lights were visible across the bay on Scraggy Neck, where the Copper King had electrified his estate, the Big House was illuminated with candles and kerosene lamps— lamps we still press into service whenever a storm knocks out the power. (Electricity would not reach Wings Neck until after World War I.) The Atkinsons spent their summer swimming at the Bluff, planting a garden, and inviting family and friends from Boston and Naushon to admire their new home. Occasionally, they'd walk down to the sandy curve in the shoreline they called the Big Cove, where *Scout*, their yawl, was the lone boat moored in the harbor.

The following summer, Langdon Frothingham, a pathologist who was my great-grandfather's neighbor in Brookline, built a house on the northeast side of the Neck. Over the next decade, five more houses were built; by the end of World War I, there were ten. They were large, shingled summer homes hidden at the ends of long driveways, inhabited by families whose names constituted a Who's Who of proper Boston: Cabot, Lee, Hallowell, Crompton, Saltonstall. No numbers or signs were needed on the dirt road; everyone knew everyone else. Paths were cut through the woods, stitching together the houses and creating an unbroken passage from the lighthouse to the community beach. A few families built clay tennis courts in the woods. Ice was cut from the millpond in winter by a Pocasset man, stored in an icehouse, then delivered in summer along the paths. Fathers came down from the city on the Dude, a private train, out-fitted with plush drawing room cars, chartered by wealthy Bostonians to deliver them faster (its top speed was a mile a minute) and more comfort-ably to their summer estates along Buzzards Bay. (The Dude was named by its first conductor in recognition of the breed who rode it.) But once they got there, there were few frills—and even fewer rules. Everyone assumed that his neighbors shared the same values and the same vision: a place where men could retreat with their families from the stresses of business in the city, a place where, as Ned Atkinson's father liked to say, they could "do nothing, and do it all the time." Although the twentieth century was well under way, Wings Neck had a decidedly nineteenth-century atmosphere. Each morning, Norwood Penrose Hallowell, the twice-wounded Civil War hero who had commanded the second black regiment after the death of Robert Gould Shaw, rode a white horse named Dickens down the Wings Neck paths en route to the post office. Hallowell was known as "the Giant" as much for his military bearing as for his six-foot-two-inch frame. Wearing a rumpled suit, bow tie, and worn leather shoes, his face embellished with a luxuriant white mustache and goatee, he'd doff his white hat as he passed the Big House, where my great-grandmother sat reading on the piazza. Trotting across the cause-way to Pocasset, he'd beckon to one of the awed village boys, ask him to fetch his mail, stow the letters in a saddlebag, and ride away.

In a recent history of Wings Neck privately published by its residents, the most noticeable theme is how little things have changed since what one resident describes as "the good old days." Then, as now, there were scavenger hunts, skinny-dipping, blueberry picking, Capture the Flag. The Big Cove was the center of social life, such as it was. The syndicate outfitted it with a dock, eight bathhouses, and an offshore float complete with a springboard and a fifteen-foot slide whose wooden surface was lubricated with seawater drawn up by a manual pump. Mornings, own-ers and their families gathered to swim, sail, and dig for clams. After-noons, as was traditional in most summer resorts, the beach was turned over (during the hottest part of the day) to the help, a flock of Irish cooks, maids, and nannies who sunned themselves and squealed with excite-ment as they were tossed off the dock by the boatmen. Several families, including the Atkinsons, kept large schooners in the lee of Bassetts Island for annual cruises Down East. Habits became traditions. There were weekly sailboat races that started and finished at the pier, where a group of mothers shouted instructions and encouragement through a bullhorn. There were fireworks on the Fourth of July at which Jack Hallowell, the Giant's son, set off rocket launchers on the beach and distributed fire-crackers to the adults and sparklers to the children. There was an annual sail for Wings Neck men and boys to a deserted point across the bay, where they swam and picnicked—swimsuits not allowed. There were end-of-summer bonfires with clams, chicken, fish, and potatoes roasted in a sandpit dug by the younger men, followed by after-dinner sing-alongs led by my great-grandfather, who never failed to offer his rendi-tion of "The Yellow Rose of Texas."

Just as pioneers of the Old West had banded together to stave off marauding Indians, early Wings Neck settlers were united by a shared enemy: the descendants of the mosquitoes that had defeated Cyrus Bartol. (They wanted the simple summer life, as long as that life was insect-free.) Not long after purchasing the Neck, the syndicate had hired what my great-grandfather casually referred to as "a gang of Italians" housed in "commodious shacks" at the Neck's east end, who cleared away several tons of underbrush and four thousand cords of wood. When that didn't solve the problem, the Neck's captains of industry and lords of State Street tried pouring oil into the stagnant ponds from which Ebenezer Wing's cattle had drunk. When that didn't work, they had the ponds filled in. This took care of the freshwater mosquitoes, but their saltwater cousins remained at large. So they had a series of drainage ditches dug in the marshes that separated Wings Neck from the mainland. "This did the trick and solved the problem except at such times as a cloud of mosqui-toes would be blown over from other places like Barnstable and bother us for a few days," wrote my great-grandfather in his 1939 memoir of Wings Neck, a large chunk of which is devoted to the ups and downs of the cam-paign. "Today we have fewer mosquitoes on Wings Neck than in the town of Brookline." (Unfortunately, his memoir doesn't tell us what became of the "gang of Italians"; today, a large WINGS NECK TRUST: PRIVATE PROPERTY sign stands where their "commodious shacks" once stood.)

Everything was low-key and informal. When they discussed the for-mation of a yacht club, the residents worried it might start them down a slippery slope toward pomp and circumstance. "Opinion is unanimously and strongly opposed to the establishment of a yacht club if it means the construction of a building . . . with a fairly commodious room for luncheons on race days . . . which might and doubtless would be used also for dancing, teas and similar entertainments," stated the minutes from their inaugural meeting. "It is felt that a club of that nature would tend rapidly to change the present simple and informal character of the community which we desire to preserve as long as possible." Despite their apprehensions, they forged ahead with what they called the Buzzards, a name that so repulsed their wives that they unsuccessfully petitioned their husbands to consider more euphonious alternatives. In the WASP tradition of understatement, the club had no clubhouse until 1954, when several bathhouse fragments, swept from the beach to the far side of the tidal creek by Hurricane Carol, were nailed together to form the Buzzards' sanctum sanctorum. (The only maritime organization on Cape Cod that was even humbler was the Quissett Yacht Club down the bay near Woods Hole, whose members proudly point out that in nearly a hundred years, it has never had a clubhouse at all.)

After the Cape Cod Canal, a project first proposed by George Washington, was completed in 1914, making a literal island of what had been a figurative one (Ned Atkinson took his family to the opening ceremony), the big excitement was to walk over to the north side of the Neck in the evening and watch the "New York boat"—a double-smokestacked, 402-foot steamer with room for nine hundred passengers—churn through the canal on its way to Manhattan. Wings Neckers, like hundreds of others who lined the length of the canal, waved, cheered, honked car horns, and shone flashlights as the sleek vessel passed by, lit up, as one onlooker described it, "like a Venetian canal at carnival time," its foghorn blowing, its searchlight browsing the canal, picking out the channel markers and occasionally illuminating pajamaed children onshore. On windless nights, my father recalls, you could hear the orchestra playing waltzes on the deck. As the music faded and the lights disappeared, the people of Wings Neck turned away and walked quietly down the paths through the dark woods back to their houses. The glimpse they'd had of the wider, more flamboyant world only reaffirmed their satisfaction with their insular little haven.

At the Big House, meanwhile, the shingles weathered silver-gray. Honeysuckle climbed the piazza rail. The catalpa tree Ned Atkinson planted by the garden grew taller than he was. The pitch pine rose along the Bluff, eclipsing the view of the bay. A pig and a goat—who pulled my grandmother and her brothers around the yard in a wagon—were added to the barn. Ned Atkinson bought the *Bagheera*, a seventy-foot schooner that he named after the cunning black panther in Kipling's *Jungle Book*, and moored it in the lee of Bassetts Island. The coachman became a chauffeur. The guest book filled, and a second volume was begun.

Last year I came across an old mailing tube in the bottom drawer of the bureau in Grandma's Bedroom. Inside it was a set of furled blueprints for a modest, fairly traditional five-bedroom house. I did not recognize the house and wondered why my grandmother had saved the plans. Then, in the lower right-hand corner, I saw these words:

House at Wings Neck for E. W. Atkinson Esq.
William Atkinson, architect

I felt the same sense of dislocation I had felt when I first came across a photograph of my father when he was three or four, and realized that he hadn't always been my father. Even to my untrained eye, it was clear that these plans described a different house from the one I had visited every summer of my life. Where was Mariah's Room? Where was the west wing? Where were the back stairs? The vast, rambling, eleven-bedroom Big House had, it seemed, not always been that vast. (Relatively speaking, that is. The original house contained 6,000 square feet at a time when the average suburban house contained 3,000 to 3,500. The average house today contains about 1,800 square feet.) Nor, for all William Atkinson's eccentricity, had it always been so eccentric. Its footprint was basically a square with a small ell. Like the hermit crabs we find in the millpond onto whose shells assorted barnacles, seaweeds, and limpets take hold, the house, with numerous additions and alterations over the years, had gradually evolved into its present convoluted form.

In 1912, his business flourishing, Ned Atkinson began to renovate the Big House. He and his wife enlarged the kitchen wing, adding a second floor with steep stairs, three small, low-ceilinged servants' rooms, and a modest balcony, with a view not of the water but of the woods, where the servants took their afternoon break. Over the following two decades the

Atkinsons expanded the dining room, added four dormers, built rooms between those dormers, and tacked on a two-story, three-bedroom wing to the west side of the house. According to my grandmother, Ellen Atkinson dreamed up most of these additions during the winters. In summer, she went outside with a local carpenter, pointed up at the house, and told him what she wanted. Perhaps this explains why the west wing—a simple gabled cube—was referred to forever after as the Doghouse.

By 1930, my great-grandparents had added six bedrooms, three bathrooms, and two thousand square feet to the Big House. The footprint was now a sort of jigsaw-puzzle piece with jogs, recesses, and protuberances that even the quixotic William Atkinson could hardly have envisioned. I remember games of Capture the Flag in which, as I crept around its perimeter to sneak up on the enemy, the house seemed to go on forever, like a shoreline with an endless succession of inlets and peninsulas. Inside, the renovations created odd alcoves and strangely shaped rooms whose purpose was never defined, like the K-shaped space on the first floor—the only room in the house without a name—that became a sort of sitting area where no one ever sat. Or the long, skinny rectangle between my grandmother's bedroom and her dressing room that was used for storage even though its three windows afforded one of the best views in the house. Or the pantry, which looked as if it had been arbitrarily cloven by the staircase to the servants' quarters, creating two routes to the kitchen: a brighter, more heavily trafficked path past the copper sink, and a darker, more somber path past drawers so brimming with silverware that only a grown-up could tug them open. There were passageways that led to unexpected places, like the second-floor breezeway from the governess's bedroom to the Little Nursery that enabled one to step from the coziness of the kitchen wing into the more austere atmosphere of the main house. I remember reading my great-grandmother's copy of *Bleak House*, sitting on my favorite couch in the dining room, and coming upon the following sentence: "It was one of those delightfully irregular houses where you go up and down steps out of one room into another, and where you come upon more rooms when you think you have seen all there are." I knew exactly what Dickens had in mind.

Like the Big House itself, the family within it developed a few interior complications. Almost from birth, it had been apparent that Ned Atkin-

son's eldest child, Edward, was slightly "slow," a condition doctors attrib-
uted to a difficult forceps delivery. He would grow into a softer, puffier
variation on the Atkinson template, a childlike fellow with thick lips and,
according to Aunt Mary, "the intelligence of a twelve-year-old." He was
unable to hold a job. He also, as my father puts it, "got into trouble with
girls." In those days, wealthy Bostonians were able to keep their scandals
hushed up, and no one in the family knows exactly what kind of trouble
young Edward got into. A fondness for prostitutes? Statutory rape?
Whatever it was, it was sufficiently serious that on several occasions his
father had to go down to the police station to bail out his namesake son.
Indeed, for a time, Edward wasn't permitted to reside in the state of
Massachusetts, although he was allowed supervised visits. He lived nine
months of the year in a rural New York town with a male nurse hired by
his father to keep him out of trouble. Mr. Cathcart, by all accounts a quiet,
nondescript man, accompanied Edward to Wings Neck each summer.
Edward slept in a vacant servant's room on the third floor, Mr. Cathcart
close by in what is now the Playroom. (My father, who slept across the
hall in the Yellow Room, wasn't quite sure who Mr. Cathcart was or why
he was there; the subject, of course, was never discussed.) Sweet, passive,
and pudgy, Edward never joined in the baseball games or tennis matches
that dominated the Big House day; in the evening he'd sit quietly with his
mother at the card table and play hour after hour of Russian Bank.

Although Ned Atkinson's other son was perfectly capable of supporting
himself—he held degrees from Harvard, Harvard Law School, and Trinity
College, Cambridge—Great-Uncle Hal was a romantic idealist who gave
up the law for the life of a gentleman activist, a career path available to
him, he acknowledged in his *Harvard Class of 1921 Fiftieth Anniversary
Report*, "only through the generosity and tolerance of a perfect father."
Long before Pearl Harbor, believing the United States should come to the
aid of her allies, Hal, at the age of forty-one, enlisted as a private in the
Canadian Army the day after his wedding. ("It's a good thing he wasn't an
officer," my grandfather observed of Hal, a notoriously indecisive fellow,
"because his men would have all been killed before he made up his mind.")
In more than three years on active duty in the Mediterranean theater,
which included storming the beach at Anzio, Great-Uncle Hal sustained
only one injury: a collarbone broken while playing touch football with his
younger messmates, a wound for which the government saw fit to award
him the Purple Heart. After the war, he and his wife worked for a relief

organization in India, where he developed a lifelong interest in nutrition. In the classic At tradition, he joined any number of crusades—for the merit system in the civil service, for the elimination of billboards from public highways, for world federalism, for curbing the indiscriminate use of X-ray machines, for birth control, and, last and most passionately, for Zero Population Growth. He never earned a salary. Supported largely by his father, he and his wife, a high-ranking, plain-faced official with the Food and Drug Administration, lived in one of the family houses on Heath Hill. They had no children. A tall, thin man with a brush mustache, Great-Uncle Hal was a reserved, slightly ethereal presence at family parties, as I recall. When asked, however, he would eagerly extol his latest cause, discuss a recent addition to his stamp collection, or gently proselytize a piggish grandnephew about the benefits of Fletcherizing (the practice, promoted at the turn of the century by a San Francisco nutritionist, of chewing each bite of food thirty-two times before swallowing).

The lady of the house, the former Ellen Forbes Russell, contributed her share of crotchets (along with wealth and social prestige) to the family mix. Shortly after her engagement to Ned Atkinson, she had a nervous breakdown and was sent away for a "rest" that lasted two years. During that time, it seems, she was permitted neither visitors nor newspapers, lest they roil her fragile sensitivities. Her mother's letters to her during her confinement include not just family news—births, deaths, marriages, who got what for Christmas, who sang what at Naushon musicales—but national news, such as the deaths of actress Fanny Kemble and ex-president Rutherford B. Hayes. I find it extraordinarily touching that, without ever once seeing her while she was "resting," my great-grandfather waited. They were married soon after she came home.

The story goes that while she was recovering, my great-grandmother was told by her doctors never to read anything more serious than Trollope and to cover her nerve endings by eating chocolate. Apparently, she followed their prescription all too well. At the Big House, she spent much of the day on the piazza, a volume of Trollope in her lap and a Whitman's Sampler on the nearby table. Within a few years, she had read all sixty volumes of Trollope—and weighed so much (family estimates run as high as three hundred pounds) that when she went to the doctor she had to stand on two scales. Elderly Wings Neckers tell me that when Ellen Atkinson came calling in her chauffeured Franklin limousine, she didn't get out of the car; the woman she was visiting would come out to sit with *her*. (Legend has it that she insisted on taking the inaugural plunge on the wooden slide at the Big Cove; if the slide could support her weight, she reasoned, it was safe for anyone.) Toward the end of her life, she could no longer manage the Big House stairs, so she slept in the Lower Bedroom on a pair of twin beds tied together with rope. I assume that she was sensitive about her weight, for though there are dozens of photos of her husband in the Big House, there is only one of her, taken long before her marriage. It hangs on the stairwell wall. Although the portrait is nearly life-sized, I paid it little notice until I was a teenager, when, newly aware of the opposite sex, I was drawn to this slim young woman, holding an open book, her raven hair parted in the middle and pulled back from her delicate face. I thought she was the most beautiful creature I had ever seen. I had no idea it was my great-grandmother.

Her nerve endings must have been successfully protected, for Ellen Atkinson never had another breakdown. Indeed, she was, by all accounts, a strong, lively woman of unfaltering opinions, accustomed to getting her way. According to Aunt Mary, when she came across a book she considered inferior—even if it came from the Bourne library—she burned it in the fireplace. (She had a particular aversion to the "modern novel"; as she put it, "I don't want to read about the hero brushing his teeth.") Our neighbor to the west, Phips Hallowell, says that when Ned Atkinson had a wide swath of trees cut down across the Neck, saying it would create a much-needed firebreak, the real reason was that my great-grandmother wanted to see the water on the north shore from her favorite spot on the piazza. Believing that reading on an empty stomach was harmful to the eyes, she had a tin of Ritz crackers placed in the room of anyone she suspected of opening a book before breakfast. She had her cook prepare the same menu every week of her married life. Her grandchildren did their best to avoid Sunday night (chicken croquettes) but made frequent visits on Friday (steamed clams and lobsters). Like most Forbeses, she possessed a fondness for jokes and a penchant for teasing—often directed at her husband. "Now, Ned, no one wants to hear you sing," she'd say. Beneath the ribbing, however, there lay devotion. Her husband wrote to her every day he was away from her; judging from the stacks in the closet of Mariah's Room, she appears to have saved every letter. Within a few months of his death, her raven hair turned iron gray.

My uncle Jimmy once told me, "When they started out, your great-grandparents were a dream couple, and the Big House was their dream house." Whether or not he felt his dream had faded over the years, Ned Atkinson managed to maintain his equilibrium—and his good humor—as his siblings asked for more money, his children pursued more erratic courses, and his wife ate more chocolate. He had built the Big House as a haven for the entire At clan, and was determined to keep it that way. My father and his siblings cherished the three weeks they spent there each August. Their grandfather taught them to sail, took them fishing, rowed them to Bassetts Island to collect wampum. They played croquet under the watchful eye of their grandmother from her berth on the piazza. (She tore a sheet into strips and tied a little bow on each wicket so they wouldn't trip over them on their way to and from the Bluff.) On rainy days they slid down the barn roof on borrowed kitchen trays. In the afternoon, they would repair to the piazza for tea, which, for the under-twelves, consisted of a pinkish concoction involving ginger ale and "Five Fruit" juice accompanied by platefuls of ginger molasses cookies. At night, as they lay in bed, they could hear their mother and grandfather singing duets, accompanied by Uncle Bill.

By the time he reached his seventies, Ned Atkinson had made a great deal of money and given much of it away. (Near the end of his life, he made a list of his contributions and noted with satisfaction that "it is safe to say that I have given away not less than $1,000,000.") Although his doctors told him that his arthritis would soon confine him to a wheelchair, he became a disciple of an avant-garde system of posture control called the Alexander Technique and soon felt sufficiently vigorous to resume ice-skating. My aunt Ellen has a photo of him taken around this time. Dressed in a three-piece suit and black figure skates, a jaunty cap on his head and a grin lifting his thick mustache, he is executing a spiral—his right leg extended, his arms opened wide. He looks perfectly happy. I like to think he had that grin when he died—and indeed he may well have, since he suffered a fatal heart attack on a December morning in 1940, at the age of eighty-one, while performing a figure eight.

At the Bluff, Susannah picks up a stone. "This is a future grain of sand," she tells me. "And I *mean* the future—more than a thousand years, did you know that?" She points to the Black Diamond Rock. "And even *this* is a future grain of sand. Millions of grains of sand. In thousands and thousands of years."

VII

Fishing

O N THE far wall of the barn, a school of paper fish swam among the racing pennants that lay like eelgrass on the rough pine walls. They were the traced silhouettes of memorable catches made by my aunts and uncles decades earlier, carefully cut from white blotting paper and inscribed in India ink with the particulars of their demise. As a child, I knew these fish so well that their shapes became almost archetypal, like the five-pointed stars or crescent moons in fairy-tale illustrations. The slim, attenuated arc of a pickerel, frozen in midleap, mouth gaping, seemed forever about to swallow the nearby knothole. *(J. D. Colt. Pickerel. Mary's Lake. July 12, 1946.)* Another pickerel floated nearby, as simple and streamlined as a jet plane, but with a desperate, wild-eyed look supplied by the yellow thumbtack that pinned it to the wall. *(Mary F. Colt. Mary's Lake. August 7, 1942.)* My favorite was a scup that my grandmother, the eternal optimist, had rendered so plump and sinuous in its translation from water to paper that for many years I half-believed she had caught an enchanted, miniature whale. *(Mary A. Colt. Wings Neck. August 21, 1955.)*

The specimens were of modest size, the setting was spartan, and I knew that paper cutouts were a poor kind of taxidermy. Yet these trophies were as impressive to me as the stuffed elephant's head I had seen on the wall of the New York Harvard Club. And as I gazed up at the blotting-paper ghosts, I harbored dreams that one day I might catch a fish worthy of joining this elite, eclectic school.

"I think tomorrow might be a good day for a little *fishing* expedition," Aunt Mary would announce, as she rushed about the kitchen serving dinner to the children. To Aunt Mary, nearly everything that took us beyond the boundaries of our property was elevated to the status of an "expedition," a title that made even a trip to the vegetable stand take on the aura of Jim Hawkins's voyage to the Spanish Main in *Treasure Island*. There were expeditions to the firebreak to pick blueberries ("We're going *berrying*," she'd announce at breakfast, handing out pails); there were expeditions to the Sandwich gristmill ("You can't make muffins without fresh ground cornmeal"); there were expeditions to the Wings Neck Lighthouse ("If you mind your manners, Mr. Flanagan might let you climb to the top"); there were expeditions to the old railroad station in Cataumet to visit Harley Chamberlain, a soft-spoken, elderly cabinet-maker who under Aunt Mary's energetic attention seemed as extraordinary as Geppetto ("He built the bureaus for the soldiers at Camp Edwards during the war—thousands and thousands of them").

Aunt Mary had been a tomboy and an athlete—some say the finest in a family of fine athletes—and in her thirties she still radiated energy and stamina. Each August on her daughter Catherine's birthday, Mary went all out for the Neck's children, organizing Pin the Tail on the Donkey, serving her famous ginger-ale-fruit-and-sherbet punch, and hanging spider-webs of endless, crisscrossing strings at the end of each of which was tied a present. "All right," she'd announce in her husky voice, "now it's time for the wheelbarrow race. Follow me!" By the end of the afternoon, the children were ready for a nap, the parents for a martini on the piazza, but Mary was still going strong. "All right, who's ready for the three-legged race?" Wherever we went, Aunt Mary seemed to know everyone—and not just the summer people, but the year-rounders—and if she didn't know them, she'd walk right up, introduce herself, and start a conversation. Visiting a neighbor, she'd open the screen door, step inside, and call "YOO-HOO!" with a persistence that impressed and embarrassed me. She always said exactly what she was thinking—"Let's not beat about the bush" was a favorite expression—a trait that at the time I had no idea was unusual in proper Boston homes. She brooked, as she put it, "no non-sense," and she herself was no-nonsense, from her appearance (she dressed plainly and wore her dark hair short) to the suppers she cooked us (hamburgers, baked codfish, corn muffins). Once, when I had the temerity to ask her to fry my hamburger a few minutes longer, she barked, "This is no short-order house!"—a remark that would become a family catchphrase for Mary's brusque style. I had heard my grandfather use the phrase "gird your loins," and though I wasn't sure what it meant, I always felt I should be girding my loins before I went anywhere with Aunt Mary.

After dinner, we'd sort through what Aunt Mary called our "fishing tackle," a phrase that not only was redolent of a more rugged sport but conferred professional status on our half dozen handlines (thick brown string wound around warped, gray, ticktacktoe-shaped wooden frames), which dated to my grandmother's childhood. Flicking off specks of dried bait from a previous expedition, we made sure that each line was free of snarls and equipped with a sinker and a wicked silver hook. (A few of the hooks were so rusty that if their barbs didn't kill the fish, tetanus surely would.) Then we'd pack them into my great-grandfather's creel, an aged, caramel-colored wicker pouch that looked just like Jeremy Fisher's. Every so often we'd study the evening sky for signs of inclement weather. It was an article of faith that if the appointed day was overcast, the fishing would be good. "Red sky at night, sailor's delight," one of us would say, although we weren't sure how this applied to fishermen. We went to bed earlier than usual, with the expectable result that, stimulated by visions of the coming morning, we took forever to fall asleep.

All too soon, I'd hear Aunt Mary tromping from room to room, rousing my brothers and cousins, whose ages ranged from four to ten during the summer I was eight. "Let's get up and at 'em or you're going to be left behind." (My father used the same threat; unlike him, Aunt Mary meant it.) Lying in bed, I'd raise the window shade a few inches. Although Bassetts Island was limned by a faint light, it was still dark outside, and the bay looked ominously black. I felt a sense of illicit privilege at being up before dawn. As we tiptoed through the kitchen, it seemed shocking not to hear the sizzle of frying bacon, not to see Grandpa standing at the stove, poking at the toaster with a fork.

Lugging a bucket of quahogs we'd dug up the day before, Aunt Mary led us down the path single file—"quiet as Indians," she cautioned us— past the still-dark Benedict and Storer houses. We carried lumpy kapok life vests covered in a canvas whose bright orange had faded to carmine. (They made us look like hunchbacks. None of us would put them on until forced to.) At the Big Cove, deserted at this hour, we squabbled over who got to pull in the outhaul, tugging on the rope that squeaked through the pulleys until our nameless, chubby fiberglass dinghy—so ungainly among our neighbors' trim Dyer dhows with mahogany ribbing—had scraped ashore. We scrambled for seats; the bow rode high out of the water and seemed infinitely safer, but whoever sat in the stern had the honor of pushing the boat off the rocky shore and heroically climbing aboard at the last second. Aunt Mary sat in the middle and rowed. With just one or two pulls, the leather-wrapped oars groaning in their verdigris locks, we were out so deep we could no longer see bottom. With a few more, we were deeper than we'd ever swum. The shore receded, the sailboats shrank at their moorings, and we headed out the channel toward Atkinson's Buoy.

I had heard of Indian tribes that believed a man's spirit could live on in a tree or a stone. I think I felt something similar about Atkinson's Buoy. Looking out from my bedroom window at Atkinson's, as we called it, I half believed that Ned Atkinson, the great-grandfather I'd never met, was, in some way, alive in that ketchup-bottle-shaped cylinder, guiding boats, keeping watch, helping to guard the sailors tossing on the deep blue sea. But now, as we approached the buoy, which from my window had seemed as small as a bathtub toy, it loomed over us, huge, impersonal, and frightening, heaving in the water, its heavy iron pock-marked under the thick red paint.

As one of us clipped our painter to the buoy, Aunt Mary shipped the oars, slid the creel from under her seat, and set to work. We were all impatient to get started. With the rock we'd picked up on the beach for just this purpose, she crushed a quahog on the floor of the boat (I always worried that this time she'd smash a hole in the bottom). Using a paring knife, she cut its rubbery orange muscle into a half dozen bits, offering them to us like hors d'oeuvres on what remained of the shell. Taking a piece, I'd fold it so that the hook's barb could pierce it twice, giving it a better chance of staying on. (Baiting hooks with clams was a relatively simple operation. Sometimes we'd use fiddler crabs, which presented elusive moving targets, and on rare occasions, we'd fish with clam worms my father bought at the marina in Monument Beach. They came in a plain white box that looked as if it might contain salt water taffy. Inside, nestled in a cozy tangle of seaweed, there squirmed a dozen iridescent sea green worms, each equipped with an arsenal of tiny, bristly feet and, at one end, a pair of cowhorn-shaped jaws capable of delivering a severe bite to a clam, a shrimp, or a finger. Although clam worms were irresistible to fish, they terrified me. Whenever my father cut off a piece for bait, the piece left behind continued to writhe.)

As I let out my line, I leaned over to watch that orange speck of clam disappear into the dark green water, the weight of the sinker pulling it deeper and deeper until I wondered whether it would ever stop. And then I felt the sinker hit bottom. I'd raise it about six inches, so that the bait lay just above the ocean floor. And then, my wrist resting on the gunwale, the brown line resting on my pointer finger, I'd wait.

It was ironic that my brothers and I, who on land could seldom go more than five minutes without quarreling, were, within the confines of the boat, as well mannered as front-pew penitents in church. Part of this came from our firm belief that the fish below us were so sensitive that the slightest sound or movement would chase them off. (Someone might let a sinker clank against the side of the boat. "*Ssssh,*" we'd hiss. "You'll scare the fish!") Part came from our respect for our captain. But I think we were also tamed by a sense of shared vulnerability. Although we were not more than twenty yards from shore, the channel seemed to us as vast and deep as the middle of the ocean. With five of us wedged aboard, the boat seemed overburdened, Malthusian. We were always aware of the water lapping at our sides, nudging us, toying with us. Occasionally a motorboat gurgled past, shedding a series of three waves that would jostle our boat alarmingly. Across the channel, the Big House seemed impossibly distant. My grandfather would be up by now, watching us from the kitchen window as he fried the bacon. For a moment I longed to be there with him, sitting at the breakfast table. And yet I was happy to be here in the boat. I had the giddy feeling of being weightless, as if we were suspended in air and were letting our lines down from a great height. Only now, thinking back on that scene, do I see how apt a metaphor it was: the small, clumsy boat loaded with my family, out in the ocean, tying our fortunes to our great-grandfather's buoy.

Water magnifies the things you see under the surface. It magnifies even more the things you can't see. As I fished, my thoughts followed my line down to the ocean floor. The sea that surrounded us seemed so dark and inscrutable that in my imagination, the legendary creatures I'd read and dreamed about swam beneath our tiny boat: the garrulous flounder from *The Fisherman and His Wife;* the Leviathan that swallowed Pinocchio; the jet-black viperfish that lived so deep in the Pacific no human had ever seen one alive. I felt it entirely possible that I might even pull up a coelacanth, the five-foot-long, prehistoric fish that was supposed to have died out seventy million years ago but that—as I knew from repeated readings of a *Life* Nature Library book—a South African man had hauled up one morning in 1938 on a fishing expedition like ours.

But as time went by, I worried that maybe nothing at all was down there. In the nineteenth century, fishing smacks from New Bedford used to ply the waters around Wings Neck. Using handlines only a little bigger than ours, they fished for scup, tautog, menhaden, and bluefish; when their holds were full, they sailed their catch to the New York markets. Midway through the twentieth century, nothing was biting, no matter what I tried. We each had our special techniques. I'd rest the line on the tip of my pointer finger, giving it an occasional judicious lift as if I were weighing something, which made the bait bob in a gesture I hoped fish would find titillating. Every few minutes, I'd haul up my line, "just to make sure the bait's still there." Sure enough, it was. I'd do this five or six times, occasionally pausing to refasten the morsel of clam. And then, the seventh time, or the tenth or the twentieth, even as someone suggested we might have better luck at a different spot, I'd haul it up again— although I hadn't felt a thing and *knew* the bait would still be there—and there was nothing on the end of the line but the glistening, exposed hook. I felt foolish—how long had I been fishing without bait?—but I didn't care. Now we knew something was down there.

And then I felt that unmistakable tug on my line, that sudden intimacy with another, unknown world. It was as if I'd telephoned China and someone, after endless ringing, had answered the line. (I think I would have been happy never pulling up the fish, just having it on the line, swimming about, maintaining our connection.) Not wanting to risk the ignominy of a false alarm, though maybe muttering "Got one" to myself, I yanked hard, hand over hand, the line tangling at my feet. As I pulled, I'd try to judge the shape and weight of the fish as it rushed toward me, a moment that has always reminded me of reaching deep into a Christmas stocking, getting my hand on something but not knowing what I'd haul up. Years later, fishing for trout in mountain lakes so clear I could practically count the scales on the very fish I sought to catch, I would think back on those mysterious moments at Atkinson's Buoy, when the blur of a fish was approaching the surface, moments when anything, even a coelacanth, was still possible.

✳

It never was a coelacanth, of course. Bottom fishing, as its name suggests, is considered a lowly form of the sport, and the fish we caught ranked high on no angler's hierarchy but our own. The scup (its name is said to be an adaptation of a Narragansett Indian word, *mishcuppauog*) was a small, silvery fish whose trim, alert look and horizontal stripe gave it an almost military appearance; when I fanned out its dorsal fin, as I liked to do, its spines as sharp and clear as knitting needles, it looked as sporty as any marlin, albeit in miniature. The tautog was, by comparison, a drab, lumpy, mud-colored piscine mutt whose undistinguished looks belied its taste. Our Holy Grail was the flounder: diamond-shaped, flat as a plate, mottled brown on top, white as snow underneath, with both eyes on the left side of its face, just like the Picasso portraits of which Aunt Mary was so fond. The flounder's elusiveness—its bite was barely perceptible—made it highly desirable; it was, after all, a fish for which our grandfather actually paid more than a dollar a pound at the Captain Harris Fish Market.

We were perhaps even more concerned with the fish we *didn't* want. Eels—slick and wriggly—were odious, but the fish we most dreaded finding at the end of our lines was the sea robin, a slimy, pockmarked, rust-colored specimen with goggle eyes, a wide, grumpy mouth, a receding chin, and so many fins, flippers, tubercles, and winglike appendages that it seemed less fish than bird or reptile. The Buzzards Bay man who named his yacht *Sea Robin* must never have seen one up close. It was so disagreeable-looking (a nineteenth-century fisherman called it a monster "who, if his size were commensurate with his ugliness, would be the most frightful of created things") and disagreeable-*sounding* (by vibrating its swim bladders, it was capable of emitting an asthmatic croak) that whenever we caught one, Aunt Mary took pity on us and removed it from our hook. Although the sea robin devoured anything edible—and was so adept at bait stealing that for many years I thought its real name was "sea robber"—it was not edible itself; before tossing it back, in fact, many turn-of-the-century anglers would bludgeon it unconscious to discourage it from biting their lines again. We didn't go to such lengths, but as Aunt Mary flung the fish over the side, we silently prayed that we wouldn't pull it up a second time. Sometimes we even weighed anchor and moved to a new spot rather than risk another meeting.

The fish most likely to be found at the end of the line was the puffer, whose goggle eyes, blunt snout, and buckteeth made it extraordinarily homely, but whose green skin, orange-lined belly, and small black tiger stripes gave it a mildly exotic touch. Although said to contain a pearl-sized gob of meat that the Japanese considered a great delicacy, it was not considered worth the trouble. And getting a puffer off the line was especially unpleasant; its body was so oily and soft that one could feel the bones inside. But the puffer had hidden talents. Parts of it were said to be deadly poisonous, an attribute we children greatly admired. And when one tickled its flabby, white belly, the frightened fish would gulp air, swelling up like a balloon in an attempt to deter predators, until it was a perfect sphere with eyes and nose on one side, a tail on the other. Here, again, was extraordinary magic! We had heard that teenagers on the Neck had tickled a puffer until it burst. Or had they stuck it with a pin? No one we knew had actually *seen* them do it, but we were sure it had happened. It made us feel sorry for the puffer, who, as we scratched its rapidly swelling belly, lay there, panting, terrified, and submissive, like the chubby kid at school who knows he's going to get picked on, so he might as well get it over with. Feeling guilty, we'd lob it overboard, the boat tipping dangerously as we leaned across to watch the fish float for a moment before it deflated and skittered away.

Now the boat hummed with activity: Oliver pulling up a fish, my brother Ned getting one off the hook, cousin Catherine rebaiting her line. Aunt Mary, in the middle, was a model of efficiency, cutting up more bait, helping unsnarl Oliver's line, telling Catherine not to trail her finger in the water, reminding us not to rest the line on the side of the boat or we wouldn't be able to feel a bite—all the while catching more fish than anyone else. Although my father would often take our fish off the hook for us, wrapping his own line around an oarlock while he attended to ours, Aunt Mary believed in self-sufficiency. At a certain age we were expected to take responsibility for our own catch. Impatient to get my line back in the water, I'd pin down the fish with a sneakered foot, grasp the end of the hook, and begin to twist, trying to ignore the sound of metal grinding against bone, the fish's impassive stare, its frantic panting as it sucked the unfamiliar oxygen, the exposed ruffle of scarlet gills. Even after I'd worked the hook free, and placed the fish in the bait bucket, invariably I'd have pulled the line up so fast that it had snarled; it took several minutes of concentrated wet-fingered work to untangle the knots.

After an hour or so, we began to run out of bait and were reduced to using the gooey, blobbish stomach of the quahog, which often fell off the hook no matter how slowly we lowered it over the side. By now, our pointer fingers were bisected by a pink runnel where the wet fishing line had rubbed back and forth. The bottom of the boat was a shallow broth of clam juice, quahog shards, crimped line, spare sinkers, and filaments of blood. Fish scales glittered up at us like the flakes of mica we found on the Bluff. Three or four fish lay atop each other in the bait bucket, giving an occasional, desultory flap. Without our noticing, the sun had climbed clear of Bassetts Island. We were sweating under our sweaters and bulky life vests. More and more boats were unsettling us with their wakes. It was time to head in.

When we got back to the Big House, hot, laden with gear, and smelling of fish, it felt as if we'd been away on a two-year whaling voyage, although the ship's clock in the front hall was just chiming seven bells. The rest of the family was in the kitchen eating breakfast, and they all came out on the porch to peer into our bucket and compliment us on our catch. We felt flushed with valor. We were fishermen, home from the sea.

While everyone else trooped back inside, we stayed out to watch Aunt Mary "clean the fish"—an expression that seemed ironic as we saw her matter-of-factly chopping off heads and tails from the sleek, pristine creatures, fingering out globs of internal organs from the tiny pockets in their bellies, teasing out the bones, as thin and fragile as dry pine needles, from the flesh. "Better do it quick, before rigor mortis sets in," Oliver and I would say. We were fascinated by the idea of rigor mortis, which we thought was one word: riggamortis. Once, when we'd accidentally let a scup go dry, we found it had curled up like those cellophane party-favor fish that purport to measure one's powers of love. We gingerly attempted to straighten it out but soon stopped, fearing it might snap in two. Splicing such field observations with bits of sermons I'd heard in church, I believed that within a certain amount of time after its death, a fish's soul would depart and its former owner would begin to stiffen. We knew that rigor mortis could set in with humans, too. And the next time I saw my grandfather, for a moment I could not help imagining him curling just a little at the head and feet.

We watched the fish slowly change in size, shape, and texture, until by the time it was in the frying pan, sizzling in butter, the small white rectangle seemed unrelated to the adventure we'd just had. Except for Aunt Mary, none of the fishermen really liked to eat fish—especially fish we had caught—but we knew we were supposed to, so we took a ceremonial nibble. "Can't get any fresher than this," we'd say knowledgeably—wishing, meanwhile, that the memory of it flopping around in the boat wasn't *quite* so fresh—and then push the rest aside, muttering something about "too many bones." While Aunt Mary, who abhorred waste, ate up what remained, we'd turn hungrily to the sausage and eggs Grandpa had ready for us. And then we turned to the rest of the day, to swimming and Ghost and tennis. The fishing expedition began to fade. But that evening, when we slipped into bed after a hot bath, our fingers still smelled faintly of fish, and as we drifted off to sleep, I would try to remember exactly what it had felt like as I'd pulled that shimmering weight up toward the light.

Who decided when a fish was worthy of being memorialized on the barn wall? I never knew. I never asked. I think I wanted to believe that it was up to some higher power, that it would be self-evident, as if the fish itself would somehow leap onto the wall and become its own paper shadow. Neither did I know the criteria. Size? Species? First fish? I had always been jealous of my older brother for being the only member of our generation represented on that wall, albeit by a six-inch scup, whose size seemed an impertinence to its larger brethren. *(August 31, 1956. Henry F. Colt III. Scup.)* It was the first of a new generation of fish and fishermen, memorialized not with blotting paper and fountain pen but with letter paper and ballpoint. Harry caught it the day before his fourth birthday.

It wasn't until I was ten that I made the grade. By then, of course, I'd already caught dozens of fish out by Atkinson's—scup, puffer, tautog—all of them puny, but equal at least to my brother's specimen. Apparently, none of them had been special enough. Then we rented a house at Naushon for the first time. Naushon had always been represented as an Eden to us, and indeed, we found a corner of the harbor where I hauled in a scup so enormous I felt guilty, because it made fishing near Atkinson's Buoy seem suddenly tame. It was then that I began to suspect that Wings Neck might not be the most extraordinary place in the entire world. Nevertheless, I was proud as my mother and I laid the fish on a section of the *Boston Globe* and traced its silhouette, which we cut out and retraced on a piece of my father's shirt cardboard. And then I wrote, in my best handwriting, *George Colt. 1964. Ten years old* (adding my age lest anyone not realize how young I had been to catch such a Leviathan). In a further act of bravado, I pinned it directly underneath Harry's diminutive scup. And yet even as I stepped back to admire it, I recall my disappointment. Pinning my fish on the wall didn't make my achievement seem larger; it made the others' seem smaller. The following summer, my scup was upstaged by a tautog so large it required *two* sheets of shirt cardboard. *(Ned Colt. Nine years old. 1965. June 20.)*

My prized scup is thirty-two years old now. Its tail is tattered and its inscription is blurred. The other fish are in even worse condition; their white blotter paper has mildewed gray and is pocked with small ferruginous circles at the eyes and fins where thumbtacks have rusted off. The inscriptions are so faded that I can decipher them, like those on old gravestones, only by tracing the indentations with my fingertips—and consulting my memory. The tail of Aunt Mary's pickerel is bent back on itself; rigor mortis has finally set in. All that remains of my grandmother's enormous scup is a half-inch scrap of blotting paper, as if it had been gulped down to its nose by one of its neighbors, perhaps Uncle Jimmy's voracious-looking pickerel.

One afternoon when Susannah and I visit the barn to hunt for a minnow trap, she asks about the fish. She wants to know who caught each one, what kind it was, and so forth.

"Uncle Jimmy caught that one," I tell her.

"When?" she asks.

"In 1946."

"But when was that?"

"Thirty years ago," I say, and then catch my mistake. "I mean fifty."

Susannah gazes up at the wall. She has mixed feelings about fishing. Earlier this summer, when we were at Naushon, her grandfather took her to Mary's Lake, where they caught a small yellow perch. She was initially delighted, but after I cooked it, she took only one bite before pushing it away and saying it made her sad.

Now she hurries back to the Big House, where she gets out a pencil and a piece of paper and carefully draws a fish—far smaller, it seems to me, than the one she actually caught. And then she writes *Susannah Colt. June 18, 1996.* She cuts out the perch, then carries it back out to the barn, where she tacks it near her great-uncle Jimmy's pickerel. She steps back to admire it. "There," she says.

VIII

The North and South Faces

WHENEVER I walk past the Big House, I see the essential selves of my grandparents, its preeminent figures during my childhood, reflected in its two faces. On the south side, where my grandmother's bedroom lay, the house looks out to sea, buffeted by the prevailing southwest breeze. The kitchen wing angles back here, and the house, thus exposed, reminds me of a defiant child who stands, firmly planted, with legs spread and arms akimbo. My grandfather's bedroom lay on the leeward side, where the front of the house faces inland, and is heavily lidded with dormers and gables, like the folds and wrinkles of his own face. On this side, the kitchen wing bends in toward the rest of the house, making the house seem stooped, brooding, wise, and melancholy, turning its back on the agitation and possibility of the ocean.

Even in her later years, as my grandmother grew old and ill in the Big House, the aura of her golden youth surrounded her as perceptibly as the scent of her eau de cologne. I remember hearing old men who had known her when she was young draw in their breath sharply in remembrance and murmur, "Mary Atkinson was the belle of Boston." When she moved through the Big House living room during the cocktail parties of my childhood, offering her guests Cheddar cheese on Triscuits from a tray of parsimonious WASP hors d'oeuvres, I could see men's heads turn. Many years later, Grandma attended my graduation from Harvard. As the annual alumni parade wound through Harvard Yard, a succession of ancient, tottering figures, marching under their class banners, stepped out of line and, almost tripping in their eagerness to reach her, said, in voices quavering with memory and desire, *"Mary."*

My grandmother was the only daughter of Ned and Ellen Atkinson, the sister of Edward and Hal. She was born in a time and place in which people of her social class were sure of their standing in the world. In her case, this sense of entitlement was enhanced by being the youngest child and the apple of her father's eye. She grew up in the Atkinson family compound on Heath Hill, surrounded by upper-class Boston society: a cocoon within a cocoon. The house was served by a squadron of Irish maids, cooks, and gardeners who treated her (as she admitted to her grandchildren, with a mixture of pride and embarrassment) "like the queen of Sheba." She had fashionable clothes, horse-drawn-sleigh rides, tennis lessons at The Country Club, vacations in Europe, camping trips in Canada, and, of course, summers at Wings Neck.

Grandma did many things well. She was president of her class at Miss Winsor's, the finishing school for daughters of prominent Brahmins. She wrote and acted in plays. At family sing-alongs, her renditions of "Where'er You Walk" and "The Braes o' Balquither" were so frequently requested that she toyed with the idea of a singing career. (In the Big House, her location was often signaled by the strains of "Lavender's Blue, Dilly, Dilly" or some other song from her youth.) At Wings Neck she swam, kayaked, fished, played tennis and baseball, sailed in races with her adoring brother Hal, cruised on the *Bagheera* with her family. In the Big House there is a snapshot of her at age sixteen or so, performing a high dive: dark, curly-haired head uplifted; arms spread wide; body parallel to the water far below. She looks so buoyant that despite her knee-length black bathing dress and thick black stockings—a costume that might seem more appropriate for a funeral than for a swim—she looks as if she might never hit the water.

"In my day even holding hands was considered of questionable morality," wrote my great-aunt Amy, recalling her turn-of-the-century Boston upbringing, "but it was quite all right to struggle as hard as possible to attract as many boys as possible." Grandma didn't have to struggle. As the family saying went, "She could charm the birds and the bees right out of the trees." I've looked at innumerable photographs of hearty young men and women picnicking on the Bluff or making human pyramids; Grandma, in a middy blouse with a silk sailor's bow, is at the center of every one. During the 1918–19 debutante season—four months of dinner parties, football weekends, theater evenings, and dances, a ritual no less grueling in its way than a Masai coming-of-age ceremony—she was, observed the *New York Tribune*, "one of Boston society's best known girls." (Although their home on Heath Hill was only ten minutes by car from Copley Square, my great-grandmother rented an apartment in Boston for the season so that she and her beautiful debutante daughter would be even closer to the dress shops on Newbury Street and the dinner parties on Beacon Hill.) There are boxes in the Big House attic stuffed with letters from besotted suitors who had danced with her at parties and were begging for a chance to see her again. One of them was a Harvard sophomore named Larrie Austin, whom she met when she was seventeen. When he went off to war, there were more than a few Bostonians who assumed that when he returned, they would marry. "You must be tired of having me say so often how beautiful everything is, but I can't possibly describe France in spring so I won't try," he wrote to her from the front in May 1918. On November 11, three hours before the Armistice was signed, Austin was killed in the Argonne. Years afterward, she hung his portrait in uniform in the Big House stairwell, near the sketches of my father and his siblings. It was the only nonfamily portrait there. I passed it thousands of times, always assuming it was some Atkinson cousin.

After Larrie Austin's death, Grandma's admirers included John "Black Jack" Pershing, commander of the American forces in France, who, in September 1919, a few weeks after returning at war's end to a hero's welcome, visited his old friend Cameron Forbes, grandson of John Murray Forbes and former governor-general of the Philippines, on Naushon. There he was treated to a typically exhausting Forbes "vacation" of swimming, fishing, hiking, playing High Seas (a strenuous game of tag on horseback), and woodcutting (not just a sapling or two but an entire grove of fifty trees). Evenings, the white-haired four-star general joined in singing the old Naushon songs, and was even dragooned into taking a role in a pageant titled "Gay Age and Gilded Youth," written in his honor by Cousin Cam. My grandmother, eighteen at the time and gilded youth incarnate, had the lead. Though the exemplar of gay age was forty years her senior, his aide, George Marshall, who accompanied him to Naushon, observed that wherever he went, Pershing still moved "like a wind blowing amid the ladies." Sorting through Grandma's papers one day, I came upon a picture of the general (medal-bedecked uniform, bearing so erect he's nearly bent backward) and a sheaf of letters that brim with disciplined ardor. In my favorite, he entreats my grandmother to teach him all the songs they'd sung together (I can just imagine Black Jack belting out "Lavender's Blue, Dilly, Dilly"); he adds hopefully, "I am sure it would take a long time." Pershing's correspondence with Grandma was one of many flirtations, most of them harmless—but flirtatious it was, for after being informed of her engagement to my grandfather, his response, in the last letter he ever wrote her, is markedly less frisky. He signs not with his usual "Always affectionately," but with "Very sincerely yours, John J. Pershing."

Although Harvard degrees were expected of all the male members of her family, my grandmother wasn't expected to attend college. Instead, like many other Boston debutantes, she sailed to Paris to study at the Sorbonne, take in the Comédie-Française, and wander the Louvre. Halfway through her second year, she surprised not a few Brahmin doyennes when she announced her engagement to a penniless Harvard senior from a small town in upstate New York that no proper Bostonian had ever heard of.

My grandfather Henry Francis Colt was such a gentleman that I always assumed he, too, had been born into an old Boston family. In fact, he came from Geneseo, a farming town near Rochester, and was descended from a long line of self-made—and subsequently unmade—men. His great-grandfather ran the Geneseo general store, a position of sufficient importance that he was later elected state senator. His grandfather was a Union soldier in the Civil War, who, after being wounded at Gettysburg, became the famously benevolent commander of the Confederate prison at Elmira; when the war ended, persuaded by some of his former prisoners to open a paper mill in Richmond, he lost all his money, and wound up back in Geneseo in the lowly position of stationmaster. His father, James Wood Colt, headed west at nineteen to work on the railroads, rising from blacksmith's helper to head contractor, responsible for much of the construction of the Chicago, Milwaukee, St. Paul & Pacific Railroad. After saving what he believed was enough money to last the rest of his life, he moved back to Geneseo, bought a five-hundred-acre farm and a string of racehorses, and built two Queen Anne houses side by side, one for his hard-luck father and one for his new wife and their growing family.

Grandpa was a storyteller, and the tales that most charmed his listeners—and seemed the most vivid to him—were the ones he told about growing up in Geneseo. To his children, the very word conjured a gentle, enchanted, turn-of-the-century world: swimming at Conesus Lake; milking the cows; sledding down the street in two feet of snow; pelting the gardener with rotten tomatoes; taking tea next door with the maiden aunt who had been born the year Napoleon was defeated at Waterloo; watching his father ride down Main Street, where the hunters and hounds gathered before the first meet of the Genesee Valley Hunt; taking the overnight train to New York to watch his father's horses run the Grand National Steeplechase (and winning the beaten-silver punch bowl, large enough to bathe a child in, that we now fill with eggnog at Christmas parties). Sixty years later, when my grandfather was an old man, the few pictures on the wall of his bedroom at Wings Neck, which was itself not much larger than a stall, were of his father and Clarence Jones, his beloved childhood groom, mounted on hunters. Indeed, I wonder whether Grandpa spent so much of his time working in the woods at Wings Neck because its rough, rural, catbrier-infested atmosphere—so different from the formal Bostonian circles in which he trailed his wife during the winter—reminded him of his boyhood home.

That phase of Grandpa's life was sweet but short: his father's money did not, after all, last forever. In 1909, needing to replenish his funds, J. W. Colt accepted a job with a commission to assess the feasibility of building a railroad from the Black Sea to the Mediterranean. At the age of fifty-two, he rode for five weeks through the Turkish wilderness to map out a possible route. He returned home to Geneseo and announced that the family was moving to Constantinople—which they did, by ship, train, and carriage, accompanied by fifty-seven pieces of luggage that had to be counted at every stop. My grandfather and his younger brother attended a French lycée and were supervised on weekends by a Greek tutor who had won a silver medal in the 1908 Olympic decathlon. But the railroad deal fell through, and, as if doomed to repeat his father's reverses, my great-grandfather lost all the money he'd invested in the project. After a year of living like expatriate royalty, he and his family retreated to the United States—not to their beloved Geneseo, but to Englewood, New Jersey, where he became a striving commuter with no servants and no horses. Over the next two decades, J. W. Colt traveled the globe, attempting a series of business ventures: financing construction projects in South America; acting as middleman in a complicated sub-rosa attempt to sell 200,000 Spanish rifles to the Russian government; negotiating to build a railroad for the czar (an enterprise that might have enjoyed greater success had the revolution not broken out while he was in St. Petersburg). None of his deals fully panned out, and some of the money he did make was gambled away at the racetrack. His long absences—during one stretch, he lived apart from his family for five years—and his financial instability would have a lifelong effect on my grandfather.

Grandpa followed his older brother James to St. Paul's School, where, like his brother, he was a "scholarship boy." When James (a fearless athlete about whom my great-uncle Chis, the youngest of the Colt boys, would observe, "He was a great leader, but the direction of his leadership was somewhat problematic") exploded a small bomb in the church tower, the headmaster had no choice but to suspend him. Perhaps partly in consequence, my grandfather became an earnest, conscientious, hardworking fellow—"a terrific Christer," says Chis, using a popular term of the time applied to people who had a firm sense of right and wrong and little patience for those who didn't. Grandpa compiled a glittering record: vice president of the senior class, star of the hockey team, president of one of the secret societies that effectively ran the school. At Harvard, his achievements were even more impressive: president of the freshman class, president of the A.D. Club, and captain of the freshman hockey team. While playing hockey during his sophomore year, he fractured his skull. Many years later, his grandchildren were told that he had been "hit on the head with a puck," an experience, it was suggested, that had caused his premature baldness. Although this was an interpretation consistent with the WASP tradition of disguising emotion with humor, the accident, in fact, was nearly fatal, and some family members looked back on it as a harbinger of Grandpa's subsequent difficulties.

At a Saltonstall coming-out party in Boston his junior year, Grandpa was introduced to the hostess's best friend, a curly-headed brunette named Mary Forbes Atkinson. He thought she was the most enchanting creature he'd ever laid eyes on. "I feel like a love-struck fool and probably look like one," he wrote her. "I feel terribly unworthy of you, darling. You are so true and noble, full of the vigour of life. I have nothing but myself to offer. Believe me, that is all yours." My grandmother was no less smitten; she later told her children that as soon as she met this handsome, accomplished man, she knew she had to marry him. By the time she left for Paris, they were secretly engaged. Their wedding was held in April 1923, at the Unitarian church in Brookline; the reception took place at Heath Hill. On their wedding day, her father presented her with a Steinway baby grand and a Stutz Bearcat.

They moved to New York, where Grandpa worked for J. P. Morgan during the day and attended law school at night. Grandma—left alone in a Gramercy Park duplex with a nanny and my infant father, the first of their five children—was homesick and unhappy in the larger social pool of Manhattan, where she was no longer the resident belle. As Great-Uncle Chis put it, "People in New York City were used to glamorous women with Stutz Bearcats." Within two years she persuaded Grandpa to move back to Boston and work for her father at Atkinson, Haserick. It is a move that in family history is generally acknowledged to be the beginning of the end for my grandfather, who was then twenty-five.

I remember walking across Boston Common with Chis on a beautiful spring day fifteen years after Grandpa's death. I was living in Manhattan at the time, but, pleasantly mellowed by our long lunch at the Tavern Club and struck by the glow of the statehouse under the afternoon sun, I idly mused about the possibility of moving back to Boston. My octogenarian great-uncle, who himself had left Boston at a young age for a newspaper job in Kentucky, whirled on me. "Don't *ever* do that," he snapped. "Your grandfather did and it was the *ruin* of him."

When I was a boy, I was fascinated by a children's book called *The Big World and the Little House*, in which a family moves into an abandoned shack in barren surroundings. The family, which itself seems to come out of nowhere, cheerfully sets to work: painting the house, installing windows, moving in furniture, planting flowers and trees. Gradually, they turn their house into a home. "'Home' is a way people feel about a place," the narrator observes. "These people felt that way about the little house."

Looking back, I can see that my interest in the book owed much to my own feelings about home. By the time I turned twelve, we had moved four times, following my father's job promotions, and had never lived in a winter house long enough to feel we truly belonged there. Summer houses are the emotional center of many Boston WASP families, and in the unstable Colt geography this was doubly true. We felt about the Big House the way the family in the book felt about the little house: it was the one place that always seemed familiar when we returned. But our vagabondage was nothing compared with that of my grandparents. Until the last few years of their married life, they *never* had a permanent winter home. Over the next several decades, they moved from place to place in the Boston area, never buying (aside from their first house, on Brattle Street in Cambridge, which they owned only briefly), always renting or borrowing. In my father's sixth-grade history book, there are three addresses written on the inside cover. "Even when they were young, my mother and father were nomads, never putting down roots the way most families do," Dad told me. "I never knew why." Perhaps Grandma's tendency toward restlessness, combined with worry over money, prevented them from purchasing a house and settling down; perhaps, because they had the Big House to return to every summer, they felt they already had a home.

At first, my grandparents were at the center of what Dad refers to as "the fast, younger set." They sang in a Cambridge chorus, joined the right clubs, and kept up a full schedule of cocktail parties and dances. Grandpa was known for his skills as a raconteur, while Grandma was a dazzling hostess and sought-after dinner companion. (Dad recalls how a besotted young John Finley—later to become a legendary classics professor at Harvard, whose last lecture I would attend a half century later in a packed Sanders Theatre—used to sit on the front steps of their house and serenade my grandmother on his accordion.) With the help of a nurse, they looked after the children, four of whom were born within eight years. Grandpa was a down-on-hands-and-knees kind of father, leading his children and their friends on merry games of Follow the Leader at parties—over beds, behind sofas, around columns. Every Friday night, he'd come home from work with a bouquet of violets for his wife.

There were, perhaps, even then, nearly imperceptible fault lines. In Boston, Grandpa was surrounded by Atkinsons and Forbeses. "I think he felt smothered by his wife's family," says Aunt Ellen. (As Great-Uncle Chis, who himself married into an even more prominent Brahmin family, puts it, "In Boston, you couldn't do anything without all the aunts coming.") And though Grandpa got along well with Ned Atkinson, it gnawed at his pride to work for his father-in-law in a job that didn't fully challenge him. His own family, meanwhile, was fragmenting. In 1931, his adored elder brother James, who had become a Santa Barbara stable manager and one of the top polo players in the country, was thrown from his mount and died at the age of thirty-five. My grief-stricken grandfather tried to contact him through séances and automatic writing. Several years later, Grandpa moved his family to Santa Barbara for a year, in part to be near his bereaved parents, in part so my father and Aunt Mary, both of whom had small heart murmurs, could recover in a sanatorium. When they returned to the East, they moved into one of the houses in the family compound on Heath Hill, in the shadow of Ned Atkinson's home.

Shortly after my aunt Sandy was born in January 1939, my grandmother (as my family puts it) "went off the deep end." Some say her mental collapse was triggered by postpartum depression after the birth of an unexpected fifth child when she was thirty-eight, an age at which most women in those days were long past childbearing. Grandpa always suspected it might have had earlier roots, in guilt Grandma felt over an affair she'd had with a family friend while living in Santa Barbara. In hindsight, of course, the fact that both her mother and her uncle had themselves suffered breakdowns suggests the possibility that Grandma had inherited a genetic predisposition. (Several years ago, when Anne was pregnant with our first child at the age of thirty-five, a "genetic counselor" asked whether there had been any history of mental illness in my family. My immediate answer was no—and then I remembered my grandmother. And my great-grandmother. And my great-great-uncle. And an aunt. And two cousins.) Grandma's milieu may also have played a role. In a memoir of her grandmother, a painter who spent years in and out of mental institutions, Honor Moore described her madness as "the inevitable result of conflict between art and female obligation in upper-class, old-family Boston." Robert Lowell put the matter more directly, writing to a friend of the "manic-depressive New England character," as if a severe climate and the Puritan sensibility were enough to drive anyone around the bend. Certainly my grandmother felt lifelong tension between her spiritual yearnings and the emotional parsimony of Cold Roast Boston.

That summer, in hopes that a change of scene might ease Grandma's anxiety, the family gathered at Naushon. It didn't help. My father, fifteen at the time, remembers only that "whenever the phone rang, Ma burst into tears." One morning, when the children woke up, their mother was gone. "Mary and family went to Naushon July 1st," wrote Ellen Russell

Atkinson in the Big House guest book, "but she left for a much-needed rest July 5." Although there were blank pages left in the book, it would be the last entry in the volume. In 1971, my grandmother would write next to her mother's entry: "That this guestbook ends in 1939 is very touching to me. My parents had many guests after that date. My 'much needed rest' was a rather long illness. Blessed parents!"

Grandma spent two years at Butler Hospital, in Providence. Butler was one of the oldest psychiatric facilities in the country, founded in 1844 as the Rhode-Island Asylum for the Insane by Nicholas Brown, Jr., the merchant for whom Brown University had been named. He was also the great-grandfather of John Nicholas Brown, my grandfather's Harvard roommate, who sat on Butler's board of trustees and was, I assume, the reason my grandmother was sent to Butler and not somewhere closer to home—McLean, for instance, where she would stay during later break-downs. Histories of the hospital do their best to make Butler in 1939 sound like a sort of low-key summer camp for adults: in addition to twice-weekly therapy sessions, there were crafts, games, carpentry, weekly dances, recitals (I wonder if Grandma sang "The Braes o' Balquither"), nature walks on 130 wooded acres along the bay (the setting may well have reminded her of Wings Neck), a patient-run literary magazine, a five-thousand-volume library (carefully culled to remove provocative volumes), and sessions of bean stringing and strawberry hulling—the hospital had a farm—to give patients "a feeling of sharing and worthwhile-ness." What the histories don't mention is that the centerpiece of many patients' treatment was electroconvulsive therapy, developed the previous year by an Italian psychiatrist who, observing that pigs in Rome slaugh-terhouses shocked by an electrical current could be stunned into uncon-sciousness (at which point they could be eviscerated without fuss), was inspired to try it on severely depressed humans. To doctors, ECT, which proved to be effective at relieving particularly obdurate depressions, seemed a godsend. To patients—strapped to a table, fixed with metal plates on their temples, given wires to bite, and zapped with 125 volts— it seemed a nightmare. Twenty sessions constituted a typical course of treatment.

My father still speaks of those years as the time "Ma was away," a euphemism that struck me as odd until I learned that, although his boarding school was a mere thirty miles from Butler's wrought-iron gates, he and his siblings were never once taken to visit her. Part of the reason was that her doctors considered it essential to keep the outside world at bay. Part of it was that, while few Brahmin families didn't have some member who'd "gone away for a rest," mental illness was a subject to be avoided or talked about only in whispers. Grandpa never mentioned Grandma to his children—nor, it seems, to anyone else. (In a letter to his mother that Christmas, he described in detail the activities of every other member of the family without once mentioning his wife.) My aunt Ellen, who was thirteen at the time, learned where her mother had gone only because a cousin told her. In the absence of information, imagination filled the gap. "I had read *Jane Eyre*, and I had this picture of Mother locked away in an attic like Rochester's wife," says Ellen. As time passed, her fears worsened. "That Christmas," she recalls, "we all made presents for our mother and gave them to our father to give to her. And then one day Harry and I were looking for the shoe-shine equipment. We went into Dad's closet and there were all our Christmas presents for our mother, unopened, that she just wasn't in a condition to receive. Of course I thought she had died and nobody was telling us."

Ellen confided her fears to her great-aunt Carla, who arranged to circumvent the rules so she could visit her mother at Butler. "I was shocked, but I was so glad to see her. She looked so . . ." Ellen's voice catches. "She was always so pretty. She had on a brown dress . . . she didn't look well in brown. It was a shock, but at least she was alive. We had a wonderful day together." In a relationship that would become increasingly brittle, this would be, ironically, one of the last easeful times Ellen ever spent with her mother.

Grandma came home in the summer of 1941. While she was away, she had changed from a charismatic young belle to a fragile, middle-aged woman. The world had changed, too. Seven weeks after she left for Butler, German tanks had entered Poland, and they now occupied much of Europe, including her beloved Paris. During those years, her father, Ned Atkinson, had died. Her father-in-law had died. Her husband had gone to work in Washington for the War Department. Her brother Hal had married and enlisted in the Canadian Army. My father had gone away to boarding school. Miss Smith, the family's longtime governess, ran the household at Heath Hill, assisted by seventy-five-year-old Uncle Bill, the architect of the Big House, now hobbled by arthritis but still composing piano sonatas, writing pamphlets, and teaching Jimmy chess. Jimmy and Mary had each grown several inches; Sandy, an infant when my grandmother had last seen her, was a sturdy toddler who had learned to walk, talk, and recite her ABC's.

Grandma's return was hardest on Ellen, who had entered adolescence. Bookish and brilliant, Ellen was also beautiful; she was often told how much she resembled her mother. Every time she looked at her, Grandma must have seen something of what she had lost—including her position as the lady of the house. Battles over Ellen's freedom—typical, no doubt, for any mother and her teenage daughter—were exacerbated by the independence to which she had become accustomed and the erosion of her mother's self-assurance during her years of ashtray-making and bean-stringing. Bitter arguments ended with Ellen storming up to her bedroom and playing melancholy tunes on the harp, given to her by her grandfather Ned Atkinson. "At fifteen," recalls Ellen, "I didn't understand how hard it was for Mother to come back and live with us after we'd learned to live without her, to slip back into a current that was going too fast for her."

The current plunged ahead, faster and faster. Less than a year after my grandmother returned, her mother, Ellen Russell Atkinson, died in her sleep at Heath Hill. (A few hours earlier, she had handed Grandma a fifty-dollar bill and murmured her last words, "Be sure the children get the very best milk.") The following year, her aunt Carla died. Her brother Hal was on active duty in North Africa. And after his freshman year at Harvard, my father, who had always been her favorite child, had enlisted in the Army Air Force. Ellen and Jimmy were away at school. The family was more scattered than ever.

In August of 1944, they made arrangements to reunite (with the exception of my father, now stationed in England) at the Big House. It would be the first time they had been together in many months. "We planned a long, fat weekend—pool our lives and relax without effort," wrote my grandmother many years later. "And a dinner Saturday night with champagne, singing, arrayed in our best. Were we excited! And homesick all! We came by diverse routes—motor, train, bus—and by early Saturday morning we were all there, our voices and spirits rising with each new arrival." Grandpa, up from Washington, was the last to reach the Big House. He looked even more weary than usual. After hugging his children, he took Grandma aside and told her that on its first bombing mission, after dropping its payload on Munich, the B-17 Flying Fortress on which my father served as navigator had been intercepted by German fighters and shot down. My father was missing in action behind enemy lines. On Sunday morning, Grandpa led a prayer service in the Big House living room.

Although there was hope (Grandpa learned that several parachutes had been seen dropping from the plane), as days passed without any news, Grandma could not help presuming the worst. After five weeks of waiting, however, the family received a telegram from London: SAFE. WELL. MUCH LOVE. HARRY.

Growing up, we never heard Dad talk about what had happened— "Oh, you want to know how I won the war single-handedly," he'd say, deflecting our questions with typical self-deprecation—and I would not learn the details until I was in college, when I came across a brief memoir, buried in his files, that he'd dictated at the insistence of a friend. I was humbled; at the age when I thought myself adventurous for patronizing Boston jazz joints, my twenty-year-old father was bailing out of a plane over occupied Belgium.

Landing in a garden in a small town overrun by German soldiers, he sprained one ankle and chipped a bone in the other. A farmer offered to hide him in his cellar, where his two daughters bandaged my father's ankles and fed him boiled beets and chicory. (Dad, who stayed in touch with the family after the war, would learn that the daughters had made their wedding dresses from his white silk parachute.) With the help of the Belgian Underground, my father escaped through the Ardennes, disguised as a local farmer and armed with nothing but three years of high school French. At one point, he found himself bicycling down a dusty road past hundreds of Nazi troops singing "Lili Marlene." (Aunt Mary is convinced that Dad's expertise at hide-and-seek and Sardines, honed at the Big House, was instrumental to his survival.) His closest call came on a railway platform crawling with German soldiers and Gestapo agents, when Dad, unaccustomed to wearing farmer's boots, accidentally stepped on the toes of a Belgian woman. "Oh, forgive me, I'm so sorry," he blurted out in English, his Boston-bred manners trumping his survival instincts. (Luckily, only the woman heard.) Eventually, he was able to reach Allied lines and, from there, England. He was informed that six of the twelve planes in his squadron had been shot down; four of eleven in his crew had died.

My father came home laden with decorations but thirty pounds lighter and emotionally spent. "I probably should have gone into a mental institution," he says with uncharacteristic seriousness. "Instead, I got married." Twelve days after he returned, he was engaged to the daughter of family friends, a nineteen-year-old with the improbable name of Babes. A year later, they were divorced. It was a marriage that ran its course so quickly and was buried so completely that not until I was fifteen, while paging idly through a Forbes genealogy in the Big House living room, did I learn that my father had once been married to someone other than my mother. Years later, I asked him about it. "She was perfectly nice, but we were both very young, and when it came down to it, I don't think either of us really loved the other." I remember being delighted by his answer because it was, at the time, the closest I'd ever heard him come to saying that he loved Mum.

In his own way, my grandfather, too, became a casualty of World War II. The war years had been the high point of his career. (He had always regretted that he had been a year too young to serve in the Great War, in which so many of his St. Paul's friends had died. Four months before Pearl Harbor, he had gone to work for "the war effort.") As chief of the renegotiation branch in the office of the quartermaster general, he was in charge of awarding contracts to mills and factories across the country for manufacturing uniforms, boots, and other supplies for American troops. It was a demanding job—he oversaw three thousand workers— in the service of a higher moral cause, and I imagine he felt fulfilled in a way he never had while placing orders for textile machinery at Atkinson, Haserick. His work earned him the Legion of Merit. Those under his command were devoted to him—to his erudition, his wit, his idealism, his sense of fair play. We children were fascinated by the huge framed caricatures his coworkers had presented to him each Christmas during the war, which hung outside the lower bedroom in the Big House. And we were impressed by the way some of his visitors addressed him as "Colonel Colt."

After V-E Day, Grandpa served as executive officer to General Lucius Clay in Germany, helping feed a citizenry on the brink of starvation, until he contracted pneumonia and had to come home. He stayed on in Washington for several years as a consultant to the army; there were those who thought he could have made a distinguished second career in government. But fearing that Grandma, who seemed as breakable as a porcelain teacup, might fall to pieces if he stayed away from Boston too long, he returned, once again, to Heath Hill. Grandpa's effectiveness in wartime, however, made it difficult for him to readjust to a calmer life. He was offered his old job at Atkinson, Haserick, but after "running his own show" during the war, as my father puts it, he was unable to settle for a subordinate position. He was also offered a job as head of the bank in Geneseo, but although he longed to return to his boyhood home, he continued to fear that Grandma's well-being depended on staying close to her roots. (At the same time, given his success in Washington, I cannot help wondering whether Grandpa's own well-being depended on escaping the influence of his father-in-law and the claustrophobia of proper Boston.) "A lot of people who'd worked for him during the war wanted to work for him again, but he never found the right niche," says Dad. "Maybe he was leery because he had done so well during the war, but he felt he had been a failure working for his father-in-law, and he didn't want to fail a second time." Only forty-eight, Henry Francis Colt would never work again. To use one of his favorite expressions, he was, both literally and metaphorically, *"hors de combat."*

Unable to act, unable to choose, Grandpa seemed to age prematurely, gradually retreating from the world and from his wife. The drinking that had begun as an expression of bonhomie at the final clubs of Harvard developed into something more pernicious. He became an exemplar of a classic New England WASP type: the handsome young man of great promise who peaked in prep school and went downhill thereafter (in his case, a slide interrupted by his exemplary war career). After Grandpa rebuffed his younger brother's attempts to help him get back on his feet, my great-uncle Chis asked Grandpa's old friends from college to intervene. They found the idea inconceivable. "How could we?" said one. "He was our *leader.*" To complicate matters, there were money worries: without Grandpa's salary, the only source of income was Grandma's modest trust fund, which was insufficient to sustain their comfortable style of living. Grandma—who was gradually reentering life even as Grandpa was retiring from it—looked for work, but, having accumulated little experience beyond hosting benefit luncheons, she could hardly start at the top and was unwilling to start at the bottom. Accustomed from her childhood on Heath Hill to doing what she wanted when she wanted, she was reluctant to consider a job from which she wouldn't be able to take an afternoon off to attend the symphony. Her makeshift résumé reveals an idealism and naïveté I find poignant. Under "work wanted," she wrote: "Work with people, preferably of different races and nationalities. Or training for future job to be done during next twenty years that will be some contribution to better human relations."

In Grandma's quest to help her husband and their family get back to normal, the Big House played a critical role. During the war, although gas was rationed and the Colts were scattered across the Northeast, they had tried to gather there whenever possible. Tennis courts went untended, few boats were in the water, and, though regattas were held, the use of starting guns was prohibited. Instead, army trainees practiced amphibious landings on Old Silver Beach, one of the bay's few sandy stretches, a few miles south of Wings Neck. Five miles east, where Ned Atkinson used to buy eggs from the old Coonamessett farm, 69,000 soldiers, many of whom were soon to die on the sands of Omaha Beach, drilled at hastily constructed Camp Edwards. (Some lucky officers were quartered in nearby summer estates, including the Eustis mansion on Scraggy Neck.) Two submarine surveillance posts were constructed on the hills of Naushon, while navy pilots took target practice by dropping fifty-pound water bombs on the nearby Weepecket Islands. With German U-boats lying in wait for American ships along the Atlantic coast, convoys bound for Europe rendezvoused in Buzzards Bay, their lights extinguished, then steamed through the canal by night. At the Big House, my aunts planted a Victory garden of potatoes and corn in the baseball diamond out front, nervously discussed the five thousand German POWs quartered at Camp Edwards (who helped pick the cranberry crop and clean up after the 1944 hurricane), and grew adept at finding their way to bed by flashlight while the blackout was in effect. Even with these changes, Wings Neck still seemed, at least for a weekend here and there, a relative haven from the chaos of the larger world.

With the war over, people wanted nothing more than to go home. Since Ellen Atkinson's death, the Big House had been without a real owner. Now, in an attempt to recapture the prewar, prebreakdown happiness, my grandparents decided to commit themselves more fully to Wings Neck. In September 1949, although worried they couldn't afford it, they purchased her brothers' shares in the Big House from the Atkinson estate for $12,500. Grandma hoped that the house would bring the Colts together as, during her father's time, it had brought the Ats; that, year after year, their children and their grandchildren would return to sit on the piazza and swim in the bay and play croquet on the lawn. "I think she wanted to go back to the old family manse," says Uncle Jimmy. For the rest of their lives, instead of visiting only during the hottest part of the summer, my grandparents would live in the Big House—which, of course, was unheated—from April through Thanksgiving. After Labor Day, aside from the lighthouse keeper, they were often alone on Wings Neck. When it grew too cold for them (which was a month or two after it grew too cold for most of their guests), they'd migrate from friend to relative to club to friend, biding their time till the first hints of spring appeared and they could return to Wings Neck.

In the summer of 1950, my grandmother ordered a new leather-bound guest book on whose spine she had printed in gold the initials of all seven members of the family. In a letter inviting a friend to visit, she revealed her hopes for the house and the people within it:

> We have a big, rambling wooden house at Wings Neck, Pocasset, Mass— this is toward the "heel" of Cape Cod. It faces up Buzzards Bay southwest and is near the edge of what we call the Bluff, where we have steps and walk down to swim at any time. The water is warm, the prevailing wind southwest, so it is very cool—everyone sleeps and children bloom. One feels relaxed—almost too much so—this is the gulf stream being near. The house is big and one has privacy; sort of a camp-like atmosphere. One whisks the broom around easily. . . .
>
> This is the first year we have been able to be at Pocasset since the war. So it is quite an event. It is a summer that is very important to the Colt family somehow. I feel we are making a new start—back to all the old serenity and gayety, I hope—but with a firmer foundation than we have been able to have during the last few years. Oh yes, the foundation was there, but it seemed to wobble a bit.

IX

The Barn

THIS AFTERNOON I wander out to the barn to fetch a minnow trap, pausing to examine the board into which Grandma carved her initials as a young girl. (My brother Ned discovered them only last summer.) Tugging open the huge sliding doors, I step inside, where I pick my way past a century's worth of accumulated detritus: old license plates; wooden lobster pots; antique shovels, scythes, and pitchforks; decaying birdhouses; rusted sash weights; broken croquet mallets; plastic potting tubs; half-empty cans of dried paint; coils of chicken wire; stacks of cedar shingles; lengths of wooden fencing; a wagon wheel; a wheelbarrow; a hand-powered rotary mower; two sledgehammers; two fishing nets; three sawhorses; three derelict bicycles; four wooden ladders; seven oarlocks; eleven mismatched oars; boxes of nails; hanks of rope; old wooden pulleys; a saw with my grandfather's initials carved into the handle; a red high chair used by a succession of cousins; my brother Harry's Little League mitt; four baseball bats, including a thirty-three-inch Bobby Doerr–autograph model Louisville Slugger; a punctured inner tube; a wooden cranberry scoop; a four-foot fluorescent lightbulb; a pile of painters' tarps; and the green-lettered E. W. ATKINSON sign that hung at the end of the driveway until my great-grandfather's death. I haven't been inside the barn since last August, and everything is as I remember it. In fact, hardly anything here has changed since I was a boy.

When I walk into the center bay, however, something seems odd. It takes a few moments before I notice that on the barn floor there are four six-inch squares where the weathered pine planking is unusually pale. It takes another moment before I understand their significance. They are the places where the elephantine legs of our pool table rested for half a century.

After dinner, my brothers and I would rush across the lawn in the fading light, our seersucker pajamas billowing in the breeze; my father and uncles not far behind, puffing on cigarettes; my grandfather, clutching a martini, trudging along in the rear. It took two children to slide open the heavy barn doors. We made our way to the middle bay, where the knotty pine walls were lined with racing pennants, nautical charts, Grandma's garden club ribbons, and a huge wheel said to have been salvaged from the *Bagheera*.

In the center of the room, suspended from a rafter on a long cord, like a ring announcer's microphone, was a sixty-watt lightbulb inside a frayed Japanese paper globe. In the dim circle of light beneath sat the massive pool table my grandmother had bought from Cousin Cam. It was the most exquisite object I knew. I loved to run a finger over its velvety surface; to trace the sharp cliffs of its cushions; to press a fingertip to the ivory disks inlaid at intervals along the rich brown cherry banks. Long before we were allowed to play, we'd participate in any way we could. Two of us lifted the corners of the translucent, plastic cover and, with the dignity of pages unrolling a carpet for a queen, slid it down to reveal the table's smooth, green expanse. Then we'd fetch cues for the grown-ups from the rack on the wall. From across the room the cues looked identical, but over the years their minute variances in length and weight—and their infirmities (some were warped, some chipped)—rendered them as familiar as our own fingers. We vied to chalk my father's cue, rubbing a powder blue cube over the tip until it generated a small azure cloud. When a shot was made, we'd race to be first to reach into the leather pocket, within which the heavy Bakelite ball lay like an egg in its nest. Most exciting was being gauged sufficiently tall and trustworthy to keep score—reaching a cue stick up to the sagging necklace of brown wooden disks strung on a wire over the far end of the table, deftly inserting the cue in the proper place and sweeping the beads to one side with a satisfying, abacuslike click. Every tenth bead had a thin, numbered shield; the shields were easily chipped, and by the time I was a teenager, only the less frequently attained fifties remained.

The real honor, of course, was to be deemed good enough (and well mannered enough) to play with my grandfather—to be asked, one memorable night, "Would you like a turn?" My grandfather was the acknowledged master of what he called "the greensward," and we were his acolytes. In his sixties, he was still a fine player; in the eyes of his grandchildren, he had no equal. Wearing his velvet smoking jacket and bow tie, he moved slowly about the table, his pumps shuffling across the pine floor, pensively chalking his cue—that he used the longest and heaviest one only added to our awe—while sizing up the leave, muttering to himself, pausing for a sip of his now-watery martini. Suddenly, he'd lean over the table, sight down the cue stick (one heavy, nearly lashless eyelid lifting quizzically), slowly draw the stick back and then thrust it forward, triggering a click, a sudden rush of balls to far corners of the table, and, invariably, the satisfying plop of a ball dropping into a pocket. (And, on his rare misses, a "Dam*na*tion," the addition of the suffix "nation," with its patriotic associations, seeming to excuse the epithet.)

We played a variation of billiards known as cowboy pool. I liked to believe that Grandpa had picked up the game in some dusty saloon out West, but he had learned cowboy pool within the wood-paneled precincts of Harvard's A.D. Club. Not for my grandfather the random chaos of eight ball, with its messy, spectacular break. Cowboy pool, which uses only the five, the three, and the one balls (the latter, for some reason I never could fathom, counted two points), seemed more refined, more exclusive: as on Wings Neck, the real estate was less cluttered. Then there was the restrained dignity of a carom, in which the cue ball must strike two other balls without sinking them; it seemed a sort of exhibitionism, as if one were saying, "I could sink a ball if so inclined, but I prefer to try something a bit more difficult."

We ached to impress our grandfather—or, at least, not to humiliate ourselves. On our turn, if there was no obvious play, we'd glance uncertainly about the table, hoping for a hint from him as to which shot we should attempt. "I wouldn't try that if I were you," he'd say quietly, as we paused behind a position he considered beyond our ability. If he disapproved of the spot at which our cue was poised to strike the ball, he'd shake his head and say, "You might want to put a little English on it, old boy." After a successful shot, however, he would bow his head in mock astonishment. "I take my hat off to you, sir," he'd say (the fact that he wasn't wearing one rendering the sentiment even more valuable), then gently tap his cue on the barn floor, in a dignified form of applause.

Others would join in, and for a few seconds the barn echoed with a gentle rumble that on windless evenings could be heard from the Big House. (Grandpa was the arbiter. If he didn't tap, there would be no tapping.) The highest accolade was to be compared with the great Willie Hoppe, who, I knew from poring over Grandpa's copy of the *Encyclopedia of Sports*, won his first world championship in 1906 at the age of fourteen, and was regarded as the finest billiard player of all time. Willie Hoppe (the name itself delighted us, having a trochaic sprightliness that brought to mind a highly caffeinated gentleman in a tuxedo) was one of a few sporting figures—Pancho Gonzales in tennis, Sam Snead in golf, and Ted Williams in baseball were others—whom Grandpa so firmly touted as exemplars that it hardly seemed worthwhile for anyone else to take up those sports. As I bent over a particularly difficult try, my grandfather would shake his head and say, "Willie Hoppe couldn't make that shot." It was his polite way of saying "you damn fool"—another favorite expression—and had a similar chastening effect. I would reconsider, try a different shot, and miss that one instead.

I remember the first time I ignored my grandfather's warning. As I drew back my cue, I could sense him shaking his head behind me. I felt sure I could make the shot, however, and I followed through. When the ball disappeared into the pocket, and I heard him murmur, "I take my hat off to you, sir," I felt both vindication and disappointment: I had proved Grandpa wrong. As I got older, the pool table would be the first place where I could see how we all conspired to maintain our belief in his preeminence. At a certain point, I realized that my father was the better player, and that he put Harry, the most skilled of the children, on my grandfather's team to keep the game close.

There was one shot we dared not attempt in Grandpa's presence. We had an unspoken agreement that the massé belonged to him and him alone. Derived from the French word for mace, a massé shot was required when the cue ball came to rest so close to another ball that in order to strike the cue ball without striking the other ball first, one had to hold one's cue nearly perpendicular to the table, suspending one's fingers in midair to form a bridge. It was a delicate, dramatic shot. The danger was that, after one hit the cue ball, the stick's momentum might carry the tip straight down into the table. The inherent risks were brought home to us one summer when we found an L-shaped gash in the green felt on the far end of the table, exposing the hard gray slate beneath. The scar—the table's only blemish—had been inflicted by a neighbor's son, a doughy teenager with thick eyeglasses. Compounding the offense, it was rumored that the young man had inflicted the injury while attempting a massé shot. But the details of the tragedy were never spoken of, his name was never mentioned, and forever after he was defined in my mind by his crime; it seemed the sum of his biography, so that I always thought of him as a kind of juvenile delinquent. A few weeks ago, at the annual Wings Neck Trust meeting, when a motion was passed thanking a certain trustee for his work on the docks, I was surprised to see a middle-aged man with glasses get to his feet. He didn't look like a criminal; he looked like me.

By day, the barn had the roasted smell of sun-drenched pine. By night, with the windows open, the darkness closing in, and the balls clicking, we could imagine—if we ignored the peepers trilling and the moths banging around inside the Japanese lantern—that it had the cool, rich gloom of a gentlemen's club. Occasionally, a delegation of women would come out to watch. (Spectators occupied several black wicker chairs so decrepit they had been deemed beneath even the modest standards of the Big House. These crunched when sat upon, a property sometimes employed to great effect just as an opponent was about to shoot.) But the barn was, I liked to think, a man's world, and after the weekday matriarchy, I found this exhilarating. Indeed, we referred to the bridge—the long wood-and-metal instrument used to support the cue when one attempted a shot one couldn't reach—as the "ladies' aid," and went to great lengths to avoid using it. Once in a while the men would step out for cigarettes. Framed by the barn door, silhouetted against the darkness, they looked like ranch hands relaxing after a long day.

When the game ended, we put the table to bed, returning cues and balls to their racks and shrouding the table in the plastic cover that a few years later would remind me of the body bags we saw in TV news coverage of the Vietnam War. Sliding the barn doors closed behind us, we stepped outside to a transformed world. The sky was black and brimming with stars. We could hear the wash of waves against the Bluff, and the Big House, with its lights on, looked as huge and luminous as an ocean liner in the night. "Watch out for wild Indians!" my grandfather would say as we started toward the house. In darkness, the lawn seemed a vast black sea, and we'd stay close to the shapes of the grown-ups. Suddenly we'd hear an unearthly "WHOOP! WHOOP!" And though we *knew* it was Grandpa—we'd notice he wasn't with us—and called out his name, our hearts would pound fast, and we'd still hear the "WHOOP! WHOOP!" and where *was* he, and suddenly one of us would break into a run, and then we were all sprinting toward the yellow pool of light at the Big House door.

Last winter, Uncle Jimmy's eldest daughter, knowing the house was on the market, bought the pool table from the estate as a wedding present for her husband. When I learned that the table had been sold, I was relieved that it would remain in the family, although the thought of it reposing in a den in Los Angeles seemed almost sacrilegious. I could imagine it nowhere but the barn, with Grandpa and his retinue of pajamaed grandchildren hovering around its green expanse.

I thought I had resigned myself to letting that table go. Now, as I stand in the barn, I feel dizzy, perhaps in part because I know this is only a foretaste of the greater losses to come.

X

Plain Living

MY GREAT-GRANDMOTHER used to describe the Big House as "just a little camp." In 1903, that remark was pure upper-class disingenuousness, but today it comes closer to the truth. All that remains of the seventy-foot yacht Ned Atkinson once plied on Buzzards Bay is a huge, rusted mushroom anchor in a corner of the barn. The chauffeur who drove my great-grandmother on her afternoon calls is gone, and his cottage behind the barn, known as Hidden House, is rented out or used for overflow from the Big House. The Faraday "Gravity Annunciator," an electric bell system that once summoned maids from distant rooms, has fallen into disrepair; in any case, there are no maids left to summon.

Behind its imposing shingled walls, the Big House exemplifies that peculiar combination of wealth and masochism which conclusively identifies it as the summer retreat of Boston Brahmins. It is furnished with that culture's traditional mix of Victorian mahogany dressers, cast-iron bedsteads, caned chairs (with *most* of the caning intact), plastic porch furniture, and 1950s Sears Roebuck appliances. The house has no indoor shower, no television, no VCR, and no stereo, although there is a battered portable radio, used primarily during hurricanes and Red Sox games. There are three stoves in the kitchen, but one is a ninety-year-old Walker & Pratt coal-burning monstrosity, used only as a refuge for mice, and another is a gas range that hasn't worked in decades. Along with the third, a semifunctional electric stove itself thirty years old, they constitute a sort of museum of twentieth-century cooking paraphernalia. The pantry contains vestigial specimens of Canton china from the days of John Murray Forbes, but no more than four settings from a single service remain, and dinner guests sit down to a mix of plastic and porcelain from three or four sets and five generations. Guests are likely to sleep in a bed made up with a pink bottom sheet, a blue top sheet, and flowered pillowcases, and, on unseasonably cold nights, to lie beneath four blankets of different sizes, colors, and materials. Nearly half of the house's sixty-seven windows have broken sash cords; various among them are propped with a wooden coat hanger, a piece of driftwood, a can of tennis balls, a small log, Ned Atkinson's mahogany-knobbed cane, and a copy of *Greyfriars Bobby*. Most of the green window shades have lost their oomph and must be furled by hand. The salt air keeps the toilet paper damp, the magazines curly, the potato chips soggy, and the salt unpourable (unless there are more grains of rice than salt in the shaker), as well as annually disabling another key of the battered Ivers and Pond piano around which Ned Atkinson and his family used to gather for after-dinner sing-alongs. At least once a month, a bat swoops down from the attic to interrupt dinner; crickets often survive weeks in the kitchen, taunting us with their bright chirping but hushing as soon as we try to track them down; anyone drawing a bath invariably finds that a daddy longlegs has taken up residence in the claw-footed cast-iron tub, whose rubber plug is as hard as a fossil.

How many Boston Brahmins does it take to screw in a lightbulb? Ten: one to put in the new bulb, and nine to reminisce about how great the old one was. If it *used* to be done this way, it *ought* to be done this way, and, by God, it *will* be done this way. We would never tolerate the Big House's inconveniences in our winter homes, but this is different: we change in the winter, but during the summer—a season in which we regress to an innocent, Edenic state by replicating the experiences we had as children— change is heresy. We bristle when guests expect, well, something a little more *deluxe*. Were we to stop washing the dishes by hand, it would mean losing not only the opportunity to watch the boats sail into the harbor, but a precious daily chunk of WASP bonding (which is performed far more adhesively over a mildewed dish towel than over a beer). Were we to replace the hypersensitive toilets, so aged that their porcelain handles are spiderwebbed with cracks, it would mean taking down the typewritten notes my grandmother thumbtacked in each of the seven bathrooms, whose words we can recite by heart now, like an affectionate family mantra: NOTHING BUT TOILET PAPER—AND NOT WADS OF THIS—TO GO IN TOILETS. CESSPOOL TROUBLE POSSIBLE, THOUGH NOT PROBABLE, IF WE WATCH.

Like Plimoth Plantation or Colonial Williamsburg, the Big House is to be preserved intact, uncontaminated either by throwing anything out or by willingly introducing anything new. Any change is likely the result of serendipity: a book left on a bedside table, a shell on a mantelpiece, a toy car on the kitchen floor. If no one removes them immediately, they will likely be granted tenure. Several years ago, an iron bedstead in the Little Nursery lost a caster. For two summers the resulting tilt was ignored. This summer we arrived to find that a copy of *Tess of the d'Urbervilles* had been placed under the shortened leg. We haven't touched it. Recently, sweeping up after a weekend of houseguests, I came across a guitar pick. For the time being, I put it in the wooden dish on the front hall shelf where the key to the Chelsea clock is kept. I know that if the house were not being sold, that guitar pick would remain there for decades, as immovable as a barnacle. My grandchildren would assume that Ned Atkinson played the guitar, and would venerate the pick as a holy relic.

Wandering through the old rooms, I have, on occasion, felt as if I were on an archaeological dig. In the bathroom cabinets there are vials of aspirin whose contents expired more than a decade ago. In the front hall closet, four different eras of life jackets jostle for space. On the utility room shelves, I find five rusty cans of Drano, six cans of lighter fluid (all with prices of less than a dollar a quart), two cans of weed killer whose toxic contents clearly predate Rachel Carson's *Silent Spring*, and five half-empty tubes of Sea & Ski from the innocent era, before people worried about skin cancer, when it was called not sunblock but suntan oil. Why have we saved these artifacts? I doubt they will ever be used. And yet when Anne suggests that we throw them out, I cannot bring myself to do it. Not on my watch.

Everything in this house breathes of the past, from the stacks of my grandfather's sheet music on the piano—Gilbert and Sullivan operettas, turn-of-the-century ballads, patriotic World War I tunes—to the globe in the Playroom whose countries include Palestine, French West Africa, and Tanganyika Territory, to the outdated tide charts under the rusted thumbtacks on the bulletin boards. The photographs in the albums are mostly of long-dead relatives. The drawers of bureaus and bookcases are lined with old newspapers, their edges yellowed and crinkly; as I retrieve a photo album from the cabinet in the living room, I am confronted by a fading headline from the May 26, 1969, edition of *The New York Times:* APOLLO 10 AIMS FOR SPLASHDOWN TODAY.

Prospective buyers of the Big House are often stunned into silence by its time-warp atmosphere. An architect said that when he stepped into the house for the first time, he was reminded of walking into the main hall on Ellis Island after it had been sealed off for three decades. I sometimes imagine that one day I'll walk into the Metropolitan Museum of Art, and there, between the Boscoreale Bedroom and the Josephine Rosenberg and Harold Kahn Rococo Room, behind a red velvet restraining rope, I will see a familiar iron bedstead with flaking white paint, sagging springs, and a horsehair mattress; a small pine dresser, painted green, with sticky drawers; a folding suitcase stand; a wrought-iron floor lamp, its shade stippled with burns; a worn set of Thomas Hardy on a swaybacked shelf; a lamp made from an Almaden wine bottle, filled with sea glass, on a rickety bedside table; a handful of jingle shells on the sill. The plaque will read: THE NED AND ELLEN ATKINSON NEW ENGLAND SUMMER HOUSE BEDROOM.

Until I grew up and moved to New York City, I did not realize that attempting to make time stand still was a Brahmin tradition. "It is no coincidence that the two American cities most widely known for their hereditary upper classes, Boston and Philadelphia, are the two most notorious for their hostility to fashion," wrote Nelson Aldrich in *Old Money*. "Patricians of those old towns never go anywhere unless they've 'always' gone there, never know anyone unless they've 'always' known them. Fashion never troubles them. Sometimes, indeed, it seems as though anything they do not inherit they do without, buying only the very plain food on their plates." There is the story of the Boston doyenne who, when asked where she got her hats, replied, "I already have them."

If one had old money, it followed that one had old things: the wealthier the Bostonian, it has been said, the more dents in his car and the more holes in his clothes. "He was scrupulously dainty about underwear," observed a daughter of John Murray Forbes about her ill-dressed father, "but habitually careless of the outer man, and loved his old raiment so dearly that one almost had to use force to get possession of it with a view to its transmission." A former neighbor of ours, the scion of an estimable Boston family, grew up thinking that those gnarly plastic scrubbers with which his mother cleaned the family's (old) pots must cost at least twenty dollars, because they were never discarded until they were in tatters. "At some point I found out they were three for a dollar," he recalls. "That was the moment when I felt I truly understood what it meant to be a WASP." Playing tennis with a wealthy Washingtonian, my cousin Henry was appalled when, halfway through the match, his host opened a fresh can of balls, explaining, "We never play more than two sets per can." (To a Bostonian, this seems as profligate as William Randolph Hearst's practice of having his San Simeon table set with new jars of ketchup, mustard, and pickles at every meal.) Henry had been raised on the Big House system, in which, every time we play, we must sort through the two dozen cans of old balls that sit, Stonehenge-like, on the chest in the utility room, holding each ball at eye level and dropping it until we come up with three that are acceptable. "Here's a decent one!" one of us will announce joyfully, as the floor thumps with the sound of bouncing balls. "I've got one here!" says another. But are the duds thrown out? Of course not. Back they go into their cans to await their next trial. "After all," points out a sardonic friend, "you never know when they might come back to life."

"The Proper Bostonian," wrote Cleveland Amory, "if he is going to be at all happy away from his work, must be comfortably uncomfortable." Hence, while turn-of-the-century New Yorkers chose to vacation on Cape Cod's Atlantic coast, with its broad, sandy beaches, Bostonians preferred Buzzards Bay, with its rocky shores, cozy harbors, and limited horizons. The apotheosis of the genre may be Naushon, where a great deal of time and money has been spent trying to keep the island as close as possible to the state of prelapsarian innocence in which John Murray Forbes found it more than a century ago. When Cameron Forbes, his grandson, was running the island, he kept the Mansion House without electricity until long after World War I. Realizing that he was having difficulty finding and retaining qualified help who wished to work in such conditions, he was eventually persuaded to permit electric lights in the servants' quarters in 1926. Forbeses and their guests had to make do with candles and kerosene lamps until 1945. Even today, Naushon has no cars (Forbeses walk or ride horses) and no stores (Forbeses shop in Woods Hole, carry their groceries across the channel by ferry, and push them home over bumpy paths in wheelbarrows). Nelson Aldrich recalls a recent visit. "The house I stayed in was a somewhat severe H. H. Richardson cottage of twenty-two rooms. The ambience, though 'old' and 'simple,' was as far removed from Kiluna Farm"—Aldrich's sumptuous ancestral summer place in Rhode Island—"as one could get without becoming actually squalid. Paint peeled from every wall and ceiling; it was a kindness to call the furniture rudimentary; the kitchen seemed well equipped for making sandwiches; everywhere was the odor of mold, carried along by brisk drafts of damp sea air." The inhabitants are no more kempt than their houses. As a child visiting Naushon, I was terrified by Forbes women with their lean, leathery bodies, wrinkled faces, long gray hair, and sharp noses, who seemed always to be galloping about on horseback or hacking their way through the woods with machetes. Their determined expressions suggested that if I got in their way, they wouldn't shrink from hacking me down, too.

The Brahmin penchant for privation derives, in part, from the Yankee credo of simplicity and practicality, passed down from the Puritans and reinforced by the Emersonian philosophy of "plain living and high thinking." (The thinking may no longer be as high as in Emerson's day, but the living is still determinedly plain.) Deep down, Bostonians consider their anhedonia to be a moral position. Like the early Christian martyrs, we feel spiritually purified by masochistic ritual; instead of standing on a pillar for thirty-seven years like Saint Simeon Stylites and encouraging worms to fester in our open sores, we embrace the thorns and poison ivy that festoon our winding paths. We assume, of course, that our skin is so thick, and our virtue so impeccable, that these irritants will have no deleterious effect. (From the Bostonian point of view, physical infirmities are a character flaw. According to his wife, John Murray Forbes was never seasick. "All such suffering from that cause," she reported, "John termed weak-mindedness.") Favorite Brahmin tales center on the hardiness of the species: the Cabot who, well into his nineties, continued to walk three miles from his home in Cambridge to his office on State Street, as he had every morning of his working life; the Lowell who, no matter how harsh the winter weather, never wore an overcoat; the Peabody who, as a prep school headmaster, insisted that his students begin each day with an ice-cold shower; the Forbes who, hoping to make it through the winter without buying a new pair of shoes, arrived barefoot at his sweetheart's door. (She shut it and chose a better-shod, if perhaps less well-heeled, husband.) Even a Bostonian's manners are a form of self-denial. There have been occasions in the Big House when I—and everyone else in my family—have let the last ear of corn on the platter languish uneaten rather than suffer the ignominy of appearing selfish.

Back to the kitchen it will go, at which point someone will surreptitiously gobble it up: in the Brahmin hierarchy of sins, greed is grievous, but waste is worse.

Could it be that these self-imposed hardships can be traced back to guilt? After all, their coatless winter walks returned these Bostonians to well-appointed and well-staffed (if not well-heated) homes. Their tribal adversities may have been a way to test themselves, to set up artificial obstacles where few natural ones existed. I doubt, for instance, that my father-in-law, who grew up contending with poverty and anti-Semitism, would have understood the moral advantages of taking a cold shower when one could afford a hot one, or why one might choose to poke around in the mud with one's bare toes when cherrystones were available at the fish market. I, on the other hand, can fancy myself a gritty survivalist as I swim at Wings Neck in October (I'd respect myself even more if it were November) or sprawl on its uncomfortable sofa, which is covered with a stained India-print bedspread, while straining to make out the type in a secondhand paperback under the dim glow of a sixty-watt bulb.

I see now that the Big House is, in some ways, downright dangerous. Its balloon framing, knob-and-post electrical system, and eelgrass insulation make it, in the words of one architect, a fire waiting to happen. (If the house *were* to go up in flames, the thick but frayed escape rope, knotted to an iron hook in the Playroom since Ned Atkinson's day, hardly inspires confidence.) Its windows, their sash cords snapped long ago, are veritable guillotines. Its threadbare lawn has a luxuriant border of poison ivy. Its porch sags so dramatically that whenever we have guests, we worry that *this* time they will end up falling through. My mother half jokingly suggests that we ask renters to sign a waiver relinquishing their right to sue in case of death or dismemberment. But, like the eternally optimistic and eternally broken barometer over the liquor cabinet that always points to FAIR, even in a roaring gale, we are oblivious to these perils.

Indeed, I have come to realize that I have unconsciously considered the Big House a kind of princess-and-the-pea test for visitors, except that the Brahmin version reverses the tale, and even a boulder under the bedding is supposed to go unnoticed. Will guests complain about the stiff horsehair mattresses, the rusty springs that bray with the slightest movement, the straw-filled pillows that crunch when you try to nestle your head on them? Will they be so gauche as to believe that beaches should have *sand* on them? Will they hesitate to take a dip at low tide, when they must tiptoe across barnacled rocks to reach swimmable water? (I confess that when a guest dons a pair of water shoes, I feel smugly superior; to Wings Neck children, barnacle cuts are red badges of courage.) When guests fail the test, I feel as if I've introduced two close friends who haven't hit it off. When they pass, I am proud. Last summer, watching my cousin's girlfriend walk toward the tennis court, our old-salt neighbor told my cousin gruffly, "She walks barefoot down the driveway. That's a girl worth marrying." (Lest we be accused of sadism, I must point out that ailing and elderly guests are quartered in the Lower Bedroom, where the paint is relatively fresh, the windows are intact, the shades are in proper working order, and the beds actually have box springs.)

My faith in the sanctity of the Big House and its insular world has been tested over the last few summers, during which we rented it out to defray the cost of taxes and upkeep. Last summer, my family stayed in Hidden House for three weeks while a family from the Midwest rented the Big House. It came as a shock that someone might not revere the web of traditions we have woven around the place. They played a boom box at the Bluff, left the house ablaze with lights after dark, and parked their cars on the front lawn. (It's not so much that they damaged the grass, which could hardly be less verdant than it already was, as that *we* never park there.)

One night I came home to see smoke pouring from the beach. I raced toward the water, certain the scrub oaks on the Bluff were ablaze and the fire would soon spread to the house. A young man sat quietly on the sand, gazing into the flames of a fire he had built among the rocks. My anger, I realized, was mixed with confusion and envy. In my forty-two years at the Big House, we had never had a cookout on the beach. I thought to myself: Why not?

XI

Money

YEARS AGO, when I was told that my great-grandfather Ned Atkinson had, for several years, paid the highest income tax in Massachusetts, I was incredulous. The information was usually imparted with some sheepishness—money, of course, was not something proper Bostonians talked about—but also with a certain amount of wistful pride, for it evoked the kind of wealth our family no longer possessed. By the time we came along, the millions that Ned Atkinson made importing cotton machinery had been given away or spent, and, as the family tree proliferated, the Forbes fortune had collected more abundantly on other limbs. We were, as the caption for a recent William Hamilton cartoon put it, "Old Money without the money." (Or, as one family member observed when her suitor was accused of being a gold digger, "There's no gold to dig.") The Boston area was full of families like ours, venerable tribes that had nothing left to remind them of their former prominence but their names—which no longer counted for much—and their ancestral summer homes. (An astonishing number of seemingly down-at-heels New England families turn out to possess grand old country houses that they'll do almost anything to save.) In fact, it is not wealth so much as *former* wealth that defines Old Money families, and is most central to people's perceptions of social class, according to Nelson Aldrich, himself a Rockefeller heir. "Once the wealth has been there, for perception, it needn't go on being there," he writes. "Indeed, it must not go on being there; it must retire discreetly behind the veil of time and disappear like the Cheshire cat, leaving a smile."

Like most Boston Brahmin families—even those who lived off their trust funds—we pretended that we cared nothing for money and, furthermore, that those who did suffered from a kind of character defect. Relatives who, like John Murray Forbes, had made their piles long ago were somehow excluded from our opprobrium—even if those piles had been made in such dubious enterprises as the opium trade. And, after all, Forbes had gone on to compile a second, more morally acceptable fortune building railroads, and then a third, with his friend Alexander Graham Bell, in telephones. Like most rich WASPs, he was appropriately embarrassed by his wealth. I was not surprised to learn from his biographer Henry Greenleaf Pearson that, after concluding that he could give his six children "every advantage which had been his own except that of poverty," my great-great-great-grandfather had vowed to "have their circle formed among families of moderate means where the children are being brought up to labor, and not among the rich alone." (Discomfiture over one's fortune was one Brahmin reaction; "pleading poverty," as Cleveland Amory described it, was another. Aunt Mary remembers a childhood visit to Home Farm, the four-hundred-acre John Murray Forbes estate inherited by his grandson James Savage Russell. Sitting at a dining table laden with priceless Canton china, carving another slice off a massive roast cooked by one of his many servants, "Savage Jim," as he was known, was complaining about how little money he had. His lament was so persuasive that my uncle Jimmy, age six at the time, tearfully insisted on sending his great-uncle his piggy bank. "That," says my aunt Mary, "was the last we heard about how poor Uncle Jim Russell was!")

Although my brothers and I hadn't inherited ancestral wealth, we inherited a wealth of ancestral attitudes toward money. We cut the subject from our conversation as completely as we cut the price from the inside front flap of a book before giving it as a gift. (I confess, however, that when the price was high, I regretted that the recipient would never know how much I'd spent on him.) And yet we had absorbed a great deal of information about money, most of which had to do with its corrupting influence. We knew, for instance, that money didn't grow on trees; that a fool and his money were soon parted; that a penny saved was a penny earned. We should watch our money, yet we should not worship the almighty dollar. "It isn't how much money you have, it's how much love you have," my mother would say whenever we complained about not having enough of the former. (Her response confused me, for in those days it seemed the family was courting bankruptcy in both accounts.)

A strange by-product of putting the Big House on the market has been the necessity of talking about money—at frequent intervals and in large quantities. Every five minutes, it seems, we toss about vast sums with the ease of Wall Street traders. Although we claim to find these conversations distasteful, I admit that I—and, I suspect, some of my brothers and cousins—find in them a certain illicit, liberating thrill. Though we never talked about money growing up, we thought about it all the time. And though prices were never mentioned—except when we were told "That's too expensive"—we knew exactly how much everything cost. Watching *The Price Is Right*, a television game show in which contestants guessed the cost of refrigerators, lawn mowers, and fur coats, we were always chagrined when we totted up all the things we would have won if only *we* had been on the show.

In Brahmin homes, the only thing more vulgar than talking about money was spending it. One of the worst sins one could commit was to manifest symptoms of trying to "keep up with the Joneses," whom I imagined to be a large family with perfect teeth who lived in a columned white mansion not unlike that rendered in plastic at Millionaire Acres on our Life game board. Yet I wanted desperately to keep up with the Joneses. Or with the Singers, my cousins, who lived in a huge, well-kept house, took ski vacations in Europe, and yet still seemed to worry about money as much as we did. Aunt Ellen's husband, Uncle Tom, was what people of my grandparents' generation, with a hint of condescension, called a self-made man, which meant that he hadn't inherited his money, he had actually earned it. (Similarly, to be called a go-getter by a Bostonian was not a compliment; it was considered more graceful not to go get things but to wait for them to come to you.) Austrian Jews, the Singers had fled Vienna just before the Second World War, leaving their possessions and arriving penniless in New York. Uncle Tom had worked his way up from door-to-door salesman to become a vice president of Gillette. He drove a Mercedes, dined at fine restaurants, knew his wines, and appeared to live what at the time I was conditioned to dismiss as "the high life." I loved visiting the Singers, and I couldn't help believing that the adversity my uncle had faced had taught him lessons about surviving in the real world that could never be learned growing up in the Colt family. Each Christmas Uncle Tom sent us a large box full of Gillette products: razors, shaving cream, soaps, and lotions, all of which my family gratefully used, but which seemed to me a CARE package that unintentionally underscored our neediness.

On the surface, of course, my feelings of deprivation were ludicrous. My family was not wealthy but, as my mother frequently reminded us, we had more than 99 percent of the people on the planet. (In the phrase favored by Boston blue bloods anxious to appear less flush than they really were, we were "too well off to be middle class, too poor to be upper class.") My father, who had himself started out as a door-to-door salesman for a small company, was a successful businessman continuing a rapid ascent up the corporate ladder. And yet, growing up in what was called an affluent suburb, we always seemed to have less than those around us. Although we lived in a four-bedroom clapboard house with a large back-yard, much of my father's salary went toward the mortgage. My brothers and I attended private high schools only by virtue of the tuition reductions allowed us through my mother's position as an art teacher. We wore hand-me-down clothes and always bought our shoes at least a size too large. "You'll grow into them" was the family mantra. We shopped mostly at Sears and Woolworth's. Major purchases were landmarks in family history; my parents debated for weeks before buying a plastic-handled carving knife from a family friend who moonlighted as a cutlery salesman; we referred to it as the Cutco Knife, in the reverential tones others might reserve for the Wedgwood china or the Ming vase. Other than to Wings Neck, we never traveled. I first set foot in a plane when I was in college. We made long-distance phone calls only on Thanksgiving and Christmas, and even then, Dad would pace the floor, sighing and taking histrionic looks at his watch until the offender hung up. We were trained never to leave a light on when we left the room, although my brothers and I had heated discussions over whether, if we left the room only *briefly*, it took more electricity to turn the light off and then on again when we returned, or to leave it on throughout our absence. In winter, Dad never allowed the thermostat to venture above sixty degrees.

There was always enough food on the table, but never more than enough; my brothers and I wolfed down our dinners in a race to get seconds before supplies ran out. (My younger brothers are convinced that their inordinate fondness for all-you-can-eat buffets is a kind of eating disorder rooted in a childhood fear of never having enough.) We used margarine instead of butter, always bought cheap cuts of meat, and for several years drank a powdered milk called Sanalac, a name whose mention still brings a chalky taste to my mouth. Our rare dinners out were usually at Howard Johnson. For a splurge, we'd go to a pseudo-

Polynesian restaurant next to the gas station on Route 1, where we'd order a Pu Pu Platter (a name intoxicating to a scatologically minded ten-year-old boy), an assortment of greasy appetizers served in a partitioned wooden bowl in whose center a can of Sterno sent up a cobalt flame. My parents celebrated their fifteenth wedding anniversary with us over a bucket of Kentucky Fried Chicken.

Our relative poverty stood in sharper contrast when we moved to Darien, the Connecticut suburb that possessed, the real estate agent proudly told us, the second highest per capita income in the country. In Dedham, under the influence of Puritan Boston, money had been something to camouflage; in Darien, which felt the gravitational pull of pagan New York City, money was something to flaunt. The town was full of Joneses we couldn't keep up with. While my classmates wore khaki slacks and penny loafers from the Darien Sport Shop, I wore rolled-up jeans and oversized Keds. While friends were ferried around town in sleek, imitation-wood-paneled station wagons known as Country Squires, we rattled about in a battered 1956 Ford wagon whose floorboards had rusted through; when you lifted up a corner of the rubber mat, you could see the road rush by beneath you. While my friends' families sat down to refrigerator-sized RCA sets encased in dark wood cabinets called consoles—the very word promised comfort and succor—we took turns standing by our small, ancient, black-and-white Zenith, pinching the ersatz coat hanger aerial, reaching into the set with a pair of pliers to change the channel, and twiddling the vertical hold button until the parallel lines stopped moving north to south, paused for a blessed moment, and started moving south to north.

I am ashamed now to remember how ashamed I felt then. I couldn't know that years later, I wouldn't want to have been raised differently, that the lessons of thrift and common sense I had learned would stand me in good stead as I began to make my own way in the world. Now, of course, I can see that my feelings of deprivation had more to do with adolescent self-pity than with any real lack. How hard my parents worked to give us all they did! How much they gave us! And how stoic they were about doing it. Sunday nights, as my brothers and I marveled at the exploits of the wealthy Cartwright family on *Bonanza*, my father bent over his desk, paying the bills. He never complained, never said a word about being strapped—"We're doing fine," he'd insist—and yet somehow I grew up convinced that we were one step from the poorhouse. I had no idea of the struggles my parents went through to provide for us until one evening, when I was a teenager, I happened to see my father's checkbook open on his desk. Flipping through it, I was terrified to realize that during the past few years, he'd never had more than $300 in the bank.

The Big House was different. On Wings Neck, our old blue Ford wasn't much more decrepit than anyone else's car—perfect for jouncy tailgate rides down the bumpy road to the Big Cove. On Wings Neck, *everyone* dressed in tattered hand-me-downs. The bare-bones style that seemed shameful in winter was the status quo in summer. There was plenty of wealth on the Neck, but it was hidden in the old wooden boats, in the high property taxes, in the cost of keeping everyone's antique plumbing in working order. Only now do I realize that it was the abundance of money that allowed people to act as if they had so little. (This phenomenon is encapsulated in an oft-told story about my great-great-great-grandfather's mentor, Thomas Handasyd Perkins. Asked by a Boston jeweler why, considering his position, his gold watch had a leather strap and not a gold fob, Perkins replied that he could afford to wear a leather strap *because* of his position.)

At the same time, despite its scruffiness, the Big House seemed the height of luxury to us. It was as big as the largest mansion in Darien. (When my sister-in-law first saw the house, she was troubled, assuming our family was extraordinarily wealthy and that my brother had been hiding that fact from her. Once she stepped inside, however, she learned the truth.) Although there was no household staff, as in Ned Atkinson's day, Martha came down from Boston to run the kitchen on busy weekends, and Mrs. Watt, a small, sharp-faced woman from Grandma's garden club, drove out from Pocasset twice a week to help with the sewing, mending, and cleaning. And did anyone who wasn't rich use finger bowls?

I assumed Grandma and Grandpa were wealthy, because they acted as if they were. That is, I assumed that money and class were one and the same. My grandparents' winter apartment-hopping I believed to be a sign of a wealthy, sophisticated lifestyle and not, as I now consider it, a symptom of their inability to settle down and their belief that they couldn't afford a permanent winter home. I assumed that the reason

Grandpa didn't work was that he didn't need to. Although there were no Stutz Bearcats or Steinway baby grands, there were fresh flowers, jewelry (inherited), evenings at the theater, the occasional trip to Paris. There was even a special pair of gold-plated scissors for cutting grapes. Once or twice a year, Grandma took us to lunch at the Chilton, the venerable women's club in downtown Boston named for the first Englishwoman to set foot on North American soil. Amid a flock of middle-aged and elderly ladies, dressed in moth-eaten fox furs over old cloth coats, all of whom seemed to revere my grandmother and therefore us, we'd sip milky tea from matching porcelain cups and nibble on watercress sandwiches with the crusts cut off, a practice that seemed the height of decadence, as it went against everything we'd been taught about not wasting food. My grandmother sent us to sailing camp, helped pay for my brother Harry to go to boarding school, promised to take each of her grandchildren on a grand tour of Europe after high school graduation. (By the time we graduated, however, she was no longer well enough, emotionally or financially, to follow through.) Like many proper Bostonians, she could be impulsively, extravagantly generous. (Brahmins are far less stingy toward others than toward themselves.) At Aunt Mary's wedding, held at the Big House, a guest admired the grandfather clock in the barn and marveled that such an antique would be used to store fishing rods. "You *must* have it, then," Grandma exclaimed. Only his most energetic protestations could dissuade her. When my mother was a young housewife, she received a shabbily wrapped package in the mail from my grandmother; inside was a ring—a large topaz (her birthstone) encircled by diamonds—that Mum had often admired but never mentioned. One summer, after I mused aloud about needing to buy a wedding present for some friends, Grandma disappeared upstairs. She returned with a sheaf of old, oversized papers. "Do you think they might like these?" she asked, handing me a set of antique folio prints of birds by John James Audubon.

The theme of my grandparents' concerns about money runs throughout their letters to each other. Perhaps my grandfather had never recovered from his childhood, in which his father's income so fluctuated that at times he had employed a staff of five and thought nothing of buying a string of new hunting hounds, and at times he had to sell off a beloved horse to pay the bills. Grandpa's experience as a "scholarship boy" at St. Paul's must have given him the same feelings my brothers and I had of being less well off than, and therefore inferior to, those around us. While he was at Harvard, where his roommate, John Nicholas Brown, heir to a Providence shipping fortune, was known by the tabloids as "the Richest Boy in the World," the family finances declined still further. Both he and Great-Uncle Chis had to drop out before graduating. When Grandpa joked about supporting his wife in the style to which she'd become accustomed (overlooking the fact that it was in fact *her* money that supported *him*, in a somewhat better style than that to which *he* had become accustomed), he was masking his very real fears that he wouldn't be able to support her at all. Despite—or perhaps because of—her gilded youth, Grandma was, if anything, even more worried about the family finances than he was. Occasionally her anxiety waxed so alarmingly that she'd hastily sell something from the Big House—an old piece of silver, the R. Swain Gifford landscape over the dining room mantel—often for far less than it was worth. In the last decades of her life, she would burst into tears and exclaim, "There's not enough money! What are we going to do?" In the end, she was right. There wasn't enough money to keep the Big House.

As an adolescent in the sixties, of course, I would scorn Country Squires and color TVs. I would crave the appearance of poverty, though never its reality. Even today, when I more fully realize the privilege of my birth, I proudly point out that I worked every summer, that I was on scholarship at Harvard, and that I had a part-time job all through college, a situation that allowed me, fatuously, to imagine that I was working my way through school. (Do I sound just like John Murray Forbes, proud of exposing his children to working-class playmates?) Behind what I thought was a philosophical stance was, of course, a psychological flaw. As a young writer, I took cost-cutting measures that made my parents look like high rollers: I fished the day's newspaper out of street corner trash cans; I wrote postcards instead of letters to save on stamps; I reused manila file folders until they were tattered; I ripped Scotch tape lengthwise to get twice as much. In my first job, from an annual salary of $8,000 I somehow managed to bank $2,000, a feat that in retrospect seems mathematically impossible. I was terrified of being penniless, and yet I felt there was something shameful about having money. For many years I found ways to avoid it. When I moved to New York, I applied for jobs wrapping presents at Macy's, working as a clerk in a toy store, waiting tables in a chain restaurant. Flipping through my résumé, potential employers would say, "I don't understand—why would you want this position?" I had no answer. Eventually, when I got a job writing for a magazine, I felt both triumphant and disappointed to be earning what seemed like a small fortune, and I had no idea how to spend it. I didn't own a suit until I was twenty-six or a car until I was thirty-seven; it never occurred to me that I might be entitled to one. I bought clothes at thrift stores and furnished my room with chairs and bureaus scavenged from sidewalks. When a burglar broke into the apartment I shared with a similarly penurious friend, he could find nothing worth stealing.

Like many Colts, perhaps in part subconsciously wanting to live a comfortable life while maintaining my own sense of personal privation, I married someone who, though not wealthy, was certainly better off than I. When I met Anne, her matter-of-factness toward money shocked—and attracted—me. Although far from a spendthrift, if she wanted to eat a steak, she did; if she wanted to phone a friend in California at 4:59 P.M., before the cheap rates kicked in, she did; if her television set broke, she bought a new one. Her father had grown up poor in Brooklyn, working after school in his parents' pharmacy. When he got his first big job as a radio host, he rushed home to his parents to boast about the size of his paycheck. Each check represented one step farther from his Brooklyn roots. Well into his nineties, he worked at his desk ten or twelve hours a day, not only because he enjoyed it but because he was determined to accumulate more money for his family before he died. Anne never drank Sanalac when she was growing up, and was learning the names of French cheeses while my brothers and I were salivating over Pu Pu Platters, yet she is no more spoiled than I; I liked her, among other reasons, because she too wore T-shirts with holes, she didn't use makeup, and she could shower and dress for a party in ten minutes. Anne, who has always supported herself as a writer, views my attitude toward money as a kind of developmental deficit, like a vestigial limb, one of the quixotic handicaps of my social class. Although I've tried to absorb some of her ease around money, our philosophies are sufficiently ingrained that we find it wise to maintain separate checking accounts. I cannot help lowering the thermostat behind her back, eating her bread crusts, and, like James Tyrone in *Long Day's Journey into Night*, wandering around the house and turning off lights as soon as she leaves the room. Anne is a good sport about it. She doesn't even complain when we dine out at Kentucky Fried Chicken.

Although my brothers and I all earn comfortable livings, we still wear socks with holes in the toe and mend tattered blue jeans until they are more patch than denim. Harry, a doctor, always checks the unit price of every item he buys at the supermarket; Mark, the recycling coordinator at a school for the blind, calls his friends (provided their area code is local, of course) to share the news when he's gotten a good deal on a new toaster; though he has had a successful career as a television journalist, Ned admits that, like me, for most of his adult life he has harbored an irrational fear of ending up homeless.

Maybe penny-pinching (which we, of course, would call good sense) simply runs in the Colt genes. A few weeks ago, before coming to Wings Neck, I took Susannah and several of her friends to a neighborhood fair, where, after we'd played a few games and ridden the Ferris wheel, she anxiously looked up at me and said, "Daddy, I don't want you to spend too much money." I assured her that I had enough. "I just get very worried," she said, "when people spend too much money." I felt guilty that I had passed on my attitudes to her—but not very. Mostly, I felt pride that she knew the value of a dollar; that she, like her father and grandfather, was becoming, as Dad puts it with a self-mocking grin, "a prudent Bostonian."

One by one, my parents paid off the mortgage, the car, the college loans. These days, they eat at nice restaurants, and though they still look at the menu prices first, they order what they want. They buy new cars every few years. They travel occasionally to Europe or Central America. Part of it is simply that they can afford to now, and part, I think, is a relaxation of old tensions. There is more money *and* more love between them. When one of his sons leaves the house, as we are saying good-bye, my father is sure to ask, "Do you need any money?" When a stranger fumbles for change at a store counter, Dad immediately rummages in his pocket, the coins therein jingling in a sound of plenty: "Do you need a quarter?" he asks. And yet some things are immutable. My parents still keep their house at sixty degrees. "Of course you're cold," Dad will say. "You don't have a sweater on."

This morning, on the way back to the Big House from the fish market, I stop by the post office. There is rarely any mail for us, and I perform the errand mainly out of nostalgia, but today, among the accumulated copies of the *Cape Cod Pennysaver,* sale flyers addressed to "Occupant," and MasterCard applications addressed to my long-dead grandfather, I find an envelope addressed to me in my father's hand. When I open it, a check for $8,000 flutters to the ground.

I learn from the accompanying letter that my parents have sent checks in that amount to each of my three brothers. When I call to thank them, my father, in a voice quivering with emotion, says, "Well, it's something we always wanted to do for you boys. During our twenties and thirties and forties, when we didn't have a pot to piss in, we couldn't, but now in our seventies, we can do it." My mother tells me Harry is thinking of spending his money on a tractor mower. Mark will make a down payment on a condominium. My first impulse—prudent Bostonian that I am—is to put the $8,000 into a money market account. But I feel I should use it to buy something special, something I've coveted for a long time. Unfortunately, $8,000—which for several years was my annual salary—won't go far toward the only thing I really want: the Big House.

XII

Sailing

Race days when I was eleven or twelve, the first thing I did on waking was look at the leaves on the sassafras tree outside my window. Were they trembling? Would there be enough wind? This morning I was especially anxious. I had been invited by a friend of my grandparents' to crew in the Saturday afternoon race—the senior race, the grown-up race, the one my family watched through binoculars from the Bluff. As I looked out my window, I saw that lack of wind would not be a problem. The tree was thrashing in the breeze. It was what sailors called a "big" wind. By afternoon, when the wind usually came up, it might be even bigger.

I was at the Big Cove an hour early. By now the morning crowd had packed up and gone home for lunch. The beach was deserted except for a lone man clamming in the millpond. I sat on the creaking swing and scanned the harbor—a mere crook in the shoreline that sheltered a few dozen small sailboats, a Boston Whaler or two, an old fishing boat, and, moored slightly apart, the *Arion*, an elegant thirty-foot sloop that was the only vessel in the harbor truly deserving of the name "yacht." It was a modest fleet, and yet I found the Big Cove as bustling and cosmopolitan a port as the young John Murray Forbes, a century earlier, must have found Canton, China. The boats nodded at their moorings, bows facing obediently into the southwest wind, halyards ticking against their masts. No less restless, I picked up a handful of stones and skipped them, one by one, across the water.

The sailors began to arrive after lunch, rattling down the dirt driveway in rusted station wagons, pedaling bicycles, a few of them trudging along on foot. Tall and lean, their wrinkled skin the color of a well-varnished teak deck, they were older men for the most part (or so they seemed to me), and yet in their baseball caps and worn shorts, with spinnaker poles and sail bags slung over their shoulders, they reminded me of boys, duffels on sticks, running away from home. State Street bankers, doctors, and lawyers during the week, they transformed each weekend into what we referred to in the Big House as old salts. They wore bright yellow foul-weather gear and worn brown Top-Siders. Rubber-encased stopwatches hung from their necks. They spoke their own peculiar language: topping lifts, jury-rigging, luffing matches, ditty bags. Of someone they didn't care for, they'd say, "I don't much like the cut of his jib"; a messy house wasn't "shipshape"; a teenager who had decided to skip college had "lost his compass" or, more charitably, was "going off on his own tack." They could tie a bowline and a sheepshank, and they not only carried marlinspikes but knew how to use them. Their living rooms were lined with racing pennants, their place mats were nautical charts, and, like family pets buried in the back lawn, their beloved old dinghies were taken home to rot in their yards. When they weren't sailing, they could often be seen in their boats at their moorings, bailing the bilge, checking the stays, their hands sure and persuasive as they performed their gentlemanly housework. On the beach, they always seemed a little awkward, shifting from one foot to the other, unconsciously edging toward the water, looking not at each other as they talked but out to sea, admiring the lines of a passing ketch ("Boy, she's a beauty"), shaking their heads at a particularly chunky stinkpot ("Jeesh—will you get a load of that one"). (To Wings Neck sailors, boats with motors weren't really boats at all, and fiberglass was anathema; a fiberglass boat with a motor was the devil incarnate.)

Each summer colony on Buzzards Bay had its star sailors, and each no doubt believed its sailors to be the best. None, I felt sure, could match up with the men (and they were men, with a few exceptions) from the Buzzards Yacht Club, whose sail numbers were as deeply ingrained in my memory as the uniform numbers of my beloved Red Sox. There was Toby Baker, a boyish-looking schoolmaster who wore his foul-weather gear even in the brightest sun. There was good-natured Bill Malcolm and his wife, Ellie, a tall, square-jawed, white-haired woman. There were the Hallowell brothers (grandsons of the Giant): Bill, a gruff, rangy, big-boned gentleman farmer, whose grizzled good looks reminded me of the Marlboro Man; Phips, a mild-looking physician who knew everything about Wings Neck and its history; and Johnny, a shy, handsome high school teacher with eyebrows as thick as mustaches and a mouth that seemed always curled in a kindly, expectant smile. All the Hallowells were fine sailors, but Johnny seemed to have an understanding with wind and water that enabled him to find a breeze in a dead calm or to pass gracefully through a fuming northeaster. Watching the Saturday races from the Bluff, we could always distinguish his boat, *Nuthatch* (H-92); it would invariably be off alone, hunting wind along the shore on a risky tack. And, invariably, half the fleet would trail after him—one could almost hear their skippers saying, "Where's Johnny Hallowell? What's he doing?"—like baby ducks after their mother. At the end-of-summer cocktail party at the Buzzards clubhouse, he would be awarded so many pennants and trophies that, after a certain point, each time his name was called, a communal chuckle erupted. Many years later, I would learn that he had suffered much of his life from depression, and I wondered whether he went off on those long, solitary tacks not just because he thought he might find a fresh breeze, but because he thought he might find some peace.

My brother Harry had once been asked to crew by Johnny Hallowell, an honor that had sent the inhabitants of the Big House into a proud tizzy. They had finished first and Mr. Hallowell had given my brother the blue pennant with a cloth *B*, a prize that was hung in the barn and soon became the object of extreme jealousy on my part. Perhaps today I'd have my chance for a pennant. The prospects, however, didn't seem good. Powell Robinson, my grandparents' friend, was not one of the Neck's star sailors. He didn't race often, and when he did he usually finished near the back of the fleet. He wasn't one of those men who stood on the beach discussing the relative merits of gaff and Marconi rigs; in fact, we rarely saw him at the Big Cove. A relative newcomer to Wings Neck, he lived in a cottage down by the lighthouse, in the shadow of the Bartol house, which was owned by his elder brother. I occasionally saw him on my paper route when I made my Sunday collection rounds. A tall, slender man with an owlish face and a formal bearing, he lacked the bantering ease with which my father and most men on the Neck seemed to treat one another. He wore squeaky white sneakers; his foul-weather gear was new. I've forgotten the name of his boat—one of those awkward, matronly-sounding names that felt thick on the tongue. (The fastest boats always seemed to have the sleekest-sounding names. How, for example, could the *Wren* [H-50] ever hope to keep up with the *Tern* [H-15], the *Doughboy* [H-90] with the *Tomboy* [H-73]?) On the other hand, I'm sure that an eleven-year-old boy from a tennis-playing family had not been Mr. Robinson's first choice for crew.

We paddled out to the boat in silence. All around us, sailors in their dinghies were pulling away from shore. With two grown men to each small boat, the sail bags in the bow insufficiently heavy to keep the vessel from riding comically low in the stern, they looked as if they were being punished, like loyalists set adrift by mutineers. Tying up to small wooden sloops not much larger than the dinghies themselves, they climbed aboard.

To Buzzards Bay sailors, wooden boats are good, small wooden boats are better, and the most revered of all small wooden boats is the Herreshoff Twelve, whose history is entwined with that of Wings Neck. The creation of Nathanael Herreshoff (the boatbuilder who, among other accomplishments, designed every America's Cup defender between 1893 and 1920), the Twelve had its origins in 1913, when Robert W. Emmons II, a well-known yachtsman and one of the men with whom my great-grandfather had purchased Wings Neck, was asked by J. P. Morgan and William Vanderbilt to oversee the upcoming America's Cup defense. In the winter and spring of 1913–14, Emmons spent many afternoons at the Herreshoff boatyards in Bristol, Rhode Island, monitoring the construction of a new twelve-meter yacht, *Resolute*. Fourteen years earlier, Emmons had managed the ordering and delivery of the first Buzzards Bay fifteen-footers, a popular racing boat designed by Herreshoff. Now he talked to "Captain Nat" about designing a smaller, more stable craft in which his children and his friends' children could learn to sail. (At the time, most people started out in catboats—chubby, single-sailed, shallow-draft centerboard vessels that were difficult to handle in the choppy waters of Buzzards Bay and that left them ill prepared, Emmons felt, for the larger, sloop-rigged boats they would sail as adults.) Emmons invited Herreshoff to Wings Neck to inspect the local sailing conditions. The result was a simple, gaff-rigged sloop twelve feet at the waterline, whose heavy, fixed ballast and abbreviated mast provided stability, while its fixed keel, drawing only two and a half feet, made the boat suitable for reasonably shallow water. "Here was a surprisingly fast little boat, quite able to take anything short of a hurricane that Buzzards Bay had to offer," commented a Beverly Yacht Club yearbook half a century later.

In the winter of 1914–15, the Herreshoff yard produced its first batch of twenty boats. The new design was called the Buzzards Bay Boys Boat, a name that would last only until the vessels were discovered to be ideal not only for boys learning to sail but for grown men (and women) racing, as well as large families embarking on picnics—whereupon they became known, with less alliteration but more dignity, as Herreshoff Twelves, or, simply, Twelves. In June 1915, a Herreshoff launch steamed up Buzzards Bay towing a string of the new boats. Of that first batch, four went to Cameron Forbes on Naushon and four were delivered to Wings Neck. My great-grandfather had ordered one of them, which he named the *Bonita*. The cost was $420.

By the time I learned to sail, the boys for whom the Buzzards Bay Boys Boat was originally designed had become middle-aged men—the men I now saw rigging their aging Herreshoff Twelves all around us. I had learned to sail in these now-venerable Twelves in an informal camp run out of the Buzzards clubhouse, a privilege that in retrospect seems as extraordinary—and risky—as a child taking violin lessons on a Stradivarius. Now, Mr. Robinson and I quietly went about our work. While he arranged the spinnaker in its bag, I untied the stays on the mainsail and jib, stowed the boom crutch, and bailed the bilge with a scoop cut from a Clorox bottle. Then we crouched in front of the mast, and while Mr. Robinson hoisted the mainsail, I raised the jib. The moment the sails started up the mast, the boat came to life. The nylon rustled and snapped in the wind, the boom began to wag, and the traveler slid noisily back and forth across the transom. I too trembled; raising a sail always seemed an act of defiance, a direct challenge to the wind. Alternating tugs on the main halyard and the topping lift, Mr. Robinson adjusted the gaff. When all was ready and he gave the order to cast off, I climbed onto the foredeck, unfastened the lobster-pot mooring from its cleat, and dropped it over the side. As I scrambled back to the cockpit, the boat fell off the wind, nodding uncertainly, sheets snapping. Then the flapping sails filled until there wasn't a crease left, and the boat, soothed, sure, and purposeful, began to slice through the water. All around us, the harbor bloomed like a garden with white sails. Behind us, our dinghy on its mooring grew smaller. Passing the Big House, I knew my family would be watching from the piazza. I forced myself not to look up.

Out in the bay, there were already a dozen Twelves gathered near the committee boat, the old wooden launch that served as one end of the starting line and on whose stern the course was posted on a blackboard. Others were still arriving from Wings Neck, or from Cataumet, the neighboring harbor with which we had a fierce but friendly rivalry. Their skippers were the genial grown-ups I saw at parental cocktail parties or at the general store, here transformed into grim-faced monks, peering intently from within their slickers. A few of them nodded or raised a hand in acknowledgment as we passed. From the Bluff, the races had always looked as quiet and orderly as a ballet. Up close, however, they seemed chaotic and violent. There was the constant thrum of water on wood, the ever-present danger of a crash as we threaded our way along the starting line, and a tension so thick that as we passed the committee boat, where race officials sipped from thermoses of coffee, I had a momentary longing to leap into its anchored safety. Some skippers sailed back and forth along the line; others stayed clear. I noticed Johnny Hallowell off by himself, casually nosing along Bassetts Island, as if he were giving a tour of its geographic features to his crew. What was he doing so far away? Would he get to the line in time? The shrill blast of an air horn startled me. Five minutes. Mr. Robinson reached for his stopwatch and headed toward the line. Another blast. Three minutes. The knot of boats tightened. Two. One. Now all the boats were huddled at one end of the line, trying to time their progress so they'd cross on starboard tack the moment the gun went off. A few boats in front had to let their sails luff in an effort not to cross the line prematurely; we were in the middle of the pack, trying to keep up speed but not come on so fast we'd ram a boat in front of us. As the starter moved toward the miniature cannon in the stern of the committee boat, I noticed a boat coming hard on port tack toward our tight pack. It was Johnny Hallowell. It seemed impossible that he could clear our bows in time. He'd have to tack—and yet he didn't seem to be aware of the fleet surging toward him. Warning shouts of "Starboard!" filled the air. A crash seemed inevitable. But at the very moment I saw the cannon recoil and a puff of smoke dissipate in the wind, he crossed the line, clearing the lead boat by a foot. We trimmed our sheets and headed up. We were off.

The first leg was a beat to windward out to the tip of Scraggy Neck. For a time we were in the midst of the pack, but one by one the other boats tacked off. We were alone. The sea around us seemed suddenly vast. All was silent but for the sound of the waves slapping our hull, the wind singing in the stays, and the occasional creak of the mast in its step as a gust bent us to its will. I clung, white-knuckled, to the jib sheet as if it were a lifeline while I studied the stylish right triangle of the sail and tried not to move a muscle, certain that the slightest shiver might slow us down or bring a reprimand from Mr. Robinson. (There were a few Wings Neckers who seemed to feel that playing Captain Bligh was an integral part of being an old salt.) But except for an occasional request to trim the jib, he was silent, leaning forward, grimly scrutinizing the luff of the mainsail for the faintest tremor to determine whether he might risk pointing any higher. Every so often, as if he'd seen a message somewhere in that sail, he decided to tack. "Ready about," he'd announce cautiously—and then, with relative exuberance, "Hard-alee!" The firm push of the tiller to leeward triggered a jangling chaos—bodies changing sides, sails flustered and undecided, bow plunging—as the boat turned into the wind. Then we fell off the wind, the traveler skittered across the transom, the sails refilled, and we headed off in the opposite direction, suddenly smooth and serene again.

From time to time, as we crisscrossed our way toward the mark, we encountered a boat on the opposite tack. These meetings seemed as serendipitous as encounters in an uncharted desert. We'd hear the shout of "Starboard!" and peer below the sail—an awkward task when the boat was heeling so precipitously—to judge whether we could safely clear the oncoming boat or whether we'd have to come about. As we passed, I'd glimpse helmsman and crew, in their own intense, self-contained world, bent forward as if in silent prayer. And then they were gone. Occasionally a boat tacked slightly to windward of us, and we'd sail along, a matched pair in unacknowledged communion. Then the other boat would tack and we'd be alone again.

The bay could get rough in a big southwest wind—sailors called it the Buzzards Bay Chop, and spoke of it with affection, as if it were a memorable cut of meat—but races were held in anything short of a hurricane. (I remember watching from the Big House one afternoon during a near-gale as a neighbor's Twelve was towed into the harbor, its three-inch-thick mast snapped to a jagged stub.) Our boat would climb a swell, then drop suddenly into the trough beyond. Occasionally a Twelve would seem to appear from nowhere, lifted by a wave from a deep furrow. At times we'd heel so sharply that, looking over the gunwale, I could see the tip of our keel nearly parallel to the water's surface, like the russet fin of a shark keeping pace alongside. Spray broke from our bow; water washed over the leeward rail. We could hear sloshing in the bilge, but bailing the boat at this angle was out of the question. Every so often a gust of wind made us cling to the coaming. One more inch, it seemed, and we'd go over.

I was even more dazzled by Wings Neck's sailors than I might otherwise have been, because my family was on the periphery of the sailing world. Our participation in the Saturday afternoon races was usually limited to watching from the Bluff for a moment on our way in from swimming. Although we couldn't be classified as downright landlubbers, neither could any of us qualify as a salt, young or old. I would have been amazed to learn that my great-great-great-grandfather Forbes had made the family fortune by sailing clipper ships around the world, or that my great-grandfather Atkinson had at one time owned a boat more than twice the size of the *Arion*. I had assumed that the *Bagheera*, the schooner in the photograph over the dining room mantel, was a famous old yacht belonging to someone else's family, and that the tattered, twenty-foot-long "Championship Second Handicap 1915" pennant that stretched across an entire wall of the barn had been a gift from a friend who'd pitied our maritime ineptitude. (In fact, it had been won by my great-uncle Hal, racing at the Beverly Yacht Club.)

But the golden age of my family's maritime history ended when the *Bagheera* sank at its mooring sometime in the twenties. The *Bonita* was sold to a neighbor not long thereafter. (I found it mortifying that our family had no Herreshoff of its own. With proper Bostonian generosity, our neighbors frequently offered us theirs; with proper Bostonian modesty, we always refused.) By the time my brothers and I came along, the Colt armada consisted of a rowboat, a kayak, a small motorboat, and a Sailfish—and even these vessels were not exactly what Katharine Hepburn in *The Philadelphia Story* would have called "yare." Our flagship, the nameless white fiberglass dinghy from which we fished, had been molded in one piece—hull, seats, and all—like a cheap bathtub toy. Its bow rode pompously high, its stern perilously low; paddled about the harbor, it resembled a newly surfaced baby beluga whale. My cousins and I loved it dearly, but each time we used it, we were reminded that we had no larger boat to row out to; our homely dinghy was an end in itself, a tender with nothing to tend. Then there was the *Humdiddy*. A slim, four-teen-foot aluminum motorboat equipped with a six-horsepower Evin-rude, the *Humdiddy*—Down East slang for a raging storm—looked seaworthy, but reacted to a light chop as if it were a Class 5 hurricane. This made for a certain excitement, but also for a certain danger. We eventually sold it for a painfully low price, but its name lived on as a family code word for ineptitude, and even today is liable to provoke a guffaw at the Big Cove among sailors of a certain age.

The *Humdiddy*, however, was a veritable H.M.S. *Victory* compared with the red fiberglass Sailfish we bought at the tail end of a Sailfish craze that gripped the Neck in the fifties. It was a purchase that placed us, technically, in the sailboat-owning class, and I recall the exhilaration we felt as we brought it to the Big Cove for the first time: lugging it down to the water; snapping its cumbersome, double-jointed tiller and rudder into place; propping its tongue-shaped dagger board above its slot; and pushing the mast up and into its hole with all the determina-tion of the marines planting the flag at Iwo Jima. Alas, within a few months—before we'd even given it a name—our Sailfish had become so waterlogged that no matter how many times we stood it on end and drained it, four grown men were required to carry it the ten yards from the community boat rack to the water, and, under way, it rode slightly beneath the surface, as if it were part submarine. (Its mysterious afflic-tion appeared to be not only incurable but inevitable; when it came to boats, there seemed something tainted about my family. It did not much surprise me to learn, from an old guest book, that in 1954, when my grandparents rented a Twelve for their children to sail, it had been hit by lightning—the only boat in the harbor to be so honored—and sank.) That summer I entered the annual round-Bassetts Sailfish race, delighted to be skippering my own boat for the first time. After leading the pack across the start, my Sailfish began to dip its bow under the water and move in a maddeningly slow motion I thought possible only in dreams. One by one, every other vessel in the fleet slid past. I ended up dropping out and pretending I hadn't really meant to enter the race at all. From then on, the Sailfish sat on the rack among its less impaired brethren, largely unused. Eventually, we didn't bother bringing it to the Big Cove at all, and it stayed in a corner of the barn. My father placed an advertisement in the *Pennysaver*, $150 or best offer, but to our shame, no one even offered. Out of the water, however, the Sailfish *looked* seaworthy, and several years ago, my brother Mark and my cousin Oliver decided to launch it one more time. After wrestling it down to the Little Cove, they sailed it—the word doesn't accurately describe its bargelike progress—as far as the lighthouse before it started to sink. Although they wrestled it to shore, the Sailfish had made its last voyage. Owing to the family-wide horror of throwing things away, it sits in the barn to this day, beneath the "Championship Second Handicap 1915" pennant, its sail peppered with mouse droppings.

By the time we approached the first mark, all but a few boats had already rounded it and headed for the lighthouse. The second leg was a broad reach, affording me the time and the equilibrium to bail the bilge. Hunched in the cockpit, struggling to keep my footing as the boat yawed in the waves, I removed the heavy wooden floorboards and set up the gray plastic pump. But no matter how hard I pumped, the water level never changed. Then I noticed: the hose I'd draped over the coaming had slipped back into the boat. I'd been recycling seawater from the bilge onto the seat and back to the bilge. As I readjusted the hose, I looked up to see if Mr. Robinson had noticed, but his eyes seemed fixed on the sail. I finished the job, using a sponge to soak up every last drop, and went back to my jib. As we coasted along the Wings Neck shoreline, I saw the Big House in the distance, looking as if it owned the bay.

After beating back out to Scraggy Neck, we prepared for the fourth and final leg; a run before the wind to the finish. A fleet of Twelves with spinnakers set is a stirring sight (this was the moment they'd reach for the binoculars at the Big House), a peacock-proud display of vast, billowing, brightly colored sails that seemed strangely ostentatious rising from the simple, no-nonsense boats. But setting a spinnaker is a delicate task, one that in a big wind can be downright foolhardy. A few of the boats ahead of us, with little chance of winning, had chosen not to risk it; with our spinnaker up, we might be able to catch them. But first we had to jibe around the mark, a potentially dangerous maneuver in which a boat changes tack with the wind at its back, causing the boom to swing nearly 180 degrees across the cockpit at high speed. Carelessly done, this can result in snapped masts, cracked skulls, and men overboard. As we approached the massive black can that heaved ominously in the swells, Mr. Robinson gripped the tiller. "Stand by to jibe," he muttered. "Jibe ho!" The moment we cleared the can, he pulled the tiller hard to windward. The boom started slowly. Then, as it caught the full force of the following wind, it swept like a scythe across the cockpit, its power nearly pulling the boat right over, and our momentum nearly carrying us back into the marker.

After the boat settled, I took the tiller while Mr. Robinson went forward to raise the spinnaker. Rummaging through the sail bag, he attached the head to the halyard and gave a tug. A thin, crinkled, pale blue sail levitated from the bag like a silk scarf from a magician's sleeve. But before it was halfway up, the wind took hold and thrashed it against the jib. Mr. Robinson jiggled the sheets, tugging first one way, then the other, trying to tame the spinnaker, but they snarled around the sail so that while the top and bottom halves filled with wind, the middle twisted in an hourglass shape. One of the boats behind us, spinnaker full, took our wind and pushed past. Mr. Robinson hauled down the spinnaker, sorted through it, and tried again. This time, a wave caught a corner of the sail and dragged it under. Panting, Mr. Robinson leaned over the leeward rail, grabbing at the sail, trying to gather it in before it went under the boat and fouled the keel. I worried he'd go overboard, but I had problems of my own. Each four-foot swell—the word, with its medical associations, seemed appropriate, as if the sea had become swollen with infection—reared up behind us, towering above our transom. Just as it seemed ready to swamp us, the wave lifted our boat as easily as a lobster buoy and sent it surfing off at an angle—our rudder partly out of the water, ineffective, the boat itself, bow and stern out of the water, seeming nearly airborne—before letting it down. It took all my strength to keep us on course. And in the back of my mind, a greater danger lurked. When we ran directly before the wind, there was always the possibility of an involuntary flying jibe, which in this wind might snap the boom, swamp the boat, or remove Mr. Robinson's unsuspecting head.

I never felt the ease of a true salt. Indeed, I could never bring myself to say the word "salt," to refer to a boat as "she," or to omit the fricative and call the wind that whipped up the bay a "sou'wester." From summer to summer, I never managed to keep straight the difference between a ketch and a yawl. My repertoire of knots consisted of figure eight, clove hitch, and bowline—and I had to talk myself through the bowline: "up the rabbit hole, around the tree . . ." I never got the knack of coiling a halyard by gathering it in loose, easy ovals like a cowboy's lariat, but had to wrap it around and around my forearm. Although I loved the ocean and dreamed that, like the boy in *Little Tim and the Brave Sea Captain*, I might one day stow away, I always felt self-conscious in a boat. Even pleasure sailing seemed a test there were a hundred ways to fail. Asked to raise the mainsail, would I remember that its halyard was on the right, or would I, to my embarrassment, hoist the jib? Would I furl the sail—that awkward, clownish process of stuffing the canvas into its own belly—so that it fit neatly between the jaws of gaff and boom? Or would the sail spill out here and there, causing passing skippers to sniff at my clumsy work? Most important of all, would I shoot the mooring cleanly? Or would I fall short and end up sculling the tiller in a frantic attempt to close the gap, before ignominiously falling off and trying again?

Compounding my anxiety was the fact that even pleasure sailing was a spectator sport on Wings Neck. At the Big Cove, an ostensibly harmless crowd of children, mothers, baby-sitters, and a few shore-bound ancient mariners constituted a critical audience that, without ever seeming to look up, scrutinized every vessel that went in or out of the harbor. Whenever anyone ran a Sailfish up on the beach a tad too fast, you could see them shaking their heads, clucking. And oh, the embarrassment of the skipper who came in too hard to the dock, so that one of the ancient mariners had to hop over and fend off, murmuring, "Came in a little strong there, eh?" I recall the smug delight with which we watched a visiting yachtsman run his fancy fiberglass sloop aground in the Gut. Although someone jumped into a Boston Whaler and raced out to pull him clear, it was too late; he'd have to wait for the incoming tide to lift him free. But the tide was ebbing, leaving the boat at an increasingly skewed angle. The hapless skipper paced the cockpit helplessly as we watched—eventually he went below, where he couldn't see the eyes watching from shore—until the tide came in and he could sneak away. The story of his ineptitude would be told and retold at the Big Cove all summer.

I felt a secret sympathy for that sailor. One morning, coming in from sailing class, we threaded our way through the boats in the harbor toward our mooring. This was always an anxiety-provoking task, and that day a brisk wind made it especially difficult. There were four of us in the boat, including my younger brother Ned. I don't recall who was at the helm—I fear it may have been me—but at some point, just as we tacked, the wind gusted and we found ourselves heading directly toward the *Arion*. It was moored on the edge of the harbor, a position that gave it sufficient scope, but that also seemed to set it apart by virtue of its superior breeding. Leaving or returning to the harbor, my friend Allen and I always liked to sail down its length so we could admire at close range its seemingly endless, immaculate white hull, its forest green cabin, the words ARION/WINGS NECK painted in gold on its attenuated stern. One of our favorite games was to swim through the harbor, touching every boat, and occasionally pulling ourselves up over a gunwale to peer into a cockpit. When we came to the *Arion*, we looked, but did not dare touch.

But now our bow was pointed directly amidships at the immaculate white paint of the *Arion*'s wooden hull. Whoever was at the tiller abandoned it. We all shouted for someone to take the helm—a quick, decisive tack might have saved us—but no one wanted to be the one at the tiller when we hit. As the eldest, I knew I should take over, but I felt immobilized. No one even scrambled to the bow to fend off—we all, in fact, unconsciously moved farther toward the stern, away from the crash point. (I'm sure we assumed that either we'd stove in the *Arion*'s hull and it would sink to the bottom before our very eyes, or—at the least—our Twelve would shatter against its imposing flank.) At the last second Ned leapt up, took the tiller, and tried to head us off. But it was too late. Our bow smacked into the *Arion* with a sickening thump, leaving, as we all turned our heads to see, an Oreo-sized dimple in her heretofore pristine side. It was only then that Ned bravely leapt up onto the foredeck to push us off, and our boat slid down below the *Arion*. Ned sailed us, silent and shocked, to our mooring.

I'm not sure what we would have done if nobody had seen us, but several horrified mothers had witnessed the whole thing from the beach, getting to their feet and moving toward us as if there were something they could do to prevent it, and we were forced to confess to the *Arion*'s owner, Dr. Reynolds, a gruff-looking man with a walrus mustache whose grandchildren were friends of ours. He was so understanding that I felt even worse when one night, a decade later, several young men slipped the *Arion* off her mooring, painted her black, and sailed to Florida, where she ended up as salvage.

I'd like to say that the rest of the race went as I'd imagined it: that we got our spinnaker flying; that one by one we picked off the boats ahead of us; that just before the finish, we overtook the great Johnny Hallowell, whose astonishment turned to awe as we shot past him to win the race. But it wasn't like that. Halfway through the final leg, we still hadn't succeeded in setting our spinnaker. We were, if not in last place, close to it. There would be no pennant. As we neared the finish line, although there was no longer any competitive reason to do so, Mr. Robinson tried once more to raise the spinnaker. He pulled at the halyard and the sail rose. He jiggled the spinnaker sheets, adjusting, positioning, and—I could hardly believe my eyes—the great blue sail began to fill. Suddenly it pulled up and out, with surprising power, and I felt the boat leap forward. I believe a modest, involuntary shout of surprise and pleasure escaped the taciturn skipper (although it may have been from the crew). The tiller in my left hand and the mainsheet in my right felt as if they were living things, gently tugging at me. I could feel the wind at the end of my line, the water at the end of my tiller. Mr. Robinson leaned back happily, sheets in hand, as if he were driving a team of horses. Earlier, we had been fighting the wind for control of the boat; now we were working in concert. We seemed not *on* the bay, but part of it, four elements in balance: sailor, boat, wind, water. This, I thought, is what Johnny Hallowell must feel. A few seconds later, we crossed the finish line in last place.

Not long after we crossed, an air horn's desultory honk marking our passage, the committee boat weighed anchor and headed home. By now, the top finishers were back on their moorings, pennants stuffed in their pockets, furling their sails. A few of them would linger, discussing the race as they stowed their gear in the backs of their station wagons. Their wives and children would have gone home to get dinner ready. The race was over. But we weren't finished. "Let's keep her up," Mr. Robinson called.

And so we did. Spinnaker flying, we ran back down the Gut toward the harbor. The sun was low in the sky. The boats that had filled Buzzards Bay, in a dozen other races like ours, were heading back to their home ports, disappearing into creases in the land. The bay was nearly empty. A lone tugboat nosed a barge toward the canal. As I looked at the sea around us, it amazed me that such a furious afternoon of sailing could leave no mark on the water. We passed the Big House. I could see my grandparents waving from the piazza. I waved back.

Most of the legendary old salts of my youth are dead now. Some have had sailing trophies named for them, given out at the Labor Day party. An aluminum flagpole in front of the clubhouse has a plaque with Bill Hallowell's name. Driving down to Wings Neck one summer day, Johnny Hallowell crashed into a tree and died. Phips, although well into his seventies and beset by heart problems, still heads out in the *Tern* once a week. Of the 364 Twelves built before the Herreshoff Manufacturing Company went out of business in 1945, some 200 remain. A half dozen of them still sit in the harbor at the Big Cove, having been sailed, in some cases, by four generations of the same family. (The Twelves are no longer used in sailing class; families understandably grew reluctant to let rambunctious ten-year-olds perform flying jibes in their family heirlooms. Fledgling skippers now take lessons in small fiberglass sloops.) They are an endangered species, and families have gone to great lengths to save them from extinction. Maintaining a Twelve costs about $5,000 a year; rebuilding one can cost four times as much. Last year a Cataumet family spent $35,000—nearly twice the cost of a new fiberglass reproduction— to have theirs restored by the local boatbuilder, a meticulous craftsman widely regarded as the only man in the area to whom one could possibly entrust a Twelve. (When a neighbor mentioned that she was considering taking hers to a less expensive boatyard, her neighbors quickly dissuaded her from such apostasy.)

The Buzzards Yacht Club still holds weekly Herreshoff races—one of the last harbors in New England to do so—and each Saturday afternoon, a dozen Twelves venture out of the harbor, Quixote-like, past the stinkpots and the Cigarette boats, to gather in the bay. The friends I grew up with on Wings Neck have become the middle-aged salts that now sail them. They no longer use a cannon to start the race, and the *B*'s on the pennants are now made of iron-on vinyl. As Henry and I watch the Twelves congregate before the start one afternoon, while Wave Runners zip back and forth around them, the scene has a dreamlike quality. These wooden boats seem to have sailed out of the past.

One afternoon, a friend invites us out on her family's Twelve. I haven't sailed in ten years, and, as I bend to raise the jib, not remembering whether its halyard is on the left or on the right side of the mast, I feel, at forty-two, a prickle of self-consciousness—a sensation that, even more than the physical act of hoisting the sail itself, brings back my early sailing days. We cast off, and it all rushes back: the sound of the water gurgling as we part it, the tickle of the wind, the tug of the mainsheet in my hand. We don't stay out long—just a few lazy reaches back and forth across the canal. Susannah so likes the bustle and excitement of coming about—"Ready about, Hard-alee," she chants as she scrambles to the other side of the boat—that she asks to tack again and again and again.

XIII
Tennis

THIS MORNING I persuade Susannah to play tennis. She has never played before, so we rummage through the utility room closet, where, under a yellow cloud of foul-weather gear, a dozen tennis rackets lean against the wall. I suggest one of the lighter aluminum models, but she reaches behind them to pull out several old wooden rackets, some of them frameless and warped, but a few still screwed tightly into their trapezoidal presses. "These are prettier," she says. "Can I use one of these?"

To my childhood self, these rackets possessed not only beauty but a mystical, almost sacred power. Even now, as Susannah and I sort through them, squeezing their worn leather grips and running our fingers over their chipped, varnished throats, they seem almost to vibrate in my hands, so resonant are they of the people who once used them. Here is the tan, serious-looking Bancroft Winner that seemed nondescript but was once capable of Bunyanesque feats when wielded by Uncle Jimmy. Here is my grandmother's expensive, chestnut-colored Silverstreak, whose name promised lightning play, but which rarely left the closet and, although a half century old, still looks brand-new. Here is Aunt Sandy's Tad Imperial Deluxe, as slim and elegant as its owner, its shaft composed of laminated wooden strips in shades of brown from beige to mahogany, like the deck of an antique sloop. (Its name, combined with its effete appearance, always made me think of Abraham Lincoln's coddled youngest son, Tad.) Here is my old Jack Kramer, as clean-cut and sturdy as the man whose signature is etched above a king's crown on its snow-white throat. Here is the assortment of Victors and Dunlops that were made available to generations of houseguests. And here is the Slazenger that, in my father's strong hands, once seemed as omnipotent as Excalibur.

On Wings Neck, there were sailing families and tennis families. There were several families that were passionate about both, which seemed slightly greedy to me, and there were even a few families that were not much interested in either, which seemed eccentric and brave. But most leaned toward one or the other. For the tennis families, there was a certain satisfaction in seeing an old salt—someone who had crossed the finish line before the rest of the fleet had even rounded the last mark in the Saturday afternoon race—out on the court Sunday morning, flailing at a tennis ball as if it were as elusive and potentially harmful as a yellow jacket. Similarly, for the sailing families, there was justice in seeing the man who'd recently won the annual tennis tournament get his spinnaker twisted as he raised it on the downwind leg of the Labor Day race. Given Cape Cod's geographic and historical intimacy with the ocean, it was hardly surprising that on Wings Neck, tennis was the lesser sport. It was also the less visible. While the boat races were held in the vast, open-air arena of Buzzards Bay, tennis matches took place on courts reached by long driveways. Walking on the Neck, hearing the rhythmic *pock* of a rally, one might follow that sound up a path through the woods to a clearing where a ferocious doubles match would be taking place. One had the feeling of stumbling on a secret, furtive ritual.

Despite the pennants on the barn wall, which attested to the few isolated successes my aunts and uncles had achieved on the water, my family was a tennis family. I recall hot, still afternoons, stretched out on my bed during "quiet time," the hour after lunch during which children were expected to nap or read in their rooms, when, punctuating the thrum of crickets and the muffled footfalls of grown-ups in a far corner of the house, I'd hear the metronomic thwacks of a rally or the iambic beat of someone hitting against a backboard. Every so often there was a pause, a cry of joy or dismay, and then the sound would begin again.

As I listened, I would try to guess which tennis court the sound was coming from. We had no court of our own. But we had permission to play next door at the Benedicts', on a rosebush-enclosed clay court they rarely used, or at the Hallowells', a sailing family who owned an ancient clay court the color of old bricks. I loved the forgiving softness of clay—

actually a mixture of clay and sand—on which the gradual accumulation of sneaker prints documented the story of each match. (Clay also left its mark on the players; by the end of the match, one's shirt and shorts were usually well smudged, making tennis appear rougher than it really was.) I even liked the postgame sweeping and rolling, a bit of ritual house-keeping that brought opponents together and wiped the slate as clean as an Etch A Sketch after a vigorous shake. It took two children to get the heavy iron roller moving, its clapper gonging mournfully like the bell buoy in Buzzards Bay.

Eventually, when I was fourteen, my father and uncles decided to have our own court built, which, for a family that rarely spent large sums, and on a property that had seen so little change, seemed enormously daring. (My father and Uncle Jimmy borrowed money from their brother-in-law to finance their shares.) We arrived the following summer to find a green, hard-surface court in the firebreak. The fact that it was made not of clay but of a cementlike material called Har-Tru seemed almost sacrilegious—yet I was impressed that my family was capable of effecting such a contemporary miracle.

In *Speak, Memory*, Vladimir Nabokov recalls the "temperamental family doubles" played on the Nabokov country estate in Russia when he was a child, in which he became "easily cross" with his mother and her "feeble serve," and annoyed by his father, an expert but slightly patronizing partner. Young Vladimir kept his butterfly net propped against the fence as an excuse to escape to less stressful pursuits. Family tennis in the Nabokov household was a fractious, fragmenting activity; in the Colt household, by contrast, it seemed an expression of familial togetherness.

Ours was a large family, and in those days there were houseguests every weekend. Games could go on all morning, players shuttling in and out, new players arriving, neighbors dropping by and being persuaded onto the court, a changing roster of spectators awaiting their turns. Before we were old enough to play, my brothers and I liked to imitate the ball boys we'd seen on television: darting across the court, snatching a ball on the run, then dropping to one knee near the netpole, suddenly still and alert as pointers, trying to exude skill and humility, being conspicuously inconspicuous. Our employment was invariably short-lived; within a game or two my brothers and I would quarrel over a ball and be summarily fired. But even on the sidelines, the game had its tactile pleasures: the faint peppermint swirl of the gut strings (we were awed to learn they were made from the sinews of cats); the latticework of nylon trim interlaced in the head that dictated "rough" or "smooth" when the racket was spun to see who got first serve; the wooden presses whose wing nuts I loved to spin madly, like the seedpods of maples as they flutter to the ground; the rainbow-colored canvas bag of practice balls; the end-of-day courtside collage of extra rackets, canvas covers, presses, empty ball boxes, car keys, change, cigarette packs, matches, and paper cups.

Although they had all had a tennis lesson or two, my father and his brothers and sisters were natural athletes who possessed an effortless grace. Family tennis was an embodiment of that grace. The court was a stage on which the family took shape in my eyes: Aunt Sandy, still in her teens, simultaneously girlish and elegant, tossing the ball so high on her serve she'd lose sight of it and have to try again. Uncle Jimmy, serious and determined, his serve a mighty swat. Aunt Ellen, intense and self-critical, muffing a shot and muttering "Oh, you fathead!" before turning her attention to the next point. Aunt Mary, who rarely played (I had the feeling that she considered tennis frivolous), but when she did, dispatching the ball with characteristic purposefulness. My father, the eldest and the ringleader, talking between points, teasing his siblings. (Over the years his sayings on the court became family catchphrases. If his doubles team lost the first few games of a match, he'd say, "We're just lulling them into a false sense of security." Down love-five, he'd invariably announce, "Okay, we've got 'em right where we want 'em." After a match, if his partner apologized for his or her poor play, he'd reply, in mock surprise, "Why, I've never seen you play better!" If there were any disputes or tensions, he would say, "Come on, it's just family tennis," as if it were as innocuous as a game of Candyland.)

Family tennis was when the Colts seemed at our most attractive. Damned attractive, in fact. It was not until I was old enough to play it myself that I became aware of the psychological crosscurrents that were as real as, and often far more accurate than, the shots that sailed over and into the net. And I began to see why there were some, especially those to whom the Colt grace did not come quite so effortlessly, who, when my father was drumming up "a little family tennis," would grimace and bury themselves in their books. But even at a young age, I sensed that family tennis served as an unspoken testing ground for guests and girlfriends. It was not a question of how well they played but of *how* they played; whether they were good sports, whether they had a sense of humor, whether they could be kidded a little, whether they cared about winning without seeming to care *too* much.

My mother had never played before she met my father, but she realized that family tennis was an important part of being a Colt. My father taught her the game, but she was not a natural athlete. Her forehand, a weak, cupping push, was erratic; after she hit the ball, she'd continue running toward the net, giving a little jump of frustration and calling out, "Oh, sorry! Oh, Harry, I'm *sorry*!" as the ball sailed out. And yet she was capable of unleashing a terrific backhand. Stepping into the shot as if she were stamping her foot, she slashed downward with her racket, a motion that appeared awkward, almost angry, but had devastating effects. Ironically, the excellence of Mum's backhand marked her even more as an outsider: the lack of a bona fide backhand in my family has been sufficiently pronounced as to appear genetic. Looking back now, I sense that those two shots were emblematic of her conflicting impulses within the family—her clumsy, apologetic forehand representing the outsider longing to be accepted; her stinging, unorthodox backhand representing the individualist who would one day break free.

Although many husbands and wives believed that marital happiness was best promoted by staying apart on the court, my parents were always partners in family tennis. And they were good to each other. My father never took shots that were rightfully my mother's, even if he knew it meant losing the point. When Mum double-faulted or flubbed an overhead, Dad never chided her. "We'll get it back, Lise," he'd say, the nickname, used only by him, thrilling and pleasing me, giving my brothers and me a hint of the private life they shared, a relationship that did not include us. Even later, as that relationship frayed, they remained a couple on the court, perhaps because in that arena the roles they'd assumed in courtship and early marriage—he the gallant master, she the adoring acolyte—still held true. At the time, I knew only that I liked watching them. On the court, they seemed more intimate, more gentle, more forgiving.

For Wings Neck tennis players, the highlight of the summer was the annual tournament that took place throughout the month of August. Although most of the entrants were our friends and neighbors, and the

stakes were pewter ashtrays or silver candy dishes—mere trinkets compared with the pedestaled silver sloops passed out among the sailors at the
Labor Day cocktail party—when I was eight or nine, the Falmouth Hospital Benefit Tournament seemed more momentous than Wimbledon.

As July drew to a close, I would pedal down to the fork in Wings Neck
Road each day to see whether the draws had been posted. One morning,
I'd arrive and there they'd be, in the cleft of the fork, thumbtacked on a
sheet of plywood that leaned against the trunk of a pine tree, having
appeared, it seemed, with the suddenness and moral force of Luther's
theses on the church door in Wittenberg. I'd kneel on the pine needles
and examine the draw for each tournament from midget singles to senior
mixed doubles, the long, vertical lists of familiar names in unfamiliar
pairings, poised like armies at the edge of a vast, virgin white field. I
always saved men's doubles for last. It was the most heavily subscribed of
all the competitions, the most fiercely contested, and the one in which
my father and uncle reached the finals almost every year. I studied it until
I nearly had it memorized: seeing how high they were seeded, charting
their potential opponents, and looking for unfamiliar names that might
signify a ringer—a word that excited me, carrying, as it did, a whiff of a
wider, less scrupulous world, and representing another obstacle over
which Dad and Uncle Jimmy could triumph.

They made a formidable team. Both had been what my grandfather
and his friends called "fine schoolboy athletes" (and Jimmy had gone on
to play varsity hockey at Harvard), but they were physically quite different. My father was tall and skinny—in snapshots of the time he looks
thin almost to the point of sickliness—but he moved with a loose, casual
ease and was quick enough to chase down almost any shot. He reminded
me of Chip Hilton, the eighteen-year-old apple-pie hero of the sports
books my brother Harry and I read. My uncle was also tall, but his mus-
cular build and slight slouch gave him an ursine languor on the court that
reminded me of the heavyweight boxing champion of the time, Sonny
Liston. Indeed, Jimmy had a way of holding back on a shot till the last
second, sizing up the ball like a boxer measuring his opponent's head for
a punch, then delivering a knockout blow. His game was based on power,
my father's on guile. My father would be all over the court, slicing, par-
rying, chasing down lobs, sending up lobs of his own, until Jimmy, as if
he had seen quite enough of this, would step in and put the ball away. To
protect his pate from the sun—like my grandfather, he was prematurely

bald—Jimmy wore a Panama hat with a plaid band. This gave him a casual, touristlike look, as if he were hardly exerting himself, that only added to his aura of potential force.

Each Friday evening after work, my father and my uncle would drive down from Boston, often arriving long after we children were in bed. And before they went back on Sunday night, they'd play a round or two in the tournament. Over the course of the month I'd bicycle to the fork in the road almost every day, tracing their path from left to right, through the draw's reductive, musical-chair mathematics, from thirty-two to sixteen to eight to four to two to one. The further they got, the more vital it became to me that they win. By the time the semifinals and finals came around on Labor Day weekend, I could hardly believe that God would grant my prayers yet one more time.

The more tense I got, the more casual my father seemed. On the morning of a big match, he would work in the woods, take a load of trash to the dump, play Ghost with us. I was amazed that he could go about his day as if it were like any other, when at two o'clock he had to play the men's doubles final. When he appeared for the match, Dad looked as if he'd just walked out of the forest, as indeed he probably had. He wore an old pair—his only pair—of canvas sneakers, once white and now gray, with a hole in each toe. His wool socks, slightly yellowed with age, drooped at the ankle. He wore brier-tattered khaki shorts and a plain white T-shirt that, while clean, had been laundered so often it was shiny. If the match was at the Benedicts', my brothers and I would watch Dad and Uncle Jimmy rally until their opponents drove up. More likely, the match would take place elsewhere; my father, even after we had a court of our own, always agreed to play wherever his opponents chose.

When I was a child, my father's ease with people astonished me. Wherever we went, he seemed to know everyone: the butcher at the general store, the guard with the paunch who told us where to leave our trash at the town dump, the man who wiped our windshield at the Esso station. And they knew him, joked with him, thought the world of him. (A few years ago, at a family gathering, watching my seventy-one-year-old father jump up to greet some arriving guests, Uncle Jimmy, who had recently been elected state representative, shook his head in amazement. "*He's* the one who should have been the politician," he said.) Before parties, his parents had always urged their children not to focus on their own pleasure but to "give other people a good time." And on the tennis court, even in a match he wanted desperately to win, Dad tried to give people a good time. He was always the first to spin his racket and offer his opponents the choice of rough or smooth; indeed, he was visibly uncomfortable if his opponent beat him to it. Between points he hurried about the court to retrieve balls, including those close to him on his opponents' side of the net. If a ball went over the fence, no matter who had hit it, he was always the one to rummage through the poison-ivy-laced woods. He never failed to compliment an opponent on a good shot. (If a long rally ended with a winner by his opponents, he'd whirl toward them and say, intensely, "That's *too* good," pointing his finger at the man who had made it.) He never hit excessively to the weaker opponent; if anything, the opposite was true. I never saw him (or anyone in the family, for that matter) decide a close call in his own favor; he always gave the benefit of the doubt to the other team, even when, to my eyes, the ball was clearly out. As one who was, even then, praying for his opponent to double-fault, I cringed whenever my father urged him to "take two" after a jet from nearby Otis had buzzed overhead in midserve. But I admired him for doing it.

Dad's sportsmanship was neither studied nor conscious; it was natural, loose, like his body. After points, he would banter with his opponents, ask after mutual friends. As they changed sides on the odd games, he might say something that would leave the other players chuckling and the spectators shaking their heads, smiling. Between sets, he'd light up a Kent cigarette and take a few quick puffs, chatting a moment with the gallery before stamping it out on the clay and heading back onto the court. People liked playing against him, and people liked watching him play. And just as I loved seeing my parents on the court together, I loved watching my father and uncle; I loved seeing what brothers could be. Little by little, sweat would spread over their shirts, as gradually as a shadow lengthens in the late afternoon, until the thin white cotton clung to them. At some point, Uncle Jimmy would take off his hat and toss it aside, as if what had gone on thus far were just a warm-up for the real contest. The tighter the match, the more intense they got. Annoyed by an error he'd made, Dad might mutter, "Come on, you dummy," or, in extremis, "Nincompoop!" But at the most crucial point, he would invariably make some flip remark that made Uncle Jimmy say, "Jesus, Harry," shake his head, and laugh his deep, booming laugh.

As the match went on, word would spread across the Neck—"the

Colt brothers are three-all with the Wrights in the third set"—and people would materialize from the woods like deer gathering at a hidden
pond: barefoot boys in bathing suits, mothers carrying their knitting or
their children's sand toys, fathers coming in from a regatta or from just-
completed tennis matches of their own. Those already there would whis-
per the score to late arrivals. Eventually two or three dozen spectators
lined the court or sprawled on the nearby grass. A few of the men might
lean, arms folded, against trees at the edge of the woods. A young mother
would disappear into the house and return with a pitcher of ice water for
the players. And then the grande dame to whom the court belonged
would slowly make her way out from the house, accompanied by a retinue
of grandchildren, wearing a long dress, a string of pearls, and a broad,
platter-sized sun hat, the crowd parting for her, a young man jumping up
to offer her his chair, my father pausing in his serve, as if in homage, until
she was settled into a position of honor, a host of barefoot and swimsuited
Wings Neckers at her feet, the whole assembly bringing to mind old photographs of Queen Victoria among the natives in some far-flung corner of
her empire.

   Afterward, no matter where the match had been played, or whether
they had won or lost, Dad would leap up and begin to sweep the court,
smoking a cigarette as he trudged between the traces of the broad,
wooden brush, which made long loops in the dust behind him, while
Uncle Jimmy, the broom looking like a toy in his huge hands, took small,
shuffling steps as he dusted the tapes, the suggestion of domesticity
slightly absurd in such a large, powerful man. If they had played at the
Benedicts', my father and uncle would invite their opponents back to the
Big House for ginger ale, which—especially on the rare occasions they
lost—seemed as unnatural to me as enemy armies sitting down for tea
after a bloody battle. (If our guests had never been inside the Big House,
they might ask for a tour. I loved hearing their admiring comments.) We
children played in the garden while the grown-ups sat on the piazza in the
late afternoon, watching the boats in the channel, talking about the Red
Sox, my father leaning against the garden rail drinking a Carling Black
Label (and, when I pestered him, giving me a sip). My grandmother
might emerge with a tray of cheese and crackers, which she'd pass around
as she engaged our guests in conversation; my grandfather might step out
to say hello, and then return to his crossword puzzle. After his opponents
left, Dad would take us all for a swim at the Bluff. And if they'd won, we'd

insist on driving down to the fork so that we could watch him write the name "Colts"—his name, *our* name—one last time on the draw.

The glory years of the Colt brothers seemed to last forever, but there were really just five or six summers in which my father and uncle played in the tournament together, reaching the semifinals or the finals. There they invariably faced the legendary Steve Wright, a balding investment banker, who, although he must have been in his fifties (he seemed ancient to me), was so canny and steady that he won the tournament almost every year no matter whom he played with. One Labor Day weekend, Dad and Uncle Jimmy finally beat him, and for a few years, they were on top. But then a new team from Cataumet—another pair of brothers, in fact, younger and fitter—began to knock my father and uncle out of the tournament. Not long afterward, Uncle Jimmy got married and began to spend his summers at Naushon. My father, in his forties now, played with other partners, but they never got far.

By then, my family's hopes for glory were transferred to a new team: my father and my older brother in the parent-child tournament—Harry and Harry Colt. (Boston WASPs recycle names as diligently as they recycle tennis balls, behaving in each case as if new ones were in short supply. The last five generations of my family have included three Ellens, four Marys, four Charleses, four Jameses, four Edwards, and five Henrys, of whom my son is the most recent but doubtless not the last.) In his early teens, my brother Harry was a fine player, an intensely competitive perfectionist who played with a quiet, inward fury. For several years, he and Dad got to the finals or semifinals, though they did not win. Then one summer, when the draw was posted, we saw that the team that usually beat them had not entered. This, we were certain, would be the Colts' year. And indeed, Dad and Harry moved easily through their half of the draw. But simultaneously, a team we'd never heard of was moving through the other half, beating even formidable opponents with alarming ease. They would meet Dad and Harry in the finals. As always, my father agreed to play the match wherever his opponents wanted. One Sunday afternoon, we drove over to the Cataumet Club, a trio of clay courts and a one-room clubhouse that, compared with the remote, isolated courts of Wings Neck, seemed a veritable tennis factory.

When we arrived, their opponents were rallying. Rather than stop, they continued until one of them missed a shot before coming over to meet my father and brother. And it was a long rally. To my provincial eyes, the Gordons, who were renting a house in the area for the first time, seemed a different species. On Wings Neck, the notion of tennis whites was almost an oxymoron; the Gordons fairly gleamed in the after-noon sun, their outfits as crisp and immaculate as the clothes in deter-gent commercials: Lacoste shirts with toothy little alligators, tight white cotton tennis shorts, white socks that were pulled up high and obediently stayed there, sneakers designed and used only for tennis. They wore Bill Tilden–ish, cable-stitched, V-neck tennis sweaters with navy blue and burgundy stripes. They wore sweatbands around their wrists. They had brought several cans of new balls. The son was a quiet, handsome, blond twelve-year-old. The father was a tall, carefully groomed, dark-haired man with the kind of buttery tan people brought back from vacations in the Caribbean. A thermos of ice water with paper cups sat on the bench; a pair of clean white towels had been draped over the net post. The father had brought two rackets to the match, something I'd never seen before. The Gordons seemed the exact opposite of my father and brother. And I was desperate for them to lose. But as they rallied, you could tell from their crisp, elegant strokes that there had been many lessons and tennis camps, that they played through the winter, and that they were very, very good.

The way they played was different, too. The father, a television executive from New York City, was unfailingly polite, but in a measured, formal way. He moved with purpose; there was no wasted motion. Between points, as Dad scurried about, Mr. Gordon walked slowly, deliberately, to pick up balls. If one was on the other side of the net, no matter how close to him, he didn't pick it up. While he couldn't be accused of flagrant poaching, whenever he had an opportunity to take a shot, he took it, instead of deferring to his less skilled son. He didn't smile or talk much, except to announce the score. And when my father laughed or bantered, he didn't seem charmed, as most people were—in fact, he seemed slightly annoyed.

Or was it that *I* began to feel that way? As I watched the match, I found myself, for the first time, growing critical of the things I had most admired about Dad. His informal attire began to seem bumpkinish next to the Gordons' whites. His urging his opponents to "take another serve," when he had accidentally returned a missed second service,

seemed more foolish than sporting. His gregariousness seemed garrulous, his jokes corny. His sportsmanship seemed a cover for his lacking
the killer instinct that his opponent clearly possessed. As the match went
on, and more and more spectators were drawn to the court, I was
ashamed to realize that I felt embarrassed by my father. He seemed suddenly older, stumbling, anxious to please, vulnerable. I dreaded the possibility that Sally, a cute Cataumet girl in my sailing class who lived near
the Community Club, might wander by and see us.

Why was I so hard on my father? I can look back now and see things I
couldn't have articulated then, but of which I may have been dimly aware.
The stresses of winter were, for the first time I could recognize, spilling
over into summer. This was the year Dad's company, a bottled-gas manufacturer called Air Reduction, had transferred him to New York City, the
year that in wealthy Darien, our down-at-heels Boston gentility seemed so
out of place. My father commuted into Manhattan, where the rate at
which he climbed the corporate ladder gradually slowed. There were
other men more ruthless, less sportsmanlike. They didn't care quite so
much about giving people a good time. But what puzzled me was Dad. He
didn't seem himself around them; his voice was thickened with what I later
realized was liquor. He had recently been beaten for a promotion by a
younger, more polished colleague. I had seen Dad lose before, but it was
the first time I had ever seen him defeated. And now, his opponent on the
tennis court seemed to represent the forces that were beating him in the
wider world of New York. To have it happen here, on the Cape, where, in
my eyes, he had never lost, seemed unbearable.

I have never cared more about the outcome of a match. At the time, I
didn't know why. Now, of course, I realize the stakes were not just the silver candy dishes that sat on a bench at courtside but my feelings about
Dad. I felt, in some inchoate way, that this father and son were taking my
father from me. Or was it that they were taking me from my father? To
make it even worse, it was clear that my brother was a better player than
the other boy. If my father could hold his own against the other father,
the Colts would prevail; yet the more embarrassed I felt, the more tentative my father seemed, and the worse he played. Dad was the weak link.

I don't remember the final score, but the match went to three sets,
and in the end, the Colts lost. It was a quiet car ride home. Dad was
apologetic—he thought he had let Harry down, let the family down. I
thought he had betrayed me; in my heart I knew I had betrayed him. I

hated his opponents for making me feel that way. And yet for months afterward there was nothing I wanted more in the world than one of those V-neck tennis sweaters the Gordon boy had worn. I finally badgered my parents into buying me one, wore it once or twice, and then never wore it again.

Today, on my way back from the Stop & Shop, I notice that the tennis draw has been posted. While Henry sleeps in his car seat, I pull over for a look. There, against the trunk of the same old pine tree, perhaps even on the same sheet of plywood, are the familiar draws. In recent years, the tournament has shrunk. As families have grown larger and more fragmented, they come to Wings Neck for shorter stays each summer; few people are here long enough to play in a tournament that lasts an entire month. There are no midget or junior draws anymore, no parent-child. There are only four entries in ladies' singles, eight in men's singles. (When I was a child, there was no adult singles competition at all, perhaps because in that less individualistic era, it might have seemed a trifle vain. That Wings Neck has not completely succumbed to the times, however, is evident in the tournament's continued use of the word "ladies" to describe its female entrants.) Only eight teams have entered the men's doubles.

There are no Colts in the tournament this year—nor have there been for some time. None of us have been down on Wings Neck long enough. But for many years after the Gordon match, my brothers and I filtered through the tournament—midget doubles, junior doubles, and so on. We added several more trophies to my father's collection in the breakfront in the front hall of our winter home. A friend and I even beat Steve Wright and a partner in the finals of the men's doubles one year, though by then he was well into his sixties. But none of us ever did as well as my father and Uncle Jimmy.

The Gordons played in the tournament a few more times before they stopped spending their summers in Cataumet. Years later, when I moved to New York after college, I occasionally saw the father's name in the newspaper as he rose rapidly in his profession and eventually became president of a television network. Not long after that, he was suddenly fired. I was ashamed to feel a quick burst of joy. He had been beaten at last.

Dad continued to play in the tournament for many years, eventually graduating to senior mixed doubles and senior men's doubles, rarely getting very far, but not caring as much as he had once and having a great deal of fun. (When he partnered Anne, an inexperienced player, in a weekend-long tournament, she said she had never played with such a good sport.) Aging but still graceful—we called him the Silver Fox for his graying hair and crafty shot making—he continued to be the ringleader of family tennis whenever we got together, although these days we called out his pet witticisms before he could say them himself: "Now we've got 'em right where we want 'em!" A few years ago, his longtime partner in the senior men's doubles, a close friend, developed a brain tumor, to which he eventually succumbed. About the same time, Dad developed spinal stenosis and could no longer play. But he still walks down to the court to watch and to joke with us from the sidelines.

A few new courts have been built on Wings Neck, most of them close to the road, one of them even equipped with a small grandstand. The old clay courts—no one builds new clay courts; they require too much maintenance—have gone to seed. The sprinkling of weeds on the Hallowell court has grown into a lush fur, and the owners now use the space for storing boats. The Benedict court hasn't been used for tennis in twenty years. It has no line tapes, no net; the net poles themselves are rusty and incline toward each other from years of net-tightening, as if they hoped one day to meet. A three-foot pine tree stands at the far service line. The rosebushes that surrounded the court have died. For the past few summers, the Benedicts have parked a huge motorboat on the court. And yet the roller still sits at the side of the court, and a sweep broom hangs on the fence, as if someone might resume play at any moment.

Our own court, too, is being reclaimed by nature at a voracious rate. Ever since the Big House was put on the market, the court, in need of resurfacing, has been patched just enough to keep it playable, but last year, with the property likely to be sold, there was no compelling reason to do even that much. It is startling to see what a year of neglect can accomplish. Ever-widening cracks meander across the surface like the fault lines of an earthquake, occasionally brimming with weeds. Here and there, mushrooms have pushed their way up. The green backboard my father and mother built one summer is intact, but winter storms have started to dismantle the fence around it. The net is pocked with holes. The painted white lines have faded to a ghostly gray. The broom, its rust-colored bristles bowed from years of sweeping, has been left out all winter under the wooden bench where my grandmother used to sit. Nine balls, presumably leftovers from last summer, are scattered around the court, so weathered now that it seems the years have rolled back to the days when tennis balls were not yellow but white. It is hard to imagine that on this court, where a section of the fence has begun to buckle, David Howell and I won the junior doubles twenty-six years ago; that where a nursery of four-inch pine seedlings has sprouted near the service line, my brother Mark and a friend took the Counihans to three sets in the men's doubles semifinal; that on this court, which ants have mottled with dozens of hills, large crowds once sat and watched Dad and Uncle Jimmy.

For Susannah and me, the court is just fine. I set up on one side of the net and place the bag of old practice balls at my feet. I pick one out and toss it to Susannah, who stands ten feet from me on the opposite side. She hefts her great-grandmother's Silverstreak and takes a swing.

annual run for the pennant—is high tide. And then the tide slowly ebbs: the days grow shorter, the nights cool, the Red Sox fade. There is a surge of false hope on Labor Day weekend, but then the streets and stores are empty, the crowds are gone. Low again.

Now, in mid-August, the tide of summer is high. The house reverberates with the padding of bare feet across the wooden floors, the punctuation of screen doors slamming, the squeals of children. The Red Sox are only three games out and, as we listen to the radio while doing the dishes, we start to believe that *this* may be the year they actually pull it off.

I know it is an optical illusion, but Susannah looks as if she's grown a few inches since we arrived. (Her toes can nearly touch the sandbar at the Bluff at low tide.) The small girl who in winter is pale, delicate, and susceptible to strep throat has given way to a nut-brown Amazonian, speckled with scabs, mosquito bites, and barnacle cuts. In the city, her life is circumscribed; even if she could figure out the locks, she would never be allowed out the door alone. Here, as soon as she wakes in the comfortable, messy nest she's made of Grandma's Dressing Room, she puts on her bathing suit and calls, "I'm going outside." She has numerous projects under way by now. She spends much of her time at the Bluff, working on her clubhouse of driftwood and stones in the lee of the big gray rock, or tending Treasures of the Sea, a gift shop stocked with crab claws, sea-glass "jewels" sorted by color, lucky stones, jingle shells, fragments of rope, bouquets of goldenrod, a white rubber boat bumper, half a horseshoe-crab shell, a chunk of milky quartz. (Everything's a bargain. Customers pay with bits of quahog shells provided by the proprietor.) She has made a terrarium of moss, lichen, earth, and small pinecones. Climbing the barn roof, jumping from rock to rock at the Bluff, or scrambling across the slippery, barnacle-covered rocks at low tide, she seems older, more capable, more fearless than her winter self. Walking on the road, she doesn't have to hold my hand, although I am pleased when she does. At the Big Cove, she knows how to swim to the spooky space under the dock, where generations of children have scratched their initials into the wood, and where the water is green and clear and she can watch small scup investigate her feet, and hear the grown-ups talking above her, their silhouettes visible between the planks. She will soon be ready to try the long swim to the diving board dock twenty yards offshore. If she doesn't do it this summer, she may never get the chance.

As I watch my daughter, I feel a parent's narcissistic pride that she likes to do the things I once did, and a relief that those things are still here to be enjoyed. She and Anne bake blueberry muffins in the ancient cast-iron tins in which, thirty-five years ago, I baked muffins with Aunt Mary. (They also bake blueberry buckle, blueberry cobbler, and blueberry cake; our teeth and tongues are purple much of the time, as they were throughout the summers of my childhood.) At the Bluff, she learns to dog-paddle to the Big Rock; to beachcomb for lucky stones; to walk along the soft furl of seaweed the tide has left. She swims at low tide. She passes the test. As I watch her play with the children of the children I once played with, the grandchildren of the children my father played with, the WASP incestuousness that once seemed so stifling now seems comforting and safe.

I am especially pleased by Susannah's affection for the Big House, where she has stumbled on the secret places of my childhood: the vast, three-windowed closet on the second floor, the crawl space on the third floor that starts in the Playroom and ends on the landing. She uses the house as an historical marker, telling me that the dollhouse Anne and I assembled last Christmas "was built in 1903, when the Big House was built" or that "the Big House was one year old when Bapa"—her maternal grandfather—"was born." I like to eavesdrop as she gives her friends tours. "This is a picture of my grandpa when he was younger than my daddy. And this is the room where my great-grandfather used to sleep." She believes the house to be haunted by a variety of benevolent ghosts; she reports that she has, several times, encountered the ghost of Ned Atkinson. I can see her trying to fit herself into the family history. One afternoon, pumping on the wooden swing that hangs from an apple tree behind the barn, she nearly sings with satisfaction: "When I grow up, if I have children, we could come here and I would tell my children, 'This swing is where I used to swing, and your grandfather used to swing on this swing, too.'"

Susannah knows we're selling the Big House. She has offered to give me all the money in her piggy bank to help us keep the place. But like me, at some level, she cannot quite believe it. "How old were you when you first walked to the Big Cove by yourself?" she asks. "Next year, can I walk to the Big Cove by myself?"

Henry, of course, has no idea this may be our last summer here. He's too busy learning the place. A late talker, at eighteen months he's making up for lost time, and he spends the day barging around in sensory overload, accumulating and repeating new words that add up to a sort of haiku on the subject of Wings Neck: Boat, Mushroom, Moon, Muffin, Shell, Hermit Crab, Fish, Moss, Stone, Pinecone, Blueberry, Feather, Corn. He loves to walk underneath the badminton net shouting, "Neath! Neath!" Whenever he hears the Chelsea clock chime, he adds "ding-ding" (a phrase that has become his word for any watch or clock). One afternoon, napping next to me in the Little Nursery, he suddenly sits up, lifts the shade, and points with excitement: "Ocean! Ocean!" He is fascinated by daddy longlegs and lets them crawl over his arms and legs while he trembles with the effort of keeping still, his face wrinkled in a tentative smile. Whenever he sees the path to the Bluff, he calls out, "Boat! Boat!" and makes a beeline for the water. Once there, he insists on navigating the steep steps on his own, and then clambering over the rocks, picking up stones and skates' egg cases, savoring the different textures. Inside, his favorite sport is climbing up and down the stairs, holding Anne's hand, from first floor to third floor and back again, over and over and over.

Anne and I had tried for years to have a second child, through two miscarriages, several operations, many months in bed, and a demanding fertility program. Whenever we pass Grandma's Dressing Room, we vividly recall having to make love according to the gynecologist's rigidly prescribed schedule, in an unheated Big House on a twenty-degree Columbus Day dawn, while Anne had bronchitis and a fever of 103. Despite the circumstances, we were excited by the possibility of conceiving a child in a place that meant so much to us both. (The effort failed.) Not long after we began to fill out adoption applications, Henry was conceived and carried to term. We named him for his two grandfathers—Henry Clifton Fadiman Colt—and joked that my father had swallowed Anne's father. There seems something miraculous about having another Henry in this house.

There is a bittersweet joy in watching my children discover this place just as we are selling it. After five summers here, will Susannah ever forgive us? After two summers here, will Henry remember anything? After ten summers here together, will Anne and I ever live in another place where we can sneak out of the house for a midnight skinny-dip and watch the phosphorescence fly from our fingers like shooting stars? During this lame-duck month I have felt a desperate yearning to breathe in as much of the Big House as possible, as a person soaks up the essence of a loved one he knows is dying. I find myself wandering the house at night, poking into desk drawers, peering into trunks, hoping there might be something else to learn. I tend to get stuck, half in the present, half in the past. Searching for blueberries in the firebreak beyond the deteriorating tennis court, I come across a tennis ball bald and blanched with age, the result of an errant shot from a match many years past. Heading toward Hidden House, I notice a faint trace of the strike zone painted on the green barn door where we used to throw a ball for hours. In the sleight of hand performed by the passage of time, the generations seem to shuffle before my eyes. As I watch my father read Beatrix Potter to his grandchildren before bedtime, I see my grandfather. As I take my daughter fishing, I become my father. And as I watch my daughter pause to listen to the wind in the Playroom, I see my childhood self. With her curly hair, delicate features, and saucy air, she also reminds me of my grandmother—thus completing a circle almost dizzying in its fullness.

Like Henry, I find myself naming things. Part of it is because Susannah asks a lot of questions to which I don't know the answers: *Are inchworms worms or caterpillars? Can I eat those red berries? Where do waves come from?* But it's more than that. On the brink of losing this place, I want to identify the trees, plants, and insects I've grown up with, to know their proper names before they are no longer part of my life. Naming things, of course, is a way of trying to hang on, of claiming ownership. I study nature guides from the living room shelf, natural history books from the library. I learn that the gnarled tree with gray berries behind the Big House is a juniper; that the small fish we call minnows are actually silversides and alewives; that the spiky green sedge we call eelgrass is more properly known as spartina; that the seaweed washing up on the Bluff comes in at least three varieties—rockweed, sargassum, and sea lettuce; that the sand pellets littering the mudflats at low tide have been kicked up by burrowing fiddler crabs; that the boat shell's proper name is the slipper limpet, and its even more proper name is *Crepidula fornicata* (which may help explain its recent proliferation on Buzzards Bay beaches). I find myself especially anxious to put names to all the faces in the old photo albums. Whenever my parents or Aunt Ellen is here, we leaf through the albums, and I am introduced to a long-dead cousin, a distant uncle, a maiden great-great-aunt.

But time is growing short. Already, in mid-August, there is a chill in

PART TWO

more difficult to keep four boys on Big House–caliber behavior; we needed a place where we could wrestle on the floor without worrying about the noise and fry clams without worrying about the grease spatter. Without my grandparents listening, my parents could say—and we could overhear—things in Hidden House that had never been voiced in the Big House. I came to think of Hidden House as a useful metaphor for all that my family kept hidden.

Sandy was the youngest by far of the five Colt children in my father's generation, the baby of the family. (She was called "the baby" or "Popsie" well into her twenties.) Born just before my grandparents turned forty, she arrived into a world on the verge of war and a family on the verge of fracture. With her mother in an institution for the first two years of her life, her father away working for the army for much of her first eight, and three of her four siblings at boarding school, Sandy had been raised largely by Miss Smith, the firm but beloved family retainer. Judging from letters I found in the closet of Mariah's Room, her early familial relationships had been conducted largely by mail. As a young girl, Sandy was a combination of beguiling innocence and beyond-her-years wisdom: at twelve she still loved to be read stories about enchanted castles and fairy princesses; at the same age, she realized that her father was drinking too much and was the one to ask him to stop. My mother recalls how, each evening, the grown-ups, playing bridge in the living room, would hear Sandy whistling in the dark on her way upstairs to bed.

Perhaps in compensation for their earlier absence, my grandparents doted on Sandy, just as Ned Atkinson had doted on his youngest child. She always got what Grandpa referred to as "first-class treatment." After Sandy graduated from Bryn Mawr, where she captained the swim team, they sent her to Paris, where she studied piano with Nadia Boulanger and took cooking lessons from cordon bleu chefs. Like her mother, however, Sandy was divided between her desire to live the well-heeled life and her desire to help—as Grandma put it—"those less fortunate." After a year in Paris, she volunteered for the Peace Corps, then in its infancy. When she finished a two-year stint in the Ivory Coast, she stayed on with the corps as an administrator, living in Washington, D.C., and traveling the world giving speeches about the corps's mission. Come summer vacation, she always returned to the Yellow Room on the third floor of the Big House. In a family of attractive people, Sandy was, perhaps, the most attractive of all. Tall, slender, and long-limbed (my mother called her "Legs Diamond"), with a friendly, freckled face that made her seem simultaneously glamorous and girlish, Sandy inspired so many wolf whistles in downtown D.C. that she kept the top up on her red Fiat convertible even on the hottest summer days. At twenty-seven, Sandy was the only one among the Colt children whose future still seemed limitless. "She would have gone far," Uncle Jimmy told me a few years ago at the wedding reception for Sandy's son, Russell. "She would have been *really something.*"

Sandy had married outside Boston. Sidney was a prominent Washington child psychiatrist, a tall, fit, cosmopolitan man eleven years her senior. The son of Russian Jews, he had converted to Protestantism. He and Sandy had met at a reading group. The book under discussion that evening was *The Last Puritan;* Sandy, arriving late, admitted that she'd read only the first few chapters, but added that she knew what it was about, "because Santayana wrote the book about my cousin." (Alas, I can find no evidence for this claim.) They were married at the church across the street from the general store in Pocasset, with a reception at the Big House. Sandy taught French at a private school, served as vice president of the Washington Opera Society, and orchestrated a complex social calendar of teas, dinner parties, committee meetings, tennis matches, and occasional trips abroad. On summer vacations at Wings Neck, zipping up the driveway in their Fiat with their West Highland white, Niccolo, she and Sidney brought a decidedly un-Boston fizz to the Big House. Dinner table conversation turned from the tribulations of the Red Sox toward contemporary art, the Washington political scene, or the need for improved medical training in Third World countries.

Sidney challenged me. At twelve, I was silently critical of the ways in which he differed from us—his awkward but effective tennis game, the pristine perfection of his tight tennis whites, his strenuously correct pronunciation of Italian—yet I could not help being impressed by his extensive travels, his brilliance as a jazz clarinetist, the rumor that he had smoked marijuana. I was fascinated to learn that while still a teenager, he had run away to join a roadhouse band: in a family of musical dabblers—who alluded to the singing careers they *could* have had, yet whose acme was a "Skye Boat Song" solo at a Naushon musicale—Sidney was a bona fide professional. I could sense that he, too, felt divided about us—leery

of our family's Bostonian insularity, but longing to be part of its graceful, assured informality. I often felt Sidney was trying too hard—at
everything—but the force of his effort made our family seem self-
indulgent by comparison. And his engagement with the wider world
made me think for the first time about how isolated the Big House was,
perched on top of a bluff on a peninsula at the end of a causeway, a
remote outpost of provincial WASP culture.

In October 1966, five months after the birth of my cousin Russell, Sandy
came down with a cold and a low-grade fever she couldn't shake. Like
most proper Bostonians, she didn't believe in getting sick, and resisted
Sidney's attempts to get her to a doctor. Finally, she agreed to go in for a
checkup. The doctor told Sidney that his wife had acute granulocytic
leukemia. She might survive several years; she might die within days.

There began a siege whose extent I would not learn until six years later,
when Sidney wrote a memoir of the ordeal. An essential part of that siege
was silence: we children were never told the truth, and neither was Sandy.
Her doctors informed her that she was anemic, although she must have
suspected something more serious as her routine of teaching, Opera
Society meetings, and gallery openings was infiltrated, and then over-
taken, by blood tests, transfusions, and trips to the emergency room. That
Christmas, against her doctors' advice, Sandy and Sidney flew to Boston,
where they were met by medical technicians with a wheelchair. The family
assembled at Uncle Jimmy's house on Christmas Eve. Although we always
got together over the holidays, it was an unusually large gathering,
including several cousins we hadn't seen in years. I didn't know the reason, of course; my parents had told us only that Sandy was sick and might
look a little different. Indeed, we were shocked by her appearance: her
aquiline features and slim, elegant figure were puffy from prednisone; her
speech was dulled by painkillers. Sandy, however, acted as if nothing were
amiss, bantering with her nieces and nephews, admiring the huge Christmas tree, singing carols (albeit less vigorously than usual), and occasionally joining in the small talk at the dinner table. It would be the last time
she would be together with her whole family.

In a cruel twist, not long after Christmas, Sandy found herself unex-
pectedly pregnant. Sidney knew she couldn't have the baby; even if she
lived long enough to deliver, she would be unlikely to survive labor. Dur-

ing the abortion, she spiked a 105-degree fever and nearly died. When the procedure was over, she insisted on seeing her baby, a perfectly formed five-inch girl.

As winter turned to spring, Sandy's body was overwhelmed by disease: her skin blossomed with black-and-blue blotches; her gums bled after she brushed her teeth; she developed ulcerations on her buttocks; her glorious legs were shrouded in support hose to help her weakening circulation; she had difficulty swallowing; she suffered excruciating pain in her pelvis and lower back; she was left nearly blind by retinal bleeding. The Georgetown home she had so recently redecorated for Russell's arrival became a virtual hospital, its rooms pervaded by the scent of alcohol, its shelves filled with medicine bottles, its floors stained with blood. There were frequent injections of morphine and several near-death emergencies. Yet Sandy struggled to hold on to what was left of her life, never complaining—although in extremis she might mutter "Godfrey's tweezers," an expression she'd picked up from her father. She spent as much time as she could with Russell, who was learning to walk. Although she could barely see, she managed to embroider needlepoint for Miss Smith. She even threw a fortieth birthday party for Sidney in their backyard, complete with tent, band, and several dozen guests. But by early June she was so weak she could not turn over without help, and the only activity she could tolerate was listening to fairy tales—stories her father had read to her at the Big House when she was a child. Visiting her, my father did his best to hide his sorrow as he bathed his once-athletic sister, gently lifting her crippled body in and out of the tub.

When it became clear that the end was imminent, Sidney suggested going to Wings Neck. Sandy was delighted by the plan. For her, the Big House had been not only her cherished family home but a haven from the social hubbub of Washington. Now she craved a haven from the emergency room atmosphere that had taken over her own house. Although she could no longer see, she wanted to feel the southwest breeze on her skin, smell the pine-scented air, hear the moo of the foghorn at Cleveland Ledge. Sidney contracted for an ambulance plane big enough to hold him, Sandy, Russell, and Russell's nanny, and made arrangements for Sandy to be transfused just before boarding. A family friend obtained clearance for the plane to land at Otis Air Force Base. Although her doctors doubted she'd survive the flight, Sandy was determined to get to the Big House one more time.

We had already arrived at the Big House for the summer. There was a strange sort of disequilibrium within. My grandparents had flown to Washington to be with Sandy, leaving a house that felt empty even though it was overflowing with people. The grown-ups kept shooing the children outside, where we'd get caught up in our usual activities— tennis, swimming, baseball—and then remember that something was amiss. Inside, our parents bustled about, making plans. My father arranged to have an ambulance from the volunteer fire department transport Sandy from the air force base to the Big House. The local Red Cross chapter was alerted to have blood on hand. Someone tracked down a stretcher on wheels so Sandy could lie outside during the day. My mother and Aunt Mary prepared the Lower Bedroom, where Sandy and Sidney always stayed, and where, two years earlier, Russell had been conceived on a summer afternoon. We children made WELCOME SANDY signs for the doors and picked pansies from Grandma's garden for her bedside table. Late at night, I'd be jarred awake by the *brrring* of the phone; I'd hear my father's footsteps and the murmur of low voices.

The flight was scheduled for Thursday. That afternoon, when we returned from swimming at the Big Cove, the house was subdued. There had been a call from Washington. In the morning, Sandy had been well enough to lie in bed, talking with her husband and her parents about the trip. Sidney had joked about maneuvering her stretcher down the steps of the Bluff so she could be as close as possible to the water. "Only until I can walk on my own steam," insisted Sandy. But in the afternoon she had become increasingly listless, eventually falling into a morphine-sodden sleep that, Sidney later wrote, "no longer seemed animated or human." (Afterward, her doctors surmised that at some point during the afternoon she had suffered a massive brain hemorrhage.) The flight was canceled.

The following morning, as we were playing Ghost, the telephone rang in the Big House. When we came in, my father's eyes were wet as he told us the news: Sandy had died at 8:41 A.M. He trudged into the den and began making calls. That afternoon, as we played a subdued game of croquet, we could hear thrashing in the woods, as Dad tore away at the catbrier that threatened to overrun the place.

It seems incredible to me now that no one ever said the words "leukemia" or "terminal" to Sandy, that she never talked with her husband or her parents about her imminent death, that she never had an opportunity to say good-bye. But at the time, the idea that such things were unspeakable was in keeping with standard medical practice. It was also in keeping with the buttoned-up ethos of Brahmin Boston. "Don't make a spectacle of yourself," I can still hear my grandfather say.

Throughout my childhood, whenever conversation at the Big House dinner table tended toward the intimate, Grandpa would head it off with the remark "We don't talk about *personal* things." (By contrast, Grandma often talked about personal things—her psychiatric hospitalization, for instance—which may have been part of the reason Grandpa was so sensitive on this point.) One didn't talk about one's feelings any more than one talked about taking out the garbage. If one were pulled into uncomfortably intimate conversational waters, one could always excuse oneself to refresh someone's drink. The reflexive reply to "How are you?" was "Fine," no matter what the situation—as in "Fine . . . except for a touch of pneumonia," or "Fine . . . aside from the divorce." Shortly after her wedding, my grandmother was invited to tea by a Bostonian grande dame. On the appointed afternoon, she spent a lovely hour with her charming hostess, only to learn later that the woman's husband had died the previous day.

I could walk down my street in Dedham, the well-to-do Boston suburb in which we lived, and know that in this house, the father was an alcoholic; in this, the retarded son had been put in an institution; in this, the wife had taken an overdose of sleeping pills. No one talked of these things, but everyone knew. Several years ago, I attended a Christmas Eve service at the Episcopal church. In the middle of the First Lesson, a harrowing moan filled the nave. The sound came from my brother's childhood piano teacher, who, suffering from amyotrophic lateral sclerosis, had been wheeled up the aisle on a gurney. Her unearthly howls, which continued throughout the service and were politely ignored, seemed to give voice to the accumulated pain that lay under the town's sleek veneer.

When young Brahmins found Cold Roast Boston too frigid, they traditionally thawed by looking outside the family circle. My great-aunt Amy was raised in a turn-of-the-century Beacon Hill home where no voice was ever raised in anger or joy. She recalled that whenever her older sister, a teenager at the time, grew frustrated by the restrained atmosphere, she'd slam the door and run over to the Italian neighbor-hood in the North End, where mothers shouted out the windows and fathers slapped or squeezed their children with equal fervor. Well-to-do WASP children often gravitated to the kitchen, where the warmth of the stove—and of the Irish servants who worked over it—provided a wel-come contrast to the rest of the house. (In the Big House, it was not only Martha Keady's cakes but her hugs that drew us to the kitchen table.) It was not uncommon for wealthy parents to take long trips, leaving even infants and toddlers in the care of a governess for months at a time. When those children grew up and published memoirs, they often wrote in greater detail, and with far greater feeling, about their nannies and cooks and maids—people whom in many cases they knew only by their first or last names—than about their parents.

None of this would surprise the authors of *Ethnicity and Family Therapy*, a recently published psychology textbook that discusses the therapeutic issues presented by Latinos, African-Americans, and other ethnic groups. (My cousin Forbes, who was reading it for a graduate school class in clinical psychology, passed it along to me.) "Anglo Ameri-cans would rather not complain," observe the authors of the chapter "American Families with English Ancestors from the Colonial Era." "They value bearing pain silently." The authors suggest that to counter the group's tendency to repress unpleasant emotions, therapists teach WASP couples how "to have small, immediate, frequent, and personal fights instead of letting it all build up." Of course, this very tendency toward keeping things inside makes it difficult to lure WASPs into therapy in the first place: "Failing to solve their own problems make [*sic*] Anglo Americans feel inadequate."

There is one situation in which my family has always managed to express its feelings, albeit in a way that enables us to convert them into a kind of joke. Whenever a guest leaves the Big House, we gather on the front porch for what has come to be known among us as a Colt Good-bye. After hugs, kisses, and final snapshots, the guests start to drive away, and we begin to wave—modestly at first, then more ardently. Some of us pretend to cry. A few younger cousins may chase after the car as if their grief at parting is so great that they intend physically to prevent the guests from leaving. My grandfather was especially spirited at these good-byes. He'd extract a handkerchief from his suit pocket, wave it wildly, mop his brow, dab at his eyes in mock-sadness, and weep crocodile tears. At times he'd get so carried away by his performance that he'd begin to laugh, a great, wheezy roar that occasionally evolved into coughing of such intensity he'd have to bury his face in the handkerchief to muffle the explosions. (These days, my father waves a handkerchief; the rest of us wave ratty beach towels, soggy bathing suits, or whatever else comes to hand.) It was a point of pride to wave until our departing visitors were around the bend in the driveway and out of sight. We never risked the chance that they might turn around and see us abandoning them, going into the house before they had disappeared from view. I think we wanted our guests' last image of us to be that of a large, loving family benevolently waving farewell in front of their extraordinary house.

Last summer, looking through the trunks in the attic, I came across several cartons of Sandy's things. For many years they had been left as they were in the Yellow Room, but at some point, someone had boxed them up and moved them here. Dying so young and so suddenly, Sandy had never had occasion to sort through them. There were her Peace Corps speeches; her Bryn Mawr diploma; a calling card—MISS ALEXANDRA COLT—from her debutante year; a rusted trophy with a tag that read TARRATINE TENNIS CLUB, DARK HARBOR, MAINE, SENIOR CLUB CHAMPIONSHIP MIXED DOUBLES, SANDY COLT–FRED DAVIES, WINNERS 1957; a high school paper on "The Format of the Saint Matthew Passion" (on which she received an 84); a school calendar she kept the summer she turned fourteen, in which she'd noted, in her chubby, youthful hand, the sails she'd taken, the dances she'd attended, the movies she'd seen ("Saw 'Duel in the Sun' with *sexy* Greg Peck. Woo! Woo!"); a cast photograph of her junior high school play, *H.M.S. Pinafore;* her sixth-grade yearbook; a snapshot of her at twelve, sitting on the Big Rock at the Bluff, looking as if she'd struck a sophisticated pose and then blushed at her temerity.

It wouldn't be fair to say that Sandy's death triggered the family-wide unraveling that was to come, yet it surely marked the end of the seemingly perfect summers at the Big House. Part of it was that as I grew older, I began to realize that those summers hadn't been so perfect after all, that our golden family was not, in fact, so golden. Although we continued our trips to the general store, our family tennis, and our Fourth of July pageants, I began to see that beneath our web of traditions a great deal was concealed. It reminded me of our games of Sardines, in which, while the children hid in the crannies of the Big House, the adults went about their business: two eerily parallel worlds. As we curled up in our grandmother's closet, we could see, through a crack in the door, Grandma writing letters at her desk a few yards away; as we huddled in the laundry room, we could hear the clatter of dishes in the kitchen as Grandpa prepared ratatouille. (Sometimes these worlds might briefly overlap. Extracting his tennis racket from the closet in which we hid, my father might wink at us before shutting the door.) Eventually, I came to think that as we swam and sailed and played pirates, a secret world was running quietly alongside the one we inhabited—a world glimpsed only rarely, in the slurred speech of my grandfather at dinner, in a flurry of cutting words overheard downstairs as I fell asleep. As I grew older, it became harder to tell which world was the more real.

The Big House itself was a library of clues to our hidden family dramas. It was while flipping through a Forbes family genealogy at the age of fifteen that I discovered my mother was my father's *second* wife. About that same time I began to wonder why, among the familiar charcoal sketches of my father and his siblings on the stairwell wall, there wasn't one of Aunt Ellen; her only childhood portrait, a smaller one by a different artist, was relegated to a spot over the chest in the utility room. Or why volume two of the guest book ended abruptly in 1939—the year Grandma went to Butler Hospital, though I didn't know that—and did not resume for several years. It was only last summer that I realized the handsome young soldier in the portrait farther up the stairwell was Larrie Austin, Grandma's first love. I did not see that Mary's name was missing from the guest book for nearly two decades. And only recently did I notice that there is not a single photograph on the Big House walls taken after 1967.

When my grandmother bought the Big House from her father's estate in 1949, she intended to make it a center for a reinvigorated family life. Her dreams had been partially realized. Summers, the house had indeed become a mecca for their children, their grandchildren, and their friends. But my grandfather had been unable to rouse himself from dormancy. His keen intelligence and wit now surfaced primarily in cross-word puzzles, puns, dinner table bons mots, verses and plays written for Tavern Club celebrations, and occasional poems penned for birthdays and anniversaries, at which, like many proper Bostonians, my family excelled, masking their strongest emotions in doggerel. (I recently came across a poem Grandpa had written to commemorate the election of a friend's grandson to the A.D. Club. Its effortless brilliance astonished me.) As he retired from the world, he retired still further from his wife. Grandpa used to sleep in the large bedroom next to Grandma's, but as he got older, he retreated across the hall to his dressing room, a cramped space whose two windows and wood paneling left it as somber as the men's clubs he belonged to in Boston. The surface of the massive oak dresser is still stippled with the prints of his martini glasses, like a shad-owy map of the solar system. The bed is not much larger than a school-boy's cot. A few photographs of horses hang on the walls. The shelves are filled with old yearbooks and class reports from St. Paul's and Har-vard, volumes of military history, and novels by Kipling, Conan Doyle, and P. G. Wodehouse describing the gentlemanly, class-conscious, Vic-torian world that slowly receded around him like an outgoing tide. Even when Grandpa was alive, the room had a museum stillness, an atmos-phere of preservation, the salt air chastened by the scent of bay rum and starched shirts.

My grandmother, meanwhile, continued to try to save the world—and improve herself—from her second-floor bedroom. She wrote letters to her congressmen, signed checks to sponsor "underprivileged" chil-dren around the globe, sent gifts to friends and grandchildren. The old date books that still lie on her desk are filled with appointments for Chilton Club lunches, trustee meetings for the New England Conserva-tory of Music, church conferences, peace vigils, prayer meetings, local political campaigns, concerts, plays, dance performances. While Grandpa read about military campaigns long past, Grandma read about the quest for social justice. Her bookcases are lined with the important and con-troversial novels of the last half century *(Cry, the Beloved Country; Black Boy; Manchild in the Promised Land);* the shelf over her bedroom fireplace is lined with old Bibles, spiritual tracts, and inspirational pamphlets. Each winter, she spent several weeks at Pendle Hill, a Quaker retreat near Philadelphia, where she churned out fiction and poetry; took classes on the history of nonviolence; and discussed global politics over nutritious meals with fellow seekers from around the world (including Euell Gibbons, who, long before he became famous for *Stalking the Wild Asparagus*, was a part-time handyman and cook at Pendle Hill, serving surprised guests blanched pokeweed from the crop he'd grown in the basement). There, the woman who at the Big House took breakfast in bed—and whose housework consisted largely of arranging flowers and rearranging furniture—rose early to peel potatoes, sweep floors, and carry out other communal chores.

Back at Wings Neck, her resolve generally evaporated. She vowed to write every morning, but never managed more than a few days in a row. (In her bedroom closet, there are dozens of unfinished poems, stories, and plays, copied out on yellow legal pads, now brown and powdery at the edges.) In the Big House kitchen, there is a large index card collection of recipes she carefully copied down from friends: "Shortbread Scrunch (Lady Forbes)"; "Fish Chowder—Tavern Club 1949. At last!"; "Chicken Baked in Cream Tracy (tried 1955 pretty good)." Yet I never once saw her cook. Her few forays into the kitchen are family legend: the time, in her desire to be resourceful, she cleaned, poached, and served an eel to her shocked family; the time, determined to make use of the ingredients available, she made a soup of spinach and grapefruit juice. "She loved the idea of leftovers," says my mother. "It made her feel that though she was a privileged woman, she knew how to economize." She hung a framed poem over the stove in the Big House titled "The Kitchen Prayer" that described Mary Magdalene and her more practical, hardworking sister, Martha. "I think Grandma struggled over that poem," says Mum, "knowing that she was a lady of leisure like Mary, yet wanting so much to have a bit of Martha in her."

Grandma was a romantic, and no matter how much evidence accrued to the contrary, she never stopped believing that she could become a better person, that her husband would stop drinking, that their marriage would right itself, that the world would find peace. For her fiftieth reunion at Miss Winsor's, asked what she had learned from the school, she wrote, at the age of sixty-eight, a year after Sandy's death, "Could optimism be the school's gift, too? During the years since graduation, I have encountered such heroism and tenderness in the pilgrims on this planet that I see hope for a better life on it. I enjoy growing older immensely, because of this beauty in people. . . . 'Greet the unseen with cheer.'"

After Sandy's death, Grandpa spent more and more time slouched in his morris chair, martini glass in hand, a pack of unfiltered Camels on the table, muttering at the ineptness of the Red Sox on the tiny black-and-white television set that graced the house in those days. "Wretched lout," he'd growl, and we couldn't be sure whether he was referring to a baseball player or to himself. To my younger brothers and cousins, he began to seem as sedentary, irascible, and potentially dangerous as Old Brown, the owl in *The Tale of Squirrel Nutkin* who is silent and unmoving until one day he pounces on the impertinent Nutkin and bites off his tail. Dinners around the big table in the dining room became tense. Although she knew—or perhaps *because* she knew—that her husband was a little "under the weather," as she put it, Grandma would prod him from the far end of the table, asking his opinion on the subject at hand when she knew he hadn't been listening, or formulating complicated questions that, even had he been sober, he would have found hard to answer. There were times when Grandpa would start a story, lose its drift, and be unable to finish. When he played pool, his cue slipped more often. Once, when my six-year-old brother Mark spilled his juice at the table, we were shocked to see Grandpa swat him. And yet there were still glimpses of the witty, generous man we loved, and who loved us. On winter mornings, in their respective Boston homes, his grown children would open their back doors to find boxes packed with Jones sausage and Keiller's Dundee marmalade. An anniversary couple would be honored by a clever bit of verse. And every so often, a dispirited grandchild, tiptoeing through the dining room after a parental scolding or a lost tennis match, trying to get to the kitchen without rousing Grandpa from his morris chair, would hear him speak. "Hello, old man, how goes the battle?" he'd say quietly, giving a look that made one feel he understood that children, too, could have cause to be sad, that he knew something about the unfairness of the adult world.

No longer was the Big House filled with guests each weekend. No longer was it even a gathering place for the family. After their marriage, Uncle Jimmy and his wife, Buffy, stayed there a few times, but though they were fond of the Big House, like Ned Atkinson they wanted a place of their own, where they could do things their own way, choose their own meals, invite their own friends. Buffy wasn't gung ho about tennis, and she and Jimmy were, as the saying went, more motorboat people than sailboat people. They began spending their summers at Naushon.

Aunt Ellen and her family weren't at the Big House either. Although we saw them frequently in the winter months—my cousins were among our closest friends and lived up the street from us in Dedham—we rarely saw them in summer. At the time I assumed they simply preferred Naushon to Wings Neck. It wasn't until many years later that I learned they would have liked to come to the Big House but were never invited. The rift between Ellen and her mother that had started when Grandma came home from the hospital in 1941 had never fully healed. Indeed, it had widened when Ellen married Uncle Tom. Even at a young age, I was somehow aware that my grandparents had opposed the marriage, though only people outside the family dared mention that the reason might have had something to do with the fact that, like Uncle Sidney, Uncle Tom was Jewish. (A genteel form of anti-Semitism was taken for granted in my grandparents' day; Jews were excluded from Harvard's final clubs, and marrying outside the WASP tribe was considered a serious affront to one's parents.) There was a rumor, in fact, that one evening, in a fit of anger, Grandpa had "taken a poker" to Tom. Although I wasn't sure exactly what that meant, and I didn't know where the incident had taken place, for a while I never passed the fireplace in the living room of the Big House without a small shiver. After the wedding at Heath Hill, Grandma told Ellen to remove her belongings from the Big House because she was no longer welcome there. (Although Grandpa adored his eldest daughter—and eventually made peace with Tom—he apparently did not object strenuously to Ellen's banishment; he was used to deferring to his wife in order to avoid conflict.) Thereafter, although she and her mother continued to see each other at family gatherings in the Boston area, Ellen never made more than brief stopovers at the Big House.

In the period of grief that followed Sandy's death, Grandma invited Ellen and her family to stay at the Big House for a month. From my point of view, it was a memorable time; the addition of five Singer children brought the house to life. There were massive games of croquet and enough baseball players for two fair-sized teams. My cousins' presence made me realize for the first time how gaping a hole their absence had been. At the end of the month, however, my grandmother took Ellen aside and told her, "I never should have invited you." It would be many years before I understood why, whenever I talked about Wings Neck, a wary look came over my Singer cousins. While my brothers and I grew up thinking of the Big House as home, the Singer children saw it as a place from which they alone were excluded.

Aunt Mary, too, would come to have mixed feelings about the Big House. As a child, she had bridled at the grim seriousness of Puritan New England. "I resolved at an early age," she says, "to get the hell out of there." After graduating from Oberlin College in far-off Ohio, she had traveled to France, where she married a poet and settled on his mother's strawberry farm. Mary, characteristically, put a good face on things in her letters home, writing of the beauty of the fields in bloom, the clarity of the light, her love for her two babies. But when my grandparents visited, they found Mary's spartan life a far cry from their proper Bostonian vision of a successful marriage: the babies seemed sickly, the medical care inadequate, their normally indefatigable daughter exhausted. In the summer of 1960, Mary was persuaded to return with her children to the United States, where they moved into the Big House with Grandma and Grandpa. Mary and her husband were divorced in 1962, a fact briefly noted in the guest book by my grandmother. (Four decades later, both Mary and her ex-husband would look back on those years in southern France as the happiest of their lives.)

No doubt my grandparents were relieved when a well-to-do, middle-aged lawyer from a prominent Nebraska family began to court her. John had met Aunt Ellen while attending Harvard Law School. It was, it seemed, common knowledge that John had been in love with Ellen, but she had not returned his feelings. He had gone on to marry and divorce, but remained a family friend, and after Mary's divorce, we began to see more of him on Wings Neck, accompanied by his four-year-old daughter. John was only seven years older than Mary, yet he seemed to belong to my grandparents' generation. A small, pale, wiry man with thinning hair, he wore old-fashioned suits, bow ties, and horn-rimmed glasses. He smoked a pipe, which he tended with great ceremony and removed to make elaborate pronouncements, larded with literary allusions and Latin aphorisms. He spent much of his time on the piazza, listening to

Grandpa's stories with an attentiveness that made it seem as if it were not my aunt Mary but my grandfather he was wooing—which I think he was, in the sense that, like many people who visited the Big House, he appeared to be in love with the idea of the Colt family as much as with any individual therein. John was a bright, well-read man, and my grandfather was surely flattered by his attention, as well as impressed by the extensive action he'd seen in the Second World War. At the same time, when John led the children in after-dinner choruses of the University of Nebraska fight song, using his pipe for a baton, Grandpa would wince, then chuckle hoarsely, shaking his head. I wonder whether he saw in John a reminder of his own provincial origins.

How difficult it must have been to enter our tribe! How judgmental I was! Three decades later, I visited Lincoln, Nebraska, to attend the wedding of Uncle John's namesake son. On his own turf, Uncle John was loved and venerated, and I ached with shame at how thoroughly I'd failed to appreciate him. Indeed, my Boston roots seemed pallid next to those of Uncle John, whose ancestors had traveled by covered wagon from Kentucky to Nebraska, battling Indians and starvation to help settle the West. And the huge tongue-and-groove barn Uncle John's grandparents had built with their own hands in 1899 made the Big House, built by a hired "gang" of Italians four years later, seem downright frivolous.

John and Mary were married in August 1963, in front of the living room fireplace. I was nine and remember the excitement into which the Big House was plunged: the florist fussing over her bouquets; the beefy men unloading a truckload of folding chairs in the garden; my mother and Aunt Mary polishing the Big House to a fare-thee-well; Martha "cooking up a storm," as my grandfather put it; John's family and friends from Lincoln, dressed in chocolate brown suits, flowered dresses, and wide smiles, touring the Big House with awe; my grandfather, armed with a crossword puzzle, seeking sanctuary on the Hidden House porch; the harpsichordist getting surpassingly drunk at the rehearsal dinner and waking to find she'd misplaced her instrument; my father organizing a search mission he dubbed "Operation Harpsichord" and finding the elusive quarry in a closet just in time for its hungover owner to mangle her way through Mendelssohn's "Wedding March." Years later, at my cousin Jonathan's wedding, several of the groom's relatives recalled how impressed they were that my grandmother, who had been unable to find shoes to match her cranberry-colored dress, had hosted the wedding in a pair of red Keds.

After seven years and three more children, however, Mary's second marriage unraveled. A few years after Sandy's death, she moved her children back East from Lincoln, first to the Big House and then, when the November chill froze them out, to a rented home on Wings Neck. Cape Cod had not yet become the year-round place it is today; Wings Neck was all but deserted. No one seems to remember exactly how and when it first happened, but the bleak Cape Cod winter, the demands of tending five children, and the stress of a difficult divorce began to erode Aunt Mary's mental health. For years, she was in and out of hospitals. Many of her fears focused on Wings Neck; at times she insisted her family had held her captive in the Big House, and she came to believe that her beloved refuge was an evil place. For several years she refused to see her parents or her siblings. Even after she recovered, her memories of that winter were so vivid that she and her children did not set foot in the Big House for nearly two decades.

My own family, meanwhile, was threatening to implode. My parents were finding out that theirs was, in many ways, a marriage of opposites. When they had met, a few years after the war, my mother had been an eighteen-year-old nursing student in her second week of classes at Massachusetts General Hospital. Although she came from an old New England family, she had grown up on a farm in rural Maryland. A dark-haired, doe-eyed beauty—she was often told she looked like Elizabeth Taylor—she was unsophisticated, painfully earnest, and filled with artistic longings and inchoate idealism. In the vocabulary of her favorite movie, she longed to be Scarlett O'Hara, but felt fated to be practical, responsible Melanie. To her, my twenty-five-year-old father—a handsome, athletic, divorced war hero—was a Bostonian Rhett Butler. When they were introduced on a Rhode Island beach, my mother, who had never had a boyfriend, hardly dared dream she could hold his attention (especially when she remembered that she had shaved her legs only up to the knees that day). They lay on the beach and talked. And though other girls wandered by, saw Harry Colt, and joined the conversation—eventually, a Busby Berkeley pinwheel of women lay on the beach, with my father at its center—at the end of the afternoon, my father asked my mother whether he could take her out to dinner the following weekend. She didn't really believe him, but gave him her telephone number anyway. "And my God," my mother says, with a quiver of excitement, fifty years later, "he called!" (My father failed to mention that in order to pick her up at her dormitory, he'd be driving thirteen hours from his job as a salesman in Pittsburgh.)

In retrospect, the itinerary for their first date seems a bit risqué, but it was, apparently, not an unusual choice for a Harvard man in 1949. After watching the dog races at Revere Beach, they took in Sally Rand's fan dance at the Old Howard, the legendary burlesque house in Scollay Square. At dinner in the Latin Quarter, my mother, who had never had a cocktail before, ordered a Benedictine and brandy. (A nursing school friend had told her it was a sophisticated drink.) One was more than enough. In the guest room at Heath Hill, where she had been invited to spend the night, Mum got the whirlies and puked all over the monogrammed pink satin bedcover. Dad appeared at her door. "Your father was *so* sweet," Mum recalls. "He led me downstairs, washed my nightgown and sheets, and put me back to bed as if nothing had happened. . . . That was it for me."

If my mother was smitten with my father, she was no less taken with his family, especially in their summer habitat. Mum's family had never had a summer place, and, in any case, didn't put much stock in spending time together. At Wings Neck, the Colts were always drumming up tennis round-robins, playing charades, singing rounds, and listening to Grandpa read aloud from Trollope. "The Colts were just how I'd always imagined a family was supposed to be," Mum says. The Colt to whom she was especially drawn was Grandma, who espoused many of the values—artistic expression, civil rights, human equality, the importance of helping "those less fortunate"—that my mother believed in but had felt unable to voice in her own family. My grandmother, in turn, must have seen, in this eager young woman who painted, sang sweetly, and was filled with unformed longings, a less-polished echo of her younger self.

My mother worked hard to fit in, perhaps never more so than one summer during the Labor Day race, the biggest sailing event of the year. It was a windy afternoon—near-gale conditions—and as Sandy and Jimmy were heading out the Gut past the Big House in the Herreshoff Twelve that Grandma had rented for the summer, the rest of the family, watching from the porch, heard them shout, "We need more weight!" My mother, who, though beautiful, wasn't built along the lines of the greyhound-like Colts, remembers that everyone immediately looked at her. Perhaps seeing this as a chance to cinch her place in the family, she dashed barefoot to the Bluff, hobbled over the rocks, and swam out through the breakers. But the boat was rocking wildly in the wind and each time she tried to pull herself over the coaming, a wave would knock her back. Fifteen-year-old Sandy, shouting, "Hurry, Lisa, we've got to get to the start—put your foot *there*," took the tiller, while Jimmy tried to haul my mother in. The longer it took, the more desperately Mum tried and the more foolish she felt. "I knew that Sandy and Jimmy, who were so lean and athletic, wouldn't have to be pulled over the side like a fat fish; they would somehow have *sprung* from the water into the boat."

Finally, with a huge tug from Jimmy, my mother fell into the cockpit. During the race that followed, she huddled wherever the weight was needed, keeping as still as possible, slipping in her bare feet and falling whenever Jimmy tacked.

Miraculously, they won the race. (A Hallowell crossed the line first, but was disqualified for rounding a mark the wrong way.) At the end-of-year prize ceremony at the Buzzards, Jimmy and Sandy were awarded an enormous pennant, which has occupied a place of honor on the barn wall ever since. It was the biggest sailing triumph in Colt family history, but over the years my mother's contribution was boiled down to a family joke: the Time Sandy and Jimmy Won the Labor Day Race with Lisa as Ballast.

Eventually, my mother found that the perfect family she'd married into wasn't all it seemed. As Grandma increasingly confided in my mother her disappointments and frustrations about her marriage, Mum came to realize that in many ways, these complaints echoed feelings she had about her own marriage. Although Dad had a good job, it kept him on the road about two weeks a month. When he was home, he also found ways to be less than fully present. "Harry arrived late last night, drunk," Sandy had noted in her Wings Neck calendar when she was thirteen. Dad was no more a member of the fifties' three-martini-lunch culture than many of his friends, but we'd know the moment he walked in the door of our suburban home if he'd been drinking: his handsome face was a little puffy and pink, his eyes glassy, his laugh a bit too quick and falsely hearty.

"What's wrong?" he'd say. "What are you looking at?"

"You," my mother would say softly.

"What's wrong?" he'd say. "There's nothing wrong."

He'd look to his children for support, but he couldn't meet our eyes, nor we his. He'd shrug with annoyance and head upstairs. Later, when we were in bed, we'd hear our parents argue at a volume that, while falling short of a Tennessee Williams play, was nevertheless unusual in our family. On several occasions, it was accompanied by the crash of a lamp thrown by my mother. At Big House dinners, my father was sometimes as "under the weather" as my grandfather.

Dad never stopped being a good provider (rising at 4 A.M. to reach his office by five) and an extraordinary father (willing to throw fly balls into the summer sky until long past dark). But we could sense the distance growing between my parents. My mother clung to her image of the dazzling man she'd met on the beach and the dazzling family she'd joined. She tried to be a good corporate wife, to attend the Harvard football games, to make the chicken à la king for the office dinner parties, to laugh at the familiar knock-knock jokes. She threw herself into the role of caretaker—not only for her four sons but for her in-laws. "I threw myself into caretaking," she says, "because I didn't have your father to throw myself into." Her sadness surfaced in her art. She wrote poems about lone seagulls flying to distant lands, sang mournful Joan Baez ballads, painted faces of ghostly, sad-eyed women on the smooth, round stones she collected on the Bluff. For a time, she was addicted to diet pills. Then, in the mid-sixties, spurred in part by *The Feminine Mystique*, she began to refashion her own life. She became an art teacher, took writing workshops, taught guitar, marched for civil rights and against the Vietnam War. She acted on all the liberal causes she and my grandmother had talked about for years. While Mum was, as her friends put it, "finding herself," she was moving further away from Dad. He continued to go to his football games and cocktail parties; she wrote folk masses and began to meditate. It was a marriage that, in its divergent faces, was beginning to resemble my grandparents'.

My parents' conflicts had been camouflaged in the vast labyrinth of the Big House, where everything, as in a game of Sardines, could be concealed. Our rooms in the kitchen wing were far from our parents' bedroom in the main part of the house, so we heard nothing of their lives once we were tucked in bed. My grandparents served as a further buffer;

to avoid disturbing them, my family figuratively—and often literally—tiptoed around the house. Within the confines of Hidden House, there could be few secrets; indeed, troubles seemed to reverberate within its plywood walls, which permitted us to hear every word of every argument. At night, I lay staring up at the old newspapers that lay between the springs and the mattress of the upper bunk (where my brother Harry lay just as silently), trying to focus on the old headlines—WILLIAMS LASHES TWIN HOMERS IN RED SOX LOSS; STEVENSON TO RUN FOR PRESIDENT—in the fading light, to distract myself from the harsh words or, worse, the loaded silence in the next room.

We children were beginning to pull away, too. Harry, the eldest and most aware of our parents' discord, hid out on the third floor of the Big House with a stack of Oz books or trudged off with the ball bag to the Benedicts' tennis court and hit hundreds of fierce serves. Ned, on the other hand, grew ever more devoted to his grandparents, ever more tied to the Big House. Mark, the youngest by six years, was often left to fend for himself in a place where the grown-ups who might have been fending for him were preoccupied with their own problems. Later, I felt sad that his experience of the Big House had been so different from mine, that he had not known his grandparents in happier days. But I was entering adolescence, and I was too self-obsessed to notice much beyond my own self.

My attempts at teenagerhood had been uniformly inept. My experience with illicit substances had been limited to choking on rum-soaked pipe tobacco with a friend at the Big Cove. My sexual CV consisted of ogling Peter Arno's scantily clad nightclub girls in *New Yorker* cartoons, rereading the racy parts of Updike's *The Centaur*, and stealing furtive glimpses of the arc where the Day-Glo orange of our baby-sitter's bikini top met the puffer-belly white of the breasts it struggled to contain. But then a new family, third cousins of ours, built a house down the road. They were from Pittsburgh, which, on Boston-dominated Wings Neck, made them appear sinfully exotic, and the four children seemed to do all the things adolescents were supposed to do, according to the songs I listened to on the radio—and, what's more amazing, they were willing to do them with me. I smoked my first joint in one of their bedrooms, muffling my coughs with a pillow while "We're Not Gonna Take It" drowned out the sound of their mother downstairs, calling up to ask what was happening but never daring to come up and see. (How we howled knowingly when Daltrey got to the line "Hey you smokin' mother nature, this is a bust"!) Instead of being offered an occasional sip of Dad's Carling, I found myself draining cans of Schlitz from the six-packs my cousins had commissioned a mature-looking sixteen-year-old to buy at the package store, and, as it warmed my insides and melted my fear, I felt a sudden kinship with my father.

One day at the Big Cove, my cousins introduced me to a friend visiting from New Jersey. Linda was a tall girl with straight blonde hair and unblinking wide blue eyes accented by what I later realized was eye shadow, something I'd never seen up close. She chewed gum. When my cousin told me, "She likes you," I was thrown into a paroxysm of excitement and panic. What was I supposed to do? One night at the Big Cove, as we were drinking beer and listening to her brother play Tom Paxton's "Talking Vietnam Pot Luck Blues" on the guitar, the others grew restless and said they were heading back to the house. "It's such a beautiful night," Linda said, turning to me. "Wanna stay on the beach a little longer?" What followed was, in retrospect, all very tame: a slow and—on my part, at least—fumbling expedition toward the previously unachieved Everest of what I believed, but wasn't certain, constituted third base. But for a teenager whose hands-on sexual experience to that point had all been solo, it was so memorable that even now, at the age of forty-two, when I recall the moment I negotiated my way past the rough snap and zipper of her Levi's and crossed the Maginot Line of her black cotton underwear, I get a little flustered.

I wouldn't know until years later, when I took a course in college on the Romantic poets, that the touch of the breeze, the wash of the waves on the sand, the immersion of the body in the ocean, had long been considered metaphors for sexual intimacy. Lying on the sand at the Big Cove, dimly aware of the gurgle of boats on their moorings and the groan of the dock as it lolled on its pilings, I thought I'd invented the connection. Oh, how I ached for her! Indeed, the extent of my yearning was matched only by the speed with which I found an excuse to hurry home as soon as she'd relieved that ache with the confident touch of her attenuated fingers, which culminated in pale pink–painted nails. I'd steal back along the familiar paths to Hidden House, trying not to wake my parents as I groped in the dark, slightly drunk, to my bed.

Linda knew nothing about poetry, she couldn't play tennis, she signed her love notes with smiley faces, and in the light of day we had little to say to each other. I lived in fear that we'd run into my parents and I'd have to introduce her. But each evening, as I ate dinner in Hidden House with my family, I'd listen for the shuffle of footsteps coming up the path as my Pittsburgh cousins came to collect me. On the beach, I would drink two beers as quickly as I could so that when Linda asked if I wanted to sit with her awhile, I wouldn't be too inhibited to say yes. "Heaven is something with a girl in summer," wrote Robert Lowell. Indeed, it seemed to me that this kind of heaven was possible *only* in summer. There was something about the wind and the water—or was it the beer and the pot?—that melted shyness and made me think I might actually be like other teenagers. In summer, I could take chances I never would at any other time, knowing that in a matter of weeks, we'd be whirled back to our separate, winter lives. (Indeed, I felt so emboldened that the following winter, I wrote to a girl I had long found attractive but been too timid to speak to, and magnanimously informed her that while I already had a summer girlfriend, the position of winter girlfriend was still available, and that I would look favorably on her application. I failed to understand why I never got a response.)

It ended unhappily, of course. Eventually, I ignored Linda so thoroughly by day that she began spending her evenings with someone else, a shaggy-haired Cataumet boy I'd known in sailing class. When I confronted her, she wept and asked me why I had paid so little attention to her. I had no answer. Now I realize that I had learned from the example of my own parents—years of watching Mum hug Dad and Dad freeze up—that intimacy was something to be feared. Dad had learned the same thing from his parents. That I was able to pay any attention to her at all, I now realize, had something to do with the gum chewing. She wasn't one of us.

The summer after I graduated from high school, I spent a week with my grandparents. One of my uncles was also there, and we had not gotten along. After returning home, I was surprised to receive a letter from my grandfather. "My dear and gallant sir," it began. Without blaming my uncle or even mentioning his name, Grandpa said that I had handled an awkward situation "admirably" and that he loved me very much.

Two months later Grandpa had a heart attack and died in his bed at the Big House. He was seventy-two. Not long ago, as I was looking through the guest book, a slip of paper fluttered out. On it, Grandma had written in her delicate script, "On Nov. 10, Henry F. Colt died at dawn, quietly. He and I had voted for Senator McGovern on Nov. 7." It tickled me that she had chosen to note that her husband had done his civic duty before he died—in support of a cause I found fittingly noble and doomed. And I was glad that after fifty years of marriage in which they had grown so far apart, my grandmother had chosen to remember something they had done together.

At his funeral in Boston's Emmanuel Church, the pews were filled with the high school and college chums—now headmasters, ministers, judges—who had once looked up to him as their leader. One of them read Yeats's poem "In Memory of Major Robert Gregory," whose haunting refrain—*Soldier, scholar, horseman, he, / And all he did done perfectly / As though he had but that one trade alone.*—struck me at first as a strange choice. I was thinking of the man who had sat for decades on the piazza, unable to rouse himself to action. But as I listened, I remembered other men: the Christer who found his cause by working hundred-hour weeks to equip the army in wartime *(soldier)*; the wit, polished at St. Paul's and Harvard, who never stopped glittering *(scholar)*; the athlete who excelled in so many arenas, but whose greatest pleasure was riding on a spring morning over the fields of his beloved Geneseo *(horseman)*.

The following summer, my family filed through the woods where Grandpa had spent so much of his time doing battle with the catbrier, to a small, quiet glade he had cleared, and buried a handful of his ashes.

XV

The Big Cove

THIS MORNING Susannah leads us single file through the woods
behind Hidden House. The path—the last viable segment of the
path that once stretched the entire length of the Neck—takes us past the
Benedicts' tennis court, winds by the Storers' barn, and emerges at a
brief pebbly stretch, curving around a cove in which a few dozen small
wooden boats nod at their moorings. Unlike the Bluff, this beach actually has sand—although, as if it had been designed to reflect WASP
values, none too much. There are two docks, a rickety swing whose
frame is made of telephone poles, a raft with a diving board, and the
shabby one-room shanty that constitutes the Buzzards Yacht Club. Several dinghies, bottoms up, lie on the shore. At midtide the beach is nearly
empty. A mother watches her children dig a moat; an older man rows out
to bail his boat; a cormorant floats above. We drop our towels and buckets and head for the water.

A visitor to Wings Neck might believe the peninsula to be uninhabited.
Except for an occasional car or jogger, people are seldom visible from the
road. The only way to know whether someone is in residence is by noting the presence or absence of trash cans at the end of the driveway on
Thursday morning—or by coming to the community beach, whose informality is so pronounced that it doesn't even have an agreed-upon name.
Most people call it South Beach, others call it the Boat Beach or the Big
Beach. To us it has always been the Big Cove. In a place where the social
scene consists of spur-of-the-moment tennis matches or chance meetings
on the paths, where cocktail parties are rare, and where I doubt the word
"brunch" has ever been used, the Big Cove is the center of Wings Neck's
action. It is where, at the beginning of the summer, people come to find

out who died over the winter, who had another grandchild, and, with increasing frequency, who is putting his or her house on the market. It is where each new generation of children is knit together by digging in the sand, learning to swim, playing sponge tag, and performing cannonballs off the dock. It is where teenagers go at night to do all the things their parents don't want them to do, where my brother Ned and his friends used to fishtail their cars, where I drank beer and made out with Linda. It is where adults go to take out their boats, to catch up on the news, to watch their children learn to swim. It is where, at summer's end, people come to say good-bye.

As the tide rises, more people are drawn to the Big Cove, some in station wagons, some on rickety bicycles, some on foot. They settle down on the same swatch of sand each day, each summer, with the precision of migrating swallows. (Even now, I unconsciously position Anne and the children just above the tide line, a bit west of the beach's center: the space my family used to stake out thirty years ago.) A middle-aged woman with curly brown hair sits against the jetty, reading a paperback, looking up occasionally to survey the scene. I see her there in the identical place each day. The only thing that changes is the title of the paperback. When I was young, this spot was taken by another woman, the mother of a friend—her presence so familiar that some of the Neck's children called her "the Beach Lady." She was there nearly every day, every year, leaning against the same rock, her towel, thermos, and straw bag encircling her like a protective moat. She died several years ago, but for a long time thereafter, whenever we arrived at the Big Cove, I half expected to see her. For several summers, as if in homage, no one sat against that particular rock. One day, the brown-haired woman tentatively settled there; doubtless, years from now, she too will be known, by a new generation of children, as the Beach Lady.

At high tide, there are more than a dozen people here. A few old salts in billed sailing caps and khaki shorts stand on the jetty, leaning on the railing, evaluating the passing boats. Several teenage girls in bikinis loll like seals on the diving-board dock, stirring themselves only to reapply their suntan lotion. A younger girl, lying on her stomach, fishes from the finger dock, gazing down into the water. The old guard, the grandsons and granddaughters of the men who bought Wings Neck, arrive for their daily swim; at high tide the journey over the boat shells and pebbles is not quite so arduous. The women still wear the kind of one-piece floral bathing suits with pleated skirts that they wore in the fifties—for all I know they're the same suits—and white rubber bathing caps that make them look like floating eggs. Picking their way across the sand, they wade into the water, where they perform a slow, deliberate breaststroke until they're a few yards offshore. Treading water, they peer quietly about them, carefully keeping their heads above the surface despite their bathing caps, with the dignified bearing of swans. The men float on their backs, chatting. The air is filled with familiar sounds: the mournful bray of the finger dock as it shifts on its iron pilings; the squawk of the rusty swings as Susannah soars high; the hum of the wind in the boat stays; the occasional flap of sails hoisted in the breeze; the thrum of a passing motorboat; the purr of the waves shed by that motorboat washing on the beach; the chortle of Henry, holding Anne's hand as he stands in the water with those waves lapping at his ankles.

The entire scene is so familiar, so languorous, it seems to be playing in slow motion. It has changed little since my youth, except for a generational shift that causes something like vertigo. Instead of station wagons lined up in the sand behind the beach, there are minivans and SUVs. Instead of my brothers and me splashing in the shallow water, it's my children. Instead of my father and his friends, it's my friends and I, hair thinning and stomachs paunching, who stand with our arms folded, shifting the sand back and forth with our feet, talking about someone's new boat, about how hot it must be up in Boston, about how time seems to go faster the older you get.

In midmorning, a gold Jaguar zips down the long driveway to the beach. Two young couples get out and survey the scene. Although no one looks up for more than a moment, everyone is aware of their presence. The equilibrium is slightly ruffled. "Anyone know who these people are?" mutters Dr. Hallowell, grandson of the Civil War hero who rode his white horse to the post office each morning, himself now stooped with age. Walking out on the jetty, the couples argue about whether the beach is sandy enough. "It's fine," I hear one of the women say. "I could put out my little chair with short legs and be happy right here." Nevertheless, they get back in their Jaguar and drive off, dust flaring in their wake. It takes a moment for the dust—and the beach—to settle.

The New York boat—the steamer that once churned through the Cape Cod Canal en route to Manhattan—made its last run in 1936; six years later, pressed into service as a troop transport, it was torpedoed and sunk by German U-boats off the English coast. By then the Dude train from Boston was long gone. It made its final appearance in 1916; with war on the horizon, such luxuries were deemed unseemly. The road from Boston was paved, two steel bridges were built across the canal, and cars poured onto Cape Cod. The Woods Hole train made its final circuit in 1963, nearly a century after it began bringing summer people to the shores of Buzzards Bay—and a few months after my father showed me how to put a penny on the rail before the train came around the bend.

Cape Cod, of course, has changed a great deal since the Big House was built in 1903, or even since I first visited in the fifties. The main road through Bourne, the town in which Wings Neck is located, was once a tunnel through pine and oak; it is now encrusted with auto dealerships, party stores, discount pharmacies, fast-food outlets, and pubs. In Pocasset, the general store I once patronized with my grandfather has been replaced by a small shopping plaza with a hair salon, a gift shop, and a modest supermarket. (I note with interest that an assortment of penny candy is the centerpiece of an exhibition honoring "old-fashioned" general stores at the Bourne Historical Society.) Much of the Pocasset Golf Club, founded by Ned Atkinson and his friends in 1916, has been carved up into quarter-acre lots with ranch houses bordering a strip of macadam known as "Windsong Circle." Nearly every year a new condominium development sprouts, named for some local nineteenth-century sea captain. There are nearly three times as many people in Bourne today as there were when I was a child, an increase that mirrors the rate of growth for the Cape as a whole. The police blotter in the local newspaper, devoted in my youth to rescued cats and the occasional stolen bicycle, has been infiltrated by assault and battery, breaking and entering, domestic abuse. Each week, letters to the editor reenact the struggle, taking place in every community across Cape Cod, between those who want to develop the Cape and those who want to preserve it "the way it used to be," which is invariably defined as the moment when the letter writer first drove across the bridge.

To outsiders it may seem as if Wings Neck is one of the few places on the Cape that has managed to resist change. But that's not the way it seems to us. In my youth, the Neck's two narrow roads saw a dozen cars a day; people walked in the middle of the road, stopping to talk to a friend in a passing station wagon. Now joggers and bicyclists stream over the causeway to enjoy the Neck's shaded thoroughfares. Trash can be found on the roadside each morning; last summer, I came across a pornographic magazine someone had tossed in the woods. Residents have arrived at the Big Cove in the morning to find strangers sleeping in parked cars. People no longer leave oars in their rowboats; too many have gone missing. The Sailfish rack is nearly empty; most people keep their Sailfishes and Windsurfers in their barns. In a place where doors were never locked in summer, state-of-the-art security systems are now common. (Of course, the most notorious local crime in memory—the painting of the word EGGS above the name BENEDICT on the stone at the end of our neighbors' driveway—was committed by the teenage children of longtime Wings Neckers. When they were discovered, the perpetrators were persuaded by their parents to paint over the evidence.)

At Wings Neck Trust meetings, there is much pained discussion about how to ensure privacy without being exclusive, or rather— although no one puts it like this—how to be exclusive without seeming to be. No one wants to go the way of Scraggy Neck and Chapoquoit, where private guards stationed at the entrance have been hired to stop every car that crosses the causeway, ensuring that only residents and their guests are allowed any farther. But over the past few years several steps have been taken. These days a spotlight shines harshly on the Big Cove all night, discouraging vandalism as well as the kind of furtive romantic groping that made the beach at midnight so alluring to me as a teenager. The one-room yacht club is kept padlocked. Parking stickers have been issued to residents and temporary passes made available to their guests. Nevertheless, so many unstickered cars were appearing at the Big Cove that a self-appointed "security committee" of residents began to paste recalcitrant vehicles with no-trespassing stickers, coated with a special glue that made them nearly impossible to remove. (The program was discontinued when one of the offending cars turned out to belong to the brother of a longtime resident.) A large sign with the words PRIVATE PROPERTY centered below the Wings Neck Trust logo (a Herreshoff Twelve) was erected at the entrance to the Neck. When that was stolen, an even larger, more sturdy, plastic-coated, graffiti-resistant sign went up in its place. (Some residents were troubled by these restrictive measures. "Why must we have that horrid sign?" wondered one elderly, longtime Wings Necker. "Instead of saying 'Stop,' the sign should say 'Go—if you'd like to see the sunset over the water.'") An off-duty policeman has been hired to sit on a folding chair near the sign each Saturday night; his car, headlights on, is parked nearby so that approaching drivers are made to feel like criminals about to undergo intense grilling. Still, the outside world cannot be kept entirely at bay. Some nights in the Big House, I wake to hear a car roaring up the driveway, careering around the circle, and, with an exhalation of shouts and laughter, roaring away.

At one end of the Big Cove, a creek winds through the eelgrass to a large tidal pool we call the millpond. It is the kind of mucky, marshy place that looks desolate, but its shallows are crammed with life: quahogs, razor clams, ribbed mussels, minnows, shrimp, snails, hermit crabs, green crabs, and fiddler crabs. When I was young, I puttered around the millpond's edges, but I rarely strayed far from shore. Grandma told us that her governess, terrified of the blue claw crabs, had never let her play in the millpond. When Mum led us there to dig for cherrystones and we wiggled our hips and feet in a motion that looked not unlike the Twist (as we sang the Beatles' "Twist and Shout"), I was always apprehensive about what pinchy creatures my toes might encounter. At high tide, my friends and I paddled Sailfish boards into the millpond, but even then, gazing down at the vast, lunar stretches of the interior, I was terrified of falling off. I thought the soft, primeval gray mud must surely be quicksand, and although the water never got deeper than waist-high, I believed that in the distant corners there lurked massive crabs, twenty-foot eels, and, perhaps, some sluggish, long-dormant Jules Verne sea monster that had been swept in with the tide hundreds of years ago and had been growing ever since.

The millpond is Susannah's favorite place on Wings Neck, and she spends hours each day moving slowly up and down the creek, armed with a small plastic collecting jar. By now she knows each corner: the rocky channel favored by spider crabs, the sandy flats where baby flounder sometimes settle, the muddy nook in which ribbed mussels cluster. Compared with my own six-year-old self, Susannah is fearless. She touches crumbly moon-shell egg cases; traps jellyfish in her cupped hands; even drapes the long, gelatinous gobs we called eelskins over her shoulders like feather boas. Each afternoon she brings home a few crabs in her jar to keep overnight before returning them the next day, as if the millpond were a maritime lending library. Her latest quarry is minnows, for whose capture she is constantly dreaming up new strategies. Now, while Henry wallows in the mud revealed by the receding tide, she wanders out into the millpond and wiggles her feet in the mucky bottom. Reaching into the water, she pulls up a glistening quahog, brings it to shore, crushes it with a rock, places some of its gooey flesh in her collecting jar, and puts the jar back in the millpond. Minute after minute, she sits quietly nearby, waiting for minnows to take the bait.

Early histories of Cape Cod describe it as a place of biblical abundance, but unbridled development has had not only aesthetic but environmental consequences. Nitrogen from lawn fertilizers and new septic systems has triggered algae blooms that have smothered the eelgrass beds and ravaged the scallops, blue claw crabs, and flounder they used to shelter. Fourteen thousand five hundred acres of shellfish beds in Buzzards Bay have been closed. Where once, according to my grandmother, you could rummage through the seaweed and gather bay scallops by the bushel, there are now none to be found. (Several years back, the annual Bourne Scallop Festival had to switch to fatter, fleshier, less-savory sea scallops, which are dredged far offshore.) Where lobsters were so numerous in my great-grandfather's day that their tails were used for bait, Wings Neckers now come home empty-handed from their lobster traps more often than not; a friend has estimated that, if he factored in the license, traps, and boat fuel, each lobster he caught last summer cost him $85. Where once Grover Cleveland could haul in fish until his arms tired, the scup and tautog are now scarce, and certain species, including the puffers that so fascinated us when we were children, have disappeared entirely. The last three decades have seen four large petroleum spills in Buzzards Bay. Although grassroots organizations have mobilized to SAVE BUZZARDS BAY (as the bumper stickers we see in the Stop & Shop parking lot enjoin us), it may be too late. Warns one environmental group, "Gradually, imperceptibly, what's already been put into the ground all over Cape Cod will devastate every shellfish bed, estuary, and bay on the entire coast."

Inhabitants of Bourne have an unusually high rate of cancer. The cause, it is said, is the accumulation of solvents and jet fuel dumped by Otis Air Force Base (whose jet fighters so entranced me when I was young), which have seeped into the groundwater over the course of decades. Boat traffic in the area has multiplied, and many skippers still dump their sewage into the bay. A beach in Pocasset was recently closed to swimmers because of a high fecal coliform level. In the Big Cove's little millpond, we bemoan the paucity of quahogs and the absence of blue claw crabs. Yet any tendency on my family's part toward ecological holier-than-thouism was undermined forever a few years ago when a hurricane eroded the Bluff and exposed a large, rusty pipe—part of the original plumbing of the Big House that in Ned Atkinson's day had pumped the raw effluence of our charming old toilets into Buzzards Bay. We built a charmless new septic system.

In midafternoon, people begin to head home. Low tide has always been considered the least appetizing time to be at the beach; the water is farther away, harder to get to, and accompanied by the dank smell of decay. Indeed, as I look at the mudflats exposed by the receding water, the millpond seems a sort of maritime graveyard, littered with empty mussel shells and the corpses of eviscerated crabs. I can almost give credence to the old superstition that links low tide and mortality, a belief that goes back at least as far as the first century A.D., when Pliny, in *Historiae Naturalis*, posited that "no animal dies except upon a receding tide." In *David Copperfield*, Mr. Peggotty, the Bristol fisherman, says, "People can't die, along the coast, except when the tide's pretty nigh out. They can't be born, unless it's pretty nigh in." Even now, we call a tide at low ebb "dead low." What my family calls "low tide smell" is the odor of decomposing plants, fish, and shellfish. But as the tide recedes, the millpond is in fact revealed to be brimming with life: a sand dab that stays just ahead of our grasp; a baby sea robin we try unsuccessfully to catch; a school of minnows that tacks back and forth in precise array, flashing silver with each turn; an algae-covered spider crab Susannah names "Hairy Harry."

A nearby bank seems to quiver. I assume it is a trick of the light—the sun shimmering on the eelgrass—and then realize that hundreds of fiddler crabs are emerging to feed. (When the tide comes in again, they will retreat into their burrows, plugging the entrances with mud.) We give chase, and they scramble away, the males brandishing their outlandish Popeye claw, which they use to court female crabs and to defend against predators, including six-year-old girls. Last year, Susannah didn't dare pick one up, but this year she is determined to succeed. Just as she is about to grab one, it folds its claw close against its chest and slides sideways into its thumb-sized hole. We turn our backs and feign lack of interest; eventually, the crab sidles back out, and Susannah pounces.

On a 1906 map of Wings Neck my brothers gave to Anne and me as a wedding present, the 395 acres of Trust land is divided into sixteen lots. A 1988 map divides it into nearly a hundred. There are many more driveways disappearing into the woods than there were in my youth, and some of those that had only one sign nailed to a tree now have two or three or four. The thwack of tennis balls and the chirp of cicadas now compete with the rasp of chain saws. Each year more boats crowd the bay, an increasing number of them made not of wood but of fiberglass, with motors, not sails. As I sit on the Big House porch, I no longer know the names and owners of all the boats going in and out of the harbor. We don't dare swim to Atkinson's Buoy, the channel marker named for my great-grandfather that lies a few hundred yards off the Bluff. A longtime resident tells me he was at the Big Cove last weekend; although it was crowded, he didn't recognize a single face.

Although no one mentions it, there has also been an unmistakable shift in the demographics of Wings Neck. In their 1904 prospectus extolling its desirability, my great-grandfather and his partners had assured prospective buyers that property restrictions would discourage "undesirable elements." (In other words, the land was divided into lots so large that only the rich could afford them.) These undesirable elements were not specified, but the desirable elements at whom the prospectus was aimed knew this was a code phrase for people who didn't come from what were known as "prominent Boston families." Initially, this was easily accomplished; the syndicate sold estate sites by word of mouth to cousins, college classmates, business partners, and clubmates. Neighbors in Wings Neck were neighbors in Boston. Reflecting on her cozy childhood summers, my grandmother wrote: "I suppose my mother thought we all needed a 'wider view' so we had one summer a house in South Dartmouth, and often visited relations at Matunuck, R.I., and Naushon." Her wider view, therefore, consisted of even-more-exclusive summer haunts, all of which were stocked with relatives. In 1949, my grandparents sold a parcel of land to a Boston doctor who was no one's brother, uncle, or even third cousin once removed. The clucking of tongues was nearly audible. And when this interloper erected a one-story snow-white cube, as shocking as a Picasso among John Singer Sargents, those tongues said, "I told you so." That the house was said to be designed by a student of Frank Lloyd Wright's made no difference—made it, if anything, even worse: after all, that Wright fellow was from Chicago.

Since then, as trust funds have dwindled, more Old Money has been replaced by New Money. Today, the $84,350 my grandfather and his friends paid for 395 acres wouldn't buy an acre, with or without a water view. Hoping to slow the proliferation of new houses, a coalition of residents has been trying to buy up property before it comes on the market, while the Wings Neck Trust is attempting to persuade owners to put land under conservation restriction. But the horse is already out of the barn. Last summer I went lobstering with a longtime resident who gave me an informal tour of the north side of the Neck, pointing out the new houses. A generation ago, newcomers would have been identified by family—such and such a place was bought by So-and-so Cabot who had married So-and-so Hallowell. These days, newcomers are described by occupation. My guide showed me a house recently built by a developer and an old estate refurbished by the largest fish wholesaler in New Bedford. The new houses are no longer hidden away at the ends of long driveways. They have carefully landscaped gardens, wooden entrance gates, fenced-in yards so well manicured they could be used for tournament croquet, house numbers painted on oars that have never touched salt water, labyrinthine play structures (in a place where children have always used rocks for jumping and trees for swinging), and, in one case, even though Buzzards Bay is no more than fifty yards away, a heated swimming pool.

Not everyone finds these aesthetic changes undesirable. Several years ago, a new Wings Neck resident thinned the woods on his property, cutting out the catbrier and the underbrush and leaving only the larger trees, so the sunlight could filter through. There was a certain amount of grumbling at the Big Cove, but each year since then, a few more residents—including some of the grumblers—have followed his example. There have also been rumors that several owners have been systematically clearing their beaches of rocks and boulders in an attempt to expose large stretches of sand, something never before seen in these parts.

While residents have been thinning the woods, they have been letting the paths that once stitched the Neck together grow wild. Indeed, although there are more neighbors, there may be less neighborliness. The boat race schedule has dwindled, and there hasn't been a Neck-wide game of Capture the Flag in years. There are signs that the inhabitants of Wings Neck no longer share the same values. A recent buyer built a grand new house blocking his neighbor's view of the water; another resident, despite protests on both aesthetic and environmental grounds, built a deepwater dock in his backyard, only a hundred yards from the communal deepwater dock at the Big Cove.

I remember the fuss back in the late seventies, when a Boston banker bought one of the Neck's oldest estates. He poured money into the property—too much money, people said—thinning out the woods, pruning the hedges, cutting down trees. One evening, as his neighbors were settling down to cocktails on their porches and watching the sun set over Buzzards Bay, they were startled by an extraordinary sound: the blare of rock music and the laughter of what sounded like hundreds of people at a very lively party. They had no doubt where the noise was coming from. The next morning, a delegation of tribal elders that included my father invited the banker for a chat on the Big House piazza. Over ginger ale, they talked about the fragile ethos of Wings Neck, about the way things had always been done—the word "haven" was used—and extracted a promise that such a breach would never occur again.

I was at the Big House that night, and I knew that behind the word "haven" lay the unmentioned fact that the banker's money was new, and that his neighbors, a studiously tolerant bunch, were magnanimously prepared to welcome him—as long as he acted as if it were old. At least he was from Boston, and thus theoretically amenable to reason. One Wings Necker, a man who could remember back to the days when the iceman still made deliveries along the paths, recently mused to his family, "Some Texan might buy one of these houses and change this place overnight."

On the Neck, of course, fear of change is nothing new. "As others bought property and built houses, we almost looked upon them as 'intruders,'" wrote a longtime resident in a privately printed history of Wings Neck. "People put up signs at the ends of their driveways and everything became more organized. It was no longer the simple life we had once become used to." She was writing about her childhood on Wings Neck before the First World War.

In the late afternoon, the sun drops behind the pines on the far side of the millpond. The surface of the water takes on a new clarity, perfectly mirroring the yellow-green grass, flecked here and there by patches of sea lavender. Gazing at the millpond, I can easily imagine that it hasn't changed since Judah Wing harvested salt hay for his cattle here in the nineteenth century, or even since the Wampanoags, centuries earlier, dug up quahogs to cut into wampum. (Even this, I know, is an illusion; since I was a child, the serpentine channel from harbor to pond has gradually been straightening itself out, carving an ever-more-direct path to the millpond.)

We are the only ones left on the beach. The tide is midlow again. We have been here most of the day. It is time to head home for supper. Susannah carefully opens her collecting jar and releases the hermit crabs she's amassed. They scramble away in what she calls a "hermie parade." Now she returns two crabs to the jar, which she clutches to her chest as we walk back through the woods to the Big House. As we leave, a great blue heron settles in a far corner of the millpond. A gull drops a clam over and over again, until it shatters on the rocks.

XVI

Missing Cards

TRYING to track down an elusive cricket in the kitchen this morning, I remove from the wall a large, framed photograph of some distant galaxy, taken in 1920, that has hung over one of the nonworking stoves as long as I can remember. I don't find the cricket, but I do find, on the back, in my grandmother's handwriting, the comment, "Nebulae in Orion—A great picture to live with! M.A.C. 1973." It is one of dozens of notes I've come across that Grandma made as she wandered through the Big House during the year after Grandpa's death, in a spate of sorting, exploring, assessing, identifying. She annotated old photo albums, putting names to the faces of her long-dead ancestors. She resumed work on the family genealogy. She updated her address file, adding entries that indicated the direction of her life: the death dates of friends, the place to buy hearing aids, the place to buy canes. She wrote on the backs of paintings the names of people to whom she intended to leave them, and she inscribed her opinions of books inside their front covers ("Too much a travelogue," she wrote in her copy of *Three Wise Virgins,* a biography of Brahmin wives). She sorted through the playing cards, so that even now, several decks are accompanied by slips of paper that say "Two cards missing: One of Hearts, Two of Diamonds, 1973." (Of course, we haven't thrown these decks out. We'd probably keep them anyway, but because they're annotated by Grandma, they're incontestably sacred.) It was, perhaps, the typical stocktaking of a new widow, but it was almost as if she were attempting to get her bearings by labeling her world.

I had always believed that Grandpa's deepest fear—that his wife's mental health was so fragile she needed his constant attention—had been exaggerated, perhaps to justify his own lack of enterprise. But he may have been right. The first few years after his death, Grandma fared reasonably well. During the winter, she lived down the street from us in a small brick house that she and Grandpa had bought a few years before his death. She continued going out to dinner, to the theater, to the symphony. She attended plays at the Nucleus Club and poetry workshops at the Unitarian church. But without her husband, she was a flame without a moth. Her children tried to persuade her to move into an apartment in downtown Boston, to be nearer her friends. But always, on the verge of moving in—in one instance, after paying three months' advance rent—she found some reason to back out. During the summer, when she could hold court in the Big House, surrounded by family, Grandma seemed more at home. Even there, though, an undercurrent of restlessness and melancholy circulated beneath her determined smile. One cold, damp autumn morning, sitting on the living room couch, she started crying and couldn't stop. "I had never seen grief like that," recalls my mother. "It went on and on for about three days, just pouring out. There was no way of making it better; you just had to sit with it. It surprised you because you had a sense that it came from so deep and so far back."

Despite many sessions with psychiatrists and regimens of antidepressants, Grandma grew more and more despondent. One night during the summer of 1975, my thirteen-year-old brother Mark, sleeping in Grandpa's Dressing Room, awakened to find Grandma standing naked at his bedside. She held a first aid kit. "I was worried you might be hurt," she said. "I thought I might be able to help you." Was this her way of saying that *she* was hurt and needed help? Was it her way of trying to be useful? Did she think that Mark was Grandpa? As her behavior became increasingly erratic, everyone in the house started living on tenterhooks. One of the large kitchen knives disappeared from the magnetic strip to the right of the sink. Everyone suspected that Grandma had taken it, but no one wanted to accuse her directly. My mother finally found it in Grandma's Bedroom. Thereafter, the sharp knives were locked away.

One midweek night, when Dad was in Boston, Mum was startled from sleep by the clanging of a bell. She hurried down the hall toward the noise, which by now included the sounds of crashing bodies, shattering glass, and Emily, the college student hired as my grandmother's companion that summer, screaming for help. In the hallway bathroom, Grandma was smashing the window with a large bronze bell, the bell Grandpa had used to ring the grandchildren in to dinner. As Mum struggled with her, Grandma thrashed about with surprising strength. Eventually Mum was able to wrestle her into the bedroom, where she pried the bell from her hand. Grandma sat on the bed, rocking and muttering; it was apparent that she had no idea who she was or what had just happened. Mum gave her a dose of the Haldol that had been prescribed for Grandma and then called Sister Hallowell, a family friend who lived a few houses down the road. (Sister's given name was Elizabeth; I never knew whether "Sister" was the product of her religion or of the incestuous spirit that led Boston Brahmins to view one another as one big family.) In the staid world of Wings Neck, Sister was known as someone who could "shake things up." A social worker and a practicing Quaker (she and her husband, Johnny, the celebrated sailor, called each other "thee" and "thou"), she had a gentle, breathy voice, a gift for listening, and a reputation for frankness. When Sister arrived that night, she pulled back the pink satin quilt and climbed into bed next to my grandmother. Wrapping her arms around her, she soothed her until she fell asleep.

In the morning, my father drove down to Wings Neck and brought Grandma to our house in Dedham to wait until a bed was available at McLean.

"One of the so-called Ivy League of mental hospitals," as a former staff member described it to me, McLean had since its founding in 1811 been a refuge for generations of what Robert Lowell, himself a frequent visitor, referred to in a poem as "Mayflower screwballs." (The definition of a proper Bostonian, it used to be said, was someone who lived on Beacon Hill and had an uncle in McLean.) Ten miles west of Boston, its Georgian brick buildings are set on 240 acres of the kind of gently rolling hills, landscaped by Frederick Law Olmsted, that makes golf course architects salivate. (Indeed, McLean may be the only mental hospital in the country to have had its own nine-hole course, available to patients well enough to be trusted with a club.)

In 1975, when my grandmother was admitted, McLean held a certain romantic allure for me and a great many other aspiring poets. Although it was hospital policy never to divulge the names of its patients, it was common knowledge that Lowell, Sylvia Plath, and James Taylor were alumni. To my twenty-one-year-old self, McLean seemed an indispensable entry on a literary résumé, a bucolic writers' colony nearly indistinguishable from Yaddo, except that instead of Beaujolais at twilight, Thorazine was served around the clock. That spring, after years of manic-depressive episodes, Lowell had made his long-awaited return to teaching at Harvard. I audited his advanced poetry seminar. Although his manner was mild and distant, it seemed as if a storm were perpetually brewing in that Rushmore-sized head, which was encircled by long, unkempt hair the color of the cigarette smoke that swirled around it. Whenever Lowell missed a class, we wondered whether he was back in McLean. Years later, I spent some time there on a magazine assignment, and my romantic illusions dissolved. All I could think of was how much Grandma must have suffered.

Her doctors diagnosed manic depression, and gave her Thorazine and other antipsychotics that eliminated her hallucinations but left her groggy. She spent her days among former debutantes and Harvard men of her era who moved through the halls, slumped and broken, unable to recognize one another. She had always longed to do something useful with her hands, and in art therapy, she made a needlepoint hanging with fat, uneven stitches and knitted a pink-and-blue acrylic scarf, lacy with unraveling yarn. On my father's visits, all she could ask was when she would be leaving. I wonder whether she feared she might be left there for years, as she had been at Butler. One day I received a letter addressed in her once-delicate handwriting, now so shaky it was nearly illegible. When I opened the envelope, a ragged slip of paper fell out. On it were written the plaintive words, "Please come when you can. I am at the Hospital of Mercy and Compassion known as McLean."

Grandma would spend the next four years in and out of McLean. She'd be perfectly fine for months—planning a luncheon party, heading to Symphony Hall to hear Ozawa conduct the BSO in Rachmaninoff, engaging in a lucid discussion of the influence of C. S. Lewis's faith on his work. When she accompanied my parents on a business trip to Holland and France, visiting the Rijksmuseum, dining with friends on the Champs-Élysées, no one could have guessed that three months earlier she'd been unable to speak a coherent sentence. For several months, she even lived alone in an apartment on Commonwealth Avenue, from which, armed with her senior citizen's pass, she ventured forth on the subway (a mode of transportation she hadn't used in decades, if ever) to shop on Newbury Street or lunch at the Chilton Club. At other times, however, the woman a teacher had once described as possessing "a goddess-like quality" was drugged into a stupor. It was like seeing a butterfly trying to move underwater. But if, in frustration, she stopped taking her medications, her self-possession dissolved into terrifying hallucinations that usually heralded a return to McLean, from which she emerged each time a little more shaky, a little more fragile. How brave she was! It was inspiring, if poignant, to see how tenaciously she kept bouncing back, trying to overcome through sheer force of will something she couldn't charm away.

In retrospect, I can see that Grandma's mind was more apt to become unhinged at the Big House, a repository of memories, good and bad, that were all too easily stirred up. During the summer of 1976, I stayed in the Sunny Room while working as a singing waiter in a Falmouth restaurant. I remember how quietly she moved through the house, like a ghost. I'd walk into a room, thinking I was alone, and discover her there, staring in silence. It would not be far-fetched to say she haunted the house. Although my family went about the usual activities—swimming, tennis, Wiffle Ball—we were in a state of constant tension, hoping that when Grandma came downstairs she'd be coherent. Once, when I introduced a friend to her, she informed him calmly, "It is Tuesday, therefore the wind is from the west." She often spoke in rhyme. Sometimes when Katy, a young family friend hired to help her that summer, brought up her breakfast tray, laden with the foods she'd just asked for, she'd refuse it wordlessly. The rattle of the southwest wind through the house, a sound that had once soothed her, now unsettled her. Only when swimming did she seem at ease, pulling herself rhythmically away from shore, as if by memory, while Katy sat on the Bluff calling, "Mrs. Colt, Mrs. Colt, don't go too far out!"

Grandma spent much of her time sitting in the living room. Katy or Mum would sit next to her, trying to coax her out of herself. "Shall I read to you?" "How about a jigsaw puzzle?" "Would you like a cup of tea?" As the summer progressed, she stopped answering, and her delusions intensified. Once she insisted that the house was filled with snakes. Another time, she said that Uncle Jimmy was being tortured in the basement. Dad made a show of going downstairs to check. "No, everything's all right, Ma," he said when he came back. "Jimmy isn't down there. He's home in Milton. Jimmy's fine, Ma." A few weeks later Katy wrote in her journal, "Grandma's so far gone, and there's so much pain in her face." The next day, Dad drove his mother back to McLean.

All her life, Grandma had been terrified that, like her brother Edward, she'd have to have a "keeper." On several occasions, she and Grandpa had stayed with us for several months—burns from Grandpa's dropped cigarettes still pocked the bedroom floor—and in lucid moments she pleaded with my parents to let her move back in with them during the winter, suggesting she could live on the third floor with a hot plate. But Mum would have had to quit work to look after her, and she was reluctant to return to the caretaker role she was finally escaping as her children grew. "As much as I loved my mother, I just didn't think we could do it," recalls Dad. Grandma had a succession of live-in helpers: college students, young married couples, middle-aged widows, all of whom were fascinated by her sparkle and intelligence but eventually worn down by her officiousness and by the demands of her illness. The Big House guest book is rife with traces of their affection: poems written on her birthdays; long, confessional entries written on their inevitable departures. "Somehow thru love will come understanding of the realities of different generations lifestyles and comedy of errors which I've been experiencing under your roof," wrote a young hippie who had moved in with a Lhasa apso, an uncertain grip on English grammar, and an inability to cook anything more sophisticated than a grilled cheese sandwich, all of which led to crossed signals. "There is room for understanding on both counts and no ill intentions intended. Many doors of perception have opened up for me with you Mrs. Colt and a chance to know and love such a warm and intelligent person as yourself. Please forgive my faults none were intended to disrupt your life."

Things came to a head with Mrs. Reilly, a fiftyish woman whose working-class background, no-nonsense manner, and limited culinary palette brought my grandmother's snobbery to the fore. Their deteriorating relationship culminated in an argument so upsetting that the woman who had worked for nonviolence and interracial harmony slapped her surprised helper and snapped, "Don't ever talk to me that way—I've had Irish maids all my life!" (I marvel at the tenacity of her prejudice, assimilated during her childhood at Heath Hill and buried under years of liberal politics.) Not long after that, Mrs. Reilly was gone. Several months later, my father ran into a friend of hers on the street who told him that Mrs. Reilly thought often about Mrs. Colt and recalled her with fondness.

By then, we had moved Grandma into a nursing home whose high cost, relative spiffiness, and water view—although the water in question was a small lake, not the ocean—did little to assuage our guilt. A two-story brick building in the woods near the strip of clam shacks and motels we drove past each summer in Buzzards Bay, the "home" was only ten miles from the Big House: a large part of the reason it had been chosen. Among the clientele were many people—retired bank presidents, former partners at venerable law firms, onetime habituées of the Chilton Club—whom in other circumstances my grandmother would have described as "attractive." Everyone in the family was encouraged when she danced one Friday night with an old grammar school classmate with whom she might well have waltzed sixty years earlier.

But Grandma made little effort to get involved. I always expected to find her surrounded by admirers in the dayroom opposite the nurses' station, where most of the residents spent their time, the more active among them watching television, playing cards, or chatting, the others dozing, talking to themselves, or staring into space. (The dayroom was said to encourage sociability; it had the added advantage of allowing the nurses to keep an eye on many patients simultaneously.) But we'd find her in her room, alone. "Ma considered herself above a lot of people for a lot of reasons and felt people there were much sicker than she was," says my father. "Then she gradually . . . became like everybody else." Except at McLean, to which the Cape Cod Nursing Home bore an uncomfortable similarity, Grandma had always been the center of attention. Here she ignored the people around her, and they, in turn, ignored her. She could be lofty with the patients and demanding with the nurses, and as she grew sicker, she occasionally threw her food. She never decorated her room—its sole personal touch was a photograph of Grandpa in his army uniform, circa 1945—because she always wanted to believe that we were about to bring her home.

How could she not have been in denial, when we were no less so? It seemed wrong for Grandma to be living inland, on the other side of the canal, in a place whose messy overflow of medicinal smells, snores, weeping, moans, and self-comforting mutters seemed so antithetical to the orderly, reserved, perfumed world in which she had always moved that I couldn't help wondering if it was a kind of punishment for repressed

Brahmins. I dreaded visiting, feared the concentrated dose of old age, the gantlet of wheelchaired elders we had to pass in the hall. "That fellow used to be head of Fidelity Trust," Dad would say softly. Then we'd walk into Grandma's room.

"Hello, Ma, it's Harry. I've come for a visit. I've brought the boys with me." We'd kiss her dutifully, tell her about our lives.

"Help me die," she'd say to Dad. "Please help me die."

"Now, Ma, don't talk like that," he'd say, patting her shoulder, in the only way he knew how to comfort her.

I was relieved when it was time to go, guilty to be leaving, guilty to be on our way back to Wings Neck.

My parents often brought Grandma over to the Big House, where they would eat lunch on the piazza. The familiar view seemed to soothe her. Sometimes Dad took her for a swim, or walked her through the empty house. My brothers and I had scattered to colleges and jobs, and when my parents weren't there, the house lay fallow for weeks at a time. For three years no one wrote a single word in the guest book.

Grandma perked up when her brother Hal came to stay at the nursing home. He had visited her there several times and, as his health failed, he, too, became a patient. Gentlemanly, chipper, and eternally optimistic, Great-Uncle Hal was a favorite with the nurses, for whom he always had a kind word or an esoteric morsel of information as he shuffled by in khaki pants, bow tie, rumpled sports jacket, and fluffy, oversized slippers (his feet were beset by bunions). His popularity raised Grandma's stock, and his devotion to her led the nurses to see her in a new light. For the first time, Hal was Grandma's claim to fame, although Hal acted as if he believed the reverse were still true. Grandma, in turn, made more of an effort, as if she had to live up to the high opinion of the doting brother who had known her in her glory days. Side by side in matching hospital chairs, they talked about things that had happened nearly a century earlier—sleigh rides on Heath Hill, wagon rides behind Major the Goat in the Big House yard, Down East sailing trips with their father on the *Bagheera*. Grandma, who no longer remembered the names of her own grandchildren, would recall the lyrics of a song she'd last sung in 1910, the color of a sweater she'd worn when she was seven, the name of a pet that had been dead seventy-five years. Inevitably, she and her brother would bicker over some small detail, like an old married couple. Grandma would insist she was right; Hal would protest briefly but ultimately defer to her, as he had all his life, gazing at his sister with misty-eyed pride. My brother Ned remembers taking them sailing at Wings Neck on a friend's Herreshoff Twelve. Wearing bulky life jackets, the octogenarians fussed companionably at each other as they tacked out the Gut past the Big House to the buoy named for their father, with whom they had sailed here so many years ago.

But Hal gradually slowed. His lanky body bent ever lower, he walked with the deliberation and decelerating pace of a windup toy whose time is running out. Eventually, his spirits, too, began to flag. One Sunday, my parents took him and Grandma to the Daniel Webster Inn in Sandwich for lunch. My mother asked Hal how he spent his time in the nursing home. "I like to recite poems I learned as a child," he said with school-boy eagerness. "I'd like to recite Keats's 'To Autumn' right now, please." He started off briskly—*Season of mists and mellow fruitfulness, / Close bosom-friend of the maturing sun*—but halfway through the long poem, he got stuck and began to weep. Not long afterward, Great-Uncle Hal, who had entered the nursing home in far better shape than my grandmother, died in his sleep.

After her brother's death Grandma had fewer moments of clarity. Soon, the distant past was all she could remember, and then even that shrank, like a boat sailing toward the horizon, and disappeared. Gradually, her mind and memory became permanently entombed by what we would recognize in retrospect as Alzheimer's disease. Now that she could no longer object, the nurses would wheel her down to the dayroom, where she sat in silence. My father still brought her to Wings Neck. I remember taking her swimming at the Big Cove. When Dad and I eased her into the water, she clung to us in terror, just as Ned and I, learning to swim, had once clung to her, and though her body was as frail as a piece of Canton china, it had a wiry strength so powerful that her clutching fingers left red marks on my arm. I worried she might drown us. But as we held her in the water—we dared not let her go—she relaxed a little and her grim expression softened. Eventually her unpredictability made even this too risky, and we'd just sit her on the piazza, where she'd stare in silence at the lawn on which her children and grandchildren had played. Sometimes we'd wheel her down the path to the Bluff and she'd look out across the bay. But there came a time when she no longer enjoyed these visits, when she would fidget and growl, and we stopped bringing her to the Big House.

Grandma's vitality had long kept her appearance youthful, but now all the difficulties of her life seemed to be expressed in her face. Her mouth curled up on one side in a sardonic twist, her lips pursed tightly, as if she had tasted something sour. The once-perfumed skin we'd loved to kiss was pale and parchment-dry. Her hair, now as sparse as the woods of Wings Neck in winter, was brushed back (to make feedings less messy) by a different nurse each day, and always had an unfamiliar look. All her life it had been said of Grandma that she ate like a bird, and now this was almost literally true; her body became so light that once, helping her from a wheelchair to her bed, and expecting a much greater weight, I stumbled and nearly fell. The woman who had looked stylish—no matter how she dressed—wore baggy, faded smocks, not much different from hospital johnnies, easy for the nurses to get on and off. Her legs were encased in brown, knee-length support stockings that reminded me of those that Martha, her cook, used to wear. She began to have nightmares, which she could not, of course, tell us about. Gazing at his mother, my father remembered how often she'd asked him to help her die, and wondered whether he should have said yes. Now, even if he'd wanted to, it was too late. She could no longer ask. And yet she clung to life with a feral stubbornness. She communicated in wordless ways: pushing her food to the floor, spitting it out abruptly. Once she tried to strike a nurse with her cane. Occasionally, she bit a nurse or a grandchild. (We learned to aim our kisses at her forehead, not her cheek.) I felt almost cheered at this evidence that somewhere within that withered husk there remained a trace of the vital, willful woman she had once been. Such was the force of her personality, and so numerous were the times she had gotten better, that until the end I half believed that the next time we visited, she'd rise from a crowd of admirers, walk toward us, and, with a glittering smile, say, "My darlings, what a *delightful* surprise."

She never did, of course. Sitting in a wheelchair, her back to us, she'd be staring toward the window, where the nurses had positioned her. My father would walk into her field of vision. "Hello, Ma, how are you feeling?" he'd ask, knowing there would be no answer. Wanting to get through it, yet not wanting to leave, he'd continue with the ritual, his voice loud and hoarse with emotion, telling her the family news, making an occasional joke. He visited at least once a week. Long after she no longer recognized the rest of us, she seemed to know who he was, to light up a little when she saw his face. And when the nurses had difficulty getting her to eat, my father could always manage it. "She'd open that mouth for him and not for anyone else," recalls Mum. Watching Dad spoon-feed pureed peas between his mother's waiting lips made me see him in a new and tender light. He may have been the only person she never bit. And sometimes, when he held her hand, she'd squeeze so strongly it seemed as if she was holding on—as my grandfather would have put it—for dear life. By then, of course, one couldn't say whether it was a conscious act of affection or a reflex, the way a newborn infant squeezes a parent's proffered finger.

Grandma hung on for so long that when Dad called me one Saturday morning in June of 1986, telling me she had died, it was hard to reach back for the memory of her earlier self. She had outlasted my grandfather by fourteen years. It seemed fitting that she had died in June, that she had waited until one more summer—her favorite season—had begun.

Ten years later, while cleaning out his files in the basement, my father came across a crinkled piece of stationery on which Grandma, in a lucid moment not long after Grandpa died, had written the following note: "I would prefer to have any notice in the papers have my full name (Mrs. Henry F. Colt—née Mary Forbes Atkinson) and have any service private; though none at all needed, and none preferred. But what I should *really* like is something like this—'It was Mary A. Colt's hope that four days after her death (let us not interfere with conventional Christian beliefs!) her friends and relatives may pause for a moment at noon, and pray for justice and peace on this planet.'" At her request, she was buried in Geneseo next to Grandpa. He had finally gotten her away from Boston.

XVII

Rain

RAIN BEGINS to fall this morning, so lightly it seems as if the Big House is surrounded by the sound of whispering. As I do the breakfast dishes, I watch a sailboat, caught out in the bay, beat back toward the harbor. There is a sudden crack of thunder, and it begins to pour. Rushing through the house, I close the windows, though the rain is so furious that the sills on the windward side are already wet. During a storm, the wind is usually out of the northeast, and on that side of the house—normally the quiet, sheltered side—the thrumming is so loud I wonder if it could be raining *inside*. The roof has so many surfaces, at so many different heights and angles (along with a Rube Goldbergian arrangement of wooden drainpipes), that the sound of the rain—like the sound of the wind on a blustery night—is different in each room. Outside the Little Nursery, drops *rat-a-tat-tat* on the tin roof. Near the Balcony Room, a one-story waterfall whooshes from a broken gutter. The drain spout next to the front porch has a puncture hole through which water roars as if shot from a fire hose.

After breakfast, we linger in the kitchen, the doors closed to retain the heat as we bake pies and muffins with blueberries we gathered in Wareham yesterday. Although the Big House sounds as if it were under attack, it feels as cozy as an ark. Indeed, with its size and patched-together feel, it *looks* a bit like Noah's ark, as depicted in one of Susannah's old picture books—although for animals, it must make do with its resident population of squirrels, mice, bats, crickets, moths, spiders, yellow jackets, and silverfish. While Susannah and a friend master the double box stitch with lanyards left over from summer camp, Henry dumps a coffee can of checkers on the floor and then puts them back in the can, one by one. Several different sets are intermixed, but they are all familiar to me, and as I retrieve errant checkers from beneath the defunct Walker & Pratt stove, I recall our childhood hierarchy: the old set made of vulcanized rubber, with concentric circles on one side and finely detailed king's crowns on the other, had a confidence-inspiring firmness and heft; the still-older wooden set seemed light and unregal; the cheap, plastic set was brought out only when we'd lost enough of the other kinds that we needed reinforcements to king an opponent. Checkers, like many other things, was better when it was accompanied by the sound of rain.

When I was young, rainy days were an excuse to take advantage of all the things the inside of the Big House had to offer. The mission-style daybed in the dining room made a fine galleon for games of pirates, and its blue cushions were large and firm enough to serve as corsairs. The oak chest in the Playroom was stuffed with costumes—a peach-colored gingham dress that had belonged to my great-grandmother, a cream-colored riding jacket of my great-grandfather Colt's, hats from my grandmother's flapper days—with which we'd play dress-up and put on plays for our tolerant parents and grandparents. The drawers in the living room cabinet were crammed with board games: Parcheesi, Scrabble, Monopoly—in older and more evocatively faded editions than those in our winter home. There were at least a dozen packs of cards. The most sought after had a royal-blue border with a star-studded blue diamond in the center; slightly less desirable was the jet-black pack with silver edges and the initials LTB, which, despite their slick, sinful look and air of mystery—who was LTB? a famous cardsharp?—tended to stick at crucial moments, or the cream-colored Chilton Club pack, which, though elegant-looking, carried a feminine stigma that made it fine for Solitaire but undesirable for games of War. The deck of last resort was a hokey-looking, fire-engine-red pack adorned with snowflakes, which was so sticky that, while ideal for building houses of cards, it was no good at all for games of Pounce. Many of the decks came in small boxes that, when one pulled a silk tab, slid open to reveal twin packs nestled luxuriously in felt-covered trays. Sprawled on the rug in front of the living room couch, we played Slapjack, Spoons, Crazy Eights, Solitaire, Old Maid, Hearts, and—inevitably—mind-numbing, seemingly endless games of War, using two or three packs per player, the games going on for hours, the hours punctuated with the repeated incantation of "One, two, three, *war*" and the thwack of cards emphatically slapped down, the stacks waxing and waning in a game nearly impossible to win outright and ending only when we'd imploded from boredom. At that point someone would invariably announce a game of 52 Pickup, spraying the cards across the living room in a momentarily cathartic shower.

Best of all, there were books. Although it didn't take rain to get us reading in the Big House (in fact, reading inside on a sunny day gave us a deliciously guilty feeling), on an overcast afternoon people would be curled up with a book in almost every bedroom, with three or four of us draped over the sofas in the living room, physically proximate yet in separate worlds.

Summer reading is different. There's no agenda, nothing assigned, nothing mandatory. One reads at one's own pace—a few pages now and then, or a sudden all-day binge. Summer house libraries are a hodgepodge. Their contents tend to arrive as haphazardly as flotsam washing ashore. Some are refugees from winter homes; others are house presents; others are brought by visitors and abandoned. One doesn't weed out summer house libraries as easily as one does a winter collection; the books belong to a larger number of people, no one of whom can be entrusted with the responsibility. The result is an eclectic collection, highbrow mixing with lowbrow, accumulated over many years. "Summer house libraries are like trifle," Aunt Ellen once observed. "They're in layers."

The thousands of books scattered through the Big House, amassed over six generations, range from *Women of the Bible*, a large, handsomely illustrated volume, published in 1849, that belonged to my great-great-grandmother, to the latest John Grisham paperback left behind by this summer's renters. They bear the marks of bookstores across the country, from the modest, dignified labels of now-extinct Boston establishments like the Old Corner Book Store, where Emerson and Hawthorne did their literary shopping, to the lurid purple stamp of the Paperback Book Exchange in Duluth, where Ned got his start in television news. They represent the tastes of many different people, from the civic histories of my great-great-grandfather Atkinson to my mother's feminist manifestos. There's something for every reader in the Big House. Indeed, I've never brought a book here unless I was halfway through and couldn't put it down.

The Big House had no one room set aside as a library, but thirteen rooms had at least a shelf's worth of books. Every bedroom and hallway had its own cache. (The only bookless rooms were the bathrooms, a policy in keeping with the WASP trait of concentrating on the business at hand.) I don't believe anyone has ever formally sorted the books in the Big House, but over the years, volumes of a loosely similar nature tended to settle in certain places, and when I was a child I knew where to turn, depending on my mood.

For a visual journey through the sweep of English literature, there was the mission oak hutch opposite the living room fireplace, where my great-grandmother's sets of nineteenth-century novelists, arrayed on the shelves, composed a kind of colorful flag: a short maroon stripe of Thackeray above the long carmine stripe of Trollope above the sea green stripe of Brontë above the olive and gold stripe of Dickens. For useful information, there was the oak cabinet across the room, whose intricately carved scroll-work I loved to trace with a finger; it held a miscellany of manuals, dictionaries, and field guides, including such indispensable reference works as *The Clans and Tartans of Scotland* and *The Sex Side of Life*, a nineteen-page how-to (but please-don't) pamphlet published in 1919. For sheer splendor, there was the bookcase near the dining room fireplace, which held the *Life* Nature Library and back issues of *Horizon*. For Francophiles, there was the Yellow Room, stocked with travel guides and French novels, many of them dating from Aunt Sandy's college years. For escapist fare, there was the kitchen wing, whose narrow, second-floor hallway was lined with W. H. Hudson, Angela Thirkell, and other authors whose books my great-grandmother deemed worth keeping but not worth keeping on the first floor, and had passed along to the maids. The bottom of the literary barrel was the Lower Bedroom, on whose pristine white shelves were interleaved four generations of beach reading, from turn-of-the-century classics like Bulwer-Lytton and Galsworthy, to between-the-wars chestnuts by E. Phillips Oppenheim, to popular mid-century authors like Ian Fleming and Ngaio Marsh. Just as wharves are eventually colonized by algae, the Lower Bedroom shelves have in recent years been infiltrated by paperback thrillers left behind by houseguests: le Carré, Follett, Higgins, Archer, and even (as I discovered one summer evening when, alone at the Big House, I was in desperate need of something juicy and undemanding) a solitary specimen of Danielle Steel. It must have been left by a renter.

Within this rough order, there was delicious disorder. The hallmark of a summer house library is serendipity. Foraging a summer house for books is like beachcombing, in which a small stretch of shoreline may yield a mermaid's purse, a rusty fishing lure, a claw from a boiled lobster, an empty milk carton. A guest staying in Grandma's Dressing Room will find, on a single shelf, a collection of speeches by Oliver Wendell Holmes; *Fairies Afield* by Mrs. Molesworth, a handbook on sprites and pixies, as straight-faced as a guide to wading birds or salamanders, published in 1911; *Paris Through an Attic*, by A. Herbage Edwards, the memoir of a young married couple living abroad at the turn of the twentieth century; a biography of Dag Hammarskjöld. A slender edition of Housman's poetry bumps up against huge bound volumes of *Punch* dating to the 1850s, which in turn rub up against *Common Sense and Bad Boys*—a book I came across as a teenager and hoped might be a raunchy potboiler but turned out to be a collection of erudite essays on juvenile jurisprudence by a distant Forbes cousin.

In summer houses, one reads books one might never otherwise read, because one would never come across them in an alphabetized, Dewey-decimalized library. Thus was I introduced this summer to *Fore*, a collection of humorous short stories about the early days of golf by Charles Van Loan published in 1911; and *Around the World Sidesaddle*, a slim, luxuriously (and privately) printed reminiscence of riding vacations by Mrs. Winthrop Chanler of Geneseo, a wealthy horsewoman and family friend. Summer is a time for literary one-night stands with authors one might prefer to see only once—witness my tryst with Danielle Steel—as well as lifelong affairs. One summer, picking up *David Copperfield*, I began a journey through Dickens, via my great-grandmother's elegant set. In a summer house one doesn't want a librarian's organizing hand. When I was twelve, I spent several days sorting the books on the third floor, filing them neatly on shelves I labeled "Poetry," "Biography," "Classics," "Essays," and so on. But when I had finished, I felt that mix of awe and regret I felt on family trips to the barbershop as I watched, in the mirror, the barber dampen, comb, and cut my unruly hair into submission.

When I was a child, the center of my literary world was the third-floor Playroom. On one side were grown-up books that had been put out to pasture—memoirs of families we weren't related to, house presents no one wanted but felt it would be rude to throw out. On the other side was a long low case crammed with every book a nine-year-old could desire: *Treasure Island, Kidnapped, Mutiny on the Bounty, A Little Princess, Mary Poppins, Bob—Son of Battle, Robinson Crusoe, Misty of Chincoteague, The Adventures of Huckleberry Finn, Greyfriars Bobby, The Arabian Nights, The Princess and Curdie, At the Back of the North Wind, Castle Blair, Uncle Remus and Friends, The Bastable Children, Captains Courageous, In the Days of Giants.* There were the Oz books. There were the Red, Blue, Green, and Yellow Fairy Books. There were the Thornton Burgess books (the author had lived in nearby Sandwich), in which a host of woodland creatures had adventures larded with wholesome morals. And there were marvelous books I'd never heard of: turn-of-the-century tales whose popularity hadn't lasted, like *The Boys of Crawford Basin, The Dark Frigate,* and *The American Boys Handybook,* a 1882 volume filled with instructions on how to make a boomerang, how to trap a mole, how to snare a partridge, how to jig for eels, and a hundred other projects I read about over and over but never quite got around to doing.

In the Big House, the books themselves seemed as extraordinary as the stories they contained. The shelves of our winter home were dominated by paperbacks, whose flimsy, generic feel made them seem transient and unsatisfying. It was even worse in our town library, where, to protect them from the pawing of countless fingers, most of the children's books had been rebound in one of three topic-coded colors—red, blue, or orange—with title, author, and call number stamped on the spine in white sans serif print. How could the Dedham Public Library copy of *King Arthur and the Knights of the Round Table* compare with its Big House counterpart, with its delicate engravings by Howard Pyle, its ornate drop initials dripping with vines and flowers, and its gold-embossed cover? The volume, published in 1903 and handed down from my great-grandfather to my grandfather to my father to my elder brother, seemed to me almost as old as King Arthur himself.

The books in the Big House were as stimulating to the touch as to the mind. There were books whose letterpress pages had a subtle, reverse-Braille texture that made them ticklish to the fingertip. There were books whose gilt-edged pages were so finely cut that when closed, the volumes seemed made of solid gold, but when riffled, they broke into hundreds of glittering, needle-thin lines. There were books with frontispieces—the word alone was intoxicating. There were books whose illustrations— by Howard Pyle, N. C. Wyeth, Arthur Rackham, Jesse Willcox Smith— so imprinted on me that I can still see Blind Pew walking down the hill from the Admiral Benbow, Sara Crewe in crow black rags peering through the bakery window. Each illustration had its own separate page, its own thick, glossy paper, smooth and cool to the fingertip. Sometimes the illustration lay under a translucent leaf of onionskin that, when drawn aside, made a slight crinkling sound and revealed its delicately engraved scene, as a fog lifts to reveal the details of a shoreline.

There were books whose pages had a fertile smell and crumbly feel that brought to mind freshly milled timber. I now know that these were volumes whose pages had been cut, but the first time I came across a book with *uncut* pages in the Big House, I assumed it was a mistake and might be worth a lot of money, like the famous 1918 upside-down air-mail stamp I dreamed of discovering for my collection. Wanting to read the book, yet not wanting to destroy a potential fortune, I ballooned the paper and peered into the Siamese'd pages as best I could. Halfway down, I tried to read my way up from the bottom. But it was awkward going, and there were five or six lines in the middle that I couldn't decipher. After several pages of this, hooked on the book but not patient enough to fetch my grandmother's letter opener, I impetuously ripped apart every last page with my fingers, leaving the edges as ragged as the coastline of Buzzards Bay. Years later, I came across that book, the first American edition of a volume of poetry by Thomas Hardy entitled *Winter Woods*. On the flyleaf, my grandmother had written, to my shame: "Whoever, whoever, whoever cut this good book like this?"

The Big House books are hardly pristine. They bear the marks of age, weather, and affection. Covers have bubbled from the humidity. Pages are stippled with mildew. Books have become tombs for mosquitoes, silverfish, and moths. Last year, we arrived to find that a mouse had spent its winter chewing through a 1924 edition of Galsworthy's *Saint's Progress*. Over the years, the books have acquired a sweet, musty fragrance that to me is redolent of mystery and adventure, but whose chief ingredients are really paper, powder, dust, paste, glue, and mildew. Library books, handled by so many different people, have an anonymous, almost odorless smell. My first act on picking up a Big House book is always to bury my nose in its pages and inhale deeply, as one breathes in a steak before devouring it. I'm always surprised that no matter how many times I open a book, it still exudes that marvelous smell—a smell so vital you'd think that, once released, it would escape like a genie from a lamp, and the book, when opened thereafter, would smell like any other. (Susannah is also partial to the smell of Big House books; I once watched her sniff her way, volume by volume, through an entire shelf.) Indeed, at the end of each summer, I like to borrow a book to take back to New York, where, in the middle of winter, I can, with one inhalation, be transported to Wings Neck.

The Big House books were also marked with inscriptions dating back to the mid-nineteenth century, graffiti that stitched us deeper into the family, to the past, and to this house. *King of the Wind* had been a present from Aunt Ellen to her horse-loving sister ("Sandra from Ellen, Christmas, 1948"); *Tom Brown's School Days* had been given to my grandmother by her parents when she was eleven ("Mary F. Atkinson, from Father and Mother, Christmas, 1911"). It gave me a curious feeling to see the words "Henry F. Colt, Jr., 40 Heath Hill," in a careful, youthful hand, on the endpaper of *Pitcairn's Island,* and know that thirty years earlier, my father had sat with this same book in his hands, read these same words, embarked on this same voyage—and that thirty years before that, *his* father had, and so on. Now that bond is extending to another generation. Last night, Anne read to Henry from the same copy of *The Tale of Peter Rabbit* that my grandfather had read to my brothers and me, while Susannah finished *The Adventures of Sammy Jay*. When she closed the book with a contemplative smile, I told her that the Thornton Burgess books she loves had been favorites of mine when I was boy. She seemed stunned. "You mean when you were a boy and came to the Big House, you read these *same* books—not other copies of these books, but *these* books?"

Reading in the Big House was different from reading in Dedham. Wings Neck itself seemed to me as untamed as any Oz, the Big House as mysterious as Miss Minchin's Select Seminary for Young Ladies. The dramatic setting made the gap between my life and the lives I read about seem not quite so vast. In the Big House, which was built in the same era in which these books were written, Dickens—or Stevenson or Burnett—became even more vivid. Conversely, imbibing these mythical tales made the Big House itself seem even more the stuff of myth. The two worlds blurred, so that even now I associate Tom Sawyer with the Big House, as if he had somehow spent his summers here. Certain books became so linked to the house that I read them *only* in summer, only there, not because I couldn't find them in my winter library, but because they seemed to be inextricably bound to that place. And indeed, there were certain books I read *every* summer during those years—a ritual, I think, to mark my return to the Big House.

One could always find an empty room, a spare bed, a corner in which to read. I often chose Mariah's Room. With its lofty view of the bay, its whistling wind, and its looming eaves, it made a particularly atmospheric setting for salt-soaked sea adventures, or tales of plucky orphans in unheated garrets. But my favorite place to read was the daybed in the bay window of the dining room. There I would lie on my stomach, legs bent, elbows on the mattress, hands cupping my chin, as if my head were about to fall into the book and effect literally what had already occurred metaphorically. Lying on my stomach, I saw nothing but the book and the patch of blue bedspread that framed it. (Nowadays, that belly-down posture looks as painful as a circus contortionist's trick. I read on my back, holding the volume at arm's length above me, prey to the visual distractions—lights, windows, pictures—on its periphery.) I was dimly aware of the ship's clock chiming, a car crackling up the driveway, the chandelier's shadow lengthening across the ceiling, and I had the strange sensation that although I was holding this small rectangle of cloth and paper in my hands, it was really holding me. My body lay there for hours, while my mind walked the cobblestone streets of London or the dusty canyons of Nevada. (Even now, when I walk past that daybed, it seems an optical illusion, freighted as it is with all the places I have traveled on it.) And then I'd turn the last page, and suddenly realize that I wasn't in the Emerald City but here in the living room of the Big House, that the shadows were lengthening, and that the rain was letting up.

In the afternoon, the rain stops and we go outside. The woods tick, ever more slowly, with drops falling from leaf to leaf. There are lakes of warm water in the old, familiar places, dotted with hummock islands. The ground in front of the barn, worn smooth over the years by automobile tires, is a vast sea. Henry picks his way through the puddles gingerly, unable to gauge how deep they might be. A few birds chirp. A corner of the sky begins to clear. The house, soaked dark, stained, dripping, looks like the decaying mansion on the moors in a story I once read on the daybed. Susannah wants to check on her clubhouse, so we walk to the Bluff. The water is still. The boardwalk is festooned with seaweed. We watch a Herreshoff head out of the harbor for an evening sail.

XVIII

The White Elephant

ONE MORNING, as we get in the car to go to the Stop & Shop, a blue Camry rolls up the driveway. It brakes twenty yards from us. A middle-aged couple sits in the front seat.

"Can I help you?" I call out. They don't respond. I walk toward them, calling—shouting, really—"Can I help you?"

If they were lost, surely they would get out and ask directions; it is likely they've heard the house is for sale and have dropped by to see it on the off chance no one is home. Although prospective buyers are supposed to come equipped with a realtor and an appointment, a house on the market is expected to be available at all times, and on several occasions we've returned to find people wandering the grounds, peering into the windows. "We heard the place was for sale," they say, "and we were in the area." I'm uncharacteristically standoffish in these situations, even a little belligerent, like some cartoon Appalachian backwoodsman confronting "revenooers," and I'm particularly annoyed by the couple in the Camry. They won't even explain themselves. Indeed, as I approach, the car backs up. I increase my pace to a trot, but before I reach it, the car abruptly turns around at the fork, near the LOOK OUT FOR CHILDREN sign, and, with a puff of dust, accelerates down the driveway and out of sight.

As I walk back toward Anne and the children, I know I have acted foolishly. I can imagine the couple telling their realtor, "We couldn't even get out of our car. A highly agitated man came out of the house and chased us down the driveway." But I feel like an animal protecting its turf.

I know, however, that if I'd really wanted to protect this house, I should have done something years ago.

X

After Grandma's death in 1986, the Big House passed into the hands of her four surviving children and Sandy's only child, Russell. For several years, no decisions were made about the property. My father continued to act as its informal caretaker, opening the house each spring, overseeing repairs, mowing the lawns, preparing Hidden House for rental, and so on. He and my mother spent weekends and all of August in the Big House. And though other family members occasionally stayed there, my parents were spending more and more time at Naushon, and the Big House often sat empty for weeks, even months. All five inheritors shared the cost of taxes and upkeep, which averaged $25,000 a year, exclusive of major repairs, a sum difficult to justify for an unheated house that was habitable for five months a year, and a sum those who weren't using the house were, not surprisingly, increasingly reluctant to pay. It became clear that a decision about the property's future must be made.

In the spring of 1990, my father and his siblings met in the living room of Aunt Ellen's house, the last piece of the old Atkinson compound on Heath Hill to remain in family hands. Uncle Jimmy presided over the meeting. He opened by quoting from a letter my father had written to the other inheritors: "The unity of Mother and Dad's children would have been far more valuable to them than any house or acreage. That is equally true for me. No matter how the situation is eventually resolved, I hope that our care for and loyalty to each other will remain undiminished."

After a brief discussion of maintenance and repair costs likely to be incurred over the next few years, each of the principals stated his or her hopes for the Big House. Uncle Jimmy said that he wasn't interested in maintaining a presence at Wings Neck; he and Buffy had established a summer home on Naushon. Although he didn't need to sell immediately, he hoped to be "out of the picture" within three years. He then said that Russell had spoken to him from Japan, where he was teaching English. Russell couldn't afford to go in on the Big House but might be interested in a small piece of the property as a way of maintaining his connection to his mother's home.

My father reiterated what he had said in his letter. He was devoted to the Big House, but couldn't afford to preserve it for his children and grandchildren. And though he loved his siblings deeply, he didn't want to be part of a family consortium sharing the house and its massive responsibilities. At sixty-six and sixty, he and my mother wanted a place of their own. But he'd like to continue coming to the Neck. He hoped to keep the Hallowell lot, a four-acre parcel, adjacent to land owned by the neighboring Hallowells, on which, eventually, to build a small house, as his portion of the settlement.

Aunt Mary said although she wouldn't be able to contribute much financially, she would like to preserve the property if at all possible, and most of her children would, too.

Aunt Ellen's first choice was that the entire property somehow be kept in the family, but if that wasn't feasible, she, too, was interested in the Hallowell lot.

Uncle Jimmy summarized by saying it sounded as if four of the five principals were interested in maintaining a presence at Wings Neck in some form. After a discussion of rental procedures, the meeting came to an end with nothing agreed on except the need to meet again.

Over the following two years, there would be several more meetings, held at the Big House, as well as dozens of informal discussions within and among families, as we tried to figure out a solution. Almost everyone wanted the same thing: to hold on to the house. But it would take the entire extended family to keep it up; no single branch could do it alone, and that was the problem. Each time my parents, brothers, and I talked on the phone or gathered for holidays, conversation invariably turned to the Big House. What about pooling our money to buy the Hallowell lot? Too expensive; even if we bought the lot, it would be many years before we could afford to build on it. What about putting up two houses on the Hallowell lot—one for Ellen and one for Dad? Not enough room. What about cobbling together an offer for the larger lot and building a few small houses for the family while renting out the Big House? Too expensive. What about developing the property ourselves? Too ambitious— and what would be left over for the family? Taking into account the financial and emotional variables of five family members and the rather byzantine town zoning requirements, the task of dividing the estate seemed as delicate as that of dividing Solomon's baby. I lay awake nights wrestling with possible strategies, as if the Big House were a sixth-grade algebra problem: If thirteen acres are divided among five children, how many acres does each child get? Or, more precisely: If thirteen acres and a nineteen-room house are divided among five children, what does each child get, given that two children want to sell the land, one child wants the house but not the land, two children want one-quarter of the land but not the house, and x represents latent sibling rivalry?

Now that I was an adult, I thought I'd finally come around to agreeing with my mother that "it's not how much money you have, it's how much love you have." But at 2 A.M. I found myself wishing I had enough money to save the day. If only I had a trust fund . . . if only I'd married an heiress . . . if only I'd gone to business school. My needs were quite modest, really. I wouldn't be caught dead in a BMW or a Brooks Brothers suit. All I wanted was a million-dollar house.

In the end, the five principals failed to agree on any plan that could keep the house in the family. In 1992, they decided to sell the entire property.

In seventeenth-century Siam, the albino elephant was considered a sacred animal. For hundreds of years tradition had held that whenever one was captured, it became the property of the emperor, who was also known as the King of the White Elephant. The emperor was the only man allowed to ride or use such an animal. An albino elephant could not be killed without his permission. Whenever the emperor desired to humiliate a courtier, he would present the man with one of the royal elephants. The cost of feeding and caring for a huge animal that he could neither put to work nor put to death would eventually bring about his financial ruin.

Over time, the phrase "white elephant" came to denote a costly but useless possession, whether it be a table with a broken leg, a piano missing a key or two, or an overlarge house that has seen better days. In 1907, Henry James used the expression to describe the Gilded Age mansions that had adorned his beloved Newport, writing in *The American Scene*: "They look queer and conscious and lumpish—some of them, as with an air of the brandished proboscis, really grotesque—while their averted owners, roused from a witless dream, wonder what in the world is to be done with them." Eighty-five years later, we would hear the phrase used with dismaying frequency when we put the Big House on the market.

When a house is put up for sale, its asking price is usually determined by performing what are called "comparables," or comps, to estimate what it might be worth in the current market. The agent takes three houses of similar size and vintage recently sold in the area, three houses recently put on the market, and three that have been on the market for a while but have not yet sold. By averaging their prices, she reaches a rough estimate of what the house might be expected to sell for. But there was nothing in the area comparable to the Big House; it was, as one real estate agent observed, "unique." There were few chunks of waterfront land this large available on the entire Cape, and its location overlooking the bay was, as another agent put it, "not to be believed." A year earlier, the property had been appraised at $1,450,000. Now, on the advice of a local real estate agent, it was put on the market for $2 million.

Had it been the mid-eighties, that figure might have been a realistic starting point. The stock market boom had minted thousands of young millionaires, many of whom, like their Gilded Age predecessors, were anxious to express their wealth through architecture. Real estate prices soared. But the crashes of 1987 and 1989 sent them back down again, and by the time the Big House went on the market, in 1992, the Northeast was flooded with ten-thousand-square-foot, multimillion-dollar contemporary houses whose paint had barely dried but whose owners could no longer afford to move in. On Cape Cod, many large houses lingered on the market for years at steadily diminishing prices. There could hardly have been a worse time to sell the Big House. We knew little of this. We assumed the house we loved would prove irresistible to all comers and would sell its first day on the market. We were both immeasurably relieved and grievously insulted when it didn't.

In fact, for two years, not a single person made a bid. Few people even came to look. We weren't bothered at first. No one in the family, even those who weren't interested in maintaining the Big House themselves, really wanted to see it sold. Indeed, the fact that we were selling it at all still seemed impossible. We weren't, as the industry saying goes, "motivated sellers." We didn't primp for prospective buyers—no fresh-cut flowers on the mantel, no coffee-table books splayed suggestively on the sideboard. We declined to let the realtors hammer a FOR SALE sign at the end of the driveway, nor did we allow them to install a lockbox on the house to enable brokers easy entry. (The brokers assumed that our reluctance stemmed from a desire not to attract vandals, but given that the Big House had no security system, was usually left unlocked, and contained, as my father often observed, "nothing worth stealing," I think the real reason was that my family considered such public exposure heretical to the spirit of the place.) My father and uncle told the brokers we were "testing the market." The Big House was clearly failing the test.

Month after month, the Big House appeared in "The Real Estate Book—Your Color Catalog of Homes," that ubiquitous brochure, found in supermarket racks and street-corner vending boxes, containing page after page of postage-stamp-sized color photos of houses, each with its own alluring headline (ESCAPE FROM STRESS; BRING YOUR BATHING SUIT AND RACKET; COUNTRY SQUIRE; WATERFRONT JEWEL; MIDSUMMER'S NIGHT DREAM!; DON'T LOOK UNLESS YOU WANT IT ALL; IT STEALS THE SHOW; IF I WERE A PUPPY I'D BE THE PICK OF THE LITTER), followed by a description as pithy and, in its way, poetic as a haiku ("Waterfront Jenkins Pond cute as a button, 24' deck, skylights, ceiling fans, wonderful retreat, $78,000"). There, between a two-bedroom condo (SPOTLESS IS MY NAME) and a three-bedroom ranch house (PUT MOM AND DAD HERE) was the Big House (REMEMBRANCE OF THINGS PAST), looking as uncomfortable as an elderly giant among apple-cheeked schoolchildren.

Several years ago, *A Trip Around Buzzards Bay Shores*, Ezra Perry's compendium of the huge estates that lined the bay in 1903, was reprinted. Under its original photograph, the fate of each shingled mansion was encapsulated in a brief epitaph: "Razed." "Burned down." "No longer standing." "Torn down." "Torn down and land subdivided." "Demolished." "Destroyed by fire." "Fate unknown." "Dismantled." "Destroyed in hurricane." "Lost in hurricane, 1938." "Torn down after a hurricane." "Demolished to make way for the A&P supermarket." Grover Cleveland's summer house, Gray Gables, had been remodeled into an inn and subsequently burned to the ground. *Boston Globe* publisher Charles Taylor's mansion had been torn down. Some of the houses had managed to survive in a transformed state: as restaurants, private school dormitories, theaters, apartment houses, or—that ironic fate of so many distinguished mansions—funeral homes. Those few that, like the Big House, existed in something like their original form were, like a boxer who has avoided a knockout punch for fifteen rounds, described as "Still standing."

Houses like ours rarely came on the market because there were so few left. Their balloon framing, outdated wiring, and eelgrass insulation encouraged many to burn to the ground. (One autumn night in 1968, an electrical fire had reduced the Hallowells' twenty-room Georgian house next door to its central chimney.) Others were leveled by hurricanes. But most succumbed to social and economic forces that worked more slowly but no less effectively. Over time, the ancestral wealth that built these houses dwindled, chipped away by the introduction of the personal income tax in 1913, and diluted as family members (and the potential for disagreement) multiplied over successive generations. Meanwhile, real estate taxes and maintenance costs soared. The old summer "cottages" became too large and too expensive for all but the wealthiest families to maintain. At the same time, families had become so geographically dispersed that they could no longer easily gather in summer. In my great-grandfather's generation, summer houses were occupied by a single family for the entire summer. In my father's generation, one branch of a family might have it in July, another in August. These days, Wings Neck is occupied largely by renters in July and by owners in August (though, in many cases, only for a week or two). With the rise of two-career couples, the time when families spent an entire summer, or even an entire month, in their house on the shore, with the wife tending the children and the husband coming down on weekends, began to seem quaint. "Summer" is no longer used as a verb.

For those families who cannot afford or agree to keep a large house, high property values make it attractive to sell and use the profits to buy smaller, more manageable houses elsewhere. In such cases, the house is said to have "passed out of the family." It is a locution redolent of "passed on," and indeed, it is a kind of death—for the family, certainly, and often for the house. Ours, of course, was not the only big summer house to have fallen on hard times. As I despaired over the fate of the Big House, I found myself paging through the "Luxury Homes & Estates" section in the back of *The New York Times Magazine* and discovering a colony's worth of ancestral summer houses on the market: Adirondack camps, shingle-style cottages in Bar Harbor, Victorian waterfront mansions in Stonington, turn-of-the-century compounds on Narragansett Bay. I recently read that Hammersmith Farm, the twenty-eight-room shingled cottage on fifty acres near Newport where four generations of the Auchincloss family had spent their summers, was on the market. This was its second time on the block; unable to maintain it, the family had sold it in the seventies to a consortium of Boston businessmen who turned it into a museum, conference center, and wedding reception site for brides who dreamed of tossing their bouquets from the landing from which Jacqueline Bouvier had tossed hers after marrying Jack Kennedy in 1953. (Like a character from *The Cherry Orchard*, Hugh Auchincloss, the great-grandson of the original owner, continued to live in a farmhouse at the edge of the estate where he was raised.) Many of these old houses on the market would undoubtedly be razed to make room for smaller houses as the estates on which they sat were sold to developers and carved into bite-sized lots. Paging through the *Times*, I saw that the former Gimbel estate, built in Greenwich in 1911, had been subdivided and transformed into a ninety-six-acre gated community, in which twenty-three "luxury stone homes" were under construction, each with its own gym, home theater, coffered ceiling, and housewide audio system.

Some families find ways to hang on to the ancestral estate. They convert boathouses and bathhouses into cottages for cousins. They lop off and sell chunks of land until their grand old summer house is, like a castle among peasant huts, surrounded by smaller homes and condominiums. They apply for conservation easements that require them to leave a certain portion of their property undeveloped in return for a tax reduction. They set up family trusts to pass vacation homes from generation to generation, appointing a trustee to administer the property, levying annual assessments to pay taxes and finance repairs. Such arrangements, in which the family becomes a kind of corporation and the house a commodity, seem contrary to the informal spirit of a summer place, but they enable families to hold on to their homes. (Negotiations for visits among the fifty-eight members of the Roque Island Gardner Homestead Corporation, who share a three-house, nine-island, 2,500-acre estate in Maine, have become so complex that two members of the board of directors do nothing but scheduling.) Several properties on Wings Neck are operated by such trusts. Since the death of our longtime neighbor Dr. Reynolds five years ago, his descendants have run the six-bedroom house as a cooperative. His granddaughter Sherry orchestrated a detailed program of arrivals and departures. After five years, however, although many members of Sherry's generation wanted to keep the house, her parents' generation decided to sell it. It was recently purchased by a Boston businessman who plans to gut and renovate it. The closing is scheduled for mid-September. Sherry and her family will be coming down over Labor Day weekend to say good-bye.

Some families ensure the survival of their house, even if it means losing it themselves, by selling or donating it to a nonprofit organization.

The Gardner estate in Monument Beach is now a spiritual retreat. The old Cyrus Bartol house belongs to Northeastern University, which turned it into a conference center. Other houses become museums. The Isaac Bell house, the shingle-style masterpiece built in 1883 by McKim, Mead and White, passed through a succession of families before it was sold to the Preservation Society of Newport County, which has opened its doors to visitors at eight dollars a head. (It is one of ten such properties the society has made available to the public.) Britain's National Trust now owns more than two hundred "noble piles," many of which owe their continued existence to the very people they were designed to exclude. Tourists pay to sip tea in the great kitchen, admire (but not sit on) the furniture by Chippendale and Hepplewhite, and browse the paintings by Gainsborough and Van Dyck. Indeed, the trust has such a long list of estates to keep up that it no longer accepts them unless the donors also supply funds to maintain them until they become self-supporting. (So many potential donors exist that there are a number of artists who, like Charles Ryder, the narrator of *Brideshead Revisited*, make a living by traveling England and painting portraits of country houses as memorial keepsakes for the families that are losing them.)

The Colts are neither wealthy nor selfless enough to donate the Big House to a nonprofit organization, and our "estate" is, of course, hardly old or grand enough to be a tourist attraction. Few people would pay to see a house in which the walls are made of Sackett Board, the most valuable paintings are by Carla Atkinson and Elizabeth Saltonstall, the rarest antique is a dysfunctional Gravity Annunciator, and the period furniture is Sears Roebuck. But they might if they spent the night and were well fed. The New England coast is lined with old shingle-style bed-and-breakfasts where guests can watch the waves play on the shore as they bolt muffins baked with local blueberries. Last year, the granddaughter of the man who built the Neck's third house converted it to a B&B. Invariably, some of us talk of turning the Big House into an inn, and though we never quite take it seriously, I do occasionally daydream about such an operation. Ned could act as general handyman and boatman, repairing broken window sashes and taking guests out on the waterlogged Sailfish. Mark would be the tennis pro, giving lessons on the dilapidated court to guests who'd play with the vintage wooden racket of their choice. After frying the breakfast bacon, Dad could continue his never-ending battle against the catbrier as head landscaper. Mum could give painting lessons on the piazza. Aunt

Ellen could give house tours, Anne could organize literary soirées, and I could wait tables. Aunt Mary, of course, would be the cook and major-domo, hauling guests off on fishing expeditions at dawn, serving them dinners of freshly caught scup around the kitchen table, and periodically reminding them that this was no short-order house. "You *can* turn back the clock!" the ad in *Yankee* magazine might read. "Sleep on horsehair mattresses! Play croquet on the balding lawn! Swim off the rocky beach! Brahmin living at its most uncomfortable!"

But when I think of the family crammed into the kitchen wing while strangers sleep late in Grandma's Bedroom, my fantasy dissolves. Last year I stayed at a Louisiana plantation owned by a member of the eighth generation of the family that had built the house in 1790. (The live oaks lining the driveway were planted from acorns her great-great-great-great-great-grandfather had brought from Haiti.) As her neighbors struggled to hold on to their antebellum mansions by turning them into inns or museums, she swore she'd never do the same. But when she faced the loss of the house, she finally opened a B&B. Although guests stayed in the old cook's cottage on the five hundred acres where slaves once picked cotton and indigo, she nevertheless felt under siege as she led them on their complimentary tour of the house, pointing out its nine fireplaces and its drawing of Fort Sumter, signed by General Beauregard. She vividly recalled the morning she cowered in her room as a German couple, dissatisfied with the continental breakfast she had laid for them, pounded on her door and chanted, *"Ham and eggs! Ham and eggs!"*

I am particularly impressed when I come across the obituary of the Marquess of Bath, the Twelfth Lord of Longleat, who owned a hundred-room stone castle that had been in his family since 1580, eight years before the defeat of the Spanish Armada. In 1949, after postwar taxes imposed by the Labor government so reduced the family fortunes that he was unable to keep up the estate, he became the first of many English lords who opened their doors to the paying public. He and his family moved into a cottage on the grounds. His sons became the parking attendants and Lady Bath served tea, while the lord himself led tours through the castle, showing off the priceless tapestries, the antique furniture, the Old Masters paintings, the 33,000 books. When that wasn't enough, the marquess turned part of his 6,500-acre estate into Europe's first safari park, where tourists could observe lions, elephants, and gazelles wandering the fields and forests where his ancestors had hunted pheasant and deer. When *that* wasn't enough, he rented out the property for rock concerts and car rallies. It is true that when he puttered around the grounds in his old clothes, tourists often mistook him for a gardener. Still, the Twelfth Lord of Longleat was able to hold on to the estate until, at the age of eighty-seven, he died there.

At a time when so many people are losing jobs, family farms, and medical insurance, I realize that the potential loss of a nineteen-room summer house is hardly likely to elicit a national outpouring of sympathy. Still, people who know the Big House are aghast when they hear it is on the market. "THINK TWICE before you destroy (for *any* reason, except *dire* financial need) a MASTERPIECE!" wrote one of my grandmother's closest friends, in a letter to Aunt Mary. But the subject strikes a nerve even in those who have never seen the house. Many of them tell me about some family place of their own that they have lost and now mourn. When they ask why we are selling the house, I get frustrated trying to explain. Part of my frustration comes from thinking that if we *really* wanted to, wouldn't we find a way to keep it? The impending loss of the house seems to fit all the historical failures in the family—the suspicion that we don't quite *get* it, that the real world is beyond our grasp.

My friends urge me, often quite forcefully, to find a way to hang on to the house. They suggest moneymaking schemes: operate a writers' colony or corporate retreat; rent it out to Hollywood studios for Merchant-Ivory-style films about venerable WASP families or for teen slasher movies set in haunted houses; lease it to advertising agencies to use as a backdrop for ethnically mixed clusters of preppily dressed teenagers in Ralph Lauren ads. I read with unease that some many-bedroomed old houses are set ablaze by fire departments wishing to hone their skills; I hear of a decrepit mansion in California that serves as a target on which SWAT teams practice their assaults. Paging through the newspaper on the daybed one morning, I come across an article about a police raid on a brothel catering to business executives, run out of Sunnymeade, a seven-bedroom, turn-of-the-century mansion in the heart of New Jersey horse country.

Our Wings Neck neighbors have a fierce interest in the fate of the Big House. Whenever we're at the Big Cove, someone is sure to ask, in the tiptoe, roundabout way one asks about the health of an ailing family elder, whether there's "anything new on the house." They vehemently hope it will never be sold. "We're so glad to have Colts in the house," they say. "That's the way it *should* be." Their worst fear is that we might sell to a developer—forgetting, of course, that my great-grandfather and his "syndicate" were, however genteel, the original developers from whom their own parents and grandparents purchased their land. Part of their concern is practical. Many of them will soon face similar decisions as the older generation dies off and a larger, less wealthy, more scattered one takes its place. For them, the Big House has become a bellwether; if it goes, then nothing is safe. But there is also a proprietary note in our neighbors' concern. Everyone has memories of sipping cocktails on the piazza, performing in impromptu theatricals, playing Capture the Flag on the front lawn, attending one of the weddings to which most of the Neck was invited. Several have even rented the house for their own weddings or anniversary parties. Most of all, I believe, they think of the Big House as representing a vanishing way of life. Wings Neck, as so many of them have put it, is "a place where time stands still." The possible loss of that place's most prominent house is an unwelcome reminder that time *doesn't* stand still.

Five years ago, we began to rent out the Big House. The experiment got off to an inauspicious start. Our first tenant was a former girlfriend of my cousin Henry's. She had visited the house several times and was looking forward to spending a month there with her husband and children. But the rocky beach, broken-sashed windows, and sagging mattresses that had seemed charming when she was a college-age guest seemed primitive and even dangerous when she was a rent-paying mother of two. When a hurricane struck midway through their stay, cutting off water, power, and phone service, she and her family were relieved, I think, to have an excuse to finish their vacation in a nearby motel. The next tenants, a young Boston couple, invited five other couples to share the house, each of which invited *their* friends. When they left, a prized aerial photograph of the house and several old books departed as well. (In defense of renters, I soon found that they brought psychological as well as financial benefits: they made ideal scapegoats. We jokingly began to blame everything—a leak in the ceiling, a misplaced spoon, a merciless cloud of midges—on "the renters," as if they were poltergeists. I finally dropped the habit when I heard Susannah, after I'd broken a plate, chirp, "It must have been the renters.")

Far more irksome than the physical damage renters inflicted on the house was the damage they inflicted on its traditions—traditions unwritten and unvoiced but so ingrained that it came as a shock that someone might not use the place exactly as we used it. For several summers, Anne and I rented Hidden House while outside tenants took the Big House, and against my will, I found myself mentally expanding the list of instructions we'd posted in the kitchen, so that in addition to knowing when to put the recyclables at the end of the driveway and whom to call when the propane tank ran low, renters would know that cars are parked in the turnaround, corn is husked on the kitchen porch, and croquet is played on the *side* lawn, not the back.

We cherished those tenants who understood. Ellie Malcolm's son and daughter-in-law had always admired the Big House, and they rented it one July. The day they moved in, Roz Malcolm called her husband, weeping, saying they'd made a horrible mistake—the house was so big that their children were certain to get lost. Within a few days, of course, they had fallen in love with the place and its crotchets. One of the children vowed to sleep in every bedroom at least once—and when the chimney was hit by lightning, the entire family piled into my grandmother's bed and sang songs; it was, they told me, the high point of their summer. They have returned each year since then, and whenever I see her, Roz refers affectionately to the house, like a boat, as "she." Last summer, the Wotkas, another longtime Wings Neck family whose house had been sold, rented the Big House in August. Ann Bement Wotka—who baby-sat for me and my brothers in our youth, helped my mother paint the signs on the bedroom doors, and took care of Grandma—had died of cancer over the winter. Her former husband and their three children wanted to stay here one last time before the house was sold. On their last morning here, the children scattered their mother's ashes off the Bluff.

In the way one might spend extra time with a lover one has just betrayed, now that we were selling the Big House we gathered here together more often. It became something of a tradition for my father, Forbes, Mark, and several other cousins to meet over Memorial Day weekend and open the house: turning on the hot water, airing out the rooms, washing the windows, mowing the lawn, putting up the tennis net, taking the summer's first swim. Anne and I began to rent the house for a few weeks each August, and other cousins took it for long weekends. Aunt Ellen and my father organized several Columbus Day–weekend reunions, to which cousins traveled from as far away as Nebraska and Montreal.

It seemed extraordinary to be here again with the cousins who populated my earliest and best memories of this place, doing the things we used to do—collecting sea glass on the Bluff, taking walks to the Big Cove, digging for quahogs in the millpond, donning sweaters and playing tennis in the crisp autumn air. At night, we slid extra leaves into the dining table, and with my father sitting in Grandpa's chair at one end and Aunt Ellen in Grandma's at the other, we ate huge turkey dinners with pies for dessert. We joked fondly about Grandpa's ratatouille and Grandma's finger bowls. After dinner, as we did the dishes, it was, we all felt, like old times, although no one put it that way. One afternoon my father asked me if I'd like to see the "real estate path" he'd cut through the Hallowell lot—the four-acre parcel that we will sell separately if no one wants to purchase the Big House's entire acreage—so its potential buyers can see the water. I followed Dad down a path that winds through curlicues of catbrier to the Bluff, where it overlooks the beach just above the Black Diamond Rock. We looked out at Buzzards Bay. "Nice view," he said.

We were lulled into thinking we could go on like this forever, but after the house had been on the market for two years without even a nibble, several family members became restive. Renting out the Big House and Hidden House during July and August didn't come close to covering the annual property taxes ($16,000), much less the maintenance costs ($9,000). While some family members could afford to make up their share of the shortfall, the others either couldn't or didn't want to. And all five wanted some resolution to the house's lame-duck status. The friend and local realtor who had been handling the property agreed that it was out of her league. The new realtor, Coldwell Banker, a large national firm, recommended that, given the realities of the market, the asking price be lowered to $1,200,000; we compromised on $1,550,000. At the same time, the house would be more aggressively marketed to a wealthier target audience, through a Coldwell Banker program known as "Previews," which, according to a letter sent to my father and uncle (the estate's trustees), handled only "the World's Finest Real Estate." Under a royal-blue-and-gold-embossed letterhead that read "PREVIEWS. Exceptional Properties," the letter began:

> *Dear Harry and Jim,*
>
> *Welcome to PREVIEWS®! We are proud to welcome you to PREVIEWS® Marketing Program. We believe it to be the finest program of services available for marketing luxury real estate. You will now receive the full benefits of the worldwide PREVIEWS® network of residential real estate services.*
>
> *—A PREVIEWS® property becomes part of PREVIEWS® International Registry, a worldwide multiple listing service.*
>
> *—PREVIEWS® brochure racks showcase PREVIEWS® properties in office entryways.*
>
> *—Your PREVIEWS® property benefits from the marketing program PREVIEWS® has designed specifically for its promotion.*
>
> *—PREVIEWS® clients benefit from PREVIEWS® national and international advertisements from PREVIEWS® direct mail.*

Clearly, the Big House had moved into a more rarefied real estate neighborhood. It made appearances in *Massachusetts Lawyers Weekly* (whose subscribers, we were informed by PREVIEWS®, had "an average worth of over $750,000") and the *Boston Business Journal* ("a prestigious weekly newsletter"). "Magnificent shingle-style turn-of-the-century seasonal residence on 13 acres boasts over 800 feet of ocean frontage with spectacular views of Buzzards Bay," the ads began. It sounded appealing, but cheek by jowl with imitation Norman castles in Marblehead and "elegant" French provincials in Dover, the Big House looked slightly seedy, and no less out of place than it had among the ranch houses of Falmouth. (Perhaps that's why in several publications, PREVIEWS® chose to illustrate the property not with a photograph of the house but with a generic shot of a sailboat at anchor.) In any case, in a single month, the Big House had, according to PREVIEWS®, been seen by 35,000 lawyers and 63,000 bankers—as well as two million readers of the *Wall Street Journal* whose occupations we did not know, but who constituted, we were assured, "an affluent home-buying audience."

Whether due to the PREVIEWS® marketing program or to the

reviving economy, the house began to receive a modest but steady stream of visitors. They were, in the words of Sally Levine, the agent who showed it most often, "simply amazed." (We made plans to do our shopping or cool our heels at the Big Cove whenever a visit was scheduled.) "When they came in the front door, they got very silent," she said. "They'd never seen anything like it—the old family photographs, the hand-carved chairs, the wooden chests, the wonderful old cast-iron stove, the fireplaces in the bedrooms, the Playroom with the old toys. One lady said it was like going to a museum." To break the ice, Levine would chuckle and exclaim, "Shades of Teddy Roosevelt!"

There was consensus on a few points: the views from the second and third floors were spectacular, the location was breathtaking, the kitchen wing would have to go, and the rest of the house was what real estate ads referred to euphemistically as a "handyman's special." Plenty of interest was expressed, but those who loved the house couldn't afford it, and those who could afford it ultimately decided it was too monumental an undertaking—whether they planned to renovate it or tear it down and build another. Indeed, anyone who chose to keep the house would likely have to rewire the electrical system, update the antiquated plumbing, replace the eelgrass insulation, and perform a hundred other tasks just to bring it up to code. Many felt it was too expensive to leave standing but too extraordinary to tear down. No one knew what to do with it. At a certain point, most visitors seemed to come more as tourists than as prospective buyers; some had seen the house from the water and were merely curious to find out what it looked like inside. In Cape Cod real estate circles, it developed something of a reputation. A friend told me he had attended a dinner party at which the conversation revolved around the Big House, and the guests, mostly realtors, discussed the problems it presented as teachers might discuss an intriguing but difficult student. "It will take someone *very* special to buy that house" was the conclusion.

The difficulty was that those with enough money to buy the Big House were largely self-made men, and they wanted something they had made themselves. And so, like the Gilded Age tycoons, they were more likely to tear down old houses in order to build what journalists called "McMansions," in a style described by *New York Times* critic Paul Goldberger as "the architecture of shrill egotism." (Ironically, many of these sumptuous houses were built in the shingle style, which was enjoying a revival after nearly a century out of favor.) What sold were spanking-new homes that, according to their ads, seemed to be constructed mostly of appliances. For about the same price as we were asking for the eleven-bedroom, eight-thousand-square-foot Big House and its thirteen acres, one could buy a four-bedroom glass box on two waterfront acres with six thousand feet of rheostatic indoor lighting, gas-log fireplace, gas grill, intercom, wet bar, Jacuzzi, central air-conditioning, central vacuuming, and advanced security system. Everything was "state of the art" and "top of the line." By contrast, the ads for old shingle-style homes employed soft-focus adjectives. They were "charming," "gracious," "historic," "classic summer retreats" redolent of "yesteryear" and "the grand old style," where one could experience "turn-of-the-century elegance" or "recapture the charm of bygone days."

"It's a case of new money coming in after the old," George Hackett, one of the agents trying to sell the Big House, told me. "Everyone loves the house because it's unique, but it's an anachronism. People today want a big family room, a big kitchen, big fancy bathrooms, and lots of glass. Your house represents the charm of the old Cape Cod. You don't see the new stuff as much on Wings Neck, Marion, or Wareham. You see it in Wianno, Osterville, Wellfleet, Chatham. They're more glitzy—the new money is coming in and paying two and three million. It's like what's happening in Nantucket, where people buy three small houses, tear them down, and build a new one. The houses are tremendous in size. But they're awful-looking houses that don't fit the scale of their surroundings. Everyone wants to build a house bigger than the next guy's, to show how rich they are. It's all keeping up with the Joneses. It's the opposite of Wings Neck. I'd rather be on Wings Neck than Nantucket, but there aren't many of us left who feel that way."

Indeed, not only the Big House but Wings Neck itself had become something of a white elephant. When Ned Atkinson built his house in 1903, the Buzzards Bay shoreline, given its proximity to Boston, was considered the most desirable real estate on Cape Cod. But the introduction of the automobile and the paving of the Old King's Highway made it relatively simple to get anywhere on the Cape, and the wealth, much of which now came from New York, turned to the long, sand-bound stretch of shoreline along the Atlantic and Vineyard Sound. (The ads of one Chatham realtor are headlined: "Chatham: Because Location is Everything," "Chatham: The Nantucket of Cape Cod," and "Absolute

Chatham"). The Buzzards Bay side is considered frumpy, old-fashioned, *Bostonian*. People paying a million dollars for a second home want a house whose magnificence can be seen, a yacht club where they can order a two-pound lobster and a rum runner. They don't want a house hidden in the woods, a one-room clubhouse without electricity.

As the Big House languished on the market, we were forced to the painful realization that the property would be easier to sell if the house didn't exist. "It is apparent that the value of this property lies in the potential subdivision," one real estate agent wrote us. (Another agent put it more succinctly: "The one thing selling it is the land, you can forget the house.") Gradually, it became clear that the only serious potential buyers were developers. As Cape Cod was chopped up into smaller and smaller pieces, thirteen waterfront acres represented a veritable mother lode. But developers faced possible difficulties in obtaining the necessary permits from the town. In addition, the Wings Neck Trust was unlikely to wax enthusiastic over the replacement of the Big House by six smaller houses. It might very well try to block development. Although such attempts usually fail, even potential opposition can turn a developer's attention to more malleable communities. These prospects invariably rekindled in me a morbid inner debate: When the property is sold, do I hope that the Big House is torn down? I cannot imagine another family moving through these halls, sleeping in these rooms. But it is even more painful to think that one day I might sail by and not see that steep, shingled roof rising above the pines.

In some ways we were treating the house as if we had already left. For decades the Big House had been patched and repaired only as needed, and now that they were selling it, my father and his siblings saw little reason to do even that much. But a new roof would soon be necessary. The ancient copper water tank in the basement might burst at any moment. Many rooms needed painting. Squirrels ran rampant in the walls. As I put another pot under a leak in the dining room ceiling after a rainstorm last week, I was reminded of the upper-class Cubans whose riches were confiscated after the 1959 revolution, yet who continued to live in their crumbling nineteenth-century neoclassical villas in Havana, waking up in bedrooms with torn paintings, peeling paint, and broken windows, and hanging their laundry in empty ballrooms with leaky roofs.

Indeed, I sometimes imagine the Big House never being sold, never being fixed, just slowly disintegrating, like the abandoned three-story mansion we passed a few days ago on an off-Neck errand. At one time it must have been among the finest homes in Wareham. Now the white paint has scraped away to gray on the clapboards, the drainpipes have rusted brown, the chimneys are pocked, there are holes the size of refrigerators in the mansard roof, the windows are boarded with plywood that has itself nearly rotted, and even the NO TRESPASSING signs are so faded as to be nearly illegible. As the house dies, life surges forth all around it and assists in its destruction. Ivy attacks it from without and within, swallows and wasps nest in the eaves, rats and squirrels doubtless make homes in the rubble inside. It was frightening to realize how quickly a place that once hummed with human life could be reclaimed by nature. Who lived here? How long had they been gone?

A year ago April, we received our first bid. A Boston-area developer offered a million dollars for the entire property, including the Hallowell lot. He said he planned to renovate the house and subdivide the rest of the land. To me, a million dollars seemed an unimaginable sum, but when I flipped through the local newspapers and saw two-bedroom bungalows boasting of a "five-minute walk to water" priced at half that, it seemed like a steal.

My father and Uncle Jimmy, who were handling the negotiations, turned him down. Although the realtor urged them to make a counter-offer, they did not, feeling that the bid was so low that bargaining would be futile. This triggered a scolding letter from one of the agents handling the property, in which she discussed the prices of houses in the area and summarized the status of ours:

> We received our first offer on April 10 for $1,000,000. The buyer has considerable experience with subdivision and is willing to rehab the house rather than raze it. He is a quality, custom builder of higher priced homes and currently has a $600,000 spec on the market in Sudbury. In spite of the fact that his preliminary discussions with the town revealed no percs on file and the probability of difficult and expensive septic, he is undeterred. We at Coldwell Banker were thrilled with a starting offer at the upper end of the anticipated selling range. We are distressed by the lack of a counter, and confused by the response that the seller is "testing the market." It is quite evident that the two year test at $2,000,000 failed. Further, all

comparables indicate that the buyer's offer is more than substantial and worthy of pursuit. Indeed, few properties over $1,000,000 sell on all of Cape Cod. Those that do are generally Osterville waterfront. Though lovely in its own right, Wings Neck is no Osterville.

The following month, my father and Mark spent the weekend opening the house. Dad had two cracks in the tennis court fixed, the Hidden House floor painted, and some sagging boards replaced on the piazza. "The place is not in good shape," he said. Neither was he. He was seventy-one and increasingly hobbled by his spinal stenosis. He sounded tired—tired of being the paterfamilias, tired of dealing with the place.

Last October, Dad and Uncle Jimmy agreed to lower the price for the whole property to $1.2 million. Dad wanted to let me know before he signed. A few months later, he told me they had received an offer of $700,000 for the property, immediate occupancy. They rejected it, and wondered if they should have grabbed the $1,000,000 when they had had the chance.

"You know what I wish?" Susannah said to Anne. "I wish they'd lower the price of the Big House to a hundred dollars, so *we* could buy it."

XIX

Full House

For the past few years Anne and I have invited several of our oldest friends for a weekend in August. They will arrive this afternoon. While Susannah assembles bouquets of Queen Anne's lace and goldenrod, Anne changes the sheets, sweeps the floors, and lays out towels in far-flung bedrooms. She enjoys the work; she says it is a Zen-like respite from her writing and a way of getting reacquainted with rooms she hasn't visited in a while. Henry and I lay in provisions from the vegetable stand, the fish market, and the liquor store. Later, we gather in the kitchen to make blueberry muffins and fish chowder. I savor this calm-before-the-storm feeling. Throughout the morning, the phone rings with friends calling for directions. Their voices, brisk with office efficiency, are punctuated by the sounds of New York—computers, telephones, car alarms, sirens. When I give them directions to the Big House, I am unintentionally vague—stay on that road about a mile and you'll get to a causeway over a marshy area, then you'll come to a fork, and so on. I realize that I don't know the names of the roads, because I've been coming here so long I know the way only by instinct. (And it occurs to me that, perhaps because I think the Big House is so special, I subconsciously feel that people should have to work to find it. After all, treasure maps rarely provide exact coordinates.)

Anne points out that it might help if, at the very least, I supplied our guests with the street number.

"What number?" I ask.

"The number on the sign at the end of the driveway," she replies.

"There isn't one," I say.

Later, driving back from the Stop & Shop, I am astonished to see that she is right.

By midafternoon, as we are engaged in a final spasm of pillow plump-
ing, the driveway begins crackling with arrivals. As car doors open, I
glimpse evidence of the outside world: a wrinkled *New York Times*, a
ketchup-splattered Happy Meal bag, a Game Boy. I feel like a customs
inspector discovering nonnative and possibly invasive plant species that
may threaten the indigenous people's way of life. Even the aromatic sack
of bagels, brought as a house gift from an Upper West Side delicatessen,
is jarring. Susannah shows our guests to their rooms, giving tours of the
house en route. "And this is the secret passageway my father fell through
when he was a child," I hear her say.

As the Big House languished on the market, the family that had lived
within it was beginning to mend. With the help of therapy, medication,
and, as she puts it, "children who never stopped loving me no matter
what," Aunt Mary had eventually—and completely—recovered. A change
in geography, she believes, was also instrumental. "I thought I'd never get
well if I stayed in Massachusetts," she recalls. "It wasn't just that the institutions I was in were so bad, but that the New England conscience had
such a grim, foreboding outlook. I'm not the Last Puritan. I live in the
present, not the past. I like a more rapid pace. I prefer the Gallic spirit."
She moved to Montreal, where, living in a studio apartment not far from
her son Oliver, she began to make a new life for herself. It would be several years, however, before she felt strong enough to venture back to New
England. There, she visited Grandma in the nursing home. It was the first
time she had seen her mother in ten years. Mary wept at the sight of her
in bed, unable to walk, barely able to see or talk. Wordlessly, they made
their peace. "She forgave me," says Mary. "The war was over." From then
on, Mary visited her mother once a month until her death.

   These days, living on a shoestring provided by her modest inheri-
tance from Grandma's estate, Aunt Mary paints, writes poetry, makes
woodcuts, and maintains an ever-expanding circle of devoted friends,
many of them artists. (It is a life that brings to mind that of the creative
Ats, but without the financial cushion Ned Atkinson provided his siblings.) She makes frequent visits to her daughter, stepdaughter, and four
sons in Nebraska, New Jersey, and Alberta, cooking them nourishing
meals, reorganizing their kitchen cabinets. She takes buses whenever
possible, sometimes for thousands of miles, not only because she can't

often afford to fly but because she meets more interesting people that way. In her sixties, with her close-cropped hair, dark eyes, and husky voice, she projects a combination of resilience and vulnerability that reminds me of the aging Judy Garland. Aunt Mary still says exactly what she feels—"I don't like to beat about the bush!"—but it's more likely to be approbatory than disparaging. Her generosity is notorious. What little money she has she's always willing to lend to friends and acquaintances, whether or not she'll ever see it (or them) again.

After keeping the family at bay for twenty years, Aunt Mary now works hard at drawing it together with phone calls, visits, and letters. I can always tell when something from Mary has arrived in the mail. Like their sender, her packages look as though they've had a difficult and interesting journey. The big tan envelopes, often recycled or homemade, are patched with stickers, labels, and tape, and quilted with disorderly rows of colorful stamps. They bulge with gifts (and not just for Christmas and birthdays): key chains and refrigerator magnets from places she's been; caps and mittens she's come across at church fairs; comfy potato-shaped slippers crocheted by a friend; poems and stories she's written; watercolors she's painted; photographs she's taken; arcane foodstuffs with suggested recipes. (Despite her best efforts at containment—and, often, despite the assistance of the postal service en route—these gifts tend to overburden their wrapping, with occasionally drastic consequences; more than once we have opened a package to find that a jar of honey or jam has shattered in transit. We have learned to handle mail from Aunt Mary with care.) Her letters are no less expansive: long, newsy travelogues brimming with historical and cultural detail. "You must come and see this place someday," she writes. "And when you do, be sure to look up my great friend . . ." (She seems to have great friends in every town in the world.) She'll enclose business cards from budget hotels, news clippings about gallery openings we shouldn't miss, addresses of apartments we might like to rent from people she's met in cities to which we've never considered moving. Her barely legible handwriting, looking as if it had been written while running to catch a bus, races across the postcard, squeezes up the sides, turns a corner, and often ends upside down, the words fairly vibrating with excitement while she explains, for example, the difference between the sandhill crane pictured on the postage stamp and its better-known cousin the whooping crane, and adds that "I'm off tonight by late train 23:30 to Edmonton." Reading her letters, with their underlinings and exclamation points, or listening to her tell a story about her latest adventure, I feel she's swept me off on another fishing expedition, and when I return home to my own life, it always seems lacking in vitality, and likely to yield only the smallest and most insignificant scup instead of a coelacanth.

For many years, even after her mind was steady, Aunt Mary's memories of that last winter on Wings Neck were so painful that she couldn't bring herself to visit. But in 1990, four years after her mother's death, she returned to the Big House with her children and grandchildren. It was the first time they'd been there since 1970. Although Mary wasn't entirely comfortable at first, her uneasiness gradually dissipated. Almost every year since, she and her family have returned to Hidden House for a few weeks each summer. Once again, she leads expeditions to the gristmill, the lighthouse, and the Sandwich doll museum, this time with her grandchildren in tow. She calls Wings Neck her home. She writes poems about it on scraps of paper: *The sea rolls over me as I lie in bed / The memories come flooding back / And I am at peace / In the quiet and silence of the night.*

"We could be such friends and we had times of such closeness, but we couldn't seem to maintain them," says Aunt Ellen of her relationship with Grandma. Both Ellen and her mother always hoped that someday they might fully reconcile, but though they saw each other often, pride and habit kept them apart until Grandma was no longer capable of recognizing her daughter, and it was too late. When Grandma died, Ellen's grief was compounded by the knowledge that the distance between them could never be bridged.

Although—or perhaps because—she felt excluded from her mother's house, Aunt Ellen has always gone out of her way to open her home to the extended family, often taking in nieces and nephews for stays during periods of emotional or financial need. And we are always welcome at the converted barn she rents in Rhode Island each August, where she leads us in the familiar family round of charades and word games. While working as a gallery instructor at Boston's Museum of Fine Arts, she has also been the family's historian and chronicler, the keeper of its stories. Each year, she sends out an updated list of addresses; I could never keep track of my fifteen Colt first cousins without it. For a time, she wrote a family newsletter that brought us all up to date on one another's comings and goings.

Slowly, her sense of family has come to include Wings Neck. After her mother's death, Ellen began to venture back to the Big House, for brief stays at first, then longer ones. She has organized family reunions there over Columbus Day weekend and visits frequently in summer. One day recently, when we were looking through unsorted family photos in the attic, I was reminded that after their breach, Ellen had made a conscious decision to call Grandma "Mother" instead of "Mummy"; to this day, she refers to her parents as "Mother and Dad." Whenever we came across a picture of Grandma taken after her return from Butler, she talked about her "mother." Then we found a snapshot of Grandma as a young married woman. She picked it up for a closer look. "Oh, *Mummy!*" she cried.

After Sandy's death, Sidney and their infant son, Russell, continued to spend a few weeks at the Big House each summer. But after Sidney remarried and moved to Denver, he no longer came to Wings Neck; Russell spent part of every summer with Uncle Jimmy's family at Naushon. It wasn't until 1991 that Russell, by then a six-foot-five-inch aspiring actor in his mid-twenties, returned with his girlfriend, Sarah, to work as a busboy at a Falmouth restaurant and spend an entire summer at the house his mother had loved. He and Sarah swam to the Big Rock, read family books on the piazza, watched boats sail in and out of the harbor, played tennis on the court his father had helped finance. Everywhere he went he came across traces of Sandy: in photo albums, in pictures on the walls, in yearbooks, in sailing pennants she'd won four decades earlier. In getting to know the house, he got to know his mother better. He peppered my parents, who came down on weekends, with questions about her. At the end of the summer, Russell and Sarah threw a party at the Big House for their friends from the restaurant. "I gave the house tour to three groups, always keeping in mind the words of both Neddy and Sarah, that sharing this house is the most wonderful way to keep it alive," he wrote in the guest book. "The comments I got were flattering—'beautiful,' 'I wished I lived here,' etc. Three separate people took me aside to say in some depth how lucky I am to have a known family history and, with that, a sense of place. Yes, I am." A year later, when the Big House was put on the market, Russell wondered whether he and his aunts and uncles had made the right decision. Part of the reason he wanted to be an actor, he says, was the outside chance that he might hit it big quickly enough to keep the Big House in the family.

My parents' twenty-fifth anniversary party had been held at the Big House in 1976. I remember it as the apex of my family's pretense that everything was okay, even though we all knew it wasn't. I have a photograph of our family, taken moments before the first guests arrived, seated on the piazza steps, all of us wearing smiles that in retrospect look more like grimaces. Grandma had been taken three days earlier to McLean. I had just graduated from college, was quarreling with my mother, drank too much, and had no job and no idea what I was going to do next. After a buffet dinner, my parents' friends and relatives read witty and heartfelt odes to a marriage that was, in fact, falling apart, and filled the guest book with encomiums to a house that had temporarily forgotten how to be happy.

A few years after that party, Mum learned that Dad had been unfaithful. Her first impulse was divorce. Indeed, after she found out, she had driven to Wings Neck, knowing it would likely be the last time she'd ever see the Big House. She went down to the Bluff, where a cold November wind stirred the bay, and found a sheltered spot where she could sit and think things over. Realizing that Dad's affair was a reflection of how far their paths had diverged, she eventually decided that if they could intersect again, she wanted to stay with him. She told Dad her conditions: he must stop drinking, he must never see the woman again, and he must tell every member of the family what he had done. (My mother had long believed that secrecy had only compounded the family's problems.) When I went home for Thanksgiving a few days later, Dad came up to my room on the third floor and haltingly told me how sorry he was, how he hoped to be able to work things out with Mum. I felt a queasy relief, as if a long-festering boil had been lanced. No matter what happened next, things were out in the open. I also felt heartsick that the gallant, seemingly indomitable father of my youth stood before me now, meek and uncertain. I had no idea how to comfort him, or whether I should; I remember asking him, fumblingly, for a cigarette, the first I'd had since quitting six months earlier. We sat on the floor of my old room, still cluttered with books, record albums, and team photos from my high school days, puffing Kents in mortified silence.

How could my family have known that this low ebb would in fact mark the turning of the tide? My father agreed to my mother's conditions. (While he was at it, he also gave up smoking.) In what may have been an even more difficult concession, he consented to enter couples therapy. And slowly, painfully, my parents did what my grandparents had never been able to do: they began to change. At an age when his own father had shut down, my father opened up. When we telephoned, Dad no longer passed the phone to Mum at the first sign that the conversation might venture beyond the weather and the Red Sox. When we hugged him good-bye after holidays, he no longer found excuses to wiggle free. One morning, when I embraced him at the end of Christmas vacation, I felt his arms tentatively reach around me; for a moment, his fingertips brushed my back.

These days, the terrible afternoon in my old bedroom is a distant memory. I thought my father had permanently diminished, like a deflated balloon; now every time I see him he seems to have grown. All the qualities I'd so admired as a child—his sense of humor, his loyalty, his generosity, his physical grace, his ability to put people at their ease—had never left him, but, no longer filtered through the occasional scrim of marital tension and one too many martinis, they shine forth even more clearly. He is—to use an adjective that had greater luster in the nineteenth century—*good*. (Once, when Anne woke at 3 A.M. and couldn't fall back to sleep, she found herself remembering a Fadiman family acquaintance who had died saving his grandchildren from a burning building. She decided, as a soporific exercise, to rank the people she knew from most to least likely to make such a sacrifice. My father was at the top of the list.) And if, during the necessary disloyalty of adolescence, I was dazzled by the glamour of Uncle Tom and the polish of Mr. Gordon, I find that today I have little desire to distinguish a Burgundy from a Bordeaux or to wear a V-neck tennis sweater. What I most want is to be a good husband and father, and I don't have to look far to find my model.

Not long before my parents' marital crisis, Dad had stepped off the corporate ladder and begun a new career raising funds for nonprofit institutions. It is ironic that this prudent Bostonian proved so adept at coaxing others to part with their money, but Dad quickly rose to the top of his profession, directing the fund-raising programs at his cherished

Harvard, then at Children's Hospital, then at the Perkins School for the Blind. All the old-fashioned, sportsmanlike virtues I'd seen him display on the tennis court had seemed less and less relevant the higher he rose in the business world, but they were exactly what his new career called for. People figured that if *he* stood behind a cause, that's exactly where they should put their money. I always enjoy visiting him at Perkins, where he has worked for the past ten years, because as he prowls the halls, he stops to talk to everyone he meets—teacher, janitor, multihandi-capped student—and knows his name, his favorite team, and the topic on which he can be most expeditiously teased.

When I was growing up my mother used to tell me that the best gift parents could give their children was to have a strong and loving relation-ship with each other. The statement was poignant then, because I knew it was wishful thinking. The irony is that in those days, everyone *else* fell in love with my charismatic parents; it was only their love for each other that seemed to have lost its magnetism. (I almost got tired of hearing my friends say, "I have a crush on your mom!" or "I wish *my* dad was like that.") Now their pull is mutual again. When Mum—who, after many years as an iconoclastic and beloved teacher of art, English, sex education, and Holocaust studies, is now working on a long memoir about her own mother—returns from a poetry reading or a weeklong silent meditation, Dad wants to hear all about it; when he returns from a football game or a lunch with a newly widowed friend, *she* wants to hear all about it. He has stopped being reflexively threatened by her intellectual curiosity; he has begun to accompany her to the foreign films she prefers; after more than five decades of peanut butter and jelly sandwiches, he has tried sushi. (He concluded that he preferred his fish cooked, but he *tried* it.) Mum, too, has learned to appreciate Dad for who he is rather than begrudge him for who he isn't: he may never write her a love sonnet, but he expresses his devo-tion by keeping her car filled with gas, bringing her coffee in the morning, and buying her favorite flavor of ice cream (chocolate). In their long pas-sage toward compromise and complementarity, they have come to know each other so well that when they go out for lobster, he trades his tail for her claws without needing to exchange a single word—and by the time they get to dessert, I often catch them giving each other's hand a surrep-titious squeeze under the table. Two years ago, when my cousin Russell and his fiancée were planning their wedding and wanted to know the keys to a successful marriage, it was to my parents that they turned for advice.

Indeed, I try to pattern my own relationship with Anne on the one my parents have forged through years of hard work: the best parental gift, the one to which my mother had referred so many years ago, at last.

As my parents were unsnarling their tangled connection, I don't think it was an accident that we began spending less time at the Big House. We gathered instead at Naushon. Although no one ever said anything, I think we felt an unconscious desire to get together at a new place, a place not freighted with, as Mum put it, "all the ancient wounds." For two or three summers, the Big House was nearly empty. But as my parents' marriage regrew, we found ourselves being gradually drawn back to Wings Neck, first for a few days en route home from Naushon, eventually for weeks at a time. For several years after my grandparents' deaths, life in the Big House had felt tentative; no one felt fully qualified to act like an owner or a host, as if appropriating those roles would be an act of filial disrespect. In the late 1980s, my parents began giving Labor Day parties, full of guitar playing, kite flying, and croquet contests, to which the entire Neck was invited. I felt they'd decided that the Big House wasn't such a sacred cow after all, and that in altering it to fit their own redefined characters, they were able to connect again with the family roots that for a time had seemed so suffocating.

Or perhaps it was *I* who was redefining my character.

I had long had divided feelings about my own heritage. As a teenager in the late sixties, I had felt embarrassed by my WASP pedigree. I wanted to be a great poet, and I believed the job description required more obstacles than had ever been placed in my path. I longed to have been born into a family beset by greater drama, whether it be the Swiss Family Robinson, Mann's Buddenbrooks, or even the dull, pathetic Louds I watched on *An American Family*. And so I rebelled, sort of. I attended private school, but circumvented the dress code by wearing my grandfather's old velvet smoking jackets and paisley ties (a remarkably reactionary form of revolt, now that I think of it). I grudgingly attended Harvard, where Atkinsons, Forbeses, and Colts had matriculated for several centuries, but devoted much of my time there to drinking—not in the final clubs my ancestors had joined but in the half-deserted afternoon bars of Central Square, where I tried to blend in among the middle-aged alcoholics. I was delighted when I "passed"—for a public schooler, a homosexual, a foreigner, a Jew, for anything that seemed more exotic than what I was. When a graduate school girlfriend, eyeing my frayed jacket and my tiny, ill-furnished apartment, accused me of lying when I admitted that I had gone to Harvard and that my grandparents owned a large summer house on Cape Cod, I was delighted.

I thought, like all would-be iconoclasts, that I was bravely rebelling against something strong. I didn't realize that the culture I was trying to reject had already grown weak. The WASP upper class, Boston Brahmin division in particular, had become a quaint endangered species, like the snail darter or the spotted owl, but one that few considered worth saving. The values it held dear—charity, loyalty, modesty, self-reliance, sportsmanship, a stiff upper lip (values I had learned, in essence, from my grandfather's repeated readings of *The Goops*)—now seemed at best naive and at worst irrelevant. In *The Dining Room*, a play by A. R. Gurney, a college student persuaded his patrician great-aunt to demonstrate the proper use of finger bowls before confessing that he was researching the eating habits of vanishing cultures for his anthropology class; more recently, the index of David Brooks's *Bobos in Paradise: The New Upper Class and How They Got There* included the entry "Wasp, crushed culture of." Brahmin decorum has become something to spoof, as in the mail-order catalog I saw recently on whose cover an otherwise naked woman photographed from behind slipped off a loosely crocheted macramé sweater. The company was named Boston Proper.

During my teens, while I was giving haircuts and decent clothes a wide berth, the Big House was somehow exempted from my scorn. Perhaps this was because on Wings Neck the WASP style was manifested in its shabbiest form—the decrepit yacht club, the creaky wooden boats, the ancient T-shirts. Its asceticism allowed me to delude myself into believing that it wasn't privileged. If Wings Neck were truly wealthy, the beaches would be made of sand, not rocks, wouldn't they? If the Big House were truly a mansion, the shower would be indoors, wouldn't it? But by the time I reached my early twenties, even the Big House seemed guilty of pernicious Establishment leanings. And I learned that my family had problems of another sort, problems not of stodginess but of instability, problems that seemed exemplified by the Big House. It was as if something toxic emanated from its mildewed sofas and salt-soaked walls that had propelled its inhabitants toward alcoholism, madness, and estrangement. I stayed away.

Now I feel that the Big House was holding a part of me in escrow, knowing that one day I'd reclaim it.

In 1985, when I was thirty-one—old enough, perhaps, to start appreciating some of the WASP values that I'd spent so many years trying to reject—I needed a quiet place to write my first book. The Big House was available and free. Why not? I ended up spending three summers there, staying well into the fall. Although my parents came down on weekends, I was alone most of the time—unless one counted the benevolent ghosts who filled the house. It was the first long period I'd spent there since my parents' twenty-fifth-anniversary summer of 1976. I swam each morning, weeded the over-grown garden, wrote all day, and at night, before bed, walked down to the Bluff to look at the stars. I was the one who called the roofer or carpenter or plumber to repair a drainpipe or fix a leak, and I felt proud when they paused in their work to marvel at the grandeur of the house and the sound-ness of its construction: its Southern yellow-pine floors, its carved wooden gutters, and its copper flashing, all of which would be prohibitively expen-sive today. It occurred to me for the first time that a house can pass through phases, and that a century-old house was bound to have had some radical ups and downs of mood, not unlike a long marriage.

At the same time, I was courting Anne. With her Jewish-Mormon ancestry, her Southern Californian adolescence, and her fondness for premium ice cream, Anne seemed to represent yet another attempt to escape my background. But the more time we spent together, the more I came to see that we were not so very different. She had spent her child-hood in New England and, like the Forbes women of Naushon, she wore no jewelry, chewed no gum, could carry a fifty-pound backpack, could tell a harrier from a sharp-shinned hawk, and knew all the words to "The Fox Went Out on a Chilly Night." Like me, she was a writer. When, with great trepidation, I first brought her to the Big House, not only was she unfazed by its raffish ambience and antiquated traditions, but she embraced them wholeheartedly. Although her tennis game needed work, she went barefoot on the driveway and she swam at low tide. She was someone with whom I could have a romance at night and conversation by day. In falling in love with her, I also fell back in love with the Big

House, as seen through her eyes. Indeed, it was at the Big House, while washing dishes at the kitchen sink, and, perhaps, feeling the tug of family gravity exerted within its walls, that I decided to ask her to marry me, although it wasn't until we were on less emotionally loaded ground— three thousand miles away and twelve thousand feet up in the Sierra Nevada mountains—that I was able to pop the question. She later told me that she'd never dreamed she'd marry someone with aunts named Buffy and Bitsy, but she accepted anyway.

It went without saying that we would hold the wedding at the Big House. I had always envisioned it—a barefoot ceremony overlooking the Bluff—and Anne was, if anything, even more keen on the idea. Having witnessed the infertility problems of several friends, however, we began trying to start a family as soon as we were engaged, and over Christmas vacation we found out to our delight that Anne was pregnant. The wedding, we decided, couldn't wait until June. Anne tried to persuade my parents that we could have the ceremony at the Big House anyway, in February, with lots of space heaters. My father gently pointed out that even two small space heaters would likely blow the antiquated electrical system, and we'd end up saying "I do" in subzero temperatures and utter darkness. In the end, we had a modest, marvelous wedding in our Manhattan loft. It would be more than a year before Anne and I returned to the Big House, this time with eleven-month-old Susannah in tow. And we have been coming back for a few weeks in August ever since.

In 1990, the year after Susannah's birth, one more secret would be revealed. Mark, my youngest brother, had been raised during the most difficult phase of our parents' marriage. Just as Sandy had been the one to confront her father on his drinking, Mark had been the one to confront our father on his. As a young man, he seemed, in some ways, the most unclouded and uncomplicated of the four brothers, a cheerful, energetic fellow his friends vied to spend time with. (Of course, preoccupied with college and career, perhaps I saw only what I wanted to see.) We were, therefore, astonished when he told us he had a gambling problem. Ever since college, he said, he'd been placing bets on athletic events, staying up long past midnight to follow baseball and basketball games in which he had not the slightest sporting interest.

Mark's confession tugged at the roots of family-wide stresses that had never been addressed—and provided the spur that forced us to address them. Later that spring, the six of us began family therapy—I taking the train up from New York, Harry flying in from Wisconsin, Ned driving out from work in Boston to meet once a month with a clinical social worker in a suburb west of the city. (I remember thinking how strange it was that an earnest, shaggy-haired young man in a new office with wall-to-wall carpeting should be putting the Colts back together. And I remember feeling ashamed of my snobbery.) Jettisoning decades of stiff-upper-lipism, we deconstructed the "perfect family" that was symbolized by the Big House, the one we had looked like to everyone but ourselves. We came to see that we were no more or less perfect than any other family we knew. My parents admitted that it was time to let go of their children; those children, all in their thirties now, admitted that it was time to grow up (always a challenge in Brahmin families, where the friends and hobbies and values of prep school are often fixed for eternity). The therapist quietly told Mum and Dad, "What I want for you as parents is to stand in the doorway of your home with your arms around each other, watching your sons drive out of your driveway, and smile as you wave good-bye." When I heard that, I realized with shock (and some disappointment) that Dad and Mum didn't need us anymore, at least not in the intense, everyday way they once had. They had each other.

In August 1992, a year after our final therapy session, my brother Ned was married at the Big House. The property had been put on the market several months earlier, and we knew this would be the last Colt wedding there. It seemed fitting that it would be Ned's. Of all the cousins, he had spent the most time at Wings Neck. Named for the man who built the Big House, he had been Grandma's favorite grandchild, and he had spent many summers alone in the house with her after Grandpa's death. A carpenter's apprentice before going into television news, Ned had also spent countless hours painting trim, replacing ripped screens, tightening leaky faucets, and generally keeping the Big House patched together while we put off major repairs. (He was the only one of us capable of writing in the guest book, "What better way to spend a weekend than fixing the windows and shoring up the porch at the Big House?") Indeed, he had spent much of the summer sprucing up the property and, as friends and family converged from across the country, everyone said the place hadn't looked so good in ages. And for the first time in years, the place was full: all sixteen beds in use, the clothesline sagging with beach towels, and every few minutes, the driveway crackling with a new arrival.

Two days before the wedding, as my brothers and I were putting the finishing touches on a celebratory song for the rehearsal dinner, Mark told us that he had been gambling again. After heated discussion, even as the bride and her relatives were arranging flowers and pinning up welcome signs, my whole family—including the groom—rushed up to Boston for an emergency session of family therapy. It was, I think, a kind of final explosion, full of tears, anger, and affirmation. We returned to Wings Neck exhausted but relieved, feeling that although Mark—and the rest of us—would undoubtedly go through many more ups and downs, as long as we didn't keep them secret, we'd get through them. (Indeed, it would be our last session; Mark hasn't gambled since then, and the family has drawn ever closer.)

On a serene, sunny August afternoon, Harry and my cousin Oliver carried eighty-nine-year-old Great-Aunt Amy—who, wearing Grandma's old gardening bonnet while held aloft in a plastic porch chair, looked like some sort of Yankee maharani—over the bumpy croquet pitch to the edge of the Bluff, where the guests were gathering. (Great-Uncle Chis, indignantly shrugging off offers of assistance, hobbled along behind his wife.) The bride and groom processed across a series of carpets borrowed from the Big House and laid down over a field that, although freshly mowed, still bristled here and there with sprigs of catbrier and poison ivy. Mark, Harry, and I served as ushers. My mother read an Indian blessing; my misty-eyed father read a Wendell Berry poem; a cousin sang "The Water Is Wide" to a chorus of chirping birds and puttering boats. Ned and Leigh said "I do" and were pronounced husband and wife overlooking the bay where, twenty-two years earlier, he and his friends had reenacted Washington's crossing of the Delaware.

At the reception, held under a tent in the backyard, Ned and Leigh led the guests in salsa dancing to a four-piece Brazilian band. The cousins who'd grown up at the Big House, some of them back for the first time in many years, sipped punch from the huge beaten-silver bowl won by great-grandfather Colt at the American Grand National Steeplechase in 1906. Their children, a new generation of cousins, piled into the hammock. I saw my parents at a table with Aunt Ellen, Uncle Jimmy, and Aunt Buffy, all of them laughing. Aunt Mary, whose wedding nearly thirty years earlier had a been a high-water mark in the history of the Neck, was chatting up a neighbor. Balloons drifted into the woods. Kites flew overhead. Looming over everything was the Big House. "What an amazing place," my cousin Oliver said. "It's stood up pretty damn well through all these years."

The same, I reflected as I looked around me at four generations of Colts—from Great-Uncle Chis and Aunt Amy, shouting out a conversation over the Brazilian music, to two-year-old Susannah, madly dancing with her cousins—might have been said about our family.

Our house-party weekend goes beautifully. It is good to see every bedroom in use, the clothesline fluttering with towels, the front porch littered with doffed sneakers, the parking circle full of cars, perhaps for the last time. We swim at the Bluff, play tennis and Ghost, bicycle to the lighthouse. Some of our guests have been coming here since high school, and they are sad the house is going to be sold. They joke that they'll haunt it so no one will buy it. At one point on Saturday afternoon, Zorba and I are husking corn on the porch, Tina is noodling on her guitar in the dining room, Anne is baking muffins in the kitchen, Bill and Katie are taking an outdoor shower together, Sylvia is curled up on the living room couch with Jack sleeping in his baby carrier beside her, Peter and Julie are building a block castle with the children in the Playroom, Todd is reading in the Lower Bedroom. Zorba looks up from his pile of corn and tells me, "It's a great gift that in this house everyone can be alone, off doing things they want to, and yet all be together under one roof." We come together for dinner at the oak dining table, whose extra leaves Anne inserted last night and which is now set for fourteen. After dinner, Peter coaxes show tunes out of the salt-soaked Ivers and Pond piano on which William Atkinson used to accompany his brother Ned, and we all sing. Later, Anne and I walk down to the Bluff at midnight. A full moon makes a wide path on the water.

Early the next afternoon, our guests begin to leave for the city. There is a flurry of packing, sweeping, wrapping up of shells and lucky stones in protective layers of Kleenex. The driveway empties until ours is the only car left. Anne and I walk slowly around the house together, closing windows, collecting damp towels, making a small pile of things our guests have left behind.

XX

Florida

L AST MARCH, a few months after Dad and Uncle Jimmy turned down the $700,000 offer on the property, everything changed. We were on vacation in Florida, where Anne's parents lived. My parents were spending a week with us in a rented condominium down the beach from the Fadiman home.

On Sunday afternoon, the day after we arrived, Uncle Jimmy called. A Boston businessman named Garrity had offered a million dollars for the Big House. He wanted to develop the land and would probably tear down the house. We had until five o'clock Wednesday to consider the bid. If we accepted, Mr. Garrity would take possession in six weeks.

Although the offer was no larger than what we'd contemptuously spurned only a year before, time had worn the family down. Jimmy, Russell, and Ellen would undoubtedly choose to accept, and my father was leaning that way. Over the last six years, he had become reconciled to the loss of the Big House, and there would be some relief that the wait was over. "It makes me sad," he said, "but we can't go on paying the deficit, since some people in the family can't afford it. And we may never get another offer like this." After the money was taxed and split five ways, Dad and his siblings would each get about $120,000.

Typically, Dad was worried about the families who had agreed to rent the property this summer, especially our friends the Driscolls, who had spent every July for seventeen years in Hidden House. Most of all, he was concerned for his children. I could tell that he was waiting to see how I would take the news. I felt numb. I had never thought this day would really come; I had also assumed that at the last minute some deus ex machina would swoop down to save the house. But at this point, divine intervention seemed unlikely.

That afternoon, Dad and I went for a swim. As he picked his way across a strand of shells at the tide line, I waded into the Gulf of Mexico. "How's the water?" he asked.

"About like Wings Neck in June," I started to call out, but stopped myself. "Pretty warm," I said instead.

After dinner, Dad called Uncle Jimmy, giving his okay to the deal.

That night I dreamed we'd already sold the Big House. I rushed up from New York to see it one last time. From the outside, everything looked the same. But I walked into the barn to find a dozen people I didn't know stripping shelves and bureaus of their contents and tossing them on the floor. I saw many familiar items in the pile: an old suit of Grandpa's, a box from R. H. Stearns, a sign Grandma had made for the front hall bathroom. I ran from person to person pleading with them to stop, but they wouldn't listen.

The following night, while we were watching the Academy Awards on television, Aunt Mary called. "Well, what do you think of this?" she blurted in her usual straightforward way. She was unhappy about the sale, and wondered whether the buyer might be persuaded to settle for the Hallowell lot. "What do you know about this person Garrity?" she asked. I said the only thing I knew was that he owned an electrical supply company. Aunt Mary said Uncle Jimmy had told her he was sixty and had grandchildren. She worried about how many houses he'd build on the property. "If he builds a lot of them, I'd be awfully embarrassed the next time I go to Wings Neck." I said it might be hard to return to Wings Neck in any case. "What we need is a white knight," she said in a tone so businesslike she might have been asking someone to pass the salt. "But the white knight would have to have one million, one hundred thousand dollars." Later, she spoke with my father. She thanked him for being chief caretaker of the house, and said that he was largely responsible for our being able to keep it in the family for as long as we had. He was very touched.

Aunt Mary's straightforwardness was, as Grandpa would have put it, a tonic. I felt bad that I hadn't called my cousins to commiserate; it was as if there had been a death in the family but its members had been too

wounded to share their grief. Mary's call, however, was only the beginning. The following afternoon, when my mother and I returned from a
bicycle trip, my cousin Henry called from London. His sister Forbes and
her fiancé, David, were trying to put together a coalition to buy the Big
House. Forbes's mother, Aunt Ellen, had already agreed to take part.
The hope, said Henry, was that the Singers could put up two-thirds of
the money and our family—my parents and however many sons and
daughters-in-law were able to join in—could contribute one-third. I was
shocked; once my parents' generation had put the house on the market,
it had never occurred to me that we might be able to buy it back ourselves. (I also felt a twinge of the old shame at having resigned myself to
the sale while the Singers were taking action.) Then I got excited.

I called David, an economist and hedge fund partner, at his office. He
and Forbes had been a couple for several years. A soft-spoken and
thoughtful man, David talked of how he had always loved the house, how
they didn't make them like that anymore. The Big House would be a way
of holding on to Forbes's roots, a place where she could always return to
be with her family. I said Anne and I would be interested—and my parents and Ned, too, if we could build our own small house on the property. (My brother Harry had his hands full with his new home in rural
Maine; my brother Mark had no money to invest at the time.) As much
as Dad and Ned loved the Big House, they had spent so much time on
its upkeep that they didn't feel they could share the burden any longer;
they wanted to be *near* it, to see it every day, to bask in its glow. David
suggested that he and Forbes put up one-third of the money; Ellen one-
third; and my parents, Ned, Anne, and I one-third. (My father's and
Ellen's contributions would include giving up their share of the profits
from the sale, which meant we'd have to buy out only Jimmy, Russell,
and Mary, thus greatly reducing the price.) Given those proportions, said
David, why not let my parents' group take the Hallowell lot and the
Singers take the Big House and the remaining nine acres? I said that
sounded great.

I spent the rest of the afternoon on the phone: with Ned, a television
correspondent on assignment in Zagreb, who said he was all for any deal
that might enable us to have a house of our own on the property; with
David, going over practical details about property taxes and maintenance
costs and figuring out on which side of the property line the tennis court,
the pump house, and the path to the Bluff lay; with Ned again; with Aunt

Mary. Dad paced nearby, supplying information as needed, reminding me that the Big House would require an $18,000 roofing job in the next few years, that the old copper water tank was on its last legs.

With each call, there was an adrenaline rush, the feeling of mobilizing for battle, of actually *doing* something to save the house. A scrap of paper on the table accumulated a scrawl of names, phone numbers, figures, and time zones: Ned's fifteen-digit number in Croatia, Henry's number in London, Jimmy's office at the Boston State House, Mary's number in Montreal, her son Jonathan's in Nebraska, David's at work in Connecticut, Forbes's in New York City. I had an image of the family scattered around the world, constellating via telephone and fax, drawn together by a house on Cape Cod. (Oddly, the conversations usually began with small talk—how's the weather, how's vacation, how's work—social niceties we were unwilling or perhaps unable to dispense with even in the urgency of the situation.) Between calls, Anne, my parents, and I talked hesitantly about possible designs of a shared house—open kitchen, exposed beams, nothing too fancy. Dad suggested that we might be able to borrow some of the Big House's spirit by putting a few pieces of its furniture into our new little house. We reminded ourselves of all the things that could go wrong. But in our minds' eyes, all of us began to see a modest cottage rise in the woods on the edge of the Bluff, not far from the Big House.

It was strange to be deciding the fate of the Big House on a Florida island where houses were painted pink, where buildings dating before 1950 were rare, where people's roots rarely went deeper than those of the gorgeous, feathery Australian pines that lined the beaches and keeled over in a storm. Having visited my in-laws here for eight years, we were considered old-timers. On our drive into town, nearly every store and development we passed had an *e* on the end—Compass Pointe, Mariner Pointe, Sand Pointe—and the names of houses, emblazoned on carved wooden signs in the shape of pelicans and scallops, included Makin' Waves, Pair a Dice, Daze Off, Shellusion, Linga Longa, and Haus Bayou. In the real estate booklets, "sunset views across the 14th fairway," "pretty beige vinyl siding," and "panoramic views of three intersecting canals" were considered premium selling points. Anne and I had grown to love Florida in part for being the visual and cultural opposite of New England—for its architectural exuberance, its profusion of wildlife, its powdery beaches, its working appliances. But the contrast seemed almost surreal. As I discussed the fate of the Big House on the phone, I glanced around our rented condo: its walls the color of strawberry ice cream, its lime green shag carpeting, its dreamy paintings of breaking waves, its pink guest book, its three television sets, its air conditioner powerful enough to cool the Sahara. I was galled by the knowledge, gleaned from the local paper, that this three-bedroom apartment would sell for more than the Big House.

That evening, I called Uncle Jimmy to alert him that before he accepted the Garrity offer, we might have a bid from the family. "But I've already signed it!" he exclaimed. Although we had until five o'clock tomorrow to accept or reject the offer, having obtained the agreement of the five principals he had seen no reason not to go ahead and sign the contract, which required the signature of only one trustee. "In real estate, if you get an offer that's close to what you're asking, you take it," he said. "If you've got someone on the line, you've got to grab it." But he wanted the house to stay in the family, he added, and if we were really serious he would look into the possibilities. But he warned me that we might have problems getting out of the deal; Garrity could sue for breach of contract, the brokers could sue over their lost commission. "Pardon me for saying this," Jimmy asked, "but why didn't someone start doing this two or three years ago? Just to speak for myself, I've spent a tremendous amount of time and effort—I've wanted all along to see the house stay in the family. But here we have a firm offer—all cash, no mortgage, clean as a whistle. . . ." I pointed out that the price had come down so far that it was the first time the notion of a family bid had occurred to anybody. "Let me be frank," said Jimmy. "I hope you understand we have *accepted* this offer. To welsh on an acceptance—and I'm not just talking about the buyer, but about the realtors who've been working with us for so long . . ." He sounded overcome by the thought. "This is not something the Colt family—how shall I put it?—we don't do this kind of thing. We keep our word, and—aside from the damages—it would really hurt our reputation in the Greater Boston area. Word gets around on something like this." But Jimmy agreed to talk once more the next day, before the five o'clock deadline. As I hung up, I felt chastened—especially because I knew Jimmy was right.

I called Forbes and David and told them that Jimmy had already signed the contract. He would be willing—though reluctant—to go back on his word only if we could come up with something in the next twenty hours, and I knew that something had to be ironclad. Could we? No.

Although there wasn't much left to say, I found myself prolonging the conversation, unwilling to let go of any sliver of hope.

After I got off the phone, my parents, Anne, and I sat up talking numbly. We felt clobbered. It was ten-fifteen, long after my father usually went to bed. I asked Dad what he was thinking. "I'm thinking about that Sailfish," he said slowly. "The one that doesn't float . . . When I woke up this morning, I was thinking about it. Maybe we should put that Garrity guy on it and send him out to sea." He was quiet for some time. "And the white dinghy, the one my mother bought. That's a wonderful dinghy—I wonder whether we should try to sell it to someone on the Neck." Our thoughts turned to how we'd get a hundred years of stuff packed up and out of the house before the closing. We agreed that it would be nice to have a few things from the house to remind us of it. "The only thing I really want is the ship's clock," said Dad. "I want it for Ned."

My mother frowned. "I've been worried about something for a long time—and now people will see it. I once wrote on the back of that Chinese painting in the living room, 'If no one else wants this I'd like it.'"

"I'll erase it, Mum."

"It's in ink."

On his way upstairs to bed, Dad paused. "I'm sorry I couldn't do anything about this." He trudged up a few more steps and then stopped again. "If only I'd stayed at Air Reduction, I would have made enough money to buy everyone out." I told him what he knew—that if he had stayed, we would all have been so miserable that if we had had a summer house, we wouldn't have had a family left to gather there.

The following morning I told Uncle Jimmy we hadn't been able to put together anything solid enough to make him renege on the deal. He said he was sorry; he didn't want to see the house go to a stranger. "But if it's any consolation, we got a very good price—not what we wanted, but very good for today's market."

After six years, it looked as if the Big House had been sold. It seemed characteristic of the family that although we'd talked for years about doing something to save it, we hadn't acted until it was one day too late. Anne said it reminded her of a man not realizing he wanted to marry his lover until she had found someone else and it was too late to get her back. I felt guilty that it had taken someone from outside the family to galvanize us, to be our putative white knight.

There were a few glum postmortem calls. But for the rest of the week, we didn't talk much about it; it was a family death too painfully recent to mention. Making sand castles with the children, however, I found myself sculpting a crude replica of the Big House.

We flew back to New York. We made the motions of moving on. We talked of mixed blessings, of learning to let go, of the importance of change. I made plans to go up to the house to say good-bye. When I mentioned the sale, acquaintances congratulated me, friends consoled me. Aunt Ellen admitted that her sadness was mixed with relief because if she had gone in on the Big House, she might have had to sell her home on Heath Hill. But she was glad we had tried; even though we had failed, our attempts to save the house had brought us all together. She talked of using her share of the sale to build a house on a small piece of land she owns in Rhode Island; Aunt Mary talked of buying a place in the country outside Montreal. Dad was excited about using some of his portion to finance a family vacation in Bermuda. He worried, however, about finding other rental houses for the Big House summer tenants. It was already April, and most of the good places were gone.

Meanwhile, I realized that we, too, should start looking for a place to rent this summer. Anne's family had never had a summer house, but even if we didn't own a car or a microwave or a CD player, I wanted my children to continue to have the same kind of summers I had had at their age—or as close as we could get. Anne and I guiltily considered new possibilities—Maine, Nantucket—and wondered if we could afford them, but I realized I wasn't ready to leave the Cape. It felt strange and sad, as April began, to be combing the local paper for rental listings. There was nothing on Wings Neck. We were about to settle for a three-bedroom ranch house on a pond in Sandwich for $950 a week—almost two-thirds as much as my family had charged for the Big House—when I got a call from a local realtor who had heard one small house on Wings Neck was still available. And so we decided to rent Goose Cottage, a stop on my old newspaper route, for two weeks in August.

I dreamed of the Big House. Awake, I kept having an image of myself sneaking onto the property after it was sold, to spend time with my grandfather's ashes as well as with the keepsakes of our two miscarriages. They would be stranded in the woods on someone else's property. How would we ever visit them again? My mother suggested we take handfuls of dirt from the clearing and put them somewhere else.

At the same time we were losing the Big House, we were losing other old and much-loved parts of our family, too. One night, Anne's father was rushed to the emergency room with a heart blockage. Although he was able to return home a few days later, fitted with a pacemaker, he was ninety-two—one year younger than the Big House—and seemed finally to be nearing the end. And Great-Uncle Chis—the last Colt of his generation—was failing. He spent much of his time in bed or in a wheel-chair, suffering from chest pains, diarrhea, sinus problems, and arthritis. "There's not much the doctors can do," he said. They certainly couldn't do anything about his most painful affliction, the loss of Great-Aunt Amy, his wife of seventy-three years. Though Chis rallied, and from time to time sounded his old provocative self (one day when I asked what he was doing, he replied with a laugh, "I'm lying around being rather surly"), depression usually colored his voice.

At the end of one phone call, I said, "We'll see you in June."

"Let's hope," he said grimly.

One Saturday afternoon in May, Anne and I came home to our New York loft to find a phone message from my father. Dad has always been uncom-fortable with answering machines, but this time his voice was so heavy that for a moment I thought that either he'd started to drink again or Chis had died. His message said the deal had fallen through. When I reached him later that day, he told me that our realtor had received a letter from Mr. Garrity's lawyer, enclosing an article from the *Wall Street Journal* about the pollution at Otis Air Force Base and its effect on local real estate values. "Based on the enclosed article," he wrote, "we are withdrawing our offer." The realtor had told Mr. Garrity that Cape Codders had been living with the situation for years, that few people paid attention to it—but no matter how she tried to explain it to him, he felt he was being cheated. I found it ironic that although we retreated from making a bid because we were con-cerned about welshing, now the buyer himself had welshed on the deal.

Anne was ecstatic. I was so stunned I didn't know what I felt, though I'm sure there was a second or two of pure fear: *We're back in the rapids.* Then I started making plans. We'd have another summer in the Big House.

The next day, when I called Dad, he sounded almost physically sick. He had been awake since three, wondering whether he could really afford to go ahead on the Hallowell lot. Pooling our money, he said, including his share from the sale, we would have enough for the lot, but not enough to build a house. "Your mother and I have gotten used to living in a certain kind of way—taking a trip every year, getting a new car every few years, going to restaurants," he said. "We've gotten to where I don't have to worry if your mother writes a check for three hundred dollars—that's as much as we used to have in our entire account. I don't want to go back to eating at Kentucky Fried Chicken on our anniversary. I just don't know if I want to be on Wings Neck if it means going back to those days." He chuckled dryly. "You know, in the middle of the night in Florida I even found myself thinking that if the plane back to Boston went down, there'd be one million dollars in life insurance and you boys would be able to buy the place."

For my father, it was a startlingly intimate speech. For the first time I saw him as a man nearing retirement, facing a back operation, spending an increasing number of afternoons attending the funerals of his friends. In Florida I had noticed how much his sense of balance had deteriorated; it had been difficult for him to tiptoe across the tide line of shells, and in the house he had occasionally stumbled over a chair leg or the edge of a rug. Everything was exacerbated, of course, by back pain, which kept him from being able to walk more than a few blocks; from his anxiety over the nine-hour surgery he would undergo in July; and from the ups and downs of the previous month. I knew he wished he had the stamina to keep fighting for the Hallowell lot, and it made me feel guilty to think of all the sacrifices he'd made for us over the years. Now we were asking him to be the all-powerful father of our youth again. "Sometimes I wish I'd never even *heard* of Wings Neck," he said quietly.

Somewhere along the line, the Big House had truly become the white elephant I so hated to hear others call it. When I told Chis that the Big House deal had fallen through, he laughed knowingly. "Nobody will buy it, will they?"

While we hesitated, Forbes and David, aided by Aunt Ellen, jumped back into the fray. They visited Wings Neck with an architect who specialized in the historic restoration of old buildings that might otherwise have fallen to the wrecker's ball. He had sailed by the Big House many times and had always wanted to get inside—and when he finally did, he was tremendously stirred by what he saw. He told Forbes and David it would be a tragedy to tear down the house. I found myself near tears when I heard of his enthusiasm—finally, someone appreciated the place! David consulted a contractor, who estimated that it would cost a minimum of $500,000 to renovate and winterize the Big House.

As they were dreaming about ownership, Forbes and David found help from an unexpected quarter. Although Aunt Mary was, of all the principals, the one who could most use the money from the sale, she wanted with all her heart to keep a toehold on Wings Neck for her children. She told Forbes that she was willing to postpone receiving her share of the profits—money that, had it come to her promptly, would have enabled her to rent a larger apartment, travel by air instead of bus, and help support her children even more than she already did—in return for access to Hidden House. This substantially reduced the price of the Big House.

In mid-June, on the boat to Naushon for a family vacation, my father told me that another bid on the property had come in, this time for $800,000, from an architect who wanted to renovate and sell the Big House. Four years had gone by without a single offer; now it suddenly seemed as if I couldn't see or talk to my father without hearing about a new bid. The deadline was nine o'clock that night. By six o'clock, the realtor had called to say the bid had been upped to $900,000. While my mother prepared dinner and the children, struggling into their bathing suits, clamored to be taken swimming, my father hunched over the phone, talking intensely to his brother and sisters. Dad and Uncle Jimmy decided to counteroffer at one million, which at least would buy some time. The following morning, Ned, back for a week's vacation from covering the war in Croatia, went up to Wings Neck and had breakfast with Forbes and David. They proposed making a family bid somewhat less than the architect's final offer, with a small amount down, the rest to be paid out by next May. Our share, if we were still interested, would be $250,000 for the Hallowell lot. All day, we sat in the kitchen, shooing away the children, trying to decipher the flurry of phone calls about the Big House from one end of the conversation. At some point, Ned mentioned that David and Forbes wanted the option to extend until next April, because they might decide to move to San Francisco, in which case they might *not* want to go ahead with the deal. We were worried by their vacillation, but we were far more uncertain ourselves. Dad looked almost nauseous with tension. His surgery was ten days away. A frightening twelve-page booklet describing the operation lay on the kitchen table. I worried that he might go into it so anxious that he'd have a heart attack on the operating table (at his age, of course, this was a risk even without added stress).

Mum was sketching pictures of pacific-looking young men with closed eyes, as if willing Dad to relax. Ultimately, Dad decided (and we agreed) that if the architect accepted the $1 million counteroffer, that would be the end of it. If he didn't, then we would think about being part of Forbes and David's offer. In the midst of all the waffling, Mum shook her head. "I think we should get everyone in one room with a therapist and talk it all out," she said. Dad grimaced. I suggested we'd need at least four therapists.

A week later, Dad and Uncle Jimmy received a faxed bid from Forbes and David for the Big House, its contents, and nine acres. A provision in their bid graciously gave us an option on the Hallowell lot until the end of October. It was, I gathered, put-up-or-shut-up time. My father wanted to know whether I really wanted to do it. I admitted that I worried about the finances—putting in $50,000 would be a stretch for Anne and me, and for the foreseeable future we would have no money to contribute toward building a house. I told Dad that I had so admired the forthrightness of David and Forbes that maybe I'd been trying to match them. Deep down I hoped they would buy the Big House, and that we would *not* buy the Hallowell lot. I felt ashamed to admit this after all the back-and-forth. I felt I'd unintentionally led my family on. I told Dad my bottom line was that I hoped the Big House would stay in the family, and that maybe Anne and I could occasionally rent it. My father's financial adviser had advised him not to go in on the Hallowell lot, and he said he didn't think he could get money toward a house for a while. He felt he was too old to wait. He would tell Jimmy he was not interested. The Hallowell lot would be sold separately; Forbes and David would bid on the Big House with Ellen and Mary; the five principals would decide between the family bid and the architect's.

That night I dreamed that I saw my grandfather through the window of the Big House. He looked younger and fitter than I remembered him. It was a miracle; I thought he had been dead for many years. I went inside to make sure it was he. He was lying on a couch in the living room, reading. But as I moved closer, I saw that he was in terrible shape. Although he was breathing, his skin looked as if it had been peeled off, and he had a huge hole in his chest through which I could see the flesh and blood inside. His face was a mass of cuts. Though my mother came and tried to tend to his wounds, we later learned that Grandpa had died. He was the Big House, of course.

A few weeks later—not long, in fact, before we drove up this summer— there was another bid, this time from a developer who wanted to tear down the old house and put up six new ones. He hoped his bid would be sweetened by his offer to name the subdivision Colt Pointe.

XXI

Leaving

W HO CAN say when the end of summer first sails into view? Is it the night in mid-August when, after sleeping under a single sheet all summer, I get out the blankets, releasing the wintry smell of mothballs from the oak chest? Is it the morning when, driving to the general store, I see a plume of smoke curling from a Pocasset chimney? Is it when the poison ivy begins to yellow? Is it when I go down to the Bluff for a swim and see that the wind has swung around to come out of the north?

This is the morning the wind changed. The water is calm, but it looks cooler, darker, metallic, a little forbidding. Instead of beating out to the bay, a sailboat may now glide easily out of the harbor before the wind. Instead of drawing us into the harbor, into summer, the wind seems to be blowing us back into our winter lives.

Over the following week, the signs accumulate. When we go for ice cream at our favorite stand, we take our cones indoors. An ever-thickening flow of minivans and SUVs—bicycles strapped to the roofs, backseats filled with children, cargo areas crammed with buckets and fishing rods and Monopoly games—heads home over the bridge. A few cars pull boats, which, out of their element, look awkward and vulnerable on their canted trailers. Sitting in the Bourne library, I see the girls' high school soccer team practicing on the field out back. The mannequins in the department store windows in Falmouth wear long pants and sweaters that make us feel hot as we drive past in bathing suits and T-shirts. The local paper publishes the lunch menu for the opening day of school: meatball subs, lightly buttered pasta, Italian mixed vegetables, and chilled fruit. One morning, while I push Henry in his stroller around the Neck, a van pulls up alongside. The driver leans out the window and asks where Middle Road is. You're on it, I tell him. "I'm the new school bus driver here," he says, "and darn, there are no street signs—I can't tell where I am."

I think of all the projects we won't get to this summer—the screens I didn't repair, the saltwater aquarium I promised Susannah we'd set up, the whale-watching trip we never took. (And I think of all the things Susannah and Henry will never get to do here: they've never played Ghost or walked to the lighthouse along the shore.) As I lie awake in the morning, my thoughts turn to what awaits us in New York: mail, bills, work, soccer practices, doctors' appointments, the subway. The number of times Anne calls home for our phone messages increases in inverse proportion to the number of days left until we leave. Delivering some departing guests to Buzzards Bay, I get a pang of apprehension when, in the message window over the windshield of their approaching bus, I see the words PROVIDENCE/NEW YORK. One morning, sitting on the piazza with a cup of coffee, I find myself biting my nails.

Before summer ends, there is the brief flare of false hope known as Labor Day. Representing both the last hurrah of summer and the beginning of fall, Labor Day is the ideal holiday for WASPs, combining, as it does, hard work (preparing the house for winter) with nostalgia (remembering July and August). All weekend, people pour back over the bridge. On Wings Neck, the final rounds of the tennis tournament are played; the Labor Day Race—the last and most important of the year—is sailed; the end-of-season cocktail party is held at the Buzzards Yacht Club. All the owners are down. At the Big Cove, I see people I haven't seen all summer.

My parents arrive on Friday afternoon. My father's back operation took place six weeks ago, and he's still frail. His balance is shaky; he has a large scab on one knee acquired from a fall. Almost as soon as he gets here, he goes into the Lower Bedroom "to lie down for fifteen minutes." I lie on the other twin bed and we talk about Great-Uncle Chis, who has been moved to a nursing home. Dad, who visits him frequently, hadn't been in a nursing home since his mother's death. "So of course it made me think of Ma," he says, eyes glistening. "It also selfishly made me think of myself." He hopes he and my mother will never get too sick to take care of themselves. "After Dad died, I always said it was a blessing he went so suddenly, but as I see my friends dying now, I *really* mean it—it *was* a blessing." We talk about his operation and its difficult aftermath. "I can be pretty demanding. And Lise has handled it with flying colors. It could have been very rough, but we both gave a lot, both tried to make things comfortable, and I think it has brought us even closer together."

In the old days, when we talked about anything verging on the serious (particularly about Mum), Dad quickly changed the subject or made a joke. Today, immobilized by fatigue and with mortality on his mind, he talks with me for nearly an hour about his work and mine, about midlife crises, about his father's death, without a single detour to less threatening topics. "Grandpa died at seventy-two," he says, "which happens to be the same age as the fellow next to you." When I bring up the Big House, I am surprised by the fervency of his hope that it will stay in the family. It's one of the longest, most intimate conversations we've ever had, and I don't want it to end.

Although my parents say they have resigned themselves to letting go of the Big House, I am touched to see them maintain their usual rituals: Dad arranging his keys and billfold on the dining room sideboard, Mum putting their clothes away before pouring coffee into her favorite over-sized blue mug, the two of them taking a short walk to the clearing where Grandpa's ashes are buried. The lights haven't been working in my parents' usual bedroom on the second floor, but when I ask Dad whether they might prefer the Lower Bedroom, he insists on their accustomed place with a vehemence that surprises me. Later, while washing dishes, I look out the window and see him raising the flag.

On Saturday afternoon, Aunt Ellen and her son, Henry, arrive. We swim at the Bluff, while the Twelves race in the bay. As we pass the house, Dad and Ellen recall climbing onto the forty-foot-high ridge of the roof and being caught there when their parents pulled into the driveway. "That was the last time we did it," says Ellen. It is low tide, and we help Dad, who is wearing sneakers, across the rocks. He swims on his back, like a sea otter. My cousin Henry, too, swims on his back, his sandaled feet up, looking just like Dad. Swimming, like doing the dishes, is a traditional place for catching up, and we talk as we paddle.

Later, I play tennis with Henry (who for years was the youngest Henry in the clan, but now, at family gatherings, is referred to as Big Henry to distinguish him from my own Little Henry). The court is in bad shape—the fence riddled with holes and beginning to collapse, the surface veined with cracks, the net-raising gear so worn that to use it is to risk decapitation. The players, neither of whom has been on a court in several years, aren't in much better shape themselves. Nervous about falling and aggravating my bad back, I'm afraid to chase down shots. Henry's game is still lovely, but he has shoulder problems, and after one set he's so tired he stands at midcourt and swats listlessly at passing balls. As we play, we talk of the glory days, of watching Dad and Uncle Jimmy in the tournament, of playing in the tournament ourselves, and of how today we'd be lucky to win a single round. A few years ago, we would have played at least three sets, but, exhausted, we stop midway through the second. How could we have aged so fast? Dad emerges from the woods, where he has been pruning the path to the clearing where Grandpa's ashes are buried, and watches for a while. Despite our protests and his doctor's admonition not to bend over, he can't help wandering into the brush to find a ball we hit out.

As the boats come into the harbor after the race, we prepare dinner. Aunt Ellen and Dad sit on the back steps, shucking corn. My mother interleaves slices of French bread with daubs of garlic butter, and makes her famous chocolate sauce for dessert. I chop onions, tomatoes, and zucchini for ratatouille, the once-reviled specialty of Grandpa's that has become one of my favorites. Anne helps Susannah set the table while keeping an eye on Little Henry, who keeps an eye on the pinecones he's collected. Big Henry tends the grill. There is a companionable buzz of activity. People move around the kitchen, finding serving bowls for the corn, pouring another glass of wine, finding excuses to taste the chocolate sauce. When we gather around the dining table, Dad mumbles the familiar "Bless this food to our use and us to thy service." I realize that this small gathering—there are only eight of us, so we have removed two leaves from the table—may be the last time our extended family has dinner together in the Big House. Afterward, as we clean up, Dad, his back hurting, lets Big Henry take over the dishwashing halfway through. It is the first time I've ever seen him relinquish his spot at the sink.

When I come downstairs in the morning, my father, who is lining up bacon slices in regimental rows on a paper-towel-covered plate exactly the way Grandpa used to—tells me that a hurricane is going to hit Cape

Cod tonight. Big Henry and Aunt Ellen left last night; Dad and Mum are driving to Dedham after breakfast, and he suggests we come with them. Hurricane Edouard, the radio tells us, will bring "torrential rain" and "heavy damaging winds," among other things; Cape residents are urged to leave. We decide that Anne will take the children up to Dedham. I will stay. I don't want to miss the excitement. In September of 1985, I was living alone in the Big House when Hurricane Gloria was promised. Although it fizzled into a gale, it was exciting nonetheless: in the attic, the wind was so loud I couldn't think; outside, I could lean at nearly a forty-five-degree angle, like Buster Keaton in *Steamboat Bill, Jr.* Secretly, I'm hoping for something even stronger this time. I have romantic images of the Big House being swept out to sea, and me, like the captain of a ship, being swept along with it. (Had I been here in 1991, when Hurricane Bob left the Big House without electricity and running water for ten days, I might not be so enthusiastic.)

Before Anne and my parents leave, they help me check the Big House's state of preparedness. There are three new candles and a dozen stubs in the drawer above Grandpa's liquor cabinet. The house has only one flashlight, and of course it doesn't work. When we go to the hardware store, the lines are two dozen long. Hastily made signs over bins of $1.99 flashlights warn us to GET READY. As we drive home, Mum recalls that when Hurricane Carol hit in August of 1954, she was en route to Cape Cod from Boston. Dad was in Texas on business; Harry and I, infants at the time, were at the Big House with our grandparents. After a journey from the Buzzards Bay train station made memorable by both the eighty-mile-an-hour gusts and the inebriated condition of her taxi driver, she arrived at Wings Neck to find the causeway impassable. The cabbie abandoned her. Mum waited at the side of the road, not sure how to proceed. And then, like a mirage, a limousine appeared on the far side of the swamped causeway. It was driven by a neighbor's chauffeur. Mum waded through the two-foot-deep water, stepped into the waiting vehicle, and was driven through howling winds to the Big House.

Back at the house, there is a sticky, gloomy, prestorm feel. When I point out to Susannah how still it is, she says, "That's because the hurricane is gathering its excitement." Dad has already loaded the car and pulled up at the front door, wanting to get going before the bridge gets clogged with traffic. I hug everyone good-bye. "Don't get struck by lightning, Daddy," says Susannah.

"Do you have your handkerchief?" asks my father. I don't, so I pull off my T-shirt and swing it over my head as they drive away.

I head down to the Big Cove, where a crowd has gathered on the beach to haul boats from the water. Everyone is a little wired, as if the storm's electricity were already charging the air. The men work briskly, their businesslike demeanors not quite obscuring their giddiness. The elders of the community stand back, watching, talking of previous hurricanes. Many were here for Bob, when the bay rose ten feet and wind-driven salt spray turned the leaves prematurely red, bringing autumn in August. A few remember Carol, when the railroad tracks washed out and boulders along the Bluff were tossed in the air and split in two. Dr. Hallowell remembers back to "the Big One" of 1938, before hurricanes even had names, when the winds gusted upward of 180 miles an hour, the high tide lapped at his back steps, and 588 people in New England lost their lives. Most people with young children are planning to leave; their cars are already packed to the gills. I have a flicker of guilt at not accompanying Anne. My friend Charlotte and her children are decamping, but her father, Charlotte tells me, is "staying with his boats"; her mother is "staying to watch over him." Shades of the *Titanic*.

All morning, the radio has been warning listeners to "batten down the hatches." So I take in the porch furniture, wash and bring in the barbecue, turn over the wooden picnic table, take down the badminton net. I attempt to fill the bathtubs with water, so they can serve as storage tanks from which to supply the toilets if the pump fails, but because the old rubber plugs are cracked, all the tubs have slow leaks. I go from room to room, sliding down the storm windows, pinching my fingers between the broken sashes and the rotting window frames. Throughout the afternoon, people call to check on the house: Uncle Jimmy, Dad, Anne. Ned, having read about the storm over the AP wire, phones from his office in London, ostensibly to remind me to put the storm windows in place, but when he calls a second time, I realize it's because he wishes he were here. He's never been in the Big House during a hurricane. From the Web he gives me the 5:23 P.M. report on Edouard, which is two hundred miles south of Nantucket at the moment. From 3,300 miles away, he knows more about my weather than I do.

When my chores are done, I wander down to the Bluff. It is dead low and so calm that I can see crabs moving along the sandbar four feet beneath the water's surface. A few Boston Whalers zip about importantly in Red Brook Harbor. A sail disappears into Hospital Cove. A cormorant hurries across the sky. Otherwise, Buzzards Bay is eerily deserted. A nearly imperceptible breeze blows from the northeast. After a swim, I sit on the piazza and watch dark clouds move in overhead. Deceived by the premature darkness, the crickets begin chirping. The wind grows stronger and begins to push the water out the Gut. Inside, the arrow on the barometer still points to FAIR, as it has through rain, snow, sleet, and hurricane for as long as I can remember. By six-thirty, it is dark and cold. With the windows closed, the house feels mid-Octoberish. Every trace of summer I see—the half-finished book on Anne's bedside table, Henry's damp bathing suit on the bedroom floor, the pot of chowder in the fridge—makes summer seem farther away. The wind is making experimental whooshing sounds on the third floor. A light rain begins to patter on the roof.

I haven't been alone for the night here in nine years, and I've forgotten how spooky it can be. I look up and see a hand at the kitchen window: a tree branch bobbing. I hear the patter of poltergeists behind the living room wall: squirrels coming in from the rain. After a dinner of leftover fish chowder, I leaf through the photo albums in the living room, from the newest to the oldest, and, as in one of those flip books through whose rapidly turned pages a horse appears to be running, the history of the Big House seems to scroll backward before my eyes. Sandy and Sidney cutting their wedding cake (in the very room in which I'm *looking* at them cutting their wedding cake). My cousin Catherine blowing out the candles at her third birthday party. My brother Harry displaying his first fish. My father and Uncle Jimmy rushing net. Grandma cutting twenty-year-old Jimmy's hair in the garden. My grinning, five-year-old father with three-year-old Ellen on his lap. Grandpa in a rocking chair on the piazza, with my infant father on *his* lap. Grandma's 1920 passport photo, taken just before she got engaged and went to France. Grandma, wearing a gay smile, at the wheel of her Stutz Bearcat in front of the barn. Ned Atkinson sailing in the harbor with Grandma and Great-Uncle Hal. The "New addition to the dining room, 1915." The crowds at the "Opening of the Cape Cod Canal, 1914." My teenaged grandmother stepping into the Atkinson bathhouse, the millpond in the background. The *Bagheera* sailing past Bassetts. The garden in 1909, looking just as it did when I was a child. Grandma and her brothers playing baseball in the front yard. Eight-year-old Grandma pushing Ellie, her favorite doll, in a pram. Ned Atkinson posing at the Bluff with his just-completed house in the background.

Prowling aimlessly from room to room, straightening paintings and bedspreads as I go, I end up in Mariah's Room. It is my favorite room in the house. It hangs high over the ocean, and the wind's howl is so keen here that when I was a child it was easy to imagine I was perched in the crow's nest of a pirate ship. As I looked out the window from that great height, everything below—a Herreshoff Twelve beating out of the harbor, a group of cousins playing croquet on the lawn, trees nodding in the breeze—seemed slowed, smoothed, becalmed. These days, Mariah's Room is rarely used. But when I get a moment alone, I like to read here, although the wind's whistle is often so strong I cannot concentrate for more than a few sentences. It is a room so saturated with the past that if I were able to capture some of its air in a bottle, it would surprise me if it were not a different color from the air outside.

Four summers ago, while readying the house for renters, we decided to squirrel away some items—of a value more sentimental than financial—in a closet in Mariah's Room. Tonight, as I do every so often, I open the closet and sort through its contents. There is a rusty tin box containing dozens of letters my grandmother had saved. Original editions of *The Arabian Nights, The Wizard of Oz, King Arthur,* and other turn-of-the-century children's books. A copy of *The Science of Nutrition, Including the Art of Cooking in the Aladdin Oven with Directions and Many Recipes* by Edward Atkinson. Several family memoirs. Copies of letters from John Murray Forbes to his wife. Grandma's blue canvas suitcase, containing strings of fake pearls, cut-glass beads, a jumble of mismatched costume jewelry, a Bible, a toothbrush, a red change purse. A leather-and-velvet case containing eight bone-handled appetizer forks. Twenty-six yachting pennants. A family tree drawn by William Atkinson in 1926. A diary my grandmother kept for a few months at age twelve. A framed photo of my teenaged great-grandmother with her sisters, brothers, and mother.

As I look over this modest time capsule, I feel lonely. Removed from their context, these objects seem shorn of meaning. I wonder whether these could really be the family treasures, the precious gleanings of five generations, that we wish above all to preserve. I wonder what, when the house is sold, we will carry with us into the winter.

By nine, I'm in bed. There is still not much wind. I fall asleep to the sound of rain.

I wake to find the Big House still standing. Edouard managed to lose its oomph by the time it reached Cape Cod, and it hit hardest to the east, out to sea. Nevertheless, a hurricane watch is still in effect, and fifty-mile-an-hour winds from the northeast are shaking the house. There are leaks over the first-floor stairs, in the dining room, and in Grandma's Bedroom; I catch the drips in the huge lobster pot, the pan we use for boiling corn, and several mixing bowls. The electricity is out. The Big House has otherwise held tight through what the transistor radio describes to my satisfaction as "drenching downpours and gale-force winds." I wish Anne and the children were here.

Outside, the olive-brown yard has turned an almost fluorescent lime green. A few asphalt shingles lie among the twigs and branches that litter the ground. The wooden shingles on the north side of the house are dark where the rain has soaked in. The wind, roaring like a train, pushes me toward the Bluff. Huge waves race madly out the Gut. In the bay itself, protected by the Bluff from the northeast wind, the water is strangely flat, although gusts make sudden shadows rush across the water. No waves break on the shore. Susannah's clubhouse, though battered, has survived the storm.

By noon, the wind is dying and the rain is letting up. I head out the driveway to fetch Anne and the children back from Dedham, pausing to drag a fallen tree out of the way. The woods look different; I realize that the leaves on the sassafras trees have been curled inside out by the wind, revealing their other, lighter face.

In Dedham, Dad and I visit Great-Uncle Chis, who has been hospitalized. One of the two beds in his room is empty. In the other, a white-haired man lies turned toward the wall. "Uncle Chis," I say softly. The man doesn't move. Assuming I have the wrong room, I walk out. The nurse, however, insists it is Charles Colt's room, so I go back in for a closer look. But this man is neater than Chis, with a long, thin face and carefully combed hair, instead of jowls and unruly white cirrus clouds. He looks like a Wellesley banker, not a garrulous old journalist. Chis has died, I think; his bed has been remade for its next occupant, and this is his former roommate. The man turns toward me and opens his mouth. He has no teeth. I step out and tell my father, nervously, that I don't think Chis is there. Dad goes in, and he isn't sure either. Then he says, "Hello, Chis," and the man turns toward him and says in a soft voice, "Hello, Harry."

Though he has been carefully groomed by the nurses, Chis is not in good shape. He is wearing a catheter. The IVs have left a purple bull's-eye on his inner elbow. Sitting on the bed, I hold his hand and tell him about the weekend at Wings Neck. While we talk, I can't be sure whether he isn't making sense or whether I just can't understand him without his teeth. He calls me Harry several times, but when I remind him I'm George, he says, "Of course." All morning I have been looking at photographs of Chis and Grandpa as young brothers in Geneseo; his life seems to have gone by in a few hours. As we leave, Chis musters his strength and says hoarsely, "It's so *good* of you to come."

Back at the Big House, Anne fixes dinner while Susannah settles into a book. I take Henry to the Bluff. He had a fever last night, but as we watch the wind blow the dark clouds to the far corner of the bay, he revives. "Ocean!" "Boat!" "Clubhouse!" Inside, he celebrates his return by walking up and down two flights of stairs. Then he settles on the kitchen floor to play with his pinecones. It is cold and windy. It feels like fall. There are only a few lights left on Scraggy Neck now, where two nights ago there were dozens, twinkling like fireflies.

On Labor Day morning, I find Susannah digging two holes. Her stuffed animals are lined up nearby. They are, she tells me, attending two funerals. One was for a dead grasshopper she found. The other? "It's a funeral for the end of summer," she says.

When I was a boy, we always left Wings Neck on Labor Day; school began the following morning. But Susannah's school doesn't start until mid-September, and as we watch cars head back over the bridge, we feel smug about staying, even if for only a few more days. We are on the verge of a Cape Cod autumn, which Thoreau likened to "the richest rug imaginable spread over an uneven surface; no damask nor velvet, nor Tyrian dye or stuffs, nor the work of any loom, could ever match it." After Labor Day, it is astonishing how quickly summer falls away. Although more and more people choose to live year-round on Cape Cod, there is still a sudden, strange lull, as when a motorboat's engine is cut and it bobs in the water, while waves from behind, generated by its momentum, push at it. SEE YOU NEXT SUMMER signs appear on the boarded-up windows of ice cream shacks, farm stands, and fish markets. Our favorite fried clam joint in Buzzards Bay is half empty; next week its back room will be closed off entirely. On Wings Neck, which even at the height of summer looks deserted, chains have gone up at the ends of several driveways to discourage uninvited off-season guests. The tennis tournament scoreboard has been removed. The lobster buoys along the Bluff have been taken in for the winter. The boat traffic is so sparse that I can skinny-dip at any hour, although the water is cold and I get out fast. (I think admiringly of Grandma, who used to swim well into November.) The Big House, so full of people just a few days ago, is unnaturally quiet. The days when our feet were tender, our skin was pale, and summer stretched luxuriantly before us seem like the distant past. Before we left New York, Susannah kept asking, "How long till we go to Wings Neck?" Now she asks sorrowfully, "How many more days till we leave?"

In this grace period, everything we do is tinged with the familiar sadness of the approaching end of our Wings Neck summer and the unfamiliar sadness of thinking that we may never have another. These two melancholies, one small and one large, vibrate against each other, each amplifying the other until I can hardly tell them apart. Taking down the hammock makes me as glum as wondering whose name will be at the end of the driveway this time next year.

If we sell to the developer, the house will no longer exist. Even if, God willing, Forbes and David are able to buy it, they will likely gut it and undertake a massive renovation; it will no longer feel "mine" in the old, secret way. So what as a child I always called our "lasts"—each summer's last tennis game, last fishing expedition, last ice cream run—now seem truly our lasts. Like me, Anne and the children want to stay home: no more off-Neck expeditions. We spend part of each day cleaning, part playing. We eat whatever's left in the refrigerator. We throw away what we can't lug back to New York, much of it accumulated over the course of the summer by the house's other tenants: half-empty bottles of ketchup, mustard, Karo syrup, vinegar, mayonnaise, olives, salsa, spaghetti sauce. (This is painful; it goes against my abhorrence of waste. On the other hand, I note with compulsive pleasure that the end of the bottle of sun goop will coincide exactly with the end of our stay.) As the days pass, the mound of blueberries in the mixing bowl dwindles, like sand from an hourglass. When we wash up after dinner, we put the pots and pans away in their rightful winter homes instead of leaving them in the dish drainer. The house's off-season tenants are preparing for winter, too: hearing scrabbling in the wall on her way upstairs, Anne opens the closet on the landing in time to see the sleek red tail of a chipmunk disappearing into the wall.

The day before we leave is the most beautiful day we've had all summer. The sun shimmers on the still water. A slight breeze nudges an occasional boat across an otherwise empty bay. Swallows chase each other across a cloudless sky.

Cleaning house at the end of the season usually has a twofold purpose: neatening up after the departing summer, and preparing it for the next. But what, and whom, are we preparing for now? This afternoon, Anne and I strip beds, return blankets to their chests, sweep floors, clear the sills of dead flies and wasps, escort daddy longlegs outside, close and lock the windows. Cleaning a room is a good way to relearn it. I see things I'd looked at for years but never really noticed: the view from the rarely used porch off the Balcony Room, where the servants used to sun themselves in the afternoon; the gilt-framed portrait in the Sunny Room of two angels, given to my great-grandmother by her aunt in 1887; the blue, pink, yellow, and white walls—undoubtedly Aunt Mary's handiwork—in Oliver's Garden Bedroom. Later, working in the garden, I notice a small window over the Little Nursery I've never seen before. To what room does it belong? Inside, I can't find the window; as far as I can tell, it is part of a crawl space above the nursery's walk-in closet. It was likely walled off during one of my great-grandparents' renovations. It is, I realize, a window whose other side no living person has ever seen.

The children are packing, too. Sorting through the merchandise in her beachside store, Susannah decides to bring home a whelk egg case, three opercula, three lucky stones, an oyster shell, a scallop, an unidentified tooth-shaped shell, a moon snail, two jingle shells, a crab claw, one piece of green sea glass, two pieces of blue sea glass, five rose-hip petals, a blue jay feather, two chunks of milky quartz, and the vertebra of a large fish. She tucks these into a Huggies diaper-wipes box, and we scatter the rest on the Bluff. Henry is bringing home twenty-six snail shells in a baggie. Deep in my luggage is an old gray wooden shingle that blew off in the storm.

On our last night, after we bake a final batch of muffins, we walk out to the Bluff. Anne shows Henry and Susannah the Milky Way and the Big Dipper. And look—over there! A shooting star! Only two homes on Scraggy Neck are lit. Turning back to the Big House, I see that only the first-floor lights are on; the upper floors grow progressively darker until I can't tell where the roof ends and the sky begins.

At 9 P.M., I suddenly remember that Henry brought a hermit crab and four minnows home from the millpond today. They are languishing in the collecting jar on the kitchen table. Susannah and I make an emergency trip to the Big Cove to release them. In the darkness, we hear a school of minnows riffling the surface. After we return, I hear Anne, in the room where Grandma used to sing to me, singing to Henry:

> *Now the day is over*
> *Night is drawing nigh*
> *Shadows of the evening*
> *Steal across the sky.*

On the morning of our last day, it's so foggy we can't see Bassetts Island. A foghorn is blowing; mist sweeps across the lawn. We do our final end-of-summer errands: to the recycling center, to the Laundromat, to the library to return a last stack of books, to the store to get snacks for the trip home (for which Susannah has made four tickets that say CAR SERVICE— MANHATTAN— I 50 THOMPSON STREET, NEW YORK, NEW YORK). Passing the Pocasset church where Sandy was married, I look up at the stained-glass window of a harp-playing angel, given by my grandparents in her memory, that watches over the front door. Back at the Big House, I ferry five barrels of trash to the end of the driveway, haul the porch furniture inside, lock the barn door, unplug the appliances. Meanwhile, armed with mop, broom, and sponge, Anne works her way down from the third floor to the second to the first, sealing off rooms as she goes. The sheets are washed and returned to the linen closet; the blankets are folded and nested in their mothball-laden chests. Eventually, all our luggage is stacked in the hallway and we are confined to the kitchen, whose floor is a mess of smooshed Popsicles and bananas, deployed to buy time from Henry.

While Anne tackles the last and largest task—the kitchen—I take the children to the Big Cove. There are only ten boats left at their moorings, and the beach is empty, but the crabs in the millpond are still plentiful. Henry, in his pajamas—he's supposed to be taking a nap—plays happily in the muck, throwing stones to see them splash, making piles of sand. Susannah patrols the creek for specimens to show her brother, keeping an eye out for Hairy Harry, the algae-covered spider crab of whom we've grown fond. We hadn't planned to stay long and we hadn't planned to get wet, but we can't help it. Susannah takes off her overalls. I strip Henry to his diaper, which eventually gets so waterlogged it succumbs to gravity and falls off. We end up staying three hours. When we finally walk into the woods, Susannah turns back a moment. "Good-bye, Big Cove," she says. "Good-bye, millpond."

As we come around the corner of the barn and see the Big House, Susannah breaks into a run. She looks so small, and the Big House so massive, that the sight of her racing joyfully across the grass toward the house, where Anne has piled all our bags beside the car, nearly breaks my heart.

I like to think that, as a waste-hater, I'm good at loading a car. I stuff a poster in a long, thin space, use a Dopp kit to plug an available cranny. But by the time the car is completely crammed, there is still a large pile in the grass beside it. I realize that the success of the entire enterprise has been hinging on my being able to fit Susannah's bike, Henry's stroller, Henry's blue backpack, a half dozen library books that have turned up since we returned all the library books this morning, and two bags of leftover groceries I can't bear to throw out, in the right front seat. (Anne will sit between the children in the back in order to entertain Henry.) I can't quite figure out where I went wrong; except for a few books and our gleanings from the beach, we are leaving with no more than we arrived with. But our dilemma may be the product of a natural law of summer: that we expand, we ripen. I fiddle with this, throw away that, and, eventually, on the umpteenth slam, the trunk shuts tight.

When we step back inside the front door, the house is so still that for a moment I am tricked into thinking that we are actually arriving at the beginning of the summer, that we are here to reintroduce ourselves to every room, that all of August lies ahead of us.

Months ago, I had thought about how I might say good-bye to the Big House—not just an end-of-summer good-bye, an end-of-everything good-bye. I fantasized about sleeping in each of its nineteen rooms on nineteen successive nights. At the very least, I imagined being able to spend time in every room, sit in every chair, examine each picture, open each book, pay homage to every last fishing lure and sandbag doorstop. How long does it take to say good-bye to a room? Three minutes? Three hours? Three days wouldn't be enough. And so, perhaps because we know it will be less painful, we rush.

"Good-bye, laundry room," says Susannah. "Good-bye, linen closet. Good-bye, kitchen. Good-bye, pantry. Good-bye, dining room."

Henry, thinking it some sort of game, points to each room and delivers a rapid-fire "G'bye! G'bye! G'bye!" Soon, we are following him as he charges ahead, shouting, "Room! Room! Room!" as if he can't quite believe there could be more.

We walk upstairs, past the portraits of my father, Uncle Jimmy, and Aunt Mary. Like the past that is said to scroll before the eyes of a dying man, scraps of memory tickle me as we hurry through: the hum of grown-ups taking a late lunch on the piazza as I napped in the Balcony Room as a child; the gurgle of the water as it began to drain from the kitchen-wing bathtub before dinner; the dawn light waking me early in the Sunny Room the summer I first fell in love and my grandmother went mad. "Remember, sometimes we hear squirrels living in here," says Susannah, who takes the lead now, as if she were giving us a tour. "And here's where Daddy's grandpa used to sleep." She peers into every closet. "Here's that little secret passage!" We all feel a certain urgency, an onward pull, as if we have never been here before and are about to discover something. "I'm going up to the third floor," she announces.

The Playroom looks especially barren. The few remaining toys constitute a pentimento of three generations: the traction engine my father played with, the wooden fruits I played with, the plastic garage we picked up for Henry at the Bourne dump. Henry runs over to the traction engine. Loading it up with wooden pears and apples, he pushes it across the floor, making motor growls that sound over the clatter of the metal wheels. Henry has no idea we are saying good-bye to the house forever; he just sees the Playroom as a place to play in. After forty years, not one slice of the pear is missing. After seventy years, the traction engine still works.

Susannah and I climb up to the attic, where we look out each small window in turn. "If I could choose any room in the world to make my bedroom in, it would be this," she says. She points to a window. "One time, my friend Roxie and I were looking all over the house for Ned Atkinson's ghost. We came up here—and saw a spiderweb right *there* with a spider on it. We said that was Ned Atkinson's ghost." I'm surprised to hear this. So many lives have been lived here, so many feelings felt that I know nothing about. After all I have learned about the house, I have so much still to learn, and no time left to learn it.

On the way down, I notice several words scrawled in red marker on the Sackett Board wall. They are so faded I can barely read them, but I recognize my grandfather's handwriting. It says "Remember," followed by a word I can't read. Is Grandpa trying to reach us? Is he giving us a last message? Remember *what*? I call to Anne and Susannah excitedly, but none of us can decipher the second word.

It is time to go. We tell Henry we have to say good-bye to the other rooms. He begins to cry. He wants to stay forever in the Playroom, as I want to stay forever in the house. I carry him, sobbing, downstairs. On the first floor, I want to wind the ship's clock once more, but there isn't time. I pull the big green door shut behind us.

We had planned to leave by noon. It is past three-thirty, and already I am imagining the snarl of traffic that awaits us on the Bourne Bridge. The sun is coming out at last. I have to take one final swim at the Bluff. Henry, sniffling, has curled up on Anne's lap. I ask Susannah if she'd like to swim. She says no. But as I walk toward the Bluff, she changes her mind and runs to catch up.

We look out over the bay. This morning I had been able to see no farther than the Big Rock. Now the weather has cleared. The cloud cover has teased apart into distinct flocks of blue and gray, and we can see down the bay all the way to Naushon and Cuttyhunk, dark strips hovering like flying fish above the water. The air smells clean, cool, freshly scrubbed. All morning the waves were large and furious. Now the water is still. A light breeze pushes out from the harbor, strong enough to fill the sails of a lone sloop beating toward us from the horizon but gentle enough so that the boat seems hardly to move. The scene has a serenity and clarity that is almost surreal, as if it were a dream or a movie. The rainstorm has ushered in the fall. I want to stay. It is time to go.

It is dead low tide. Susannah and I help each other over the periwinkle-studded rocks, her increasing strength now making her as necessary to me as I am to her. And then it is deep enough to let go. I swim out to the sandbar, Susannah close behind. When I turn to look for her, she is standing on tiptoes on the sand, smiling, her mouth just enough above water to announce in a tight-lipped but triumphant shout, "I can touch now!"

We turn and face the shore. The Big House rises from the pines like a galleon, green waves shed from its prow.

And then I notice a large black boat churning toward us from Scraggy Neck, a boat I've never seen before. It looks like an iron-hulled fishing vessel or a small freighter. It comes on surprisingly fast, like a police car about to pull over a speeding driver, so that for a moment I wonder whether it is coming for *us*. As it approaches, I see on its side the words U. S. COAST GUARD. We swim toward shore until our legs scrape bottom, then crawl over the rocks, pulling with our hands. We squat beside the Big Rock and wait.

The boat heads straight for us, but when it reaches Atkinson's Buoy, it cuts its engine. There are four men on deck. Two of them attach chains to the top of the buoy, and, using a hydraulic arm, they begin to winch it out of the water. What are they doing? Are they taking it away? Will even the buoy named for the man who built this house disappear? The buoy is surprisingly long; like an iceberg, it lies mostly below the surface. The bottom two-thirds is shaggy with algae. The crewmen swing it toward the boat until it is suspended over the deck, where they begin to scour it with long brushes, as if it were a massive tooth. When they finish, it is fresh and clean again, and ready for the new century. Then they winch it back over the water, where it hangs for a moment before it slides in, bobs, and settles.

Epilogue

INDIAN SUMMER

Six weeks after Labor Day, Great-Uncle Chis died at the age of ninety-four. "I always say it's a blessing in a case like this, but it's still quite a shock," said my father. Although he didn't say so—and I didn't ask—I knew that the loss deeply shook Dad, for whom Chis was a father figure as well as that generation's last direct link to his own father. Dad was now the eldest Colt.

A few days later, I took the train from New York to Boston for the funeral. It was a warm, Indian summer day in late October, and the city, its banks of brownstones copper in the sun, looked seductive and smug. As I walked across the Common, I recalled the afternoon many years ago when Chis warned me not to move back to Boston, not to make the same mistake my grandfather had made. The service was held at Christ Church in Cambridge, a simple gray wooden building in which—as I could imagine Chis pointing out—Colonial troops had been quartered during the Revolution. The same familiar faces that had gathered for Great-Aunt Amy's funeral nine months before were gathered again, a little older now, to recite the same prayers and sing the same hymns— "Abide with Me," "The Strife Is O'er," and, of course, "Now the Day Is Over." Chis's granddaughter, one of the eulogists, said, "We loved to hear him tell the family stories, most of which turned out to be true: that his father had been in St. Petersburg in 1917 when the revolution began; that he had lived in Paris and Constantinople when he was young; that he had a brother who had been killed playing polo; that he had married the belle of Boston of 1920, and his brother had married the belle of Boston of the year before."

Great-Uncle Chis was buried next to Great-Aunt Amy under a single headstone that read "True Love."

Over the course of the fall, Forbes and David reaffirmed the solidity of their offer on the Big House, but when the trust received a $1.1 million bid on the property, the highest thus far, it was not immediately refused. The leap in price could not help but make some family members wonder whether the market was reviving, whether the house might be worth more than they imagined. My father, Uncle Jimmy, and Russell believed the offer should be seriously considered. Aunt Ellen and Aunt Mary made it clear they were not interested. Because four of the five legatees had to agree to a sale, two could block a transaction. With Ellen and Mary able to veto any agreement, it seemed unlikely that another deal would ever go through—and one by one, all the principals realized that they didn't *want* another deal. The wrangling was over. All five agreed that even though a greater profit might be made by selling to an outsider, it was more important to keep the house in the family. Forbes and David's offer was therefore—finally, incredibly—accepted.

For months, I had been praying that the house would stay in the family. It looked as if those prayers had been answered. I was scared to believe it, lest the deal fall through; my hopes had been raised and dashed so many times that I didn't think I could bear another disappointment. I was filled with admiration for Forbes and David for moving ahead where we had not. Also, though I admitted it to no one—not to my parents, not to Anne, and not to myself—I was terribly, terribly jealous.

The deal did not fall through.

On a bright windy afternoon in May, the day before the closing, Dad, Aunt Ellen, Aunt Mary, Uncle Jimmy, and Sandy's son, Russell, gathered at the Big House. (I came too; so did Forbes and Aunt Buffy, Uncle Jimmy's wife.) Forbes and David were buying the house with its contents included, but had agreed that each of the principals could choose five items—what the real estate lawyer referred to as "tangibles"—from the house. It was the first time they had all been together at the house since deciding to sell it five years earlier. As we lunched on pizza and soft drinks in the garden, sitting in a circle on plastic porch chairs, we caught up on family news; but, knowing what we were here for—each of the principals was clutching a list of items he or she hoped to leave with—

there was a slight awkwardness. My father, I knew, wanted to get this over with quickly. "I'm just worried someone might get a little *emotional*," he had said as we drove to the Cape that morning. (The someone he was most worried about, I suspect, was himself.)

It was decided that Aunt Ellen would choose first. She consulted her list. "The red upholstered chair in the living room," she said firmly. Everyone nodded approvingly. And so, just as my brothers and I used to have first picks on baseball cards, she and the other principals proceeded to go around the circle, declaring their dibs.

Amazingly, everyone got almost everything that he or she wanted. (It reminded me of the 1902 Boston meeting during which the twelve members of Ned Atkinson's syndicate had each named his favorite lot on Wings Neck, and discovered, to their surprise, that no two men wanted the same one.) Uncle Jimmy systematically worked his way through the nineteenth-century hunting prints from Geneseo that had hung in the living and dining rooms. In addition to the red chair, Aunt Ellen chose the bureau in Grandpa's study, a small wooden chair in the Playroom, a silver pitcher won by one of J. W. Colt's racehorses, and a set of Jane Austen. Aunt Mary chose things for her children: a casserole dish with a snail on the lid for Catherine, and, for Jonathan, who was furnishing a new home in Nebraska, Grandma's double bed, the daybed in Grandpa's study, and a pair of painted green bureaus from the Little Nursery. (The items were old, battered, and practically worthless—Jonathan could probably buy new furniture for what it would cost to ship this stuff to Lincoln—but Aunt Mary had never been one to let anything go to waste.) Russell, who had spent little time here since he was a toddler, chose toys from the Playroom—the globe, the wooden blocks, the miniature rocking horse with worn leather ears—as well as a set of Hans Christian Andersen and an old steamer trunk that had belonged to his great-great-grandfather. Dad's list was short. The one thing he cared about was the Chelsea ship's clock; he had hoped to give it to Ned. A week earlier, when he had heard that others wanted it, too, he had changed his mind and suggested that the clock—the house's most visible symbol—be left in the front hall. There was nothing he wanted for himself ("I've already got pictures of Ma and Dad," he told me, "and I don't need anything else to remind me of them"), but my mother had urged him to choose something to remind him of the house, so he selected the high-backed blue corduroy chair she called his "throne." He also chose my grandfather's dictionary stand for

Mum. That was more than enough, he said; but Forbes suggested that Ned, the best sailor in the family, might like the photograph of the *Bagheera* on the dining room mantel, and I selfishly pointed out that I'd always coveted the set of Dickens Ellen Atkinson had brought to Wings Neck in 1903.

During the first few rounds, everyone was nervous, vigilant, slightly competitive. On several occasions someone jumped the gun and started to choose before his or her turn, triggering gentle "ahems." There were murmured compliments on everyone's choices—especially when those choices were items in which the murmurers had no interest themselves. But everyone grew increasingly generous. When Dad chose Grandpa's dictionary stand, there was general agreement that the old *Oxford Universal Dictionary on Historical Principles* should go with it. When Dad's next turn came, he said, firmly, quickly, the way he does when he's emotional (and he *did* get emotional, just as he'd feared): "The Trollope set, and leave it in the house." His eyes were moist as he added, "Because my grandmother *loved* reading Trollope." There followed a discussion of the merits of Trollope, the relative readability of *Barchester Towers* and *The Warden*, and the quixotic nature of Ellen Atkinson's reading habits. This brief literary interlude seemed to loosen things up. More people picked items on the condition that they stay in the house, as if wanting to ensure that, despite the coming changes, the Big House would remain the Atkinson/Colt repository. (Forbes welcomed this. She hoped photocopies could be made of the family portraits, which, it had been agreed, belonged to their subjects and were thus exempt from the divvy. Aunt Buffy volunteered for the task.) There were remarks on how pretty the garden was, how lovely the weather, how a hint of the forthcoming summer was already in the air. During a lull, Uncle Jimmy turned to Forbes and said with sudden feeling, "I'm really glad you're buying the house. *Really* glad."

After the formal choosing was over, people began to wander through the house. Uncle Jimmy emerged from a bedroom brandishing a copy of Zane Gray's *The Shortstop*. "I knew I recognized this one," he said triumphantly, pointing to the name written on the inside cover in his own childhood hand. Dad held up a small brown suitcase, which promptly fell apart. "God, I remember Ma using this all the time," he said in disbelief. Aunt Mary, opening a Forbes family memoir, was startled when a photograph slipped from its pages. "Look at this!" she said, picking up a picture of her twenty-seven-year-old self at her first wedding. Dad came downstairs holding something behind his back. "Jimmy, we've come across an item of extraordinary value, but we all agree it's too precious to bid on, so we want you to have it." He presented his brother with a battered old music book Jimmy had used in elementary school. As I watched Dad and his siblings grow increasingly relaxed and affectionate, I almost felt I was back in the Big House in 1963, watching them kid one another in the kitchen. By contrast, Russell, who had flown in from Los Angeles on the red-eye that morning, seemed tired and forlorn, excluded from the intimacy he would have enjoyed had his mother been alive. He was thirsty for pieces of family history, as if by acquiring some of the "tangibles" he could acquire some of the intangible past that had been stolen from him. "Would anyone mind if I took this?" he said, holding up a copy of Edward Atkinson's biography.

We worked our way up through the rooms until there was no place left but the attic, where we hunched under the eaves, poking through old bags and boxes while plaster fell and wind whistled. Russell unlatched a trunk. Inside, there were hundreds of dusty, curling photographs, many of them from the branch of the family after whom he'd been named. "Who's that?" Russell asked. "That's your great-great-uncle Jim Russell," said Ellen. "And that's your great-great-uncle Howland Russell." And so on, until, realizing that it would take days if we were to go through every photo in that trunk, we closed the lid. We opened another trunk. Hundreds more faces peered up at us.

And then we began to pack up, leaving gaps in the bookshelves, empty spaces in the pantry, and ghostly, dust-framed rectangles on the walls. I winced when Uncle Jimmy, Aunt Mary, and Dad took down the sketches of their youthful selves from the stairwell, literally removing themselves from the Big House.

Before we left, we walked to the Bluff. Standing on the platform above the beach, a brisk southwest wind rippling our hair and clothing, we watched waves crash on the Big Rock. It was high tide. We all knew this was likely the last time that all the siblings, who ranged in age from sixty-four to seventy-three, would be together at the house. "We should get a picture," someone said. "Does anyone have a camera?" Aunt Mary did. Aunt Buffy volunteered to take the photo. We put our arms around one another.

"What's that peninsula across the water?" asked Russell, while Buffy started snapping.

"Scraggy Neck," said Uncle Jimmy.

"I heard Grandma used to swim there from Wings Neck," said Russell. "Did she really do that?"

"Before breakfast every day," said Uncle Jimmy. "She could have done it with one hand tied behind her back." We headed back toward the house. "God, she could swim, such a long crawl, she cut through the water so smoothly." Jimmy's voice was fierce. He shook his head at the memory.

A few weeks later, a friend asked me for the telephone number at Hidden House. I had recently lost my address book and couldn't remember the number. Calling directory assistance, I explained that there were two numbers for H. F. Colt in Pocasset, one for the main house and one for the cottage; could I have the cottage? No, she said, there were no H. F. Colts in Pocasset. Puzzled, I asked her to try Bourne. Nothing there, either. In fact, she added, there were no H. F. Colts listed in all of Cape Cod. There must be some mistake, I said—the number had been in the telephone directory for at least half a century. And then it dawned on me. I asked her to try my cousin's name. That number was listed—but it was completely unfamiliar.

Although it was only natural that Forbes and David, the new owners, should have the phone number changed, it felt strange nevertheless. Phone numbers are the fingerprints of a house. For nearly forty years, long after the numbers of other places I'd lived had blurred to an unintelligible jumble, the Big House phone number—563-6883—had been etched into my mind: the hopeful uplift of the first two digits; the playful ricochet of the 6-3-6; the pleasing symmetry of the twin eights; the reassuring return home to three. Familiarity made its sequence inevitable; to change even one digit might, it seemed, divert a caller to Nantucket or Nome. How many times had I dialed that number and heard not the prissy trill of a contemporary Touch-Tone phone but the stolid, deliberate, old-fashioned burr I knew so well? Sometimes in winter I dialed 508-563-6883 from New York, though I knew there would be no answer. I just wanted to hear that ring, to invoke the pleasant dissonance between the hum of the city and the silence of the house, in which the ringing of the phone echoed so intimately that I almost felt I could walk into the pantry and answer it myself. In the dead of winter, it was the sound of summer.

I'd forgotten the Hidden House number, but I would never forget the

Big House number. Refusing to believe the operator, I dialed it for the last time. I heard a piercing *beep-beep-beep*, mimicking the climbing do-so-do tones of a French ambulance, and then that bright, patient, no-nonsense fifties-mother voice which simultaneously comforts and chides you: "The number you have reached"—slight attention-getting emphasis on the word "*num*ber"—"five-six-three-six-eight-eight-three"—the digits enunciated separately, as if they were as unrelated as lottery numbers—"in area code five-oh-eight has been disconnected."

I felt disconnected, too.

For years, my parents had talked about what they might do with their share from the sale of the Wings Neck property. Over Christmas, we had gathered at my brother Harry's house in rural Maine, where he worked as a doctor. We talked of how nice it might be to spend summer vacations near his family, where a fine old house on ten acres sold for a quarter the price of the Big House. Armed with a sheaf of brochures from a local real estate agent, we trooped through a succession of lakeside cottages, trying to be polite about the fake paneling, the acoustic tile ceiling, the hollow-core doors, the wall-to-wall shag carpeting.

There was a flurry of excitement after we saw a white clapboard farmhouse set on seventeen acres of lakeside meadow. In our imaginations, family members gathered there from afar: Dad and Mum walking at dusk through the wildflowers; Anne and I reading on the porch; Ned turning the barn into a workshop in which he would build his dream boat; Mark riding a tractor mower against the horizon; Henry, Susannah, and their cousins racing toward the lake in their bathing suits. Although the mud lay inches thick after a sudden winter thaw, all we could see was summer.

There followed a heady few months of return visits, faxes, phone calls, and e-mails. Mum told Anne that her own family had never had a gathering place, a place to pass on from generation to generation, and she felt so lucky to have married into a family that had one. (Anne told her that was just how *she* felt.) Now that Wings Neck was gone, Mum wanted to be able to provide a place like that for her grandchildren. "I think of it as a sort of bridge to the future," she said, and the phrase stuck. The white clapboard farmhouse became the Bridge to the Future, the initial tint of self-protective irony in our voices gradually fading.

But as we talked of making a bid, my fears began to surface. How could Anne and I sink our savings into a summer house when, as writers, we would both have unpredictable incomes for the rest of our lives? Even if we could afford it, would I be able to get up to Maine often enough to tend the place? I was not the only one with doubts. When we talked about the Bridge to the Future, Dad's voice acquired the pinched tone it had had during the Big House negotiations. He worried that, at the age of seventy-three, he wouldn't be able to do his share of the caretaking either. Gradually, it became clear that what my parents really wanted—I'm not sure they even realized it themselves—was not a Maine version of the Big House but a small, manageable place of their own. *I* wanted a bridge to the future; they wanted a modest, private present. A few weeks later, Dad mentioned, almost in passing, with a casualness that seemed a measure of the wisdom of the decision, that they had bought a three-bedroom cottage on one acre, on a lake not far from Harry's. "Dad and I walked in and it felt right," Mum told me. "It was so freeing to be in a house with no past, no family history. I didn't feel all that weight."

A few months later, we drove up to Maine to see my parents' new house. A simple, twenty-year-old clapboard box not much larger but far more orderly than Hidden House, it had little to distinguish it from thousands of other cottages on hundreds of Maine lakes. It was the antithesis of the Big House. Yet within a few months my parents had made it their own. This wasn't a sacred cow; it was a small, warm, casual place whose furnishings—the collage Mum had made with driftwood scavenged from the Bluff, a coffee table Grandma had made at McLean, the patchwork quilts Anne had brought home from an assignment in Karachi—were related not by style or era but by sentiment. After so many years without boats at Wings Neck, I was somewhat startled to see two kayaks and a canoe on the dock. Ownership seemed to have released my parents, and they had gone, relatively speaking, on a spending spree. Indeed, when Mum was trying to pay for the canoe, the storekeeper apologetically informed her that her credit card had been refused. The bank explained that $2,400 had been charged during the previous few days, a spending pattern so unlike hers that it was assumed the card had been stolen.

My parents spoke of the joys of freshwater swimming, of owning a house that required so little maintenance, of having a lawn that took three minutes to mow. They already had favorite spots for their chairs on the deck, where they liked to sit, binoculars in hand, watching a pair of loons build a nest on the west side of the inlet, just as they were building theirs on the east. As we backed out the driveway, Dad and Mum stood on the porch and waved. I remembered what the family therapist had once said: "What I want for you as parents is to stand in the doorway of your home with your arms around each other, watching your sons drive out of your driveway, and smile as you wave good-bye." (I was glad to see my father embellish that prescription by pulling out a handkerchief and giving us a Colt good-bye.) I was happy that although my parents still missed the Big House keenly, they had been able to leave Wings Neck behind. Yet I felt a little left behind myself, the only one unable to let go.

That summer, Forbes and David invited us to spend a few weeks at Hidden House before the renovation of the Big House began. I'm not sure whether the prospect of returning to Wings Neck made me more excited or more scared. As we arrived, I could see that although work had not yet begun in earnest, there were already changes. The honeysuckle and ivy that lapped against the Big House had been cut away, leaving it as vulnerable-looking as an old ram after the spring shearing. In the driveway circle, the forbidding tangle of catbrier and poison ivy, once a Bermuda Triangle for foul balls, had been thinned, revealing three thriving rhododendrons Ned had planted years earlier. The biggest change was out back: all the brush along the Bluff had been removed, leaving a handful of isolated, wind-bent pines. As I looked through the vertical bars of the remaining trees at the glittering bay, I was struck by two conflicting feelings: first, that the very pruning I so deplored at other houses on the Neck had happened here; second, that it revealed a shockingly beautiful view.

The following night, Forbes and David invited us to dinner. Although we felt sufficiently informal with them to use the back door, it was the first time I could ever recall knocking on it. I felt brittle and shy. Inside, I looked around cautiously. The kitchen seemed hollow, and I realized that the big square table was gone; our cousin Jonathan, said Forbes, had taken it back to Nebraska for his new home. The items selected by the five principals were, of course, missing. Even more unsettling than what was not there was what had been added: *The New York*

Times strewn on the living room table; the bowl of fruit in the kitchen; the unfamiliar cereals in the cabinet; the television set in the dining room. Like an old lover meeting his replacement, I envied these signs of new life. I could also see that the current relationship was a thoroughly happy one—that my former beloved was in good hands—and that made me feel even more miserable.

Forbes and David were practical about all kinds of things the rest of us hadn't been. They had had the tap water tested and learned that the level of coliform bacteria made it unfit to drink. We began buying bottled water or driving to Sandwich to fill gallon jugs from the public spring. One day we returned to find our beloved rotary telephones gone. Forbes and David told us that when they started receiving the Wings Neck phone bills, they'd learned that for more than fifty years, the family had been paying five dollars a month to lease each phone from AT&T. I couldn't help laughing. It was so very Colt to have carried our aversion to change to such an extreme, and also so very Colt not to realize that we had done so. I had mixed feelings about these improvements. The new phones would save money, the bottled water might save us from cancer, but, like an unrepentant sinner, I wasn't yet ready to be saved.

Staying in Hidden House felt somehow appropriate; it mirrored the family's Chekhovian decline from being wealthy enough to employ a chauffeur to feeling lucky to rent the chauffeur's cottage. We grew used to seeing strange trucks parked out front, and I gradually stopped bothering to introduce myself to the various carpenters, electricians, and glaziers. The name George Colt meant nothing to them until I added, "I'm Forbes's cousin." I had, I realized, become a renter.

Occasionally, walking down a path, I'd hear a rustling in the woods, and for a moment I'd think it must be my father. Then I'd see David, head bobbing as he bent over with gloved hands to uproot another tenacious shoot of poison ivy. It was comforting to look up from a tennis match and glimpse Forbes and David taking a run around the Neck, or to see them floating on the waves at the Bluff. Gradually, I began to notice some of the good things that only change could render visible. "Once we accept the fact of loss, we understand that the loved one obstructed a whole corner of the possible, pure now as a sky washed by rain," wrote Camus. Mum sent me that quote many years ago, when I was suffering over a lost girlfriend. Anne turned out to be one corner of the possible; another was the ability, for the first time in memory, to sit on the stone bench above the Bluff without risk of contracting poison ivy. One afternoon, Anne, Henry, and Susannah returned to Hidden House with handfuls of blueberries. Miracle of miracles, the clearing of the brush near the kitchen porch had uncovered a long-forgotten, ten-foot-high, fruit-bearing blueberry bush. "Taste them, Daddy, taste them!" squealed two-and-a-half-year-old Henry, his mouth smeared with purple, reaching toward me with stained hands. That bush had been right under my nose for years and I hadn't seen it. How could there be something about this place I did not know?

One evening, Forbes, David, and Aunt Ellen invited us to dinner to look over the architect's plans for the renovation. After bluefish and corn on the cob, we sat on Grandpa's couch, the one on which he read us *The Goops*. While Forbes gave Henry rides atop the rolling kitchen cart, David spread out six blueprints on the table in front of the fireplace. It was strange to see the Big House address in neat letters on the side of each sheet, and stranger still to see the house flattened into an abstraction of razor-straight blue lines.

It took me a while to understand what I was seeing. But the essential changes were these: realizing they needed both to introduce some modern improvements and to bring the house down to a reasonable size (one that could be heated in winter, for they planned to make frequent visits throughout the year), David and Forbes had decided to take off the kitchen wing and the Doghouse. A new kitchen would be built. The diagonal chimneys would also come down, in part because the architect believed they put too much strain on the roof beams. The house would be gutted, rewired, and insulated. A large deck would wrap around the kitchen and living room. (I felt a twinge; it would be a *deck*, not a piazza.) Four of the dormers would be removed. Mariah's Room would go, too. The rambling eleven-bedroom house would become a more straightforward five-bedroom house.

On the other hand, the central core of the house would remain substantially the same. Grandma's Bedroom would stay intact. So too would Grandma's Dressing Room. Grandpa's Dressing Room would become a guest room. The Little Nursery would be transformed into a den with a cathedral ceiling and a small balcony—a place for reading, watching television, and listening to music.

After not changing so much as a dish drainer for decades, I felt dizzy—and so did Forbes and David. Forbes said they'd worried about these plans, knowing they had to make the house smaller, yet not wanting to tamper *too* much. But when they saw the original blueprints, the architects had pointed out that most of the elements they were removing—the kitchen wing, the west wing, several of the dormers, Mariah's Room—had not been part of William Atkinson's original design. They had been added in subsequent renovations. Even the new kitchen ell would resemble the size, shape, and angle of the original. And the house would be reduced from eight thousand square feet to its original six thousand.

I asked Forbes what aspects of the house she most wanted to save. "The one thing I always remembered from coming here when I was young," she said, "was that the house had so many twists and turns—you'd go around a corner and there'd be some new surprise, some other room, some secret space or closet. I worried we'd lose that feeling of unpredictability, so I asked the architect to put in some surprises, like closets with doors leading into other closets. The most important thing is to maintain the spirit of the house—whatever that means. I don't know if we've done it, but I hope so."

As they talked, I began to feel like an idiot. While I had been grieving over the possibility that the Big House might be changed, Forbes and David had been making the difficult decisions that would enable it to be saved. They said that at first they had been reluctant to alter a thing, but the architect kept telling them gently that they had to be realistic. David treasured some of the same things I did: the strange interior window on the first floor; the tiny, head-thumping bathroom under the front stairs. I was touched when he told me that when they had first discussed losing the kitchen wing, he felt an almost physical sickness. Forbes and David had become so attached to the bedroom they share—my parents' old room—that he could hardly bear the thought of taking down the Doghouse. They were like surgeons discussing an imminent amputation, knowing a limb must be sacrificed for the patient to survive. I saw how much time and thought and love—in addition to money—they had invested, how big a risk they were taking, how much care they'd put into hundreds of small decisions: whether to add a window in the living room to admit more light (yes); whether to close off one side of Grandma's bathroom to give it more privacy (yes); whether to eliminate the tiny closet in the front hall (no).

I began to realize how much courage it took to transform what was, after all, both a white elephant and a sacred cow, and how sensitive they had been not only to the house but to those who had cherished it. I also realized how hard it must have been to invite us to stay in Hidden House, when they might feel that we were watching everything they did. (They were right.) As I realized that Forbes and David were really making a home here—*their* home—my envy began to mutate into gratitude that the house was in such capable, loving hands. And even though I recognized that this would be the last time I'd ever have dinner in the Big House I knew, I felt a percolation of excitement at the thought of what the house would become.

All summer, David, Forbes, and Aunt Ellen had been going through the house, sorting through a century of accumulated stuff before demolition began. On Labor Day weekend, a few days before we went home, David called. He and Forbes had weeded through the books; would I like any of the discards? I walked over from Hidden House and found twenty-nine brown plastic grocery bags ("Bonus Savings Club—Pick up an application at A&P") lining the laundry room floor. One by one I hefted them atop the washing machine. There were travel guides from the thirties and forties; gardening manuals; biographies of formerly important politicians; privately printed memoirs by wealthy Brahmin wives; art books given to my grandmother when she was in Paris; novels by L. Alan Harker, Archibald Marshall, and other forgotten writers of the twenties; paperbacks from the Lower Bedroom—Turow, le Carré, Anne Tyler; an unreadable history of the Jordan Marsh department store. Here was my great-grandmother's set of Galsworthy, as well as her 1936 copy of *Gone with the Wind*. Here was Aunt Mary's twelfth-grade English textbook and Dad's sixth-grade history textbook. Within these volumes, one could trace the ups and downs of my grandparents' relationship: books they had purchased together in the euphoric early years of marriage (*Classic Myths in English Literature and Art*, "Henry F. Colt, M. A. Colt, Jan. 1927"); books reflecting their diverging interests (Grandma's collections of poetry and spiritual inspiration, with titles like *Healing Now, The Inward Journey,* and *Deep Is the Hunger*; Grandpa's World War II memoirs, biographies of Churchill, and Rex Stout mysteries); and books Grandma had bought in a vain attempt to rouse her dormant husband (*Just One More—Concerning the Problem Drinker* and *Now or Never—The Promise of the Middle Years*).

I wanted to keep *all* the books, not because of any intrinsic value, of course—the hundreds of dusty volumes might bring twenty dollars at a used bookstore—but because they were links to people no longer available to me, pieces of a house that would no longer exist in its present form. The books I didn't take would end up, like the dishes, at Dorothy's Take It or Leave It Shop at the Bourne dump, where they would languish among the broken toasters and the Monopoly games (minus Ventnor Avenue and Boardwalk) and, eventually, scatter to dozens of destinations. It was disheartening to think that years from now someone would pick up *The Life of Benvenuto Cellini* by J. A. Symonds and read the inscription ("Paris, October 1921, Mary Forbes Atkinson") without knowing that the book had once belonged to a beautiful twenty-one-year-old Bostonian who had just arrived in France, full of dreams; or *The Place and Scope of Psychotherapy*, by Arthur Ruggles, inscribed "To my Good Friends Mary and Harry Colt 1/23/53," without having any idea that one of the "good friends" had been confined for two years in the mental hospital supervised by the author.

Torn between taking everything and taking nothing, I filled four bags with books that I associated with certain people: a few novels by E. Phillips Oppenheim, the memoirs of Black Jack Pershing, Ned Atkinson's 1908 hymnal, my great-grandfather James Colt's worn leather Bible, Dad's copy of *Tom Brown's School Days*, a children's fable Grandpa had read to us, and a pamphlet on knot tying, with a pipe-smoking sailor on the cover, that Ned and I had pored over as children. After much hemming and hawing, I left the Galsworthy, wondering how long he'd last in Dorothy's Take It or Leave It Shop.

Three years later, on a warm August afternoon, we drove toward Wings Neck. Forbes and David had invited us to stay in Hidden House. They had invited us before, but the past two summers we'd promised to visit my parents in Maine. I suspect, however, that I was also reluctant to see the Big House in its transformed state. But as we drove toward Wings Neck, all was reassuringly familiar: the raffish carnival of Buzzards Bay, the lift of the Bourne Bridge, the plunge into the woods across the causeway, the familiar driveway—wider and flatter now, but still recognizable—the LOOK OUT FOR CHILDREN sign. . . .

And then the Big House came into view. It didn't seem quite so big anymore. The Doghouse was gone, of course, and so was Mariah's Room. The trim was white, not green. The house was different and yet familiar, like a Picasso portrait in which the features had been rearranged to more conventional positions. But it was still recognizably itself. Indeed, it looked remarkably like the photograph in Ezra Perry's book *A Trip Around Buzzards Bay Shores* taken shortly after it was completed in 1903. It was once again the graceful, slender home William Atkinson had designed.

Inside, Uncle Bill might have found himself in less familiar territory. The three old stoves and two old refrigerators had been replaced by a six-burner Viking range and a huge Sub-Zero fridge, both of them set among ocean blue Brazilian granite counters. The Faraday Gravity Annunciator had been replaced by a state-of-the-art intercom system; each of the five bedrooms was equipped with built-in speakers, with consoles in the walls so that its occupants could listen to any of one hundred compact discs. A small satellite dish in the backyard beamed more than a hundred channels into the thirty-inch Sony TV that was built into a console in the former Little Nursery. Mariah's Room, the Playroom, the Yellow Room, and the attic had been combined to make a spectacular master bedroom with floor-to-ceiling skylights framing a breathtaking view of the bay. Once cooled by the wind seeping through its leaky windows, the house was now equipped with central air-conditioning in addition to central heating.

And yet, while bringing the house into the twenty-first century, Forbes and David had worked hard to retain a great deal of the nineteenth. At dinner, we sat on the original dining room chairs (refinished and rerushed) around the original oak dining table (restored to a lustrous honey gold). Next to the glassed-in showers, I recognized the old claw-footed bathtubs, reglazed and refitted. The architects had used as many of the old solid-core five-panel doors—doors that aren't made anymore—as possible. The mission-style bookcase that held the family albums in the living room had been refinished and, to everyone's surprise, had turned out, under its lugubrious dark stain, to be made of cherry. The Little Nursery's iron bedsteads, repainted, had been moved to Grandpa's Dressing Room; the Arts and Crafts bed from Grandpa's Dressing Room, refinished, had migrated to a third-floor guest room. Although much of the upholstered furniture had been rendered unusable by mice or by decades of damp, cold winters, Ellen had had Grandma's chaise longue reupholstered and returned to its old spot near one of the east windows. The original pine floors, sanded and refinished, looked like new. Forbes and David had even asked the contractor to leave intact a patch of the old green bead board in the entrance hall. Near the new washer-dryer in a second-floor alcove, I recognized a battered old wicker basket with the word "Soiled" in Grandma's spidery hand. Elsewhere, Forbes and David had retained ideas from the old house—the lattice on the walls, the canted rails on the porch—but redone them with sturdy new wood. Several rooms—Grandma's Dressing Room, Grandma's Bedroom—had changed hardly at all. The Chelsea clock, reinforced with a sturdy new back, would soon reclaim its position in the front hall. And although it was elegant, the house, aside from the kitchen, was anything but fancy. The impression was not of shelter-magazine luxury but of light and air—an impression so strong that I found myself wondering why we'd put up for all those years with such a dark, wet house. And I was especially relieved to see a few new nooks and secret places, like the child-sized alcove in the master bedroom with a fire ladder leading to David's study below. Children would still be able to play Sardines in the Big House.

Parts of the house, we learned, lived on elsewhere. One of the sub-contractors had grown so fond of the kitchen wing that he took it apart, transported it to Buzzards Bay, and reconstructed it as an addition to his own house. (Watching it pass by on a flatbed truck, a Wings Necker telephoned her neighbor to say, "I just saw a piece of history go down the road.") The bay window in the Little Nursery had become a school bus shelter on County Road. Of the claw-footed tubs for which there had been no space, two were given to the architect for his own hundred-year-old home and a third to Forbes's sister for her Manhattan loft. Ellen Atkinson's writing desk, the kitchen cupboard, a toilet, and numerous plates and dishes ended up in Hidden House. The warped COLT sign that had hung at the end of the driveway for forty years was thoughtfully dispatched to my parents for their Maine house. That left the barn still crammed with possessions awaiting reassignment: bookshelves, stacks of vintage LPs, the orange life jackets we'd worn on fishing expeditions with Aunt Mary, the carved wooden deer head, the old Walker & Pratt cast-iron stove, the Ivers and Pond piano, Ned Atkinson's fishing creel, Grandma's old kayak paddles, Grandpa's couch, a photograph of James Colt from Grandpa's Dressing Room, a pair of andirons, a pile of sailing pennants, Ned Atkinson's canes, a stack of yellowing envelopes with embossed three-cent Washington stamps.

The whereabouts of other familiar Big House fixtures was less apparent. Even on blustery days, the southwest wind was silent, unable—yet—to find a way around the new Thermopane windows. And the animals hadn't yet burrowed through the new shingle siding to their own ancestral haunts. (While gutting the house, the carpenters had found numerous nut-filled squirrels' nests in the walls, and one afternoon a bat flew out of the chimney they were dismantling.) I'm not sure yet where the ghosts have gone, but I have a feeling that, like the squirrels, they'll be back.

Elsewhere on Wings Neck, there was change. The neighbors to the east of the Big House, longtime residents, had installed the Neck's second swimming pool, surrounded by a chain-link fence, and thinned the woods right up to the property line; Hidden House was no longer hidden. The Hallowell lot had been bought by a department store executive who was putting the finishing touches on a four-story home that, because it was so close to the Bluff, now dominated Wings Neck from the water and relegated the Big House to runner-up status. Our old tennis court, which served as a staging area for construction, was buried under mountains of dirt and rock. At the old Reynolds property down the shore, the buyer had promised he would renovate the existing house, but one morning a neighbor had heard a thunderous crash and hurried through the woods to investigate. All that remained of the fourteen-room home was the central chimney and the reminder that, had Forbes and David not bought the Big House, a similar sight would have lain at the end of our own driveway. On the other hand, a branch of the Hallowell family had recently bought the massive old Lombard house, saving it from the wrecker's ball. And though the old Bement house had been bought by a Texan—my neighbor's worst fear come true—the interloper had surprised his neighbors by preserving the house's original charm through just the sort of careful renovation they would have wished for their own houses, had they been able to afford it.

The first time we walked the familiar path to the Big Cove, we were stopped short by a split-rail fence. It had been put up by a relative newcomer who had decided that his neighbors' summer tenants had walked across his property one time too many. For the rest of the summer, we detoured down the Benedicts' driveway toward the road, our bare feet cringing on the pebble-strewn dirt.

Susannah was eleven now. I had worried that she might have outgrown the simple pleasures of Wings Neck, but she went right to work catching hermies in the millpond; making a new store on the Bluff; climbing the barn roof; and picking mint from the garden that Mary (who, just as she'd hoped, had become the *maîtresse* of Hidden House) had planted near the little screened porch. Henry, now six, traded sea glass with his sister, swam to the Big Rock, built a driftwood fort called the Shark Hotel, and cruised the millpond in search of the fearsome blue claw crab, which had, apparently, returned to its former haunts. Using quahogs from the millpond and Ned Atkinson's old lines, Anne and Henry fished off the dock at the Big Cove. After pulling up his line six or seven times only to find his bait had been stolen, Henry hauled up a glittering scup, his first fish. "I got one! I got one!" he shouted, performing a joyous, hopping jig. Back at Hidden House, before we cleaned and cooked his catch, Henry painstakingly traced it on a piece of cardboard.

Even if we weren't living in the Big House ourselves, I could still glory in the sight of the striped beach towels draped over the back porch; the extra leaves in the table; the new red leather guest book with the words WINGS NECK embossed in gold, filling with entries, photos, and drawings. Aunt Ellen, feeling excluded from Wings Neck for so many years, had made a triumphal return; the room she had chosen—I took this as touching proof that she had made retrospective peace with her mother—was Grandma's. The house had become the holiday gathering place for the entire Singer family. Already a web of new traditions had begun. At the Bluff, David had cleared the rocks beyond the boardwalk to make a path to the sandbar. At first, I felt an instinctive resistance, but as I walked easily along the path, my feet sustaining not a single cut even though it was dead low tide, I felt a rush of gratitude for what the Singers called "the Superhighway" (a name I felt confident would join the Bluff, the Big Rock, and the Bathtub as an unquestioned landmark in the family geography). Over the following days I found that these changes gave me permission to make a change myself: I began to wear sandals when I walked along the Bluff to and from the Big Cove (though only, I told myself, so I could keep up with my barefooted children).

One night, after dinner at the old Big House table, we all decided to swim at the Bluff. It was high tide. The wind was from the north, but the water was perfectly calm. The moon over Scraggy Neck was close to full. The sky was crammed with stars. The light from Cleveland Ledge swung toward us every nine seconds. As we dove underwater, phosphorescence poured from our reaching fingers.

Walking up the Bluff steps, I caught sight of the Big House, glowing with a brilliance that the Colts, with their meager collection of sixty-watt bulbs, would never have permitted. I thought to myself, *What a beautiful house.* Its first century had ended, but its second was only beginning. As the ebbing tide, at some indiscernible moment, begins to turn, the house, too, had reached an ebb, and was slowly filling up again.

Just before we left the next day, Aunt Ellen, Forbes, and David came out of the house. As they hugged us, I could tell that each of them was holding something behind his or her back. Standing in front of the Big House, they pulled out towels and washcloths and napkins and waved them at us wildly as our car turned down the long driveway. Susannah and Henry peered through the rear window as the figures grew smaller and smaller, sending us homeward with a Colt good-bye.

Notes on Sources

This book's most important raw material was memories—my own and those of friends and family members, drawn from interviews and conversations as well as from letters, journals, photographs, scrapbooks, and other family papers. In attempting to place the Big House within a larger cultural and historical perspective, however, I have also availed myself of hundreds of published sources. I will cite here only those on which I relied most heavily.

Judging from library and bookstore shelves, it may seem as if everyone who has ever visited the Cape has been inspired to write about the experience. I made it my pleasurable business to read as many of these works as I could find. Those to which I turned most often include: *We Chose Cape Cod* (originally published in 1953; reprinted in 1969 by Chatham Press), Scott Corbett's account of his family's decision to live year-round on the Cape; *Where Land Meets Sea* (Chatham Press, 1972), Clare Leighton's impressions, in words and woodcuts, of bluefish, cranberries, hurricanes, and other staples of Cape Cod life; and *Father to the Man* by Christopher Hallowell (William Morrow, 1987), which, literally and figuratively, covers some of the same ground as *The Big House*. Although it takes place not on Cape Cod but in Westport Point, Massachusetts, I also drew sustenance from *A Joyful Noise* (Partners Village Press, 1999), Janet Gillespie's celebration of her childhood summers. I borrowed from two fine anthologies of Cape literature: *Sand in Their Shoes*, edited by Edith and Frank Shay (Houghton Mifflin, 1951, reprinted by Parnassus Imprints in 1982), and *A Place Apart*, edited by Robert Finch (Norton, 1993). Among the many natural-history primers and field guides I paged through with muddy fingers, my favorite is *The Outer Lands* (W. W. Norton, 1978), a lucid, lyrical exploration of Cape Cod marine life by Dorothy Sterling. I owe my greatest literary debt to Thoreau's *Cape Cod*, in whose shadow all other books about the region are doomed to stand.

II   The Family Tree

For background on my Forbes and Atkinson ancestors, I consulted *Letters and Recollections of John Murray Forbes*, edited by Sarah Forbes Hughes (Houghton Mifflin, 1899); *American Railroad Builder: John Murray Forbes* by Henry Greenleaf Pearson (Houghton Mifflin, 1911); and *Edward Atkinson, the Biography of an American Liberal* by Harold Francis Williamson (Old Corner Bookstore, 1934). *The Old Brookline Trunk* by Louise Andrew Kent (Houghton Mifflin, 1955) contains a charming chapter on Edward Atkinson's childhood that draws on material from *Edward Atkinson: His Egotistography*, an unpublished memoir dictated by my great-great-grandfather into an Edison phonograph near the end of his life.

Like most people who have written about Brahmin Boston within the last half century, I found it impossible not to borrow heavily from *The Proper Bostonians* (E. P. Dutton, 1947), Cleveland Amory's infamous guide to the species. Although their influence may be less apparent, I was also inspired by *About Boston* (Little, Brown, 1948), a collection of David McCord's essays on the city he loved, and by *The Gentle Americans* (Harper & Row, 1965), in which Helen Howe displays Brahmin discretion while providing an honest, affectionate portrait of Boston's literary circles. (In the interest of full disclosure, to say nothing of familial pride, I should mention that Howe is a distant cousin of mine.)

IV   *The Discovery of Cape Cod*

My discussion of Thoreau's sojourns on Cape Cod is drawn primarily from Walter Harding's biography *The Days of Henry Thoreau* (Princeton Paperback, 1992) and Joseph J. Moldenhauer's Introduction to *Cape Cod/The Writings of Henry David Thoreau* (Princeton University Press, 1988). Fortunately, just as I began collecting material on the history of attitudes toward the seashore, Viking (1998) published *The Beach* by Lena Lenček and Gideon Bosker, a trove of information on that very subject. I also found John Stilgoe's *Alongshore* (Yale University Press, 1994) helpful.

In writing about the development of summer resorts in this country, I relied on early gazetteers, travel guides, and old magazines; *The Cornhill Magazine*, *Harper's Monthly*, and *The New England Magazine* were especially valuable. After finishing the chapter, I found much of this material—and a great deal more—synthesized in Cindy Aron's *Work at Play* (Oxford University Press, 1999), a history of vacations in the United States. Back issues of *Spritsail—A Journal of the History of Falmouth and Vicinity* contained useful information on Cape Cod's summer growth. And every community on the Cape should be lucky enough to have a resource like the comprehensive *Book of Falmouth* (Falmouth Historical Commission, 1986). I also drew from two books that describe the evolution of summer resorts elsewhere in Massachusetts: *Old Mattapoisett* by Edward F. R. Wood Jr. (Quadequina Press, 1995), and *Boston's North Shore* by Joseph Garland (Little, Brown, 1978).

Among the dozens of books that explore Cape Cod's past, I found *The History of Cape Cod—Annals of Barnstable County* by Frederick Freeman (W. H. Piper, 1869) to be a mother lode of useful material. I am also indebted to Betsey D.

Keene's *History of Bourne* (Charles W. Swift, 1937). William Root Bliss wrote two helpful books about early settlers: *The Old Colony Town and the Ambit of Buzzards Bay* (The Riverside Press, 1893) and *Colonial Times on Buzzards Bay* (Houghton Mifflin, 1888). In describing the summer colonization of Wings Neck and the surrounding area, my job was made easier by the Bourne Historical Commission, which has published several oral histories: *Memories of Monument Beach, From Pocasset to Cataumet*, and *Bourne Village*. I am particularly beholden to *A History of Wing's Neck* (Bookcrafters, 1994), compiled and edited by Nicholas J. Baker, which, in telling the story of Wings Neck in the words of those who have lived there, not only summarizes the history of each house on the Neck but captures the spirit of the place.

V   *Rooftree*

When I started work on this book, I didn't know a gable from a dormer, a shingle from a shake. I am thus indebted to numerous books and architectural journals, of which I would like to single out a few. My discussion of shingle-style architecture cannot help owing a debt to *The Shingle Style and the Stick Style* by Vincent J. Scully, Jr., the man who identified and named the style (revised edition, Yale University Press, 1971). My description of Gilded Age homes was helped by Clive Aslet's sumptuously illustrated *The American Country House* (Yale University Press, 1990). My account of the design and construction of the Big House was immeasurably improved by my reading David Owen's *The Walls Around Us* (Villard, 1991), a primer on how a house is put together. For information and inspiration, I turned again and again to Tracy Kidder's *House* (Houghton Mifflin, 1985).

VII   *Fishing*

While writing this chapter, I was grateful to be introduced to *Carter's Coast of New England* (New Hampshire Publishing Company, 1977, originally published in 1864 as *A Summer Cruise on the Coast of New England*), *New York Tribune* journalist Robert Carter's classic account of an 1858 voyage from Boston to Maine. My description of the sea robin owes much to Robert Farnsworth's poem "The Sculpin."

XI   *Money*

Although its influence may be most evident in this chapter, my entire book has been enriched by reading and rereading *Old Money* (Knopf, 1988), Nelson W. Aldrich Jr.'s examination of inherited wealth.

XII   *Sailing*

My discussion of the Herreshoff Twelve benefited greatly from *Capt. Nat Herreshoff, the Wizard of Bristol* by L. Francis Herreshoff (Sheridan House, 1996, first published in 1953), and *Herreshoff of Bristol* by Maynard Bray and Carlton Pinheiro (Woodenboat Publications, 1990). Also helpful were *Sailing Days at Mattapoisett, 1870–1960* by Edward F. R. Wood Jr. (Reynolds Printing, 1961) and "The Herreshoff Fifteens," an article by David Cheever (*The Log*, summer, 1972).

XIV   *Hidden House*
Many of the details about my aunt Sandy's life, illness, and death are taken from my uncle Sidney Werkman's lovely memoir *Only a Little Time* (Little, Brown, 1972).

Memoir cannot help being an invasion of privacy. In an attempt to reduce the level of invasion outside my family circle, I have changed the names of a few peripheral figures: the Gordons, Linda, Mrs. Reilly, and Mr. Garrity. All other names in this book are real.

Acknowledgments

Like the Big House itself, *The Big House* owes its existence to many people.

I would like to thank Kathy Holub for helping me begin to think of the house as a book; Leigh Haber for bringing the book into the Scribner fold; Barbara Haber for telling me about the New England Kitchen; Gwendolyn Wright for shedding light on nineteenth-century construction practices; Paul and Heidi Barclay for sharing research on their William Atkinson–designed house; the late Luise Vosgerchian for her memories of William Atkinson; George Waterston for furthering my understanding of the Ats; Phips and Jane Hallowell for a memorable afternoon reminiscing about Wings Neck; George Hackett and Sally Levine for their insights into the Cape Cod real estate market; Tim Mansfield for his architectural expertise; Patricia O'Toole, coordinator of the Hertog Research Assistantship Program at Columbia University, for introducing me to Julie Sheehan; Julie Sheehan for ferreting out hundreds of delicious details, from the origin of the phrase "white elephant" to the wood used in tennis rackets of the 1950s; Moe Finegold and Simon Mozr for patiently explaining how they brought a house built in 1903 into the twenty-first century; Monica Gregory for her caregiving skills, without which this book would have taken twice as long to complete; Rachel Sussman, Erin Curler, and Sarah McGrath for helping shepherd *The Big House* through the publishing process; and Bill Abrams, Todd Brewster, Dawn Evans, Campbell Geeslin, Eliza Hale, Katy Hutchins, Peter Lerangis, Peter Mansfield, Mark O'Donnell, Bill Shebar, Ed Shneidman, Rod Skinner, Friederike von Stackelberg, Bob Sullivan, and Lydia Weaver for encouragement along the way.

Special thanks to Amanda Urban, my agent, for clearing the path so that I could concentrate on the journey; and to Gillian Blake, whose childhood summers on Cape Cod and deft literary skills made her the ideal editor for this book.

For reading part or all of the manuscript and offering counsel and correction, I am grateful to John Bethell, Terry Estes, Rob *(il miglior fabbro)* Farnsworth, Peter Mansfield, Julie Salamon, and, especially, Jay Lovinger, who, as he has done so often, gave my prose and my spirits a boost when they most needed it.

While researching this book, I was fortunate to be able to draw on the resources of many institutions. I would like to thank the Jonathan Bourne Public Library, the Falmouth Public Library, the New York Public Library, the University of Rochester Library, the Sandwich Public Library, the Boxford Historical Document Center, the Manchester Historical Society, the Massachusetts Historical Society, the Herreshoff Museum, Butler Hospital, the Harvard University Archives, and, especially, the Bourne Archives.

I am particularly beholden to my family. Anyone who writes memoir practices a sort of literary imperialism, laying claim to places and events that belong just as much—and often more—to a host of other people. Each member of my family has his or her own version of the Big House, and each, no doubt, would write a very different book from the one you hold. And yet each has graciously contributed to my version by sharing memories; in many cases, by reading and commenting on the completed manuscript; and by supporting me with innumerable acts of generosity, for all of which I am exceedingly grateful. I will never forget the dozens of warm conversations about family history that I had with Charles and Amy Colt before they died. I would also like to thank Georgia Bullitt and Russell and Sarah Werkman for sharing their memories of the Big House with me; Mary Forbes Colt, Jimmy and Buffy Colt, and, especially, Ellen Singer, for cheerfully submitting to many long interviews, and for the love they have shown this nephew over the years; my beloved, bighearted brothers, Harry, Ned, and Mark Colt, for making me feel that having a writer for a sibling wasn't such a bad thing; Sandy Bell Colt for being such an affectionate reader and sister-in-law; Susannah and Henry Colt, for enabling me to see the Big House through a child's eyes again; Oliver Haeffely, for late-night remembering and eagle-eyed proofreading; Henry Singer for being such an encouraging and honest best friend throughout this project, as he has been throughout my life; Forbes and David, for giving the Big House a second life while supporting my attempt to document its first life. Writing *The Big House* has made me realize all the more how blessed I am to have been born into this family.

I have been equally blessed by the family into which I married, one that has also been invaluable to *The Big House*. I am grateful to Kim Fadiman for his thoughtful questions and his careful reading of several early drafts; to the late Annalee Fadiman for keeping me and my family well nourished with mail-order steaks and for giving the manuscript her expert scrutiny; to the late Clifton Fadiman for offering encouragement at every turn with a gentle wisdom I will remember always. I wish only that I could give my parents-in-law a finished copy of the work they did so much to nurture.

It would be impossible to enumerate all the ways in which my wife, Anne Fadiman, has contributed to this book. But I would like to thank her for a few of them: for falling in love with the Big House—and the family within it—at first sight; for helping the book take shape in my mind and on the page; for staying awake as I read each newly completed chapter aloud late at night in bed; for lavishing her matchless editorial skills and boundless enthusiasm on every word of each successive draft; for patiently explaining the difference between restrictive and nonrestrictive clauses for the umpteenth time; for bringing home—and often cooking—the bacon during the years I wrote this book; and, above all, for warming my heart with hers.

I owe my greatest debt to my parents. Eight years ago, when I told them I wanted to write a book about the Big House, there was a moment's silence. "Are you sure?" they asked. Once they knew I was sure, their support never wavered—as it has never wavered throughout my life, whatever I have chosen to do. This project has cast them in two potentially conflicting roles: loving parents and (occasionally) reluctant book subjects. They have nonetheless sat for hours of interviews, recalling events joyous and painful with equal candor; tracked down old letters and documents; listened to me talk about the book, occasionally asking gentle questions, always nudging me deeper; and read several drafts, each time offering valuable suggestions and corrections. My mother, a writer herself and the one responsible for getting me interested in books in the first place, also served as a perceptive editor. These alone have been gifts for which I can never thank them enough. But even more important—and more generous—was the love they continued to show me in a thousand ways, all expressed with a grace and patience and selflessness that—as Grandpa used to say—"unmans me."